A HISTORY OF THE UNIVERSITY
OF CAMBRIDGE

GENERAL EDITOR
C. N. L. BROOKE

A HISTORY OF THE UNIVERSITY
OF CAMBRIDGE

General Editor: CHRISTOPHER BROOKE

*Dixie Professor of Ecclesiastical History, University of Cambridge, and
Fellow of Gonville and Caius College*

This four-volume series will comprise the first substantial history of the University of modern times. Each of the volumes will carry extensive original research and a synthesis of modern scholarship, and will explore the institutions, studies, scholarship, society, sports and buildings of the colleges and University, without neglecting the schools and social context from which the students came. Although not planned on the massive scale of series such as the current *History of the University of Oxford* or the *Victoria History of the Counties of England*, the series will chart afresh and in detail a remarkable passage of history, bring current scholarship into the light of day, and inspire a new generation of students and scholars to fresh endeavour.

Volumes in the series:

1 The University to 1546
   DAMIAN RIEHL LEADER

2 1546–1750
   VICTOR MORGAN
      Forthcoming

3 1750–1870
   PETER SEARBY
      Forthcoming

4 1870–1990
   CHRISTOPHER BROOKE

A HISTORY OF
THE UNIVERSITY
OF CAMBRIDGE

VOLUME 1
THE UNIVERSITY TO 1546

DAMIAN RIEHL LEADER

CAMBRIDGE
UNIVERSITY PRESS

Published by the Press Syndicate of the University of Cambridge
The Pitt Building, Trumpington Street, Cambridge CB2 1RP
40 West 20th Street, New York, NY 10011–4211, USA
10 Stamford Road, Oakleigh, Melbourne 3166, Australia

First published 1988
Reprinted 1994

Printed in Great Britain by the University Press, Cambridge

British Library cataloguing in publication data

Leader, Damian Riehl
A History of the University of Cambridge
Vol. 1: The University to 1546
1. University of Cambridge – History
1, Title
378.426'59'09   LF109

Library of Congress cataloguing in publication data

A History of the University of Cambridge.
Bibliography.
Includes index.
Contents: v. 1. The university to 1546 / Damian Riehl Leader.
1. University of Cambridge – History. 1. Brooke,
Christopher Nugent Lawrence.
LF109.H57   1988   378.426'59   87-25586

ISBN 0 521 32882 9

UP

For my family
'semper fidelis'

CONTENTS

Contents

Contents

ILLUSTRATIONS

(now the site of the University Registry), one of the few parts of the proposed college that King Henry actually built. (Willis and Clark, IV, 13, fig. 3)

GENERAL EDITOR'S PREFACE

Cambridge is a beautiful city created by man, with little help
from nature; and of all the medieval universities Cambridge is
the one whose site is least readily explained. In a celebrated
passage in his diary, John Evelyn wrote that 'the whole town
is a low dirty unpleasant place, the streets ill-paved, the air
thick and infected by the fens...'[1] – surrounded, we may add,
by land which is flat and dull, though not unprofitable. In
truth, by 1654 when Evelyn wrote, man had already raised a
city of great beauty here and a university of renown. This is an
obvious challenge to a historian; no further excuse is needed
for launching four volumes on the *History of the University of
Cambridge*, to chart afresh a remarkable passage of history, to
bring current scholarship into the clear light of day, and, if our
hopes are truly fulfilled, to inspire a new generation of students
and scholars to fresh endeavour.

In former centuries historians treated the University of
Cambridge with loving care. In the fifteenth century Nicholas
Cantelow furnished it with many centuries of fictitious pre-
history, and in the sixteenth Dr Caius added to the store of fact
and fiction. In the seventeenth Thomas Fuller wrote his brief,
delightful jewel of a book; and in the eighteenth Robert
Masters' *History of the College of Corpus Christi* illustrated what
a mighty college history might be. Late in the nineteenth
century James Bass Mullinger began his trilogy, which carried
the story from the age of fiction to the seventeenth century –
the first modern attempt at a general scholarly history, packed
with useful information but also, especially in the earlier cen-

[1] Evelyn, *Diary*, 31 August 1654, quoted in L. and H. Fowler, *Cambridge Commemorated*
(Cambridge, 1984), p. 110.

xiii

turies, dated and flawed. More lasting was *The Architectural History of the University of Cambridge and of the Colleges of Cambridge and Eton* by Robert Willis and J. W. Clark. This great classic, published in 1886 and still the envy even of Oxford, opened the rich stores of archival evidence for the sites of the colleges as well as describing the buildings with lavish care. Its message has been splendidly continued by the two volumes of the Royal Commission on Historical Monuments, published in 1959, and by Pevsner. Meanwhile, 1959 also saw the appearance of a full-scale history of the university and colleges in the third volume of the *Victoria History of Cambridgeshire*, edited by J. P. C. Roach. This, and a stack of studies of various aspects of university history – and a sheaf of college histories, showing new growth also in this ancient plant – revealed that there is a lively interest in Cambridge history still in the late twentieth century.

Yet there is a feeling of unease. The historians of Cambridge have observed, with many emotions including admiration and envy, the launching of a mighty dreadnought in Oxford. Three volumes of *The History of the University of Oxford* have appeared: what can Cambridge offer? Such observations may stir the conscience; they are a poor basis for serious scholarly endeavour. Yet current interest in the history of universities at large is extremely active – as a highly fashionable branch of intellectual, cultural, social and religious history; and that too is a challenge to us in Cambridge. In truth, much is astir, as the recent histories of the University Press and the University Library have shown;[2] and it came as a fitting indicator of current scholarship when Dr Damian Leader offered the Cambridge University Press a book on the history of the university from 1209 to 1546. He is a US citizen and a graduate of Toronto, and he reminds us that serious study of Cambridge is an international endeavour, neglected only – if at all – in Cambridge. It was a most welcome offer, which inspired Michael Black, the University Publisher, to seek other volumes

---

[2] M. H. Black, *Cambridge University Press, 1584–1984*; J. C. T. Oates, *Cambridge University Library, A History*, I; D. McKitterick, *Cambridge University Library, A History*, II (Cambridge, 1984, 1986, 1986).

General Editor's Preface

to follow it. Victor Morgan will navigate us from 1546 to 1750; Peter Searby from 1750 to 1870; I myself hope to bring us into harbour (in volume IV) somewhere in the late twentieth century. Leader has done pioneer work especially on the arts courses and in other fields of academic intellectual history; and this book combines much that is unfamiliar with much that has been deeply studied before; thus we hope in all four volumes to seek charted and uncharted waters. Perhaps beside the great battleship launched by the Oxford Press there is room for a modest, serviceable frigate, sent from Cambridge.

We launch it in the spirit felicitously expounded by Thomas Fuller in the 1630s:

> Wherefore I presume my aunt Oxford will not be justly offended, if in this book I give my own mother the upper hand, and first begin with her history. Thus desiring God to pour his blessing on both, that neither may want milk for their children, or children for their milk, we proceed to the business.[3]

Perhaps in the 1980s a historian whose privilege it has been to serve more modern universities as well as Cambridge may enlarge this prayer to all the universities of the land, dedicated to a common task and caught in a single net of misunderstanding and neglect.

Cambridge, Lent 1987   CHRISTOPHER N. L. BROOKE

---

[3] T. Fuller, *The History of the University of Cambridge*, ed. J. Nichols (Cambridge, 1840), p. 4.

PREFACE

This book was conceived as a personal exercise: I wanted to tell the story of early Cambridge as I understand it, to explain how it became a great university. I began during some free months in Indiana, and finished under less leisurely circumstances in the West Indies and Belgium. I am honoured that it will be included in the present series.

Many people helped me on this project. Professor Christopher N. L. Brooke's assistance is especially appreciated for being so freely given before I wrote a word. His later criticism of the manuscript was invaluable. He gave me countless hours, and his patience was unending.

I am also in the debt of the Reverend J. K. McConica, CSB, who introduced me to university history and directed much of my research in the Cambridge libraries and archives. The late Reverend J. A. Weisheipl, OP assisted with the sections on logic and science. Professor D. E. Luscombe criticised part of the manuscript. Other help was given by the Reverend L. E. Boyle, OP, Mrs Catherine Hall, the Reverend and Mrs David Hoyle, Miss Marienza Lio, Dr Michael Parker, OSB, Dr H. C. Porter, Professor J. R. Shinners, and Mr M. Underwood.

Dr Dorothy M. Owen and Dr Elisabeth Leedham-Green, the Keeper and Assistant Keeper of the University Archives were of great assistance. The governing bodies and archivists of the following corporations graciously allowed me to consult their archival materials and libraries: at Cambridge, Trinity, King's, St John's, Peterhouse, Pembroke, Gonville and Caius, Corpus Christi, Queens', Jesus, Christ's, Magdalene, and Sidney Sussex Colleges; at Oxford, the University Archives, and Balliol, Merton, Oriel, New College, Lincoln, All Souls, Magdalen,

Brasenose, and Corpus Christi Colleges. Dr T. A. R. Evans, Dr Gregor Duncan, and the late Mr T. H. Aston of the History of the University of Oxford Project provided computer concordances of A. B. Emden's *Biographical Registers*.

While researching this topic I enjoyed the hospitality of St Edmund's College and the Blackfriars community in Cambridge, and Campion Hall, Oxford. Support also came at one point from a travel grant of the US National Endowment for the Humanities. Some of the material was collected while working under a grant from the Social Sciences and Humanities Research Council of Canada. Parts of this book appeared in earlier forms in *History of Universities, History of Education, Sixteenth Century Journal,* and *Humanistica Lovaniensia*.

I would also like to acknowledge those without whose encouragement I would never have pursued history: the late Msgr Philip Hughes, Dr Otto Bird, Mr Donald Fiwek, and Professors Matthew Fitzsimons and Fredrick Pike.

A reprint enables me to amend minor misprints, and to make a correction on p. 250: Caius Auberinus was the English poet John Kay, as I shall explain in a forthcoming paper. See meanwhile *DNB* III, 673.

Embassy of the United States of America   D.R.L.
Brussels

ABBREVIATIONS

Annals	C. H. Cooper, *Annals of Cambridge*. 5 vols. (Cambridge, 1842–1908)
BA	Bachelor of Arts
BCL	Bachelor of Civil Law
BCn.L	Bachelor of Canon Law
BL	British Library
BRUC	A. B. Emden, *Biographical Register of the University of Cambridge to 1500* (Cambridge, 1963)
BRUO	A. B. Emden, *Biographical Register of the University of Oxford to AD 1500*. 3 vols. (Oxford, 1957–9)
BTh.	Bachelor of Theology
CAS	Cambridge Antiquarian Society
CCCC	Corpus Christi College, Cambridge
CCCO	Corpus Christi College, Oxford
CJC	*Corpus Juris Canonici*, ed. E. Friedberg 2 vols. (Leipzig, 1879–81)
CUA	Cambridge University Archives
CUL	Cambridge University Library
CUP	Cambridge University Press
CWE	Collected Works of Erasmus, ed. J. McConica (Toronto, 1974–)
DCL	Doctor of Civil Law
DCn.L	Doctor of Canon Law
DC and Cn.L	Doctor of Civil and Canon Law
DNB	*Dictionary of National Biography*
DTh.	Doctor of Theology
Docs.	*Documents relating to the University and Colleges*

	of Cambridge, ed. HM Commissioners 3 vols. (London, 1852)
GBk A	*Grace Book A*, ed. S. M. Leathes. (CAS, 1897)
GBk B	*Grace Book B, Part I and Part II*, ed. M. Bateson. (CAS, 1903–5)
GBk Γ	*Grace Book Γ*, ed. W. G. Searle (Cambridge, 1908)
HUO	*The History of the University of Oxford*, I, ed. J. I. Catto and R. Evans (Oxford, 1984); III, ed. J. K. McConica (Oxford, 1986)
LP	*Letters and Papers, Foreign and Domestic, Illustrative of the Reign of Henry VIII, 1509–47*, ed. J. S. Brewer and J. Gairdner 21 vols. (London, 1862–1910)
MA	Master of Arts
MD	Doctor of Medicine
MGram.	Master of Grammar
NCE	*New Catholic Encyclopedia*. 17 vols. (New York, 1967–79)
OHS	Oxford Historical Society
OUA	Oxford University Archives
OUP	Oxford University Press
RCHM	Royal Commission on Historical Monuments, England, *City of Cambridge*. 2 vols. (London, 1959)
Reg. Aa	*The Register of Congregation, 1448–63*, ed. W. A. Pantin and W. T. Mitchell. OHS n.s. 22 (Oxford, 1972)
STC	*Short-Title Catalogue of Books Printed in England, Scotland, and Ireland and of English Books Published Abroad 1475–1640*. First compiled by A. W. Pollard and G. R. Redgrave. Second edition by W. A. Jackson and F. S. Ferguson. Completed by K. F. Pantzer. Vol. I (London, 1963); Vol. II, I–Z (London, 1976)
TCBS	*Transactions of the Cambridge Bibliographical Society*

Abbreviations

VCH	*Victoria History of the County of Cambridgeshire and the Isle of Ely.* 8 vols. (London, 1938–82)
Willis and Clark	R. Willis and J. W. Clark, *The Architectural History of the University of Cambridge and the Colleges of Cambridge and Eton.* 4 vols. (Cambridge, 1886)
X	Decretals of Gregory IX ('Liber Extra')

INTRODUCTION

Oxford and Cambridge, like Parliament, are medieval institutions which have survived and adapted themselves to the modern world. Whether viewed as 'cancers' on the British educational system (in the words of the Labour Party in 1982) or as examples of what is most admirable in the Anglo-Saxon achievement, they are undeniably the envy of the world. Not even Cambridge's New World daughter Harvard can claim parity with either ancient institution. Within England they held a monopoly on university training until the 1820s, a situation unparalleled in any other western country. They are now nearly 800 years old, and have for much of that time been central to the intellectual, social, political, and religious life of England. With the expansion of the Empire in the nineteenth century they served as exemplars of higher education in many parts of the world.

In spite of this position in the unfolding of English history, the scholarship directed towards both Oxford and Cambridge often suffered, until recent years, from antiquarianism, parochialism, and chauvinism. Many histories of individual colleges were little more than self-congratulatory accounts of their founders, the buildings, and short lives of the prominent members of the foundation. To this could be added appendices, or even separate volumes, on the boat club or college plate. The university histories written in the sixteenth to eighteenth centuries were partisan attempts to assert the superiority and anteriority of one place over the other. After Oxford claimed foundation by King Arthur, Cambridge replied with a Spanish prince 'Cantaber' who sailed north to establish a school that later housed Pythagoras and Anaxagoras. These mythic foundations did not survive the scrutiny of nineteenth-century scholars, who were aided by the royal commissions which published so many of the early statutes and muniments. Many reasoned institutional histories were written which, while giving little attention to intellectual life, provided a framework from which others could proceed. In 1886 Willis and Clark's superb four-volume architectural history of Cambridge appeared, for which no other university has an equal. The past twenty-five years have been the most productive ever, with much valuable work published on both universities.

Even so, Cambridge has long differed from Oxford in being noticeably less curious about its past. Oxford had a university archivist before the Civil War, whereas Cambridge felt no such need until 1949.[1] Oxford has always had more than its share of antiquaries and amateur historians engaged in self-examination to an extent dismissed by many Cantabrigians as morbid. Recent years have seen an *Oxford Book of Oxford*, and *The History of the University of Oxford* series, Cambridge scholars are quick to point out, will rival in sheer bulk the *Oxford History of England*. Why the two universities have differed so markedly in their attitudes to their own pasts is a variant on the centuries-old parlour game of comparing the two places. There are many frivolous explanations: Cambridge is more scientific and less sentimental and romantic; it is more 'protestant' in spirit and less interested in the authority of the past; its puritan ethos has always emphasised the supremacy of the individual conscience over the corporate spirit ('Oxford produces prime ministers and Cambridge Soviet spies'). To this is contrasted Oxford's 'dreaming spires' and 'home of lost causes'. Neither of these two models is accurate, nor do they explain the many exceptions that can be brought forward. But even the casual visitor to the Isis and Cam will quickly realise that very different *genii loci* animate England's ancient universities, and that explaining its own past was not an important part of the Cambridge mystique.

---

[1] An honorary keeper was appointed in 1949, a deputy keeper in 1953, and in 1958 the offices were combined. Before that the archives were kept by the university registry, who was sometimes very active in archival work. H. Peek and C. Hall, *Archives of the University of Cambridge* (Cambridge, 1962), p. 23.

Introduction

Until recently a singularly neglected area of Cambridge history has been the three centuries from its foundation to the Reformation. There are several probable reasons. First, little evidence was thought to have survived the destruction of the university muniments during the Popular Revolt of 1381, and the historian was confronted with much to conjecture and little with which to substantiate it. The most recent book solely dedicated to medieval Cambridge was written in 1873 by J.Bass Mullinger. Of its over 600 pages, perhaps two-thirds discuss the medieval world, the continental universities, and what is known of Oxford for the same time. Remarkably little of substance is actually said of Cambridge.

Secondly, to this dearth of evidence was added the feeling that the topic did not warrant much attention. In Hastings Rashdall's great three-volume *The Universities of Europe in the Middle Ages* (published in 1896, revised in 1936, and still unsupplanted) Cambridge is given only 50 pages out of nearly 1,500; and that in a work written by an Englishman. Rashdall is blunt in dealing with 'the medieval insignificance of a university which at present divides so exactly the higher education of this country with her more ancient rival'. In short, 'Cambridge was a third-rate university', and 'not a single schoolman can be shown to have taught at Cambridge'.[2] He then merely itemises ten points in which it differed from Oxford (expanded by later editors to sixteen) and gives brief accounts of the founding of the colleges.

Thirdly, the strong protestant tradition at Cambridge found little to glorify in its Catholic past. Even as early as 1550, reformers like Hugh Latimer were reminiscing about the idle monks they remembered in the university of their youth.[3] To this was added the avalanche of humanist polemic against medieval education, a reaction which antedated the Reformation by several decades and was expressed by such orthodox Cambridge men as John Fisher and Erasmus. This humanist and reformed perspective dominated Cambridge history until recent

[2] H. Rashdall, *The Universities of Europe in the Middle Ages*, ed. F. M. Powicke and A. B. Emden (Oxford, 1936), III, p. 284.
[3] H. Latimer, *Sermons*, ed. G. E. Corrie (Parker Society 26), I, p. 153.

years. The various college histories were always eager to celebrate their medieval founders, but the religious, not to say chantry aspects of the medieval colleges rarely have been emphasised. And the houses of Dominican, Franciscan, Carmelite, and Austin mendicant friars which constituted such a large part of the early university have no tradition of old boys writing with filial piety of their medieval benefactors.

Besides Willis and Clark's *Architectural History*, the pre-World War II works of continuing value are the editions of early college library catalogues, monographs on specific aspects of university administration, and registers of medieval alumni such as J. Venn's for Gonville Hall, and the monumental *Alumni Cantabrigienses*, which Venn began.

The post-war years have seen Cambridge turn more systematically to its medieval past. Care has been given to the University Archives, and several of the colleges have realised the value of their previously neglected (and often abused) muniments. Recent scholarship has made reappraisals possible. A. B. Emden's *Biographical Register of the University of Cambridge to 1500* (Cambridge, 1963), which followed a similar project for Oxford, allows the student of medieval Cambridge access to a myriad of connections and relationships that would otherwise be unrecognisable. This ever-growing register is now computerised (as part of the History of the University of Oxford project), making it all the more useful. In 1959 the earliest known statutes of Cambridge were rediscovered in a Roman library, and their careful edition by M. B. Hackett with extensive commentary (Cambridge, 1970) is invaluable. 1967 saw volume III of the *Victoria History of Cambridgeshire*, which brings together university, college, and town materials. A. B. Cobban, first with *The King's Hall* and later with several articles on colleges, has, in recent years, been the most active scholar of the medieval university.

Given this flurry of interest, and the 115 years that have passed since Bass Mullinger's *History of Cambridge to 1535*, it is time for a reappraisal of the early university. The present volume will attempt to make the wealth of specialised scholarship more accessible by presenting it in a broader context.

Attention will be given to the institutional, social, intellectual, and religious life of the university, to provide a more complete image. Comparative aspects of Oxford will be included to show how the two responded to similar influences.

Rashdall's appraisal of medieval Cambridge as 'third-rate' is harsh but not entirely unwarranted. When compared with Paris or Oxford, Cambridge was a small, provincial university in its first two hundred years. But, by the foundation of Trinity College in 1546 and the death of Henry VIII shortly afterwards, it was undeniably of the first rank in both wealth and prestige. Its graduates were to dominate the life of the Elizabethan Church and State, and many of its scholars enjoyed international reputations. To understand how this remarkable transition came about requires an examination of the small East Anglian university from its founding and early growth through the reverses of the Black Death. That was prologue. The one hundred years from the founding of King's College in 1441–43 to the royal foundation of Trinity College in 1546 saw the fulfilment of Cambridge as one of the world's great universities. It was a time of renewal and reform that restructured its relationship to both the Church and State, and within Cambridge the relationship of college to university along lines which are still recognisable today. These were developments which by 1510 brought it to the vanguard of the northern renaissance, changes which antedated the Reformation. It is a unique story of university development, and one in which Cambridge should take pride.

Chapter 1

ORIGINS

THE TOWN

If on a clear day you begin at Cherry Hinton Spring about two miles south-east of Cambridge and walk up Lime Kiln Road onto the high ground, you will be rewarded with a lovely and instructive view of the district of Cambridge. The chalk hill you stand on had a prehistoric defensive enclosure. To the south rise the Gog Magog hills, similarly fortified before the coming of the Romans. In front of you the Cam flows north-east past Castle Hill and off into the Fens to Ely and, forty miles away, the Wash. The Roman road known as the *Via Devana* coming up from Colchester passed over the Gogs and into the gentle valley, forded the river at the defensible spot under Castle Hill, and then ran straight towards Huntingdon and connections to the north. Another road, 'Akeman Street', entered the vista from the south-west and crossed the first by Castle Hill and continued north-east to the Isle of Ely.

These salient features explain why Cambridge was settled by the Romans, and why it survived their retreat and was resettled successively by Angles, Danes, and Normans. Contrary to what is often said, Cambridge is not in the Fens, but on the edge of them; the site of the ford and later bridge by Castle Hill was the easiest point of passage between much of East Anglia and the north and west, while the river provided (until the nineteenth century) the main route for traffic through the Fens to the sea.[1]

Roman Cambridge was a four-sided fort of about twenty-five acres on the high ground of the Castle End district north-

[1] RCHM, I, p. 1; *Atlas of Historic Towns*, II, ed. M. D. Lobel and W. H. Johns (London, 1975), Cambridge.

7

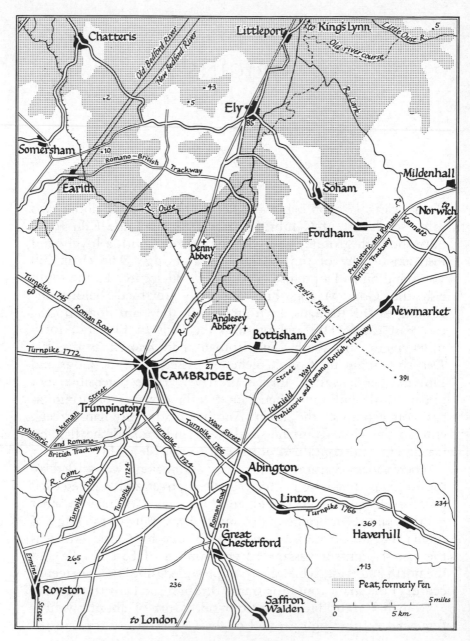

1 Cambridge and the neighbouring Roman roads.

west of the bridge (or possibly only a ford). It was divided into quadrants by the intersection of Akeman Street and the *Via Devana*, the latter the present day Castle Street and Huntingdon Road. The site was defensible because of its height; anyone who has regularly bicycled up Castle Street will contest the popular image of Cambridge's unvarying flatness. The Romans were building by at least AD 70, and their fort was surrounded by a ditch and wall, which by a later date was made of tile-laced mortared rubble. Only a few important buildings would have been made of stone, with the rest of the town built of wood, clay, and thatch. Outside the walls there were dwellings on both banks of the river and scattered throughout the vicinity. However, Roman Cambridge seems never to have been more than an important local junction and market. We are not even certain what its name was; possibly *Durolipons*.[2]

Roman occupation persisted until the early fifth century and the recall of the last legions. The Anglo-Saxons who succeeded them continued to settle on the Castle Hill site, as well as on the other bank around what is now Market Hill. The river perhaps served as the frontier between East Anglian and Middle Anglian territory in the sixth and seventh centuries, which emphasised the 'dual nature' of the early medieval town. After 634 the whole district came increasingly under Mercian control, and in the next century the linking bridge was rebuilt, possibly under King Offa (757–96). Cambridge was not at this time an important place even by contemporary standards. The Venerable Bede writing in the late seventh century described it as 'a desolate little city called Grantacaestir', a name that must not be confused with that of the present village to the south, celebrated by Rupert Brooke's poetry. The river was called the 'Granta' or 'Ree' or 'Ee' in the middle ages, and our town 'Grantebrycge' from the ninth century until the thirteenth. The first use of 'Cantebrig' does not appear until the twelfth century. The euphonic change of 'nt' to 'm' to produce the city's modern name did not happen until the fifteenth century, and the river is only called the 'Cam' (by backformation) after

[2] RCHM, I, pp. xxxvi–xxxvii, lx, lxv–lxvi.

1600.[3] Parts of the river above Cambridge retain the name Granta still.

Cambridge was swept again by invasion in 875, this time by the Danes, and in 878 passed into the Danelaw. The town prospered in the 200 years preceding the Conquest, despite being burned in 1010 during the northern invasions. The market centre was firmly established on the right bank of the river and Castle Hill, although still inhabited, was commercially unimportant. The Danish settlement, called the *holm*, centred in the church of St Clement (a common Danish dedication) and the wharves of the international traders lined the river nearby. The city filled the area enclosed by the 'King's Ditch', which was possibly first dug at this time.

The Saxons reconquered the area *c.* 917, and during the next hundred years developed the land along the river, south of the Danish settlement. Merchants' houses and wharves appeared. From the tenth century until the Conquest, Cambridge also had a mint, striking coins with the placename abbreviated to 'Grant'. The foundation of the older city churches along St John's Street, Trinity Street, King's Parade, and Trumpington Street possibly dates from this period of prosperity, including St Bene't's (perhaps *c.* 1000), whose pre-Conquest tower survives.[4]

The effects of William's victory at Hastings were fully felt in Cambridge in 1068 when the Conqueror, having ravaged York, marched south, leaving a trail of castles in Lincoln, Huntingdon, and Cambridge. For the last he chose the old Roman site which controlled the river, road, and market town. The castle itself was a motte and bailey structure (the motte survives) that required the destruction of twenty-seven houses to make room for it. The Domesday account of 1086 shows a prosperous town of ten wards under the control of William's appointed sheriff. It was taxed at ten times the rate of the average Cambridgeshire village. The town already had two mills, and the sheriff pulled

---

[3] RCHM, I, p. lxvi; J. W. Clark and A. Gray, *Old Plans of Cambridge* (Cambridge, 1921), pp. xi–xii; for an alternative explanation, see A. Gray, *The Dual Origins of the Town of Cambridge*, CAS, Quarto Publications, n.s. 1 (Cambridge, 1908), pp. 31–2.

[4] RCHM, I, p. xli and 263–6; J. Haslam, 'The Development and Topography of Saxon Cambridge', *CAS, Proceedings*, 72 (1982–3), pp. 12–29.

down more houses to build a third. These were on the site of the later 'King's Mill', marked now by the weir above the Silver Street bridge. Cambridge remained the central port of the shire, and under Henry I all landing of goods in the shire and collecting of tolls on them was restricted to the city. [5]

By 1200 Cambridge was securely established as an entrepôt for commerce between the shire, the fenlands, and the sea beyond. The city, bounded on the right bank by the King's Ditch, had three principal streets. The *Via Devana* (now Castle, Magdalene, Bridge, and Sidney Streets) entered past the Castle, went over the bridge (which, as Maitland remarked, is the only one to give its name to a county) [6] and continued through the town to the Barnwell Gate at the King's Ditch. The gate is commemorated today by the bend in the street next to Lloyd's Bank; the road turns to pass obliquely through the ghost of the medieval gate. Much of the commercial life of the town lay along the second principal thoroughfare, the medieval High Street (now St John's, Trinity, King's Parade, and Trumpington Streets), which branched from the old Roman road in the Jewish quarter and ran south to the Trumpington Gate, and London. A third street of somewhat lesser importance ran parallel to the High Street but nearer the river. Called Milne Street, fragments of it survive as Trinity Hall Lane and Queens' Lane.

Most of medieval Cambridge's numerous churches can still be seen today. The visitor entering the city by the Castle and continuing to Trumpington Gate passed eleven churches, and four lay just out of his sight. The first Norman sheriff established a small group of Austin Canons at St Giles Church south of the Castle in 1092, and his successor increased that foundation and moved it to a new site north-east of the town at Barnwell, where it was to flourish. Beyond Barnwell there was also a leper hospital dedicated to St Mary Magdalene, whose chapel has miraculously survived. [7] (Of the whole Barnwell Priory complex of the Austin Canons only a small fragment exists

---

[5] F. W. Maitland, *Township and Borough* (Cambridge, 1898), pp. 54–7; RCHM, I, p. xli.
[6] Maitland, *Township and Borough*, p. 37.
[7] *VCH*, II, pp. 234–49; C. N. L. Brooke, 'The Churches of Medieval Cambridge', in *History, Society and the Churches*, ed. D. Beales and G. Best (Cambridge, 1985), pp. 49–76.

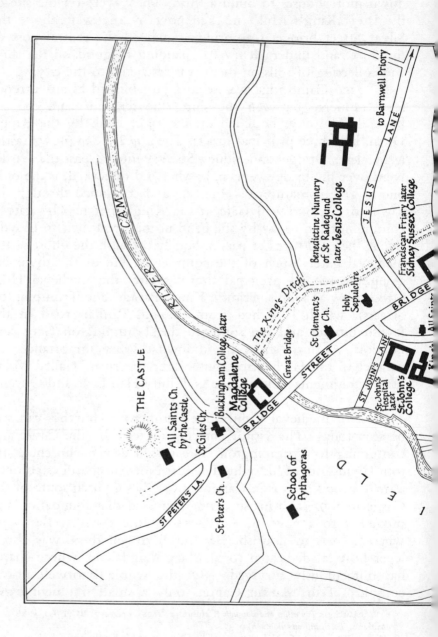

THE CASTLE

RIVER CAM

All Saints Ch. by the Castle

St Giles' Ch.

Buckingham College, later Magdalene College

The King's Ditch

Great Bridge

St Clement's Ch.

Holy Sepulchre

Bendictine Nunnery of St Radegund later Jesus College

JESUS LANE

to Barnwell Priory

Franciscan Friary later Sidney Sussex College

BRIDGE

St John's Hospital later St John's College

ST JOHN'S LANE

BRIDGE STREET

St Peter's Ch.

ST PETER'S LA.

School of Pythagoras

FIELD

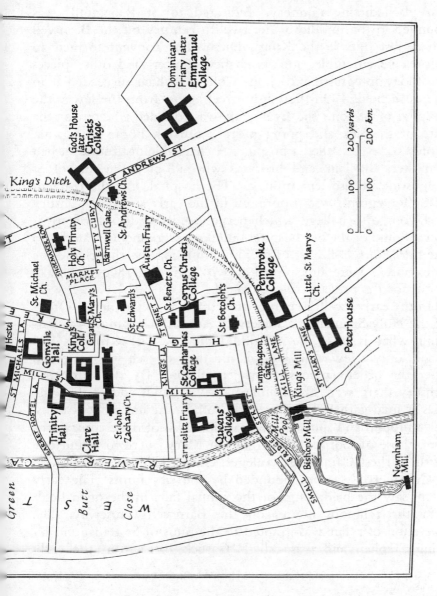

2 Cambridge c. 1500.

Green

Butt Close

RIVER CAM

King's Ditch

God's House later Christ's College

Dominican Friary later Emmanuel College

ST ANDREWS ST

St Andrews Ch.

PETTY CURY

Barnwell Gate

Holy Trinity Ch.

SHOEMAKERS ROW

MARKET PLACE

St Michael Ch.

Hostel

ST MICHAELS LA.

Gonville Hall

King's Coll.

Great St Mary's Ch.

Austin Friary

St Edward's Ch.

St Benet's Ch.

Corpus Christi College

ST BENET ST

KINGS LA.

St Botolph's Ch.

Pembroke College

Little St Mary's Ch.

Peterhouse

SCHOOL STREET

HIGH ST

Trinity Hall

Clare Hall

St John Zachary Ch.

MILL ST

St Catharine's College

Carmelite Friary

Queens' College

BRIDGE STREET

SMALL BRIDGES

Bishop's Mill

Mill Pool

Trumpington Gate

MILL LANE

King's Mill

ST MARY'S LANE

Newnham Mill

St Margaret Hostel La.

200 yards

200 km

100

100

0

0

13

today, an outbuilding in the midst of terraced houses near the gasworks.)

A Benedictine nunnery, dedicated to St Radegund, was founded in the middle of the twelfth century off the Barnwell Road, just outside the King's Ditch. The convent formed an impressive ensemble, and its chapel, cloister, and other pieces are today integrated into Jesus College, which succeeded it in the open fields.[8] On the High Street across from the Jewry the hospital of St John the Evangelist was founded *c.* 1200 for the care of the sick and poor; more a nursing home than what would today be called a hospital. A charitable institution, it had a master, chaplain, and brothers who adopted the rule of St Augustine. It also lent money.[9] The hospital, like the convent of St Radegund, was suppressed in the early sixteenth century in favour of a college which perpetuated the dedication to St John. Some of the old hospital buildings were incorporated into the first court and most of them, comprising the chapel and the 'labyrinth', were not pulled down until the 1860s to make room for the present college chapel.

In the early twelfth century the 'small and ephemeral' Order of the Holy Sepulchre, a society of Augustinian canons regular, built what is now the 'Round Church'. The Crusades had begun only a few years before, and their church was patterned after the order's namesake in Jerusalem.[10] By the thirteenth century there were also numerous civic guilds and confraternities as men gathered together for both social and pious reasons, for temporal and spiritual mutual aid. Two of these confraternities, those of Corpus Christi and St Mary, were to found one of the earliest Cambridge colleges, Corpus Christi.

Commerce was not bounded by the city limits. The early 1200s saw the beginnings of the annual fairs in the open fields near the religious houses on the Barnwell Causeway. The operation of a fair was granted to the nuns of St Radegund by King Stephen and was called 'Garlick Fair' from the early

[8] A. Gray, *The Priory of Saint Radegund, Cambridge*. CAS, Octavo Publications, 31 (Cambridge, 1898).

[9] *VCH*, II, pp. 303–7; M. Rubin, *Charity and Community in Medieval Cambridge* (Cambridge, 1986), pp. 148–246.

[10] *VCH*, III, p. 124; Brooke, 'Churches of Medieval Cambridge', p. 56.

3 Jesus College, successor of St Radegund's Convent in the fields outside
medieval Cambridge.

name for Park Street, where it was held. The canons of
Barnwell acquired the right by royal charter in 1211 to hold a
fair on 22–5 June, a fair which gave its name to Midsummer
Common. It survived the suppression of the canons at the
Reformation and in the eighteenth century was a fashionable
event that coincided with Commencement.[11] Midsummer Fair
continues today, a noisy carnival that is probably close to the
spirit, if not the local economic value, of its medieval ancestor.

By far the greatest Cambridge fair was the Stourbridge, first
granted by King John to the leper hospital of St Mary Magdalene. The hospital ceased to function by 1279 but the fair
continued to grow, lasting from 24 August to 29 September.
By 1589 it was called the 'largest and most famous fair in all
England', and it is the 'Vanity Fair' described by Bunyan in

---

[11] *VCH*, III, pp. 91–2.

Pilgrim's Progress. The city and university exercised joint control, the latter arresting exhibitors for such things as 'shewing oliphants' without licence. Stourbridge Fair declined from the eighteenth century and was last proclaimed in 1933 to an audience of three: one vendor, a mother, and her daughter.[12]

Cambridge was a thriving community in 1201 and 1207 when charters of King John consolidated the town as a corporation. It was the market for the immediate area, as well as being an emporium for commerce throughout the Fenlands, and had its own community of Jews who, along with St John's Hospital, could provide loans. It was not a cathedral town, however, and since 1109 was subject to the Bishop of Ely sixteen miles away (it had previously been in the diocese of Lincoln). There were grammar masters who taught in the town, and were, by canon law, under the jurisdiction of the ordinary.[13] We know little of these grammarians, except that neither they, nor the canons of Barnwell, formed an incipient university. The University of Cambridge began *ex nihilo* with a handful of masters who arrived down the Huntingdon Road, crossed the bridge, and settled in rented lodgings in the neighbourhood of Great St Mary's Church. They were from Oxford, and had just escaped serious troubles there.

THE FOUNDATION OF THE UNIVERSITY

By 1209 the struggle between Pope Innocent III and King John had put England into a state of ecclesiastical confusion. The death of the Archbishop of Canterbury in 1205 had led to a disputed election in which the Pope supported Stephen Langton as primate, a candidate unacceptable to the King for political reasons. The resulting quarrel led to an interdict on England in March 1208, and to John's excommunication in 1209. All but one bishop left for the continent, leaving the country's law courts and government in chaos.

---

[12] *VCH*, III, pp. 92–5; CUA, Comm. Court v/1, Documents relating to Stourbridge Fair, 1610–1854.
[13] Canon 18 of the Third Lateran Council, *CJC*, X.5.5.1.

The foundation of the university

In the academic year 1208–9, during these national troubles, an incident of apparent local importance occurred in Oxford; a scholar killed a townswoman with an arrow. Whether this was an accident depends on the bias of the several chroniclers who recorded the event. The mayor and townsmen, unable to apprehend the scholar in question, seized two or three of his housemates and, with the consent of King John, hanged them outside the walls of Oxford. This clear violation of the privilege of clerics – all scholars were by definition clerics – was not lost on a society that still remembered the death of Becket thirty-nine years earlier. The scholars of Oxford ran for their lives.[14]

Dispersals of medieval universities were frequent when local authorities infringed upon their privileges. The medieval universities were corporations of masters and their apprentice scholars. During the subsequent decades of the thirteenth century their legal positions were defined more precisely in England and on the continent, usually as a result of troubles such as those at Oxford in 1209. A *universitas* had the right to elect its own head, to own property, and to sue and be sued in court. It could make constitutions and statutes that were binding by oath on its members.[15] The university was its members acting in concert, and had nothing to do with buildings, quadrangles, or external financing. All the property Oxford University owned in common in 1209 could probably have fitted into a single chest: some account books, a little cash, and perhaps a few books, vestments, or vessels bequeathed to it by recently deceased masters. The masters rented their lodging and classrooms, and when they assembled they used nearby churches.

[14] R. W. Southern, 'From Schools to University', in *HUO*, I, pp. 26–32; C. E. Mallet, *A History of the University of Oxford* (3 vols. Oxford, 1924–7), I, pp. 31–3; H. Rashdall, *The Universities of Europe in the Middle Ages*, ed. F. M. Powicke and A. B. Emden (3 vols. Oxford, 1936), III, pp. 276–8. The source is Roger of Wendover, *Flores Historiarum*, ed. H. G. Hewlett, Rolls Series 84 (London, 1886–9), II, pp. 51, 94, which was used by Matthew Paris, *Chronica Maiora*, ed. H. R. Luard, Rolls Series 57 (London, 1872–83), II, pp. 525–6, 568–9, and *Historia Anglorum*, ed. F. Madden, Rolls Series 44 (London, 1866–9), II, p. 120. We have unfortunately to rely on the unreliable Wendover for this incident; cf. R. Parker, *Town and Gown* (Cambridge, 1983), p. 18, 'Cantabs may find it slightly embarrassing to admit that the University of Cambridge possibly owes its origin to the murder of a prostitute by an Oxford Student...'

[15] M. B. Hackett, *The Original Statutes of Cambridge University: The Text and its History* (Cambridge, 1970), pp. 49–50.

So, given a situation of very real danger, they simply left and rented rooms in another town, where they continued teaching and collecting fees from their students.

The usual pattern for dispersals was to go to towns or cities which already had schools of some sort, but not universities. This occurred in Paris in 1227 when a brawl occasioned by a disputed tavern bill escalated into a dispersal to Orleans, Toulouse, and Angers and the establishing of daughter universities there. The Oxford dispersal of 1209 was slightly different; some of the scholars went to Reading, a town undistinguished by any earlier schools, but one which had the advantage of being handy to Oxford for the day when ecclesiastical order might return to the realm and allow a return to Oxford. Others went east, bypassing Northampton which already had schools that would have been fertile ground for a new university, and settled instead in Cambridge, which was no centre of studies.[16] Many stayed and formed a new university. 'I understand that it is still there', Lord Dacre has written, and he continued by quoting Rashdall, 'what attracted them to that distant marsh town, we do not know'.[17] We can now suggest a plausible explanation, thanks to the meticulous scholarship of A. B. Emden and M. B. Hackett.

An examination of the Bishop of Ely's charters for the early thirteenth century shows a sharp increase in *magistri* who acted as witnesses to episcopal charters. This was obviously the result of the influx of Oxford masters into the diocese in 1209, and three of these masters can be shown to have been at Oxford earlier. Furthermore, some of these witnessing masters were from important Cambridge families. John Grim, doctor of theology, was master of the schools of Oxford in 1201, the chief official before the institution of the chancellorship *c.* 1216. As Hackett has written, 'his standing at Oxford coupled with his Cambridge background, assuming that he was born in the town, and the influence which his family could be depended upon to lend were possibly decisive factors that persuaded his

[16] H. G. Richardson, 'The Schools of Northampton in the Twelfth Century', *English Historical Review*, 56 (1941), 595–605.
[17] H. Trevor-Roper, *The Rise of Christian Europe* (London, 1965), p. 151.

fellow masters to set up business in Cambridge for the term of the *suspendium* at Oxford.'[18] This involves some conjecture, but seems plausible. Men from Cambridge families were probably able to strike good bargains with their fellow townsmen for lodgings and classrooms. Besides, Cambridge was convenient for ex-Oxonians of eastern origin. Among the earliest Cambridge masters we find names like John of Foxton, Adam of Horningsea, John of Stortford, and others with nearby place-names.[19] Cambridge continued until the twentieth century to recruit very heavily from the eastern counties.

Four years passed before King John made his submission to the Pope and ecclesiastical relations were once again regularised in England. The citizens of Oxford, having lost the protection of the King, were forced to seek out the papal legate and make peace with the clerks. By a legatine ordinance of 1214 the townsmen were required to perform considerable spiritual and financial penances – including annual payments which survived until 1984 – and the university was reconvened on a more secure basis in Oxford. Scholars returned from their exile in Reading and elsewhere, and many probably left Cambridge at this time.[20] But other members of the nascent university on the Granta were comfortably situated in the market town near their home villages. They stayed behind and continued to teach and be taught. They were the founders of England's second university.

THE GROWTH OF THE UNIVERSITY

The word 'university' today defines very different kinds of institution in Cambridge, Colchester, Cairo, and Kalamazoo. The word described something equally different in the middle ages. A *universitas* was a group of persons, as broadly defined as the subjects of a kingdom or as specific as a guild of men engaged in teaching. Thus, the expression used to specify what

[18] Hackett, pp. 46–7.
[19] *BRUC*, pp. 241, 272, 315, 560.
[20] Southern, p. 30; Mallett, *History of Oxford*, I, pp. 32–3; G. Pollard, 'The Legatine Award to Oxford in 1214 and Robert Grosteste', *Oxoniensia*, 39 (1974), 62–73; C. H. Lawrence, 'The Origins of the Chancellorship at Oxford', *Oxoniensia*, 41 (1976), 316–23; for cancelling the annual payment, see *The Guardian*, 29 June 1984, p. 1.

we are discussing was a 'university of masters and scholars' or a 'university of studies'. Similarly, a college, or *collegium* in the thirteenth century could mean any established community or corporation, a definition that survives in the College of Cardinals and the Royal College of Physicians.

The word used to specify a teaching guild as recognised by civil or canon law in the thirteenth century was a *studium generale*. A *studium generale*, as the concept developed, had several salient features. It was a school that possessed at least one and preferably several of the superior faculties (theology, law, or medicine), in addition to the foundation faculty of the liberal arts and philosophy. A *studium generale* had at least several masters in these fields, and it attracted students from outside its immediate district. The original *studia* that included these elements were not founded, but developed in the twelfth century out of the free association of scholars into centres of learning without charters. The definition followed the practice. These proto-universities included Bologna, celebrated for law, Paris, for arts and theology, and Salerno and Montpellier for medicine. They varied considerably in their constitutions, from the Bolognese model where the legal corporation was the students, to the Parisian (and Oxford) model where the masters formed the corporation, and the scholars stood as apprentices to them. There were also *studia particularia* in many cities, often ancient centres of scholarship like Laon or Chartres, which lacked the multiplicity of faculties or masters to qualify as *studia generalia* or 'universities'.[21]

It was only about 1200 that the *studium generale* began to take on a legally defined character, usually as a result of trouble with the civil authorities over questions of privilege and jurisdiction as at Paris and Oxford. In such quarrels appeals were made to higher authorities, usually the Pope or Emperor, who soon became active in founding universities as well. In 1224 Frederick II by decree produced a *studium generale* in Naples, and in 1229 Gregory IX chartered the recently-arrived scholars in Toulouse. By the second half of the thirteenth century universities no

---

[21] A general introduction to these concepts is found in Rashdall, *Medieval Universities*, I, pp. 1–8.

longer developed out of the free association of scholars, but relied on papal and imperial charters to define where and when they existed; and so it has remained to the present between governments and teachers.

Beginning in 1233 the papal charters included a clause that attempted to put the newer foundations on an equal footing with the earlier *studia*. Called the *ius ubique docendi*, or 'right to teach anywhere', it meant that a master of that university could freely teach in another without further examination or study. In practice this was rarely if ever the case, but the idea was respected and the *ius ubique docendi* was soon included in all the new charters of foundation, and often acknowledged retrospectively in papal relations with older universities.[22] Cambridge was so treated in a bull of John XXII in 1318. Oxford requested the *ius ubique docendi* in 1296, but the appeal was never granted. Nevertheless, it was universally regarded as a *studium generale* with the *ius ubique docendi* throughout the later middle ages by custom, and on the strength of Henry III's royal writ.

Both Oxford and Cambridge drew their legal standing in large part from royal writ, and in particular from the interest of Henry III. His long-term support of university education was probably due to a desire for trained clerks, along with the honour a university could bring to a kingdom. In 1229, when Paris dispersed, he invited its scholars to come to England. His particular interest was Oxford (he regularly stayed at his Beaumont palace just north of the city), but Cambridge benefited as well. His earliest privilege of 1231 extended to both universities, and it was followed by others. Also important for the future of Oxford and Cambridge was their monopoly on university education, again supported by Henry III. In 1265 he suppressed the incipient university of Northampton, in part because of episcopal and university pressure. This monopoly was assured again in 1334 when the masters at Stamford were suppressed. England was unique in limiting higher education so rigorously until the nineteenth century.[23]

[22] Rashdall, *Medieval Universities*, I, pp. 8–17.
[23] C. H. Lawrence, 'The University in State and Church', in *HUO*, I, pp. 125–32.

The Oxford masters who migrated to Cambridge in 1209 brought with them a model of the *studium generale* which they in turn had taken from Paris. The university was still more an idea than a legal corporation, and because of the close links of Paris with Oxford, and of Oxford with Cambridge, the English universities developed almost simultaneously, although different relationships with their respective bishops made their constitutions different from the Parisian model. In broad strokes, Oxford and Cambridge were by 1250 guilds of masters who taught their trade to apprentices.[24] Within these guilds there were several faculties, the largest being the faculty of liberal arts. The entering scholar began by putting himself under the discipline of a master of arts, whom he paid. The master put his name on the *matricula* (class list), which made him a legal undergraduate. He attended lectures and scholastic disputations, and after four years, if he had learned well, he was presented to the congregation of masters of arts and given permission to 'determine', that is, to be tested in a public disputation. Performing this act made him a bachelor of arts, in effect a journeyman master who partially shared in the masters' privileges of lecturing and presiding at disputations.

After three more years of study the bachelor could supplicate the chancellor for a licence to 'incept', or begin his career as a master. The masters of his faculty then made depositions, oaths that he was a suitable candidate for the *magisterium* both by his learning and character (*in scientia et moribus*). With permission obtained, the candidate, now called an 'inceptor', was authorised to lecture, dispute, and perform all of the duties of a master. The actual 'inception' was a two-day affair in which he was invested with a ring, robe, and hat of his office, swore oaths of fidelity to the corporation, gave a banquet for the other masters, and formally mounted the steps (*gradus* – hence graduation) to the master's chair and became a master himself by the act of practising his trade. He was obliged by oath to continue teaching for one or two years, a period known as his 'regency'. This assured the university of a supply of teachers. The newly-

---

[24] See Adam Smith, *The Wealth of Nations* v.3, art. 2; E. Gibbon, *Memoirs of My Life*, ed. B. Radice (Harmondsworth, 1984), p. 77.

created master of arts could then become a member of one of the superior faculties, such as theology or law, and passing through similar steps of bachelorhood, enter the *magisterium* in one of those faculties as well.

Thus medieval Oxford and Cambridge bear, from a constitutional point of view, a closer resemblance to the Worshipful Guild of Fishmongers than they do to the modern University of Sussex. Any appraisal of the acts and exercises of these medieval universities must always be seen in the light of the medieval guild or confraternity, and the relation of the scholar to his master as that of an apprentice to an artisan or a squire to a knight. The role of the bachelor was essentially the same, whether he stood in relation to a master or a knight.

The language of the *studia*, Latin, was shared by the initiates. The academic costumes and order of precedence were those of a caste system, albeit one that served to advance talent. The master was a brother within a mystery; he swore oaths, had privileges, and shared ritual equality with other masters, and they prayed for each other's souls. The guild limited membership to those whom they themselves alone approved. The inception of a new member was marked by processions, evening ceremonies, prayer, investiture, rings and the sharing of a banquet. It was a time of initiation, of beginning and end, and was marked by the many universal symbols of such a ritual passage.

The university was a unique medieval development, separate from the oratorical schools of the ancient world and the *scholae* of the earlier medieval monasteries. The schools of Socrates, Cicero, and Quintilian were concerned with the development of both the ethical and political man, an ideal which found its fruition in the citizen orator. The *studium generale* had no such broad social goal, no dialogues in the agora or forum. This is not to deny that schoolmen had a place in the corridors of secular or ecclesiastical power, but it was not exercised, practically or theoretically by means of oratory, public persuasion, or personal ethical example. The logical and metaphysical intricacies of the disputations, although artifacts of a culture where the dissemination of learning was in part oral, had a different purpose from the *Tusculan Disputations*. They had few echoes in the political life of England, and were the rites of passage of a closed society, comprising only a fraction of the population, and a very small percentage of the landed nobility who generally educated their children at home or in neighbouring households.

Most university men were preparing for careers in the Church or in the growing royal bureaucracy. The advanced faculties of theology and law provided specific training for ecclesiastical work, and most of the arts students in the later middle ages went into parochial work. Although studies in grammar, rhetoric, logic, and philosophy had application for the cure of souls (particularly for preaching) the foundation provided in the arts course was generally a high culture product, of interest only within the company of other scholars. This education did have a value in itself, for the advancement of the human understanding of God's creation served the Christian commonwealth. The arts curriculum, however, was not vocational training in any direct form, and it was the arts faculty that was usually the largest in Cambridge. Its curriculum was thought to include the finest products of human reason, which prepared the scholar for the study of the divine. That it was valuable was unquestioned; a parallel can be seen in the belief held until recently that first-class honours in classics was a solid preparation for service in the Foreign Office or the Treasury.

How did Cambridge develop as a *studium generale* in its early years? As historians have written, the early years are 'shrouded in the mists of time'. Roger of Wendover's *Chronicle* tells us only that in 1209 some of the Oxford scholars went 'apud Cantebregge' and that in 1213 the Oxford burghers sought to make peace, which was accomplished by a legatine ordinance of 1214.[25] As Hackett has written, 'how recently a faculty of arts, the oldest and most powerful faculty all through the medieval period, developed, or how soon a university in the corporate and academic sense evolved we cannot say'.[26]

---

[25] Roger of Wendover, *Flores historiarum*, II, pp. 51, 94. [26] Hackett, p. 47.

What is clear is that Cambridge in its first fifteen years continued to consolidate itself and attract the attention of those outside its immediate district. About 1226 the young Order of Friars Minor thought it an important enough place to send several brothers to found a house. The previous year the existence of a chancellor is first recorded, where he appears as a judge in an ecclesiastical court outside the university.[27] This mention is within ten years or so of the first appearance of a chancellor in Oxford (*c.* 1216), and we may presume, with the close contact of the two communities, the men of Cambridge and the Bishop of Ely were aware of developments in Oxford and Lincoln. The diocesan connections are important here, because education was licensed by the diocesan bishop acting through his executive officer, in the case of Ely through the archdeacon. It is not clear when this began, but by 1225 the Bishop of Ely was treating the university as a 'distinct canonical society' within the diocese, and had created by fiat an official, the chancellor, who acted as its head. Thus, 'the *studium*, although founded by the masters who led the secession to Cambridge in 1209, received its title and its capacity to act as a *universitas* from the bishop'.[28] With this status came other privileges such as the right to elect its own officers, hold property, to sue and be sued, and to make constitutions and statutes binding under oath.[29]

Cambridge as a corporation or *universitas* next appears in the decree of Henry III in 1231. The writ, addressed to both universities, granted them several important corporate rights. The universities were allowed, in conjunction with representatives from the towns, to fix the annual rent of the houses let to scholars for lodging and classrooms – a most useful privilege in assuring the stability of the young institutions. Secondly, all scholars were required to register with a master within fifteen days of arrival at university, to have their names placed on the *matricula* of that master, or face arrest. And finally, Henry III

---

[27] *BRUC*, p. 367 (Richard de Leycestria *alias* Wethringsette); *Curia regis rolls*, pp. 9–10, Henry III, xii (1957), pp. 129–30, no. 646. In *HUO*, I, 1214, 1215, and 1216 are variously given for the first Oxford chancellor. For the Franciscans, see J. R. H. Moorman, *The Grey Friars in Cambridge* (Cambridge, 1952), pp. 1–18. He inconclusively argues for a 1225 arrival.
[28] Hackett, p. 52.   [29] Hackett, p. 49.

provided legal machinery to enforce these rules, and required the town sheriff to arrest at the request of the chancellor any troublesome students.[30]

The rights and judicial identity of Cambridge were further strengthened by a bull of Pope Gregory IX in 1233, given at the request of the university. Addressed to the 'Chancellor and University of Cambridge', it acknowledged their university status and gave them the *ius non trahi extra*, which prohibited any court outside of the diocese from summoning a member of the university, provided he appeared before the chancellor or his bishop. This grant expired in three years and was never formally renewed, but Cambridge continued to exercise the prerogative throughout the middle ages.[31] Called the 'characteristic university privilege' by Dean Rashdall, it identified Cambridge in canon law as a full university with all of the rights of self-rule that the status implied.[32]

Within twenty years of this papal instrument of 1233 Cambridge produced its first constitutions and statutes, perhaps the first university to do so. When the scholars arrived in 1209 they had governed themselves by the customs they had learned in Oxford, and in the medieval world custom had the force of law. But by the mid-thirteenth century the masters of Cambridge felt the need to codify this tradition to help its enforcement, and make it binding by oath and the threat of perjury on those who violated it.

These earliest known statutes of Cambridge, properly edited only in 1970, can be dated from *c.* 1250. Probably written by a canon lawyer, they were possibly promulgated by the masters and chancellor meeting together in convocation. They are organised into thirteen rubrics, and run to only 251 lines. They deal with the university officers, masters, the hours of lectures, and funerary obligations. There is no mention of what anyone was specifically to teach or study, as that and much else were

[30] *Educational Charters and Documents*, ed. A. F. Leach (Cambridge, 1911), pp. 148–53.
[31] *Les Régistres de Grégoire IX*, ed. L. Auvray. Librairie des écoles Françaises d'Athènes et de Rome (Paris, 1908), I, p. 779, no. 1389; quoted in Hackett, pp. 26–7, 54.
[32] Rashdall, *Medieval Universities*, I, pp. 342, 418, n. 5; Hackett, p. 53.

left to custom. These statutes show the influence of Oxford practice, but not directly of the continental universities.[33] Oxford had remained in contact with its daughter through the interaction of masters, particularly the friars and those who had come to Cambridge in a second migration from Oxford in 1240.[34]

The university acting in concert was called convocation, which by these early statutes meant only the 'regent masters', that is, those graduates still actively engaged in teaching. By 1304, however, it included non-regents (graduates who had ceased teaching) as well and the term congregation referred to the body of regents. Convocation was formally summoned by the chancellor, and by 1300 (and probably much earlier) used Great St Mary's Church as its assembly hall, since the university owned no large hall of its own before the beginning of the fifteenth century. Convocation could also act as a canonical court when meeting.[35]

The head of convocation was the chancellor. Elected by the direct vote of the regent masters and (until the fifteenth century) subject to confirmation by the Bishop of Ely, he exercised in his court ordinary jurisdiction over all of the members of the university, as the archdeacon did for the bishop within the diocese and as individual masters did over their own scholars. The chancellor's jurisdiction also extended over those scholars who held cure of souls in the town and would otherwise have been subject to episcopal control. After 1305 this jurisdiction was defined to include cases between scholars and townsmen as well. By the earliest statutes the chancellor was empowered to delegate these powers to a commissary, although if the chancellor were absent for more than two weeks this power would be exercised by a vice-chancellor (the term originated in Cambridge) who was appointed by the regents voting in congregation. Thus the chancellor was not a separate estate within the university, but its chief executive officer, expressing the corporate will of the masters. The chancellor gave aspiring

[33] Hackett, p. 87; cf. W. Ullmann's review in *Journal of Ecclesiastical History*, 22 (1971), 134-9, which casts doubts on the 'official' nature of the statutes.
[34] Hackett, pp. 69-70.   [35] Hackett, pp. 143-6.

masters the licence to incept, but the candidate only became a regent himself by the act of being inducted by the other regents.[36]

The other university officers whose duties were defined are the rectors (soon to be known as proctors) and the bedells. The two rectors were by the statutes of *c.* 1250 appointed by the direct vote of the chancellor and convocation, although by 1302–7 this franchise was restricted to the regent masters of arts. Whichever candidate received the most votes became the senior proctor (or rector) and the runner-up the junior proctor (or rector). Their terms of office were one year, and they were responsible for acting as the taxors (with two townsmen) who assessed the rents of the houses used by the university. They were also to oversee the sale of bread, ale, and wine to prevent monopolistic practices and exorbitant pricing by the townsmen. The proctors' duties also included the scheduling of lectures, disputations, graduations, and funerals.

This dual office was possibly the result of tension between the 'nations' of northerners and southerners within the university. This extrastatutory distinction was the result of the traditional rivalry between Englishmen; it was far more apparent at Oxford, and had parallels in the four nations that made up the University of Paris. The two nations rioted at Oxford in 1252 and at Cambridge in 1260 hostilities broke out when southerners from Norfolk, Suffolk, and Cambridgeshire attacked the northerners, who in turn withdrew to Northampton where they set up their own university. Peace was made in 1265 when both Oxford and Cambridge imposed an oath on all inceptors that they would not teach anywhere other than the two established universities, nor recognise any masters who did so. Cambridge also followed Oxford's lead in requiring an oath from all incepting masters that they maintain the peace. It is possible that the custom arose at Cambridge, as at Oxford, that the two proctors would always be from different nations, although much research would be necessary to prove this.[37]

---

[36] Hackett, pp. 104–18.

[37] Hackett, pp. 152–8 and 225; Richardson, 'Schools of Northampton', pp. 595–605; A. B. Emden, 'Northerners and Southerners in the Organisation of the University to 1509', in *Oxford Studies Presented to Daniel Callus*, OHS, n.s. 16 (Oxford, 1964), pp. 1–30.

In addition to the proctors, the statutes recognised two lesser university officers, the bedells. Immediately answerable to the proctors, they were responsible for seating and general order in the classrooms, announced the decrees of the chancellor and convocation, rang the bells for the lectures, and collected the tuition fees from the students. They were to be present at all university assemblies, funerals, and academic acts, carrying their maces as signs of their office. One of the bedells was accredited to the faculty of arts, and the other to the superior faculties. The medieval bedells were usually non-graduates, and sometimes married.[38]

Among the scholars themselves discipline was established by requiring all to matriculate within a fortnight of their arrival, and to continue to attend all prescribed lectures and acts.[39] Otherwise, the scholar could not enjoy the privileges and immunities that came with membership in the university. Those expelled from Oxford, burglars, assaulters of women, and any who flouted the university rules were not to be so accredited, and if they already had been, they were to be expelled.

The statutes regulated the annual rhythms of academic life.[40] A calendar outlined the three terms, which throughout the middle ages and renaissance were known by a myriad of names. The first, Michaelmas (or Winter, Autumn, and Christmas) began the day after the feast of St Dennis (9 October) and lasted until 'O Sapientia', the sixteenth of December (so-called from the antiphon in vespers for that day). Lent term (or Hilary, Easter, and Annunciation) began the day after the feast of St Hilary (13 January) and continued until the Friday before Palm Sunday. Easter term (or Summer, Ultimo, and St John the Baptist) began on the Wednesday after the first Sunday after Easter and continued until the feast of St Margaret (20 July). By the early fourteenth century this term was shortened back to 6 July, the Vigil of the Translation of St Thomas of Canterbury. This Easter term was divided by a ten-day break

---

[38] Hackett, pp. 159–62; H. P. Stokes, *The Esquire Bedells of the University of Cambridge (1250–1568)*, CAS, Octavo Publications, 45 (Cambridge, 1911), esp. pp. 49–80; *Annals*, I, p. 131 (1386).
[39] Hackett notes three surviving lists, in Gonville and Caius MSS 385/605, 465/572, and 593/453 (pp. 167, 348–9).   [40] Hackett, pp. 142–3.

from the Friday before Pentecost until the Monday after Trinity Sunday.

By the fifteenth century there was a non-statutory fourth term at Cambridge during the long vacation. Known as the *terminus autumnalis* it was frequently mentioned in the late medieval records. Although statutorily no ordinary lectures were given in this term, work was done that the university considered serious enough to count towards graduation. There were lectures available within hostels and colleges and, by the late fifteenth century, from salaried university professors as well. Credit for this autumn term was variable, ranging in worth from a one to one correspondence with the other terms, to as little as three autumns for one term. This term gave a scholar more flexibility in his scheduling and in fulfilling his lecture requirements.[41]

Days in term were divided between *dies legibiles* and *non legibiles*, and *dies disputabiles* and *non disputabiles*, days set aside for lecturing or disputing, the dual essence of medieval university work. Legible days were those on which ordinary lectures were read in the Schools, and disputable days allowed for the solemn disputations of masters. Statutes in the middle ages also reserved days for reading cursory lectures, and also distinguished extraordinary lectures.

Ordinary lectures were to begin after the hour of prime (about 6 a.m.) and last until terce (about 9 a.m.), with the rest of the day reserved for extraordinary lectures and informal exercises. Ordinary lectures were delivered by regent masters for at least one year after their inception. They could be attended by both undergraduates and bachelors. The master was required to wear a prescribed habit, and the lecture was to consist of a 'diffuse, authoritative, *questiones* commentary based on an exact and profound understanding of the text'.[42] The amount of profound understanding doubtless varied from one master to the next.

---

[41] e.g. *GBk* A, p. 8 (1455–6) and p. 25 (1459–60). By 1501–2, eighteen of twenty-seven recipients of the BA counted autumn terms towards their course work, thus allowing the scholars to complete their course in three years, rather than four.

[42] Hackett, p. 134.

The habit worn at ordinary lectures was the *cappa clausa* or *pallium*. The former was a sleeveless, cope-like garment worn over the regent's clerical dress, and the *pallium* was identical except for having two slits for the arms, rather than a single opening in the front. They were both black, except for the secular doctors (those not members of a religious order) in canon law, who wore red.[43] The academic robes familiar today, with separate hoods, developed in the late middle ages and were elaborated in modern times. Dress was controlled for all scholars, and foppery was reckoned a recurring problem in medieval Cambridge. Formal complaints were made to the Archbishop of Canterbury in 1343 about long hair and gaudy gowns, and in 1444 the university passed further sumptuary legislation.[44]

Extraordinary lectures included any lecture not in the ordinary category by reason of time, person, or method. An extraordinary lecture could be read by a master or bachelor on any day other than a *dies legibilis*, read outside the Schools, cover any text, and be given without wearing the prescribed habit. They included those given within hostels and colleges, as happened increasingly by the fifteenth century. It was forbidden for any master to change an ordinary lecture into an extraordinary one, or vice versa, if he wanted it to count *pro forma*, that is, as part of the requirement for a scholar's degree. The distinction between ordinary and extraordinary lectures should be seen as primarily one of time and sponsorship, as they could be identical in content and method.[45] Extraordinary lectures included all those given in the non-statutory autumn term.

'Cursory' lectures were textual readings which 'served a useful purpose in the times when books were scarce, before the invention of printing'.[46] They were meant simply to transmit

---

[43] Hackett, p. 202.

[44] *Annals*, I, pp. 94–5 (1442), 355 (1532); Statutes 24 Henry VIII, c. 13, ss. 2, 7; *Docs.* I, no. 147, pp. 387–8; *Docs.* II, pp. 538–40; *Enactments in Parliament*, ed. L. Shadwell, OHS 58 (Oxford, 1912), I, 1–2.

[45] J. A. Weisheipl, 'Curriculum of the Faculty of Arts at Oxford in the Early Fourteenth Century', *Mediaeval Studies*, 26 (1964), 166, n. 83; T. Gascoigne, *Loci e libro veritatum*, ed. J. E. Thorold-Rogers (Oxford, 1881), p. 141, '...ita quod modus praedicandi ad populum sequatur modum legendi doctorum quando legunt ordinarie aut extraordinarie lecciones suas in scolis, declarantes in una leccione unam vel duas vel tres materias, vel contenta in eisdem'.

[46] *GBk* A, p. xxiv.

the contents of the book, not to analyse it as a master did. By a statute of the fourteenth century they were restricted to those bachelors who had finished determining, and their seniors. [47] This restricted anyone from sharing the masters' prerogative unless he had at least a BA. With the coming of relatively inexpensive printed books by 1500, the need for cursory lectures disappeared.

The original Cambridge statutes were concerned with administration and jurisdiction, and are silent about the real work of the university, teaching. This first set was modified and increased as problems arose, growing from the original thirteen into several hundred by 1500. In addition, by the fifteenth century a scholar who wanted to take a degree supplicated congregation for permission, and was awarded a 'grace'. The grace indicated in which ways his *forma* (course of studies) conformed to the statutes, and from which requirements he requested exemption. In this way the statutes were modified in individual cases to adapt to changing ideas on what was most useful. The statutes themselves were never considered immutable, but were a living tradition that was always supplemented by custom. It would be a mistake to assume that what was passed as a statute by congregation as a requirement for a degree in a given year was still being followed in practice fifty years later.

Nevertheless, the statutes are the touchstone for any discussion of Cambridge's history, even more so than the parallel statutes of medieval Oxford. Cantabrigians have long had a love of statutes, and throughout the middle ages and renaissance they reorganised and repromulgated the statutes several times. Cambridge has always seemed less willing than Oxford to allow custom to stand unaided by legal definition.

The earliest statutes describe the workings of a small corporation of scholars who taught through lectures and sharpened their learning in disputations. When these statutes were written down around 1250 there were only three faculties. The oldest and largest was the faculty of liberal arts, whose studies by ancient tradition included the trivium (grammar, logic, and

---

[47] *Docs.* I, no. 142, p. 385.

rhetoric), the quadrivium (arithmetic, music, geometry, and astronomy), and the three philosophies (moral, natural, and metaphysics). A scholar had first to take the degree of master of arts before proceeding to the superior faculties, although by the later middle ages lawyers rarely did so.[48]

The second early Cambridge faculty was theology, the Queen of Sciences. 'The highest distinction in the academic world', the doctorate in theology was, before the fourteenth century, obtainable only at Paris, Oxford, and Cambridge.[49] The Cambridge theology faculty could well date from the first decade after 1209, as those migrating Oxford scholars included several theologians. Theology was, by the end of the century, dominated by the mendicant friars, especially the Franciscans and Dominicans.[50] The third faculty was canon law, which also dates from the beginning of the university. Richard of Leicester, possibly the first chancellor, was a canon lawyer. Degrees in civil law were also given by 1257 although civil law was not, strictly speaking, a separate faculty from canon law. The two were twinned, with study in both required for every master of law regardless of specialisation.[51]

This was the basic structure of the early university. The scholars grew in strength and number throughout the century. The Franciscans were soon joined by other mendicant orders: Dominicans in the 1230s, Carmelites in 1247, possibly the Friars of Bethlehem in 1257, Friars of the Sack in 1258, Friars of St Mary's in 1273, the Austin Friars before 1289, and Gilbertine Canons in 1291. The increase of all kinds of scholars, secular and religious, was not without incident. A riot between town and gown in Lent 1249 led to multiple deaths and a partial migration back to Oxford. A similar row ensued in 1259, and in 1261 a brawl between northerners and southerners was soon joined by townsmen and degenerated into the burning and

[48] *Docs.* I, no. 124, p. 377; Hackett, p. 222.   [49] Hackett, p. 131.

[50] They even claimed to have founded the faculty. See J R H Moorman, *The Grey Friars in Cambridge*, p. 235. They are given significant credit for building up the theology faculty by A. G. Little in 'The Friars and the Foundation of the Faculty of Theology in the University of Cambridge' in *Franciscan Papers, Lists, and Documents* (Manchester, 1943), pp. 122–43. The Oxford Congregation in 1465 attributed the foundation of their theology faculty to the Benedictines (*Epistolae Academicae Oxon.*, ed. H. Anstey, OHS 36 (Oxford, 1898), II, 375–6).

[51] Hackett, pp. 29–32.

plundering of houses, with the migration to Northampton resulting. The King's justice was severe on the townsmen, with sixteen executed; many students were convicted and later pardoned, and those who had formed the university in Northampton were ordered by the King back to Cambridge in 1265.[52] Over the next ten years there were several steps taken to defuse this tension. By royal intervention a pact between town and gown, assured by oaths, was promulgated in 1270–1.[53] The sheriff was again given the power to punish malefactors at the request of the chancellor, and tournaments, jousting, and other distractions were prohibited within five miles of the town. The university tried to put its own house in order by passing a statute in 1275 giving the proctors additional power to enforce the peace within the university and among the townsmen.[54] This was the first of many statutory efforts to regulate the conduct of scholars and provide for a more tranquil community. It was, as will be seen, a continuing problem.

THE MEMBERS OF THE UNIVERSITY

Determining exactly who made up the medieval corporation of scholars in Cambridge, and how many there were in a given year, is impossible. Only fragmentary *matricula* of individual masters survive, and it can not be said how thoroughly the enrolment requirement was enforced. The impression from early fifteenth-century Oxford and Cambridge is that many unmatriculated and hence unsupervised students were disrupting the universities, and on that ground all scholars were required to belong to a hostel or college.[55] No complete class list for Cambridge survives before 1575, and contemporary population estimates were fantastic.[56]

---

[52] *Annals*, I, p. 45 (1249), 47–8 (1259), 48 (1261). For a popular account of these battles until the twentieth century, see Parker, *Town and Gown*.

[53] *Annals*, I, pp. 52–3 (1270); *The Privileges of the University of Cambridge*, ed. G. Dyer (2 vols. London, 1824), I, p. 66.   [54] *Annals*, I, p. 55 (1275).

[55] *Enactments in Parliament*, I, pp. 14–24; *Statuta Antiqua Universitatis Oxoniensis*, ed. S. Gibson (Oxford, 1931), pp. 60–1 (by 1275), 208 (c. 1410).

[56] e.g. Chancellor Thomas Gascoigne of Oxford, c. 1460, claimed that before 1349 Oxford had 30,000 scholars, 'ut vidi in rotulis antiquorum cancellariorum' (Gascoigne, p. 202). The first

The members of the university

The total number of pre-1500 members listed in A. B. Emden's *Biographical Registers* is over 7,000 for Cambridge and about 15,000 for Oxford. However, both these registers increase substantially in the fifteenth century when records become more numerous and thorough, at Cambridge especially after 1453 when the nearly unbroken series of proctors' accounts begin. They list all the scholars who were given permission (that is, a grace) to take a degree. Before these records begin, the sources are weighted towards the religious orders, college fellows, those promoted to ecclesiastical livings, and men who later achieved some degree of prominence. The son of a yeoman who studied for a few years and left without taking a degree or entering a college or a superior faculty had little chance of being included. Even Thomas More, who went up to Oxford from 1492 to 1494 from the household of Cardinal Morton, did his elementary studies and then returned to London to pursue common law without leaving an archival trace.

In spite of this often scanty documentation, some general conclusions can be drawn about the size of medieval Cambridge on the basis of detailed computer evaluations of the known alumni.[57] As at Oxford, the size of the university fluctuated from year to year, and the figures are only approximately calculated. Unfortunately, no estimates can be made for Cambridge before the Plague of 1349. In 1377 the university had perhaps between 400 and 700 members, while Oxford had about 1,500. Of the Cantabs about a third to a half were friars.[58] The university expanded from that point on, and by the mid-fifteenth century numbered roughly 1,200–1,300 (Oxford then had about 1,700) and continued to grow into the sixteenth century, closing the gap with Oxford. It then suffered a decrease in size between 1530 and 1560. The important fact

complete class list to survive at Cambridge is from September 1575 (BL Lansdowne MS 20, ff. 200r.–215v.). There is a much damaged tax assessment from 1522 in the Public Record Office, printed (as much as possible) in *LP*, Addendum, I, part 1, pp. 105–10.

[57] T. H. Aston, 'Oxford's Medieval Alumni', *Past and Present*, 74 (1977), 3–40, and T. H. Aston, G. D. Duncan and T. A. R. Evans, 'The Medieval Alumni of the University of Cambridge', *Past and Present*, 86 (1980), 9–86. The methodology of this computer analysis is explained at length in 'Cambridge Alumni', pp. 9–13.

[58] Aston *et al.*, 'Cambridge Alumni', pp. 11–27.

to note is that for most of the middle ages Cambridge probably never exceeded 600 or 700 members – fewer than the average modern secondary school in Britain or the United States.

The aspiring scholar usually began his education at a song school at about seven or eight (learning the alphabet and plainsong), and then did a year of basic grammar. The grammar course proper might then begin at the age of ten to twelve, and lasted five or six years.[59] Thus the normal age for a boy to enter university would be fifteen or sixteen, with exceptional boys starting earlier, and some rather later. The statutes of most of the Oxford and Cambridge colleges allowed entry between the ages of fifteen and twenty. There was no minimum age mentioned in the university statutes. It might have been fourteen years.[60] John Major's 1520 description of the scholars as *adulti* implies that most were at least eighteen years old.[61] Thus the old impression of medieval university students as 'boy clerics' must be modified. They were younger than university students are today, but were rarely 'children'. The case of Thomas Wolsey, BA *c.* 1489 of Oxford at age fifteen was exceptional enough to earn him the sobriquet 'boy batchelor'.[62]

In medieval Oxford and Cambridge 'very possibly more than half' of the scholars never took a degree.[63] These included those who came only for basic training in grammar and logic before pursuing common law (like More), those who left to become grammar school teachers (without degrees), and those whose financing failed. Even of those promising and well-prepared men who came up from Winchester College to New College, Oxford, one in seven left before completing two years, and of the remainder the same proportion left before taking the

---

[59] N. Orme, *Education in the West of England, 1066–1548* (Exeter, 1976), pp. 20, 60–2.

[60] Hackett, p. 167. Some consider the normal age fourteen or fifteen. See J. A. Weisheipl, 'The Structure of the Arts Faculty in the Medieval University', *British Journal of Educational Studies*, 19.3 (1971), 266, and S. E. Morison, *The Founding of Harvard College* (Cambridge, Mass., (1935), p. 32.

[61] John Major, *Historia majoris Britanniae* (Paris, 1521), ff. 8r.–v., quoted in translation in Aston *et al.*, 'Cambridge Alumni', p. 12, 'In both universities you will find four or five thousand scholars, all adults, carrying swords and bows, and for the most part of gentle birth'; *BRUC*, pp. 384–5.   [62] *BRUO*, III, p. 2077.

[63] Aston *et al.*, 'Cambridge Alumni', p. 27.

BA.[64] As these men were financially secure, the attrition rate must have been even higher among the less fortunate scholars. The New College records also show the role that death played among these young men; 10 per cent of the fellows died before taking their BA. In addition to this heavy rate of attrition for undergraduates, one quarter to one third of the bachelors left without becoming masters.[65] The same factors of poverty, death, and more happily, outside employment, drew them away. In general, the idea that a 'drop-out' was a reprobate seems absent.

The average scholar who survived the unhealthy climate and secured financial support could thus be expected to take his MA in his early twenties if he was industrious. From then on he could remain for a long time if he so cared, especially if he was on a college fellowship. The King's Hall had a clause exempting students from giving or hearing lectures if they were senile, and some of the fellows remained for fifty years.[66] Two university graces from the end of our period exempt masters from academic duties *propter senilem etatem* and *ingravescentem senectutem*.[67] But most masters left Cambridge promptly to seek their fortunes elsewhere, and the long-term teacher was very much the exception.

We are on more solid ground when speaking of the scholars' provenances. The original members were exiles from Oxford, many of whom were natives of the eastern counties, men from Cambridgeshire, Norfolk, Suffolk, and Huntingdonshire. This eastern recruitment was supplemented by north countrymen, and Oxford's recruitment provided the complement to this distribution.[68] Colleges were sometimes exceptions because their fellowships were often reserved for particular counties, or the kin of founders. In the fifteenth century Cambridge recruitment changed as there was an increase in northerners among non-

---

[64] R. L. Storey, 'The Foundation and the Medieval College, 1379–1530', in *New College, Oxford, 1379–1979*, ed. J. Buxton and P. Williams (Oxford, 1979), p. 18.
[65] GBk A, p. xxix; Aston, 'Cambridge Alumni', p. 25.
[66] A. B. Cobban, *The King's Hall* (Cambridge, 1969), pp. 89–90.
[67] GBk Γ, p. 253 (1530–1), 368 (1541–2).
[68] Aston *et al.*, 'Cambridge Alumni', pp. 28–31.

collegiate students, with a decrease in easterners (men from York diocese increased from 13 per cent to 30 per cent, while those from Norwich dropped from 39 per cent to 13 per cent). The extent of this trend may be exaggerated by the inadequacy of the evidence. The major exceptions to these trends in the fifteenth century were the fellows of King's College, where 31 per cent were from the south and south-west, and Gonville Hall, Corpus Christi College, and Trinity Hall, which drew respectively thirty-two of thirty-nine, fifteen of twenty-four and twenty of twenty-one known fifteenth-century fellows from Norwich diocese. Surprisingly, students from the south and south-east are consistently under-represented at both Oxford and Cambridge.[69]

Both universities were overwhelmingly English in their recruitment. Oxford drew only 6 per cent of its known medieval alumni from Wales, Scotland, and Ireland, and Cambridge had barely 1 per cent, but many foreign scholars no doubt passed unrecorded. Of these percentages, most were Welsh. The Irish seem to have had such a bad reputation that in 1413 Henry V banned all Irish who were not students from England. Henry VI repeated this interdict in 1422. The Scots had three universities of their own by 1500, and when they did go elsewhere it was usually to Paris, a link which may have reflected France and Scotland's sometime alliance.[70]

There were few scholars from the continent at either Oxford or Cambridge, and of these most were friars studying theology. Of the seventy-four known Cambridge foreign alumni, sixty-one were friars. The Franciscan rules even demanded that the lector in their *studia* be a foreigner every third year.[71] Both the

---

[69] Aston *et al.*, 'Cambridge Alumni', pp. 30–2. Since all Kingsmen were old Etonians, the college followed the pattern of Eton's recruitment.

[70] Aston *et al.*, 'Cambridge Alumni', pp. 35–6; *Enactments in Parliament*, I, pp. 14–15, 18–24; at Oxford, William Nangull, BA, was dispensed with his determination in 1514 'quia est pauper Hibernicus habens paucos amicos', OUA, Reg. G, f. 209v; R. Hays, 'Welsh Students at Oxford and Cambridge Universities in the Middle Ages', *Welsh Historical Review*, 4 (1968–9), 325–61.

[71] Moorman, *Grey Friars*, pp. 81–2 (bull of Benedict XII in 1336); Aston *et al.*, 'Cambridge Alumni', pp. 35–6; in the fifteenth century there were foreign workmen in the town, including Dutch, Flemish, and even a *Magnus de Islandia laborarius*. E. C. Pearce, 'College Accounts of John Botwright, Master of Corpus Christi, 1443–74', CAS, *Proceedings*, 22 (1917–20), 82.

hardening of national borders and the Hundred Years War increased England's insularity in the late middle ages.

There was frequent interchange of scholars between Oxford and Cambridge, and at least one college, Peterhouse, even had statutory provision for fellows to study for limited periods in Oxford.[72] The graces from the fifteenth century often record scholars who completed part of their requirements at the other university, or took their degrees there and desired to be incorporated in the same standing. Usually the congregations considered the terms roughly equivalent, although for incorporation it was usual to require a lecture or disputation as well as payment from the supplicant.[73] Of those incorporated at Cambridge between 1454 and 1500, about three-quarters came from Oxford, and were mostly in theology and law, especially the latter. The movement was more in the direction of Cambridge; perhaps Cambridge had a more prestigious law faculty at that time.[74] This trend came to a peak between 1500 and 1510, when between 10 and 15 per cent of the students' graces mention terms kept at Oxford. There was also some movement due to plagues, as scholars tried to avoid whichever city was infected.

There was a variety of sources of financial support that a scholar might seek; few of them were consistently reliable. Recent scholarship indicates that 'family support was probably the most important single element in the maintenance of scholars at medieval Cambridge, and Oxford as well'.[75] Most of these were from the more prosperous peasant and yeoman classes that could afford the two or three pounds a year (minimum) needed to support their son; 'administrators and the *literati* of village and manorial society, stewards, bailiffs, reeves, even local scribes. And, shading into the upper reaches of these groups, the lesser gentry'.[76] There is later literary evidence of this. Describing the university of *c.* 1520 both

---

[72] *Docs.* II, 23–4.   [73] e.g. *GBk* Γ, p. 48 (1505–6).

[74] Aston *et al.*, 'Cambridge Alumni', pp. 36–7; Aston, 'Oxford Alumni', p. 26.

[75] Aston *et al.*, 'Cambridge Alumni', p. 50; see also G. F. Lytle, 'Social Origins of Oxford Students in the Late Middle Ages', in *Les Universités à la fin du Moyen Age*, ed. J. Paquet and J. IJsewijn (Louvain, 1978), pp. 426–54.

[76] Aston *et al.*, 'Cambridge Alumni', p. 50.

Thomas Cranmer and Hugh Latimer speak of 'none of us here being gentlemen born', and 'for by yeomen's sons the faith of Christ hath been maintained chiefly. Is this nation taught by rich men's sons? No, no.'[77] The dunning letters, addressed to fathers, found in medieval epistolary collections were intended for parents who came from these ranks.[78] Sometimes scholars could obtain support from other relatives and friends, who provided money, books, and household effects either while living or by bequest.[79]

For the clever child of the classes without family resources, the most frequent path to university lay in the mendicant orders, or in those colleges that made special consideration for poorer students. On the other end of the spectrum, nobles and friends of the powerful were given special consideration at both Oxford and Cambridge. At Cambridge, mandate degrees and those to 'honourable persons', their sons, and those related to the sovereign – with little or no need for academic work – first appear in 1416, reached their greatest excesses under Queen Elizabeth I, and were not abolished until 1825.[80] There was no reason, however, for a noble to bother with university (apart from the love of learning), as the careers in government and the Church that university led to would have been accessible to him anyway.[81]

Individual grants were sometimes made by bishops and lesser ecclesiastics, as well as by the crown and the aristocracy, although this form of patronage was rare. The more significant and enduring support came from the kings, queens, and bishops (and wealthy rectors like Edmund Gonville and William

---

[77] T. Cranmer, *Miscellaneous Writings*, Parker Society 15 (Cambridge, 1846), pp. 396–9; Latimer, *Sermons*, p. 102.

[78] W. A. Pantin, 'A Medieval Treatise on Letter-Writing, with Examples from the Rylands Latin MS 394', *Bulletin of the John Rylands Library*, 13 (1929), 326–82; C. H. Haskins, 'The Life of Medieval Students as Seen in their Letters', *American Historical Review*, 3 (1897), 203–29. [79] Aston *et al.*, 'Cambridge Alumni', pp. 47–8.

[80] e.g. *Docs.* I, no. 135, p. 382; Peek and Hall, *Archives of Cambridge*, pp. 32–4; *GBk* A, p. 14 (1458–9); cf. *GBk* Γ, p. 355 (1540–1), 'Alverico Vuedall...(quoniam pater eius vir nobilis Regi a conciliis hoc vehementer petit et diutius hic manere non potest sine gravi incomodo)...'

[81] Fourteen young nobles are included among Cambridge petitioners for benefices, 1372–90. E. F. Jacob, 'English University Clerks in the later Middle Ages: The Problem of Maintenance', *Bulletin of the John Rylands Library*, 29 (1946), 305; see also Henry Percy, Earl of Northumberland in *GBk* Γ, p. 234 (1527–8).

Bingham) who founded colleges which provided support in a corporate setting. The Church provided an important source of funds by allowing unordained rectors to take licensed absences from their benefices for study up to seven years. This was under the provisions of Boniface VIII's bull *Cum ex eo*, or for two years under the earlier decretal *Licet canon*. The rector was required to provide a vicar to serve in his absence, and he also had to return and serve in his parish after he had completed his studies.[82] Although this absenteeism was deplored by some, in this way scholars were supported and the parochial clergy made more learned.[83]

References to *cura animarum* are regular in the surviving graces of both universities, if relatively few in relation to the total student body. At Cambridge, John Barfoot was excused from processions in 1477 when he was occupied *circa curam suam*.[84] Thomas Scrawsby was excused two disputations for his MA in 1505, 'because he is required to reside in his vicarage'. He had been ordained priest in 1503 and served as vicar of Broadchalk, Wiltshire, a parish presented to him by King's College in 1505.[85] When Elias Moody took his BA in 1506 he had already missed three terms 'because of Masses which he was required to celebrate outside the university'.[86] He was probably a chantry priest. Richard Betingson, the vicar of Stratford, was allowed to count his admission to responding to the question (the first step in taking the BA) as his complete BA, excusing him from determination, because 'he is not able to be absent from his parish duties, especially during this time of Lent'.[87] There are other examples from Oxford which are

---

[82] L. E. Boyle, 'The Constitution *Cum ex eo* of Boniface VIII', *Mediaeval Studies*, 24 (1962), 263–302.

[83] Gascoigne, p. 198; in the diocese of Lincoln from 1495–1520, 35.5 per cent of non-resident curates were graduates. For 1521–40 this figure drops to 7–10 per cent. M. Bowker, *Secular Clergy in the Diocese of Lincoln 1495–1520* (Cambridge, 1968), pp. 85–109; and *The Henrician Reformation in The Diocese of Lincoln* (Cambridge, 1981), pp. 116–17.

[84] GBk A, p. 126 (1477–8); *BRUC*, p. 37.

[85] *GBk* Γ, p. 37 (1504–5), 'quia tenetur residere in vicaria sua'.

[86] *GBk* Γ, p. 50 (1506–7), 'ob missas quas extra universitatem tenebatur celebrare'

[87] *GBk* Γ, p. 249 (1530–1), 'propterea quod ab eius pastorali cura abesse nequeat precipue hoc quadragesimali tempore'. See also Thomas Dixon, BCn.L, who was dispensed with lecturing 'quia impeditur per curam animarum', *GBk* Γ, p. 54 (1506–7), and Master Gyllat, BTh. in 1539, 'propter animarum curam et quam alit familiam', *GBk* Γ, p. 337 (1538–9).

even more specific. especially about those who had to be elsewhere to hear confessions during Lent. [88]

More senior scholars, bachelors working towards the MA, or those already in the superior faculties, were in part supported by the fees they received for lecturing more junior scholars. [89] Others taught grammar while completing their degrees. In the *Grace Books* from the end of the middle ages examples can be found at both Oxford and Cambridge of men excused from academic duties because 'he taught grammar to relieve his poverty', [90] or 'he is a teacher in Banbury; teaches the children of the Duke of Norfolk; teaches the sons of the Marquess of Dorset; he works at studying and teaching grammar and poetry'; [91] and 'lacking maintenance he is a grammar teacher in the country and is not able to remain here unless he ignores his duties there, to his great loss'. [92]

There were other outside activities which engaged scholars. Members of colleges, particularly officials, received exemptions from coursework because of their work loads; 'because of cares he has in overseeing the operations of his college', or 'because of business which he has for St John's College', or 'because he is a tutor in King's College'. [93] Religious in the superior faculties often had other duties calling, in their monasteries, visitations, or chapters. A BTh. graduate was excused an act 'because of service which binds him to the Archbishop of York' (Cardinal Wolsey, in fact). [94]

---

[88] e.g. Reg. Aa., pp. 8–9 (1449), 33 (1449), 99 (1452), 225–6 (1456), etc.

[89] *Medieval Archives of the University of Oxford*, ed. H. E. Salter, OHS 73 (Oxford, 1921), II, 274–5, 282; *Docs.* I, no. 76, p. 356 (1415); by 1500 masters were also paid for their ordinaries if they held professorships, e.g. *Docs.* I, p. 425 (*c.* 1514); *GBk* B II, pp. 33, 76, 81, etc.

[90] *Registrum Annalium Collegii Mertonensis, 1483–1521*, ed. H. E. Salter. OHS 76 (Oxford, 1923), I, p. 433, 'doceat grammaticalem unde posset suam paupertatem relevare'.

[91] OUA, Reg. G, f. 111r. (1511), 'est informator apud Banburiam'; *GBk* Γ, p. 283 (1533–4), 'in erudiendo liberos ducis Norfochiae', p. 304 (1535–6), 'in erudiendis pueris nobilissimi viri, domini marques Dorsett'; Reg. Aa, p. 365 (1462), 'laboravit in poematibus et gramaticalibus studendo et docendo'.

[92] OUA Reg. G, f. 299v. (1516), 'caret exhibitione est ludipreceptor in patria et non potest hic permanere nisi omittat officium suum, in detrimentum maximum eius'.

[93] *GBk* Γ, p. 67 (1507–8), 'preter [*sic*] solicitudinem quam habet in superindendis collegii sui operariis'; p. 97 (1511–12), 'propter…diversa negocia que habet circa collegium sancti Johannis evangeliste'; p. 118 (1513–14), 'quia conductus erat in collegio Regali'.

[94] *GBk* Γ, p. 127 (1514–15), 'propter servicium quo astringitur archipresul Eboracensi'; see also p. 9 (1502–3), p. 57 (1506–7), and p. 80 (1509–10).

University study was by legal definition a clerical profession. However, 'clerk' does not always imply sacred orders, but simply a literate tonsured man who as a member of the university was protected by the authority of the Church and subject to ecclesiastical courts, in this case the chancellor's court. A scholar could lose this status simply by leaving the university.[95] This immunity of scholars partially survived the Reformation and the privilege was gradually extended to others until by 1856 it embraced even the servants who worked for the university, and their families.[96] Since the documentary evidence is weighted towards those who ultimately took major orders, we have few examples of married graduates, but they existed. John Paston was married while an undergraduate at Peterhouse in 1441.[97] In fifteenth-century Oxford and Cambridge the illustrious physicians Robert Yaxley, John Somerset (twice), Thomas Rede, John Faceby, and Gilbert Kymer were all married (although it was claimed that Kymer left his wife to be promoted to higher orders).[98] William Duffeld, MA, MGram., was married and taught privately in Cambridge. Of the early fellows of King's College at least six married, including Philip Morgan, physician to Lady Margaret Beaufort, who was ordained after his wife's death.[99] In 1532–3 John Pykerell was already married when he became a bachelor in civil law and was allowed to act as a proctor in the university courts.[100] Marriage caused three masters of Merton College, Oxford to resign their fellowships at the end of the fifteenth century, including Richard Holt, MA when, unlike his contemporaries who were promoted to benefices, Holt was 'promoted to a lovely wife'.[101]

---

[95] Weisheipl, 'Structure of the Arts Faculty', p. 266, n. 1.

[96] By 1589 husbands of college laundresses were included. Peek and Hall, *Archives of Cambridge*, pp. 48–9, 57–9.

[97] *BRUC*, p. 443; *Paston Letters*, ed. N. Davis (Oxford, 1971–6), I, p. 215–16.

[98] *BRUC*, pp. 664–5 (Robert Yaxley); 540–1 (John Somerset); 475 (Thomas Rede); *BRUO*, II, 663 (John Faceby); 1068–9 (Gilbert Kymer).

[99] *GBk* A, p. 96 (1493) and *BRUC*, p. 197 (William Duffeld), *BRUC*, p. 26 (Simon Aylward), 20 (John Ashwell), 411 (Philip Morgan), 139 (John Clerke), 163 (Robert Cottrell).

[100] *GBk* Γ, p. 268 (1532–3).

[101] *Merton Register*, ed. Salter I, 201 (1496), 'promotus erat ad pulcram uxorem'. Earlier Holt had gone down after being warned for frequenting suspect places, idleness, and playing

Some scholars entered the royal service, a trend that the poet William Langland had criticised in the late fourteenth century.[102] The King's Hall, founded by Edward II in 1317, was a college founded for the boys of the royal chapel. Most of the scholars, however, were looking forward to ecclesiastical careers, yet those Cambridge men who aspired to the episcopacy were usually disappointed. In the thirteenth century only 2 per cent of the English and Welsh bishops were Cambridge graduates (against 34 per cent for Oxford); in the fourteenth century 5 per cent (59 per cent for Oxford); and in the fifteenth century 21 per cent (70 per cent for Oxford). This 'poor, not to say dismal performance of Cambridge men' was to be reversed in the early sixteenth century during the first great flowering of Cambridge.[103] But, for the first 275 years Cambridge men had little impact in the highest circles of the English Church, and their performance was little better in deaneries, prebends, and the major ecclesiastical offices.

Most scholars would have been happy with more modest positions, and the correspondence of both universities has frequent requests directed to Canterbury and Rome asking for benefices for graduates. The surviving evidence indicates that about one-third of Cambridge alumni received some sort of preferment. The hope of a rectorship or vicarship was one of the 'main attractions' of taking even a degree in the faculty of arts.[104]

tennis and dice, pp. 132, 156, 162, and 170 (1490–3). See also Gascoigne, p. 136, on undergraduate carnal desires.

[102] Students in arts and theology were said to 'serven the kyng and his silver tellen / In Cheker and in Chancerye chalengen his dettes'. *Piers Plowman*, Prol. B, 92–3.

[103] Aston *et al.*, 'Cambridge Alumni', pp. 69–76; *BRUC*, p. xxx; J. B. Mullinger, *The University of Cambridge from the Royal Injunctions of 1535 to the Accession of Charles I* (Cambridge, 1884), p. 18.

[104] See also Thomas Hoccleve, *De Regimine Principum*, ed. T. Wright (London, 1860), p. 189:
Alas! so many a worthy clerk famous
in Oxenforde, and in Cambrigge also
stonde unavaunced.

Chapter 2

HOSTELS, CONVENTS, AND COLLEGES

Cambridge university men lived in a variety of situations, although from the early years the options were regulated and controlled by statute. Secular students (that is, those not members of religious orders) lived in hostels, as did most monks and canons during most of the middle ages. Mendicant friars lived in their orders' convents. With the founding of colleges after 1280 some of the more fortunate scholars lived in them. Until the later middle ages college residents were predominantly senior members of the university. These institutions will be examined in turn. The terms are often ambiguous. Hostel, house, hall, and college were sometimes used interchangeably and vary in meaning, and some hostels were owned by colleges, and other hostels became colleges.

HOSTELS

As we have seen, student housing was regulated as early as 1231 by royal writ. Rent of buildings used by scholars was to be determined by a committee of two masters (the proctors) and two townsmen. This was repeated by letters patent in 1266.[1] These rent-controlled lodgings, called hostels (or in Oxford, halls) were often quite long-lived institutions. A late thirteenth-century statute provides a picture of how they operated.[2] The

[1] *Docs.* 1, nos. 65–7, pp. 349–51, Mullinger, *The University of Cambridge*, 1, pp. 218–20 and appendix C; H. P. Stokes, *The Mediaeval Hostels of Cambridge*, CAS, Octavo Publications, 49 (Cambridge, 1924), pp. 32–4; *The Privileges of the University of Cambridge*, ed. G. Dyer (London, 1824), 1, p. 63.

[2] H. Bradshaw, 'An Early Statute concerning Hostels', *CAS, Publications*, 2 (1864), 279–81; *Docs.* 1, no. 67, pp. 350–1; Mullinger, *Cambridge*, 1, pp. 218–21; A. B. Emden, *An Oxford Hall in Medieval Times* (Oxford, 1927); *Calendar of Patent Rolls, Henry VI, 1422–1429* (London, 1901), p. 475.

student members chose from their number a principal, who on St Barnabas' Day (11 June) met with the landlord and gave him a caution (money or a valuable object) to assure their year's rent. If the landlord refused to accept the caution the principal of the hostel could appeal to the chancellor, who was empowered to force the landlord into compliance. Later statutes elaborated on this practice, and included provisions making the principal solely responsible for paying rent, and prohibited the landlord from demanding more. Once a lodging became a hostel it could not be reclaimed by its owner unless he needed it for his personal use. At Oxford, hall members had a perpetual option on letting the property if they followed the prescribed rent procedure.[3] The law clearly favoured the universities, and was a constant source of aggravation for the townsmen.

Many of the hostels survived for several centuries. Although lacking charters, statutes, endowments, and the right to hold possessions in mortmain and thus having none of the permanence of colleges, they were more than simple boarding houses. They could often be larger than colleges. Some of them, like Physwick and St Bernard's had their own halls, chapels, libraries, and galleries.[4] They sometimes received gifts from their members. Bryan Kiddal, MA 1495, bequeathed a dictionary to be chained in the chapel of St Thomas' Hostel in 1502, and John Hall, MA *c*. 1445 gave St Mary's Hostel a codex of Aristotle's logic.[5] But this stability should not be overemphasised, for hostels never had the holdings, either literary or material, on the scale of even the poorer colleges. All hostel members paid their room and board, since there were no foundations to support them.

Hostels had a corporate spirit, and fought with their neighbours in the streets. The proctors' books from *c*. 1500 speak of a two-night battle between St Nicholas' Hostel and Christ's College, and of St Clement's Hostel against all comers.[6] Dr John Caius described a particularly colourful example from

[3] Hackett, *Statutes*, p. 171.
[4] Aston *et al.*, 'Cambridge Alumni', p. 17, n. 22.
[5] *BRUC*, pp. 281 and 342; Gonville and Caius MS 466/573.
[6] *GBk* B I, 112 (1497–8) and p. 236 (1508–9); Stokes, *Hostels*, pp. 39–42; for a battle between The King's Hall and Clare Hall, see *Annals*, I, 111 (1373).

1521, when scholars of Garret Hostel and Ovings Inn together with other north countrymen attacked Gonville Hall, burnt the west gate, burst into the college, and poured out all the liquor they found in the buttery. No doubt they consumed some as well.[7] Whether hostel men were rowdier than college members is hard to prove; given that they were generally younger and under looser discipline, it seems likely. The Cambridge chancellor and his deputies had the right of visitation of the hostels, and could depose any principals they felt were unsatisfactory.[8]

Scholars naturally associate with those of similar interests, and, accordingly, particular hostels attracted members of particular faculties. When John Rous made a list of Cambridge hostels in the middle of the fifteenth century, he gave the academic tone of twelve of them: six for artists and six for lawyers. The remaining five seem to have been primarily for artists as well.[9] That makes sense, since the faculties of arts and law included all of the junior members of the university. The theologians were mostly either friars, monks, or college fellows.

Although the size of hostels varied, it seems that in the fifteenth century they averaged twenty-five to thirty residents for the eleven for artists, and about eighty in each of the six hostels for legists. Oxford halls, by contrast, were smaller but more numerous. Thomas Fuller also claimed that the Cambridge hostels were better fitted than Oxford halls.[10] By the late

---

[7] J. Caius, *The Annals of Gonville and Caius College*, ed. J. Venn CAS, Octavo Series, 40 (Cambridge, 1904), p. 13.　　[8] *Docs.* I, no. 18, pp. 316–17.

[9] L. T. Smith, *The Itinerary of John Leland, 1535–1543* (London, 1908), II, 157; Aston *et al.*, 'Cambridge Alumni', p. 52; T. H. Aston, 'The Date of John Rous's List of the Colleges and Academical Halls of Oxford', *Oxoniensia*, 42 (1977), 226–36.

[10] T. Fuller, *The History of the University of Cambridge*, ed. J. Nichols (London, 1840), p. 79; Aston *et al.*, 'Cambridge Alumni', pp. 15–18; see also W. A. Pantin, *Oxford Life in Oxford Archives* (Oxford, 1972), pp. 9–18, and 'The Halls and Schools of Medieval Oxford; An Attempt at Reconstruction', in *Oxford Studies Presented to Daniel Callus*, OHS n.s. 16 (Oxford, 1964), pp. 31–100; A. B. Emden, *Oxford Hall*, and 'Oxford Academical Halls in the Later Middle Ages', in *Medieval Learning and Literature: Essays Presented to Richard William Hunt*, ed. J. J. G. Alexander and M. T. Gibson (Oxford, 1976), pp. 353–65; H. E. Salter, 'An Oxford Hall in 1424', in *Essays in History Presented to R. L. Poole*, ed. H. W. C. Davis (Oxford, 1927), pp. 421ff.

All scholars were required to live in a controlled hostel or college (*Docs.* I, no. 18, 317), but even in the early sixteenth century there were some scholars who lived alone in rented rooms. How many is hard to say. See M. Parker, *De antiquitate Britannicae ecclesiae* (London, 1572), unpaginated appendix. See Aston *et al.*, 'Cambridge Alumni', p. 19.

fifteenth century the hostels (and Oxford halls) began to disappear as colleges took in undergraduates who paid for their room and board.[11]

CONVENTS

The students in regular orders were divided between monks, canons, and mendicant friars. They occupied a unique position within the university (especially the friars) and were perceived by the secular scholars as a threat to their privileges. Their suppression at the Reformation marks the medieval university as something very different from what came later. The clerical nature of the college fellows remained unchanged, but the great mendicant convents, churches, and the internationalist men that they housed, were no more.

The distinction of monks from friars is rarely made in the minds of some modern members of Cambridge, who conceive the medieval university as being full of monks. Actually, there were very few in Cambridge; of the 7,000 recorded medieval alumni, only eighty-four Benedictines and three Cistercians can be identified (there were, of course, many more who are unrecorded). Unlike Oxford with its three important monastic colleges, Cambridge had none before the fifteenth century. When Pope Benedict XII in 1335 ordered the Cistercians to send scholars to the universities, most British ones went to Oxford.[12]

Those monks who did attend Cambridge were, as expected, mostly from Ely and Norwich dioceses, with some from Yorkshire. The first provision for monastic students occurred in 1340, probably as a result of Pope Benedict's bull. The prior of Ely Cathedral established a hostel for the monks of Ely studying in Cambridge, a group that then numbered only two, along with two Benedictines from other abbeys. This hostel for monks moved several times, and by the 1420s was thought to be unsatisfactory. At the general chapter of the Benedictines in 1423 the prior of the Cambridge house petitioned for funds to

[11] See chapter 11.
[12] Aston *et al.*, 'Cambridge Alumni', p. 55 and n. 125; M. D. Knowles, *The Religious Orders in England* (3 vols., Cambridge, 1948–59), II, pp. 24–6.

build a permanent home. Nothing was done, and the succeeding prior renewed the request in 1426. This time action was taken, and in 1428 under the direction of the abbot of Crowland land was acquired and a house for Benedictines studying theology and canon law was founded.[13] This house, never very large, became known by 1480 as Buckingham College, so named for the benefactions of the Duke of Buckingham. Which duke, however, or even what the benefaction was, is not certain. It was not in our sense a college, since it had no legal identity apart from the abbeys which owned it, although it was spoken of as a college in all the sixteenth-century documents. In this community Thomas Cranmer lectured *c.* 1516 after resigning his fellowship at Jesus College during his brief marriage. The history of Buckingham College at the dissolution is murky, but it evidently ceased to exist as a corporate body when its parent abbeys were suppressed in 1538. In 1542 Thomas Audley founded Magdalene College in the disused building that is today its first court. The individual staircases are thought to have been built by the Benedictine houses that sent students up to college; the coats of arms above the doorways indicate what is conjectured to have been the contribution of each. The 'monks' rooms' in staircase E are perhaps the most intact medieval scholars' rooms in either Oxford or Cambridge.[14]

Not all the monks lived in Buckingham College, and throughout the middle ages there are references to them in hostels and colleges, such as Thomas Maldon of Colne Priory in St Margaret's Hostel in 1390.[15] Norwich Cathedral Priory in particular was granted papal permission in 1481 to continue to send monks to live in Gonville and Trinity Halls as pensioners (non-college members who paid their way). At Gonville Hall (excluding its dependent, Physwick Hostel) monks possibly made up half of the twenty-five or thirty residents in a given year, and the practice continued until the Reformation.[16] The

---

[13] *VCH*, II, pp. 207 and 312.
[14] R. W. McDowall, 'Buckingham College', *CAS, Publications* 44 (1951), 1–12.
[15] *BRUC*, p. 386.
[16] J. Venn, *Biographical History of Gonville and Caius College, 1349–1897*, III (Cambridge, 1901), pp. 332–3; J. Venn, *Early Collegiate Life* (Cambridge, 1913), pp. 60 and 65–79; Aston *et al.*, 'Cambridge Alumni', pp. 54–5.

'merry monk' that Hugh Latimer remembered lived with him in Clare College. [17]

In addition to the monks there were canons regular who studied in Cambridge. The largest group of them were Austin Canons, who could live at their order's priory at Barnwell, but it seems few of the scholar canons availed themselves of the advantage of this geographical proximity. Erasmus certainly did not. The Augustinians of Butley, Suffolk in the early sixteenth century rented an *honesta camera* in Gonville Hall, a college which also sheltered canons from Westacre in Norfolk. There was a community of Austin Canons in Cambridge who ran the Hospital of St John, some of whom over three centuries might have belonged to the university. [18] The Canons of St Gilbert of Sempringham established the Priory of St Edmund in 1291 outside the Trumpington Gate on the present site of Old Addenbrooke's Hospital. Although the history of the priory is obscure, it was the principal *studium* of the order and survived until the Reformation. At least some of its members attended the faculty of theology. On Rous' list of religious colleges in the mid-fifteenth century, these *canonici albi* are listed directly after the four orders of friars. [19]

The mendicant friars were, like the universities, something new in thirteenth-century Europe. Unlike the monks with their stability, ownership of property, and, ideally, seclusion from the world, the founders of the orders of friars envisaged men who made their home in the market-place and lived on the alms that they could beg. For St Dominic, the ideal was preaching and teaching orthodoxy against heresy; for St Francis it was the renunciation of all worldly pride and gain, and a life of apostolic poverty. The value of university study was always apparent to the Dominicans, and the order set up *studia* across Europe to train the brothers for their work. Those at the *studium* of Saint Jacques in Paris soon became important members of

---

[17] Latimer, *Sermons*, I, p. 153.
[18] *VCH*, II, pp. 303–7. The privileges of the university were extended to members of the hospital *c.* 1470 to protect them from the townsmen; *BRUC*, p. 198 (John Durham); *Annals*, I, p. 254 (1500); M. Rubin, *Charity and Community in Medieval Cambridge* (Cambridge, 1986); the hospital cartulary is now in St John's College archives.
[19] *VCH*, II, pp. 254–6; cf. Aston *et al.*, 'Cambridge Alumni', p. 54.

that university. St Francis himself was inimical to higher education as something which led men to the sin of Pride. But his followers were more pragmatic, and after his death in 1226 they too set up *studia* in all their provinces and eventually had friars take university degrees in theology.

The first Franciscans, or Greyfriars, arrived in Cambridge about 1226, the year of their founder's death. They begged from the townsmen and were given half of the former house of Benjamin the Jew, located near where the Guildhall now stands. It would have been humble enough for Francis himself; the other half of the house was the town gaol, and gaolers, prisoners, and friars shared a common entrance. These first Cambridge Franciscans – three friars and a few lay brothers – were attracted to the town not so much because of the opportunities for study, but for the crowds of young men around the university. From among these scholars, often as young as fourteen and away from home for the first time, the friars found fertile ground for recruiting.[20]

From the late 1220s the Franciscan house had a lecturer who instructed the members in the basics of the liberal arts and theology, which were necessary for their preaching work. The first lecturer, Vincent of Coventry, came from Oxford, as would six of the Franciscan lecturers before 1300. Paris provided two, including the great Roger Marston *c.* 1270. Cambridge's faculty of theology was granting degrees by at least 1250 and, as one of only three such faculties in Christendom, it attracted Franciscans from other friaries who sought the theological instruction to enhance what they had already learned from the lecturers in their home *studia*.[21] The Franciscan convent grew, and a new house was built in the middle of the thirteenth century on the three-acre site now occupied by Sidney Sussex College. It included a large hall – church for preaching, which in the late middle ages was also used for university commence-

---

[20] J. R. H. Moorman, *The Grey Friars in Cambridge, 1225–1538* (Cambridge, 1952), pp. 1–18. See also A. G. Little, *The Grey Friars in Oxford*, OHS 20 (Oxford, 1892).
[21] Brooke, 'Churches of Medieval Cambridge', p. 73; Moorman, pp. 30–3; A. G. Little, 'The Friars and the Foundation of the Faculty of Theology in the University of Cambridge', in *Mélanges Mandonnet*, Bibliothèque Thomiste 14, Paris, 1930, pp. 389–401; *BRUC*, pp. 393–4 and 164.

ments. Fresh water was provided by building a conduit from the high ground at Madingley, three miles west of town, which ran downhill, crossed under the river, and passed across the site of the present Trinity College. It also served the public through a standpipe outside the friary. By 1277 there were about thirty Franciscans in Cambridge, a number which grew to seventy by 1290 before levelling off at between fifty-five and seventy in the fourteenth century. Among the friars in the late 1290s was John Duns Scotus, perhaps the most influential philosopher in later medieval England.[22]

The Franciscans were probably joined in the 1230s by the Dominicans, or 'Blackfriars'. Their earliest years in Cambridge are obscure, but by 1238 they were building a church and convent outside the Barnwell Gate on what is now the site of Emmanuel College. Like the Greyfriars, they had their own *studium* separate from university control and also sent members to study in the faculty of theology. By the end of the thirteenth century there were sixty to seventy Dominicans in Cambridge, and they rivalled the Franciscans as the most influential mendicant order in the university.[23]

There were other orders as well. The Carmelites, or 'White-friars' settled first at Chesterton and then Newnham in the 1250s, apart from the university in keeping with their contemplative tradition. But they too soon turned more towards preaching and hearing confessions, and in the 1290s moved into the thick of things by settling on Milne Street on what is now the site of the Walnut Court of Queens' College.[24] The fourth of the important mendicant orders was the Order of the Friars of Saint Augustine, more popularly known as the Friars Hermits or Austin Friars (not to be confused with Austin Canons). Their convent, established in the 1280s, was on a large site around the Old Cavendish Laboratories. Although not as numerous as the other three orders in Cambridge (they had about thirty-six

[22] Moorman, pp. 33 and 39–46; *BRUC*, pp. 198–201.
[23] W. Gumbley, *The Cambridge Dominicans* (Cambridge, 1938); *VCH*, II, pp. 269–76.
[24] *VCH*, II, pp. 282–6; see also K. J. Egan, 'The Establishment and Early Development of the Carmelite Order in England' (unpublished Ph.D. thesis, University of Cambridge, 1965), p. 145.

friars in 1297), this, the order of Martin Luther, was to play a central role in the early Reformation in Cambridge.[25]

There were two other mendicant orders with houses in Cambridge, but which were forbidden to receive new members following the Council of Lyons in 1274. The Friars of Saint Mary lived in the Castle End, and the Friars of the Penance of Jesus, or 'Friars of the Sack', lived outside the Trumpington Gate on the present site of the Fitzwilliam Museum. Both of these communities died out in the early fourteenth century.[26]

The total number of friars who were members of the university is difficult to determine, as not all of the members of the convents were necessarily matriculated. However, since the Cambridge (and Oxford) houses had an 'essentially educational role', the total of mendicant alumni was substantial. All together there are 1,136 recorded friars, including 344 Franciscans, 281 Dominicans, 225 Carmelites, and 224 Augustinians. These friars accounted for 28 per cent of the recorded fourteenth-century alumni, and 16 per cent in the fifteenth. If we examine just the late fourteenth century we find that of the perhaps 600 to 700 scholars in Cambridge (the figures are very speculative), about 200 were mendicants. Nearly all of these friars were in the faculty of theology, whereas the secular scholars followed a faculty distribution pattern of 50 per cent in arts, 40 per cent in law, and only 10 per cent in theology.[27]

This domination of the faculty of theology by the friars caused considerable friction with the seculars, who were otherwise numerically dominant in arts and law. The friars, even outside the university, had been often viewed with some envy and suspicion by the secular clergy since their earliest days. Organised and aggressive, they attracted many of the brightest

---

[25] *VCH*, II, pp. 287–90; D. H. S. Cranage and H. P. Stokes, 'The Augustinian Friary in Cambridge and the History of its Site', *CAS, Publications*, 22 (1917–20), 53–75; F. Roth, *The English Austin Friars 1249–1538*, 2 vols. (New York, 1966), esp. I, pp. 136–78 and II, pp. 240–1; Brooke, 'Churches of Medieval Cambridge', pp. 60–1.

[26] *VCH*, II, pp. 286–7 and 290–1.

[27] Aston *et al.*, 'Cambridge Alumni', pp. 55–62. The arts faculty for various reasons was probably closer in size or larger than the theology faculty in most decades. The seculars in the arts faculty were much less likely to be recorded than the friars in theology.

young men to their ranks, operated outside effective diocesan control, were popular confessors and preachers, and attracted benefactions and burial fees that would otherwise have gone to the parishes. Within the universities they often recruited the youngest scholars, accepting oblates as young as twelve and fourteen, 'seducing' boys who did not know better.

From the beginning, the friars' *studia* in Paris, Oxford, and Cambridge had been semi-autonomous and thus anomalous before the rise of colleges. No one denied them the right to educate their members within their own houses in both arts and theology; it was when they became students within the universities' theology faculties that the troubles started. The seculars objected to having friars accept the rights and privileges of the university while simultaneously claiming exemption from obeying the corporate wishes of the university. At Paris this came to a head in 1251–2 when the university passed a statute limiting each order to only one master and one school, and allowing no bachelor of theology to be admitted to the doctorate unless he lectured in the school of a master recognised by the faculty. As Rashdall puts it,

> The exact extent of the authority claimed by the university should be clearly understood. No one denied the right of a friar duly licensed by the chancellor to teach theology to members of his own order or to others. What the masters asserted was the hitherto unquestioned right of the university to impose its own regulations upon its own members, to refuse professional association to masters who did not choose to comply with them, and to exclude from their society the pupils of such unrecognised extra-university masters.[28]

This quarrel at Paris flashed on and off for decades. A kindred dispute arose in Oxford in 1253 over the right of friars to incept in theology without having graduated in arts (since they did their arts studies in their own *studium* rather than in the faculty).[29] This question was peacefully settled at the time, but

---

[28] Rashdall, I, pp. 378–9, quoted in Moorman, p. 27.
[29] A. G. Little, *Grey Friars in Oxford*, p. 38.

further problems between the friars and seculars were to erupt again in early fourteenth-century Oxford and Cambridge.

At Cambridge the spark that set off the trouble was a set of three statutes passed by the university meeting in convocation in November 1303. The first ruled that the formulating of statutes and the granting of dispensations could only be made by a majority vote of convocation, that is, both the regents and non-regents, a body dominated by the seculars. This took all legislative power away from the faculty of theology, in which the mendicants had a majority. The second statute dealt with the preaching of periodic university sermons in Great St Mary's, and the third required everyone who incepted as a doctor of theology to preach publicly in Great St Mary's on a day appointed by the chancellor.[30] This was particularly offensive to the friars, who were accustomed to preaching in their own churches. Since the sermons were required for admission to the degree of doctor of theology, the friars correctly sensed the danger that these statutes had for them.[31] The Franciscans and Dominicans protested to the university, and then in March 1304 friars representing both orders were sent to Rome to present their appeal. The Cambridge convocation, not surprisingly, objected to this attempt to subvert their autonomy, and had the superiors of both orders expelled from the university.[32]

The friars continued their appeal nonetheless, listing their objections to the three statutes, and singling out for censure an Augustinian friar who had taken the side of the seculars in the dispute. Specifically, they claimed that the statutes violated the customary way of doing things and put them at the mercy of the rector of Great St Mary's, who could refuse to let them preach in his church, and thus prevent their taking theology degrees. The case was never decided in Rome, as within a few days of filing the appeal in July 1304 Pope Benedict XI died, and during the long interregnum the friars and the university

---

[30] Moorman, pp. 35–6 and 277–8; Hackett, *Statutes*, pp. 240–4; A. G. Little, 'The Friars vs. the University of Cambridge', *English Historical Review*, 50 (1935), 687.

[31] Hackett, *Statutes*, p. 242.

[32] Moorman, p. 230, '...a beneficio societatis in magistralibus totaliter privaverunt'.

were reconciled. A compromise was agreed in Bordeaux between the chancellor and the heads of the Franciscans and Dominicans, through the mediation of Cardinal Jorz (a Dominican). The three statutes remained on the books, but riders were attached which excused the mendicants from the more obnoxious parts, and allowed them to preach their sermons in their own churches.[33]

Fifty years later anti-mendicant feeling again took statutory form, with Cambridge and Oxford acting in concert. The friars in the 1340s and 1350s had been the subject of an increasingly noisy campaign by Richard Fitzralph, Archbishop of Armagh. A champion of the rights of the parochial clergy, Fitzralph publicly denounced the mendicants' recruitment of scholars who were too young to know better. In 1358 Oxford passed a statute prohibiting the religious orders from accepting oblates under eighteen years of age. Cambridge followed suit shortly afterwards, and then in July 1359 passed two more restrictive statutes; only one friar from each order could take a degree in a given year, and two bachelors or doctors of theology from the same order could not lecture concurrently. Exceptions were to be allowed only with the unanimous consent of convocation.[34]

The Cambridge friars were furious, and again appealed to the papal court. In November 1364 the Pope ordered the Archbishop of Canterbury to summon together Cambridge's chancellor and the other interested parties and make them annul the age limitation statute if it was as the friars said. Whether the Archbishop did this is uncertain, but in July 1365 the Pope ordered the Archbishop and the Bishops of Llandaff and Bangor to make the chancellors and convocations of both universities show why the anti-mendicant statutes should not be revoked. Included was a list of four statutes, the first two of which were specifically attributed to Cambridge:

1 no one was to become a doctor of theology without first having been a regent master of arts

[33] Little, 'Friars vs. Cambridge', p. 688; *Docs.* I, no. 167, pp. 397–8.
[34] S. Gibson, *Statuta Antiqua Universitatis Oxoniensis* (Oxford, 1931), pp. 164–5; *Docs.* I. nos. 163–5, pp. 395–7; Moorman, pp. 107–12.

2 no two members of the same convent could give their regent lectures concurrently

3 no one could lecture on the *Sentences* of Peter Lombard (the regent lectures of a doctoral candidate in theology) unless he was examined publicly in the Schools by all the regents in theology

4 if any prelate or prince ask for a grace for a member of any mendicant order, and the grace be refused, and the university be put to expense by reason thereof, no member of the order shall be promoted to any degree until the said expense be refunded or guaranteed by the said order or the person promoted.[35]

Oxford and Cambridge still did not back down (again, whether the meeting ordered by the Pope ever took place is uncertain). The following May 1366, the issue was settled by Edward III in Parliament. The King ordered that:

1 all parties should in questions of graces and academic exercises 'use each other in a courteous and friendly manner'

2 the age limitation on recruiting friars should be repealed

3 the universities should pass no laws prejudicial to the mendicants without good cause

4 the friars should renounce all bulls and processes they had received from Rome during these disputes

5 the King should settle all future disputes between the parties, and might 'punish all offenders against the present ordinance'

Clearly, the day went to the friars in this return to the *status quo ante*.[36]

There were to be more statutory attempts against the friars during the fifteenth century. The statutes prohibiting two members of the same order from taking degrees in the same year remained, but exemptions were granted by grace. Friars and monks enjoyed certain limited exemptions from the

---

[35] *Calendar of Papal Registers*, IV, pp. 52–3 and 91, quoted in Moorman, p. 109.
[36] *Annals*, I, pp. 108–9 (1366); Dyer, *Privileges of Cambridge*, I, pp. 71–2.

payment of fees on taking degrees, and were not required to matriculate in arts before entering theology.[37] Financially they were much better off than at Oxford, where the friars paid as much as £10 to take the doctorate, while the Cambridge fees varied from £2 to £8. This matter reached the King in 1460, with Oxford claiming untruthfully that their degrees were no more expensive than Cambridge's. By 1478 Oxford dropped the charge on friars to £6 13s 4d and £13 6s 8d for monks.[38]

COLLEGES AND THE SCHOLAR'S LIFE

The collegiate system gives modern Oxford and Cambridge a unique constitutional and social character, setting them apart from the early continental foundations and most of their successor universities elsewhere in the world. It is the autonomy of the colleges that allowed the intimate nature of the tutorial system to evolve. To the modern visitor it is the hushed courts and quads with their heavy gates, towers, and gothic chapels (as often as not neo-gothick) that is the very essence of Oxbridge.

Not so medieval Oxford and Cambridge. Most students lived in hostels or religious convents, and in 1310 there was still only one Cambridge college, with provision for fifteen senior members of the university and three choristers; in reality, it was too poor to support even those statutory numbers. In the next fifty years seven more colleges were founded, but before the fifteenth century the impact of the colleges was due primarily to the seniority of their individual members within the university, for in absolute numbers they were a small minority of the total masters and scholars. This was even more the case at Oxford.

A university college was, and is, an endowed community founded to provide support for a select group of scholars. The motivation of the college founders, who were important ecclesi-

---

[37] *GBk* A, p. xxxi; Moorman, pp. 119–20.

[38] *GBk* A, pp. 3–5, 9, 18, *passim*; *Epistolae Academicae Oxon.*, ed. Anstey, II, pp. 352–4; H. E. Salter, ed., *Mediaeval Archives of the University of Oxford*, p. 274. The final Cambridge fees, set in 1523, were £6 13s 4d for monks and £5 6s 8d for friars, *Docs.* I, p. 434.

astics, royalty, or pious women, was to improve the national
clergy by promoting learning. Whether this learned clergy was
primarily for parishes, church courts, royal service, or teaching
in grammar schools depended on the founders' wishes, which
were usually vaguely expressed in the charters. Most college
fellows, that is, full members who were supported by the
foundation, were required at some point to take major orders,
and fellows were in most cases required to pray and celebrate
Masses for the intentions specified by the founder. This usually
included praying for his soul and those of his family. This
chantry function should never be overlooked, for it was central
to the existence of the colleges, and based on the Catholic belief
that the prayers of the living are efficacious for the souls of the
dead. That was why the college founder was willing to support
the studies of the fellows; they did him an invaluable service
for generations to come. Following the Reformation prayers
for the dead were discouraged, and the improvement of a godly
clergy became the central reforming ideal. But the chantry
aspect is still echoed in the continuing annual chapel services
for the commemoration of benefactors. The medieval university
as a whole was equally concerned with corporate prayers for its
deceased members, and the statutes on these points were explicit
and enforced.[39]

The first English academic colleges were founded in Oxford
(in imitation of Paris) and the idea was implemented in
Cambridge as a direct borrowing from its parent university.
The first provision for an Oxford college was made in the will
of William of Durham, Archbishop-elect of Rouen, in 1249.
He left 310 marks (£206 13s 6d) to be invested in rents for the
support of ten or more masters of arts to pursue theology.
Oxford was slow in implementing this benefaction, and the
house of study, the later University College, was probably not
realised until 1280.[40] In the meantime John de Balliol founded
the college for bachelors of arts seeking the MA, a penance
imposed on him by the Bishop of Durham for outrages against

[39] *Docs.* I, nos. 180, 184–6, pp. 404 7 and 411–15. [40] Rashdall, III, pp. 176–8.

certain churches in the northern marches. This college was established by 1266, although it was not put on a permanent legal basis until 1282 by his widow Dervorguilla.[41]

The first English college to exist *de jure* as well as *de facto* was founded between 1262 and 1264 by Walter de Merton, later Bishop of Rochester. Supported by the revenues of estates in Malden, Surrey, the college was governed by statutes of 1270 that regulated all aspects of fellows' lives. The permanence of Oxford was not certain in those turbulent years, so Merton purchased a manor house in Cambridge against the day when his foundation might have to migrate. Now known as the 'School of Pythagoras', this patrimony was not alienated by Merton College until 1962 when St John's College, Cambridge, paid handsomely for it to complete their fifth court.[42]

It was the Oxford exemplar of Walter de Merton that was the pattern for the first Cambridge foundation. In 1280 Hugh de Balsham, Bishop of Ely, obtained a royal licence to found a college of the 'scholars of the Bishop of Ely in Cambridge...*pro utilitate rei publice*', who were explicitly to follow the statutes of Merton College. The first members were housed in the Hospital of St John, but the college was not to prejudice the rights of the brethren (Austin Canons) and the inmates already there. Balsham also provided some joint endowments. Not surprisingly, the secular scholars and the religious hospital community did not live together tranquilly. Four years later a second royal decree acknowledged that since 'various causes of dissension had arisen' it would be mutually beneficial for the communities to be separated.[43] By an elaborate division worked out by the bishop, the scholars were removed to two hostels outside the Trumpington Gate and were given (among other things) the neighbouring church of St Peter's (now Little St

---

[41] Rashdall, III, pp. 180–2.
[42] Rashdall, III, p. 193; called variously Merton Hall/Stone Hall/School of Pythagoras, it was sold to Henry VI for King's College in 1446 and then reacquired by Merton College under Edward IV in 1462. There is no evidence that Merton scholars ever used it as a place of studies. See J. M. Gray, *The School of Pythagoras – Merton Hall, Cambridge*. CAS, Quarto Publications, new series 4 (Cambridge, 1932).
[43] *Docs.* II, 2; Rubin, *Charity and Community*, pp. 271–5; Brooke, 'Churches of Medieval Cambridge', pp. 59–60.

Mary's) which had belonged to the hospital. The hospital was very unhappy about this and litigation continued for the next sixty years before it was settled that the college owed the hospital 20s annually, a right inherited by St John's College and still paid. [44] The church in question gave its name to Peterhouse, Cambridge's proto-college.

The original Peterhouse statutes have not survived, and the earliest that we have are those promulgated by Simon Montacute, Bishop of Ely, in 1344. As with the original set they used Merton as the exemplar, but with modifications to suit this smaller and poorer foundation. They make frequent reference to the paucity of resources at the college's disposal, and speak of an ideal situation that might be realised when the college grew wealthier. They outline the duties of the college officers, the selection of the fellows, the domestic economy and living arrangements, and the spiritual duties to be performed for the benefactors.

The master of the college was to be chosen annually by the Bishop of Ely from two candidates nominated by the fellowship. He was the ruler of the house, but was to seek the council of all of the fellows, old as well as young, whenever he made important decisions. When the college had sufficient funds his salary was to be £2, in addition to his income as a fellow. His perquisites included a personal servant and a horse, since it would be below his dignity to go about the college business on foot or in 'hackeneys'. The master was also allowed an extra room in which to conduct college business, in addition to his private bedroom. [45]

The master was aided in college administration by two deans, elected annually, who were specifically charged with regulating the daily readings from the Bible and other theological works in hall, caring for the library, and regulating the disputations of the scholars. [46] The statutes also provided *ad instar Aulae Mertonensis* that when funds were available there were to be two bursars to keep the accounts, and an almoner for the indigent.

---

[44] *VCH*, III, p. 334; ex info. Mr M. Underwood.
[45] *Docs.* II, 11. The provision for election at Peterhouse was unusual. In most English colleges the fellows had the right to choose their head.   [46] *Docs.* II, 17.

The college officers were to be assisted by servants when they could be afforded, and a porter. The porter was charged with preventing undesirable persons from entering, and with closing the gates during the hours decided by the master and deans.[47] The usual practice was to close the colleges at 8 p.m. in the winter and 9 p.m. in the summer. The medieval English were highly suspicious of anyone who went out in the evenings, 'noctivagation' as it was called. Most of the distractions of the town were prohibited by university authority anyway, and the proctors patrolled the street and pubs, arresting university members who were in violation of the regulations (as they did until the 1960s). The college statutes provided punishments for the college members caught outside after the gates closed for the evening.[48]

Peterhouse provided for fourteen fellows, or 'scholares' as they were called in the statutes, to be chosen by vote and named by the Bishop of Ely. The fellows were to have completed their BAs and be working towards higher degrees, and each had a year's probation before being fully taken into the fellowship. When funds allowed there were also to be two or three indigent grammar students who were to serve in the chapel and hall, read the lessons during the meals, and pursue studies determined by the deans. If they proved industrious they might later become fellows, after taking the BA.[49]

Such young Bible clerks were a feature of many of the medieval colleges. Although the older clerks might be members of the university, most were still doing preparatory studies under a grammar master before entering the faculty of arts. The two Bible clerks of Michaelhouse were established in 1429 by Sir Robert Turk and Bartholomew Seman, a goldbeater of London, an early example of the lay patronage that characterised Cambridge by the end of that century. The Bible clerks were to be two poor scholars of good life able to read and chant and proficient in grammar. As in Peterhouse, they were to read the

---

[47] *Docs.* II, 17–19.
[48] St John's College had penalties in their 1516 statutes for climbing-in. See J. E. B. Mayor, *Early Statutes of the College of St John the Evangelist in the University of Cambridge* (Cambridge, 1859), p. 353; for attitudes towards the night, see K. Thomas, *Man and the Natural World* (New York, 1983), p. 39.   [49] *Docs.* II, pp. 19–22.

Bible in hall, but also wait on tables. They could hold their positions until they reached the age of twenty-one. The three Bible clerks at Queens' College at the end of the fifteenth century were by contrast always undergraduates in the arts faculty. Thus the Bible clerk, supported through the foundation while serving at table was in some instances the forerunner of the 'sizars' and 'sub-sizars' of more recent collegiate life.[50]

There was no provision in the Peterhouse statutes for undergraduates who paid for the privilege of living in college, the later 'pensioners' or 'commoners'.[51] Pensioners would not be important numerically until the fifteenth century. The importance of most medieval colleges within the university was not in the number of their members, but in their members' seniority.

Peterhouse was physically quite small in its early years, and today remains one of the smallest colleges of Cambridge. When Bishop Balsham moved it in 1284 the new premises were two otherwise undistinguished houses next to St Peter's without-Trumpington Gate. At his death two years later he bequeathed the college £200 which was used to buy adjacent land and begin building a hall. Expansion was slow in the next 150 years, and it was not until the fifteenth century that a recognisably 'collegiate' ensemble of buildings were grouped around a court.[52]

Bishop Balsham's use of existing tenements to house his foundation was typical of the earliest colleges. The quadrangular court, incorporating hall, chambers and often chapel was a natural development in medieval institutions that was gradually adopted at Oxford and Cambridge. The exemplar was not necessarily monastic, as country houses of the later middle ages often followed the same plan.[53] More immediately, the large medieval inn with its two storeys of chambers and stables around a court had the same inspiration; they all have as a common

---

[50] A. E. Stamp, *Michaelhouse* (Cambridge, 1924), pp. 31–4; Queens' College Archives, *Journale*, I, *passim*. At Queens' a special bequest was made by Richard Andrew *alias* Spycer, a local burgess, for a 'clericus ad legendum Bibliam ad prandium et cenam infra collegium'. W. G. Searle, *The History of the Queens' College of St Margaret and St Bernard*, CAS, Octavo (1867–71), I, p. 66.

[51] Outsiders were restricted to two-week stays. *Docs.* II, 27.

[52] Willis and Clark, I, pp. 1–2.   [53] Willis and Clark, III, pp. 270–3.

ancestor the Roman atrium house that was known throughout the Empire. The first planned closed court in Cambridge was Pembroke College in the 1340s, while the first such court realised was that of Corpus Christi College in the 1350s, which happily survives largely intact. [54] This model reached its most influential form in William of Wykeham's New College, Oxford, founded in 1379. Wykeham, possessor of the wealthy see of Winchester, founded a great public school there and New College, Oxford for Winchester graduates. The scale and detail of his plans heavily influenced most subsequent colleges, both in internal organisation and external form. The closed court became the unchallenged collegiate plan until Elizabethan times, when Dr Caius prohibited his court from being closed on the south end, 'lest for lack of free ventilation the air should become foul, the health of our college...impaired, and disease and death be thereby rendered more frequent'. [55] Caius Court, with the whimsical Gate of Honour on the south side, still embodies this salubrious ideal.

Peterhouse never had a gate tower to awe the visitor or late-returning undergraduate, its entrance remaining a simple door on the street until early modern times. However, again following Wykeham's example at Oxford, many Cambridge colleges soon included this element with even more warlike posturing than was common in the parent university. The King's Hall in 1426–7 was the first, and its King Edward's Tower survives in a new location in the Great Court of Trinity. This Cambridge prototype, with its four angle turrets, was repeated at King's College (1441; now part of the University Registry), Queens' College (c. 1448), Christ's (c. 1505), St John's (c. 1510), and Trinity College (c. 1518 in The King's Hall, and the Queen's Gate in 1597), and in a less exact form in several other colleges. [56] They served no real defensive purpose (except to keep out undesirable townsmen and women), but were, and remain, psychologically imposing, a symbol of the pride and growing importance of the late medieval colleges. They echo the late medieval castles.

[54] Willis and Clark, III, pp. 255–6.
[55] Venn, III, 364; *Docs.* II, 262; Willis and Clark, III, p. 275.
[56] Willis and Clark, III, p. 289.

4 The fifteenth-century gate tower of Queens' College: warlike posturing.

The interiors of the towers have seen many uses, perhaps the most appropriate being to house the college muniments and treasure where they could be safe and dry. The university muniments were kept in the tower of Great St Mary's Church until 1400, and the collegiate pattern was begun by Wykeham when he had a special tower constructed for this purpose. Cambridge imitators included King's, Queens', St John's, and Trinity (although not in the gate tower, but in a 'lesser' tower).[57] Although not demanded by statute, the muniments of Christ's College were stored in the gate tower, where they remain today. Accessible by a narrow stone staircase and opened by an enormous key, the treasury still guards the heavy oak and iron chests in which the most precious documents remain.

The first purpose-built room at Peterhouse was its hall, the indispensable part of every college. The medieval hall served not only for meals, but for academic disputations and dramatic productions as well. The almost universal form was a rectangular room with a raised dais at one end for the high table. The other tables were placed at right angles to it, and often there was a musicians' gallery over the lower end. The ceilings were of open timberwork, and the windows in some halls were unglazed at the bottom and closed with shutters. The unpanelled walls could be covered with tapestries or, by the sixteenth century, maps of the world. The halls were often decorated for plays and college festivals, as in Roger Ascham's days at St John's in the 1520s and 30s. Sometimes there were fireplaces, but more frequently in the late middle ages a brazier in the middle of the reed-strewn floor. Other furnishings could even include stocks for recalcitrant students.[58]

All medieval colleges recognised the importance of gathering together for meals, and even the master could not regularly absent himself. It was the rule that Scripture or other edifying books were read during meals, with conversation either prohibited or restricted to Latin or French (the Latin requirement was reiterated at Queens' as late as 1676).[59] The schedule of meals

---

[57] Peek and Hall, *Cambridge Archives*, pp. 1–6; Willis and Clark, III, pp. 475–80.

[58] Willis and Clark, III, pp. 354–6, 363–4, and 371–2; for musicians in hall see A. B. Cobban, *The King's Hall within the University of Cambridge in the Later Middle Ages* (Cambridge, 1969), pp. 222–7; R. Ascham, *Epistolae* (Oxford, 1703), p. 228 (Oct. 1550); for decoration, see Queens' College Archives, *Journale*, I, f. 158r. (1501–2), 'Johni Love pictori pro coloribus et pro labore suo circa pannos pro ornamento aule colleg' £4 0s 2d'. For flogging of scholars, see *Docs.* II, 556–9 (King's College) and II, 191 (Christ's College). See also *Paston Letters and Papers*, ed. N. Davis, I, 41–2 (Jan. 1458), Dame Agnes to her son Clement's tutor Magister Grenefeld recommending whipping him if he misbehaved. Clement was fifteen years old (*BRUC*, p. 443).   [59] Willis and Clark, III, p. 367.

varied during the middle ages, but usually consisted of the main meal at 10 a.m., a lesser meal at 5 p.m., with a light refreshment early in the mornings and possibly later in the evening. The fare relied heavily on bread, meat, and beer, with fish during the many fast days, but it could be varied with vegetables, fruit, salt, honey, almonds, pepper, rice, garlic, mustard, saffron, and much else.[60] For the college fellow meals were included in his 'commons'. The additional food and drink he bought from the college buttery were called his 'sizings'. The quality of the food and drink must have varied among the colleges and hostels, and from decade to decade. Only the complaints seem to have survived: Thomas More on Oxford cuisine, and Erasmus' condemnation of Cambridge beer.[61]

The meals themselves were prepared and served by a growing corps of servants, who by the sixteenth century were supplemented by younger scholars who served at table. Medieval college accounts are full of cooks, bakers, butlers, barbers, brewers, laundresses, janitors, under-cooks, and book-bearers.[62] Most of these offices were held by men; an exception could be made for the laundress, although it was thought best for her to be old and ugly.

After the evening meal on a holy day the college members might be allowed to stay in hall and gather around the fire for songs, storytelling, or reciting poems. Card playing was sometimes allowed at Christmastime. The lighting of the evening fire was something special in the colleges, where the chambers of the scholars did not have fires and many had unglazed windows. Since the average temperature was lower in the later middle ages than it is today, the penetrating cold and damp must have slowed the spirits of many a Cambridge man. This was compounded by the lack of anything more than candlelight on those long, dark, late Michaelmas term afternoons when dusk fell around 4 p.m. Fortunately the 'common cold' does not seem to have been prevalent in medieval England, but cold

---

[60] See Cobban, *King's Hall*, p. 124.
[61] CWE, *The Correspondence of Erasmus*, II, no. 226, p. 169; N. Harpsfield, *The Life and Death of Sir Thomas More*, ed. E. V. Hitchcock and R. W. Chambers, Early English Text Society 186 (London, 1932), p. 144.   [62] e.g. Cobban, *King's Hall*, pp. 231–40.

feet were a problem discussed by several sixteenth-century masters of St John's, and it was said that the poor scholars of Trinity College had to run upstairs before bedtime to warm their feet.[63]

The solution to this chilly environment was the Cambridge combination room, attached to the high-table end of the hall, where fellows could gather about a fire in the evening for warmth and companionship. Called a *parlura* at The King's Hall in 1423–4 (a place to talk) or in other colleges a *conclave* or *cenaculum*, these were originally very simply furnished.[64] By the sixteenth century some colleges even had endowments to maintain their fires.[65] The combination room, now so integral to collegiate life, was curiously not adopted at Oxford until the seventeenth century.

The chapel, again an inseparable part of any college in most minds (until Newham College in the nineteenth century) was not included in the plans of the earliest colleges. Canonically, the college residents were obliged to worship in the local parish church, and the rectors were not eager to lose their right to the tithes and oblations of these collegians. Although the early colleges had oratories, they used their parishes for the sacraments, and some of the colleges had even closer relationships with their parish churches.[66] At Peterhouse the college was attached by a gallery to St Peter's, and the church was rebuilt in 1340–52 to accommodate both collegians and parishioners in a divided chancel. The present Peterhouse chapel was not built until 1632.

Corpus Christi College was physically attached to St Bene't's Church, as it was statutorily when it was founded as an academic chantry by a civic guild located in that parish. Corpus Christi was commonly called 'Bene't College' until modern times. Trinity Hall, and probably Clare College, had chapels in the fourteenth century, but they used the parish church of St

---

[63] T. Lever, *Sermons*, ed. E. Arber (London, 1870), p. 122; Rashdall, III, p. 414; *Desiderata Curiosa*, ed. F. Peck (London, 1779), VIII, p. 339; Mullinger, *Cambridge*, I, p. 371.
[64] Willis and Clark, III, p. 376–86.
[65] Willis and Clark, III, p. 385; for Trinity Hall in 1562, see *Warren's Book*, ed. A. W. W. Dale (Cambridge, 1911), pp. 256–7, 260.   [66] Willis and Clark, III, pp. 498–9.

John Zachary for the sacraments. When that church was moved in the 1440s to make way for King's College Chapel, Henry VI rebuilt the east end of St Edward's Church to accommodate the needs of Trinity Hall and Clare. Michaelhouse, founded by Hervey de Stanton in 1324, used their eponymous parish in the High Street, which was rebuilt to serve as college chapel, parish church, and chantry for the college founder.[67]

The early colleges often had close relationships with the town parishes, and the citizens alternated between support for the material and spiritual benefits the colleges provided, and deep antagonism against their perceived arrogance and privileges. Both factors were present, and neither was always predominant.

The movement to separately licensed chapels followed in the wake of Queen's College, Oxford, where the founder's statutes of 1340 provided for a chapel (which was not consecrated until 1420). At Cambridge the foundress of Pembroke College, the widowed Countess of Pembroke, was able to bring enough influence to bear in the papal court to obtain a licence for a chapel. Even then all the financial privileges of the parish church (St Botolph's) were to be preserved, and burials were not allowed in the chapel.[68] Soon other colleges obtained similar privileges, but often with surprisingly long delays. At the royal King's Hall, founded in 1327, the members worshipped across the street at All Saints in the Jewry, and a chapel was not consecrated until 1498 9. At Clare College the Marian visitors in 1557 found that the chapel had never been consecrated.[69]

King Henry VI's King's College, founded in the 1440s, had a fully independent chapel from its inception (as possibly did Trinity Hall in the previous century).[70] King's College Chapel was and is unique in more important ways. The last great monument of the Old Faith in England, it has given centuries of visitors a false idea of what a college chapel is. King's College Chapel was not necessary for the corporate worship of the provost and seventy fellows; it was begun grandly as a

---

[67] Willis and Clark, III, pp. 495–7, Brooke, 'Churches of Medieval Cambridge', pp. 62–8.
[68] Willis and Clark, III, pp. 512–13 & 492–3.
[69] Willis and Clark, III, p. 512; J. Foxe, *Acts and Monuments*, ed. G. Townsend (1843–9; rpt. New York, 1965), VIII, p. 275.　　[70] Willis and Clark, III, p. 514.

monument to Lancastrian ambition and it was finished magnificently as a symbol of Tudor legitimacy. Until the eighteenth century the college that it served was housed in the humble little court that is now the University Registry. Even Henry VIII's Trinity College, far wealthier and with many more members, was satisfied with a smaller chapel.[71]

Following King's, all newly founded colleges included an independent chapel as an integral component, and earlier foundations often added them as well. At Godshouse, another college aided by the Lancastrians, funds for the new chapel of the 1480s were raised by the Bishop of Ely offering indulgences to contributors.[72] Late medieval chapels often included rood screens, lofts, organs, and chantry chapels. In the sixteenth century the changing liturgical practices under Henry, Edward, Mary, and Elizabeth can be charted in college accounts by payments alternately to tear-out and then rebuild altars, roods, pixes, and statuary, and for the buying and selling off of vestments and liturgical vessels.[73]

The chambers in which college members lived were always part of every college plan. They were usually in two storeys and grouped around staircases, as they often still are. They were, however, a far cry from the gracious (if often shabby) elegance that characterises them today. There were usually two or three fellows in each chamber, with senior members assigned to oversee their more junior 'chamberers' (hence the word 'chums'). The communal bedrooms had small studies or carrels in the corners, for in reverse of modern sensibilities, privacy was more prized when studying than sleeping.[74]

The chambers were sparsely furnished, often with unglazed, shuttered windows, floors of clay or tile, and unplastered walls and ceilings. The furniture was spartan: a few shelves, a washbin, desk table, stools, and trundle beds for the junior

---

[71] The Trinity chapel is, incidentally, the only important ecclesiastical building of the Marian restoration.

[72] CUL, Ely Diocesan Archives, Alcock Register, f. 37r. Parallel indulgences were offered in 1457 for the repair of Great St Mary's (Gray Register, f. 21v.) and in 1491 for the chapel of the Hospital of St John (Alcock Register, f. 72r).

[73] See H. C. Porter, *Reformation and Reaction in Tudor Cambridge* (Cambridge, 1958), pp. 109–10; A. Gray and F. Brittain, *A History of Jesus College, Cambridge* (London, 1979), pp. 45–6.

[74] Willis and Clark, III, pp. 297–327.

members which were rolled out from under their seniors' beds. Room assignments, then as now, were regulated by statute, with only doctors eligible in some colleges for single rooms.[75] It was only with declining numbers in the seventeenth century, and an increase in gentlemen, that these accommodations were gradually made more elegant, and that privacy was eventually made available to the fellows.

The master's lot in most medieval colleges appears not to have been significantly better than the fellow's. The post had few of the perquisites that are so familiar today. He had to eat with the fellows, and although he had the pick of the best chamber, its furnishings were usually no more sumptuous than in other rooms. There were exceptions by the fifteenth century, however. Bishop Lawrence Booth, master of Pembroke and chancellor of the university seems to have lived in college for a time during the political troubles of 1462–6, and kept a significant household. By *c.* 1500 more colleges chose similarly distinguished figures as master. The splendid galleries of Queens' and St John's colleges were built for men who led more elegant and elaborate lives than their medieval predecessors. When masters married after the Reformation, they began more frequently to live apart from the fellows in separate, self-contained lodges.[76]

Peterhouse required the two deans to care for the library, regulate the distribution of books, and take the oaths of the members that they would not steal them and would return them on time.[77] The care of the library would have taken little effort, as it initially meant only a few codices kept in a chest. Later this collection grew and was given a separate room with presses and lecterns. The colleges rarely purchased books, but relied instead on gifts from alumni and external benefactors. Thus, the college libraries reflected to a large extent the interests of the donors which were sometimes, but not always, different from what was most current in the university. Since access to the libraries was restricted to the fellows who were beyond their first degree, the introductory texts of the arts faculty were

[75] Willis and Clark, III, pp. 297–327. [76] Willis and Clark, III, pp. 328–53.
[77] *Docs.* II, 17.

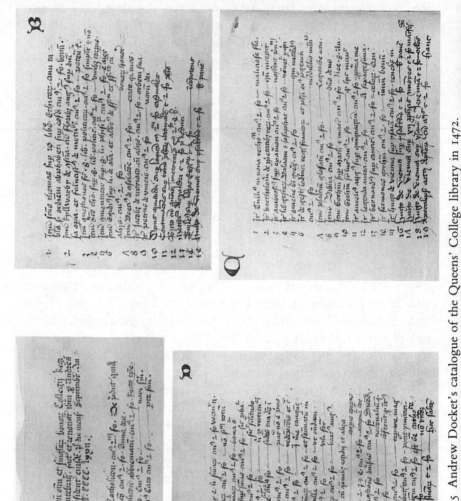

5　Andrew Docket's catalogue of the Queens' College library in 1472.

usually under-represented. Often the least expensive books and the most used within the university, very few have survived in relation to their educational importance.

The library books were as a rule divided into two classes: the *libri concatenati*, the standard works and more expensively executed books which were chained to lecterns to prevent their wandering off, and the *libri distribuendi*, duplicates of these and other less expensive books that could be borrowed by the fellows as needed, or distributed in bundles among the fellows at periodic *electiones*. In an *electio* the circulating books would be collected in lots (of five, as in the case of Merton) and given out to the fellows, presumably by seniority.[78]

In addition to benefactions, colleges acquired books through the *caucio* system. Many of the colleges had chests (called hutches) which comprised the medieval provision for student loans (the university had several). A benefactor would give a chest and cash to be kept in it. At Peterhouse such a loan chest was endowed by Thomas de Castro-Bernardo in the early 1400s, from which the fellows were allowed to borrow up to £2 and the college up to £6 13s 4d corporatively. In return, the borrower had to place in the chest a pledge or *caucio* of comparable value. Often these pledges were jewellery, liturgical vessels, or books. The books, if unredeemed, often were eventually placed in the college library.[79]

The medieval collections of Pembroke, Gonville Hall, and Peterhouse are all well represented in their modern holdings, and the fifteenth-century catalogues of Peterhouse survive. The Peterhouse manuscripts are especially interesting for the many codices with notations on the flyleaves listing previous owners, users, and when and by whom they were placed in caution.[80]

The statutes of the mid-fourteenth-century foundations of Trinity Hall and Gonville Hall spell out more clearly the care

[78] F. M. Powicke, *The Medieval Books of Merton College* (Oxford, 1931), pp. 12–18; J. W. Clark, 'On the History of the Library', in M. R. James, *A Descriptive Catalogue of the Manuscripts in the Library of Peterhouse* (Cambridge, 1899), p. xx.

[79] G. Pollard, 'Mediaeval Loan Chests at Cambridge', *Bulletin of the Institute of Historical Research*, 17 (1939–40), 113–29; Corpus Christi College Archives 'Registrum ciste mri. Billingford' contains lists of cautions from 1471 onward; *Docs.* I, nos. 181 and 183, pp. 407–11 for university chests.   [80] e.g. Peterhouse MSS 143 and 183.

of the library.[81] The books were to be audited twice a year, and never lent to outsiders. College members were only allowed to take them off the premises when going to the Schools, and were not to borrow them by quires for the purpose of copying.[82] In addition, the books of the doctors of canon and civil law, the most important studies of Trinity Hall, were to be kept chained at all times.

In the late fourteenth and early fifteenth centuries many colleges built separate rooms for their libraries, as did the university in a room in the Schools (it was tended by the university chaplain and open to the masters).[83] These were typically on the first floor to keep them dry, and varied in size from about 35 × 15 ft. to 60 × 20 ft. Most were orientated east – west for maximum sunlight, and they rarely faced a noisy street on the front side of the college. The windows were set at regular intervals with two-sided lecterns extending from the walls at right angles. The lecterns had sloping desks on each side, and the chained books were stored on their sides on the shelves below. As there were no librarians in the medieval colleges the fellows were often issued with keys so they could use the collections at their convenience.[84] A surprisingly large number of inventories of late medieval college libraries survive, showing that the lecterns were organised by subject matter, and that occasionally globes, maps, and astrolabes could complement the collection.[85] Trinity Hall built a library on the medieval

---

[81] *Docs.* II, 236 and 432; Venn, *Biographical History*, III, pp. 188–95, 351.

[82] This practice, called the *pecia* system, was practised in Paris where the scholars rented the quires from stationers. At Cambridge the school books were copied by the users themselves (e.g. John Capgrave, *BRUC*, pp. 121–2) or, less commonly, by commercial scribes. For example, the Swedish scribe *Teilmannus filius Clewardi* worked in Cambridge and produced Gonville and Caius MS 114/183, Corpus Christi College Cambridge MS 68 (part of which is now King's College MS 9), and Peterhouse MSS 188 and 240. The Dutch scribe Tielman Reynerzoon was active in Oxford and produced Balliol MSS 28 and 35B (R. A. B. Mynors, *Catalogue of the Manuscripts of Balliol College, Oxford* (Oxford, 1963), pp. xxvi–xxvii; see also G. Pollard, 'The University and the Book Trade in Medieval Oxford', *Miscellanea Mediaevalia*, III (Berlin, 1964), pp. 336–45).

[83] H. P. Stokes, *The Chaplains and Chapel of the University of Cambridge*, CAS Octavo Publications 41 (Cambridge, 1906), pp. 39–40.

[84] P. Gaskell, *Trinity College Library: The First 150 Years* (Cambridge, 1980), pp. 4–6; Willis and Clark, III, pp. 397 and 414–16; *Docs.* II, 601.

[85] See the list of library inventories in the bibliography.

6 The library of Queens' College. The cases were rebuilt in the seventeenth century, but the lower halves are fifteenth century. Some window glass (not shown) is from the neighbouring Carmelite house, demolished at the Reformation. The medieval chest is still used to store college documents.

model *c.* 1590, and it gives a clear sense of the scale and atmosphere of its many predecessors.

Halls, kitchens, and chambers were common to all colleges, and by the later middle ages chapels and libraries could be found in most as well. Some of the richer colleges had other elements. King's College had a barber's shop, and some dovecotes, vineyards, summer houses, vegetable gardens, and huts for swanherds.[86] What the medieval colleges did lack was

[86] Willis and Clark, III, pp. 588–99; for college rights to swans, see A. H. Lloyd, 'The College Game of Swans' in *Christ's College in Former Days*, ed. H. Rackham (Cambridge, 1939), pp. 64–75.

the landscaping now such a part of their attraction, for landscape gardening was not a medieval passion. But by 1500 Queens' College had a president's garden, and was paying for the cleaning 'of the garden where the crocuses grow'.[87] A more personal touch is found in Nicholas Ridley, reminiscing before his execution, on having first learned the Epistles of St Paul in a protestant manner in the orchard of Pembroke.[88]

The scholar's life in college was closely regulated. His comings and goings, attendance in chapel and hall were all determined by statute, as were his amusements. Falconing, dice, cards, dogs, fishing, and shooting arrows were almost universally banned, at King's College in part owing to the damage they could cause to the buildings and windows.[89] Some sports were encouraged, however. Corpus Christi had a handball court by 1487, Queens' a tennis court in the next century, and Ridley played tennis with his pupils when at Pembroke in the 1530s (an activity considered scandalous at Merton College in 1492).[90] Public dancing was prohibited by university statute by 1300, as was swimming in 1571.[91]

The great college celebrations in medieval Cambridge centred on Christmas. Many men stayed up for the winter holidays, especially those from the North who faced difficult roads.[92] At Queens' in 1501 it was already a college custom to serve roast boar at Christmas.[93] The holidays were a time of relaxed rules, of card playing, when fires were lit every evening in hall and a 'king of the beans' might be chosen.[94] A boy bishop was elected at King's College on Childermas and a celebration held which was repeated on Epiphany.[95] This custom at St John's

---

[87] Queens' College Archives, *Journale*, II, *passim*; Willis and Clark, III, pp. 579.

[88] *The Works of Ridley*, ed. A. Christmas, Parker Society 35 (1841), pp. 406–7.

[89] *Docs.* II, 542–3.

[90] Willis and Clark, III, pp. 568–75; A. L. Attwater, *Pembroke College*, ed. S. C. Roberts (Cambridge, 1936), p. 36; *Registrum Annalium Collegii Mertonensis*, ed. Salter, I, p. 156.

[91] *Docs.* I, no. 47, p. 335; *Statuta Academiae Cantabrigiensis* (Cambridge, 1785), pp. 453–4.

[92] Although King's College sometimes helped pay for their choristers to visit their parents. King's College Muniments, *Mundum Book*, I, f. 144r.

[93] Queens' College Archives, *Journale*, I, f. 158r.

[94] e.g. *Registrum Coll. Mertonensis*, ed. Salter, pp. xviii–xix.

[95] *Annals*, p. 197 (1446) claims that this was prohibited in King's on Childermas. But see King's College Muniments, *Mundum Book*, IV, f. 99v. (1467) and *passim*.

led to such excesses that it was suppressed after the Reformation.[96]

Charivaries parodied academic life and institutions. It was a tradition within the colleges for incoming freshmen to be subjected to burlesques of disputations, with senior scholars acting as masters. Those neophytes who performed poorly were sconced with salted beer, a custom that survived into the early modern university.[97] Every Ash Wednesday there was a university-wide election of a mock-chancellor, proctors, bedells, etc., until the practice was suppressed by statute.[98]

The life of the medieval Cambridge scholar was more violent and less comfortable than it is today. Murders and assaults were more frequent, and highwaymen haunted the road to London.[99] The light was bad for most of the year and candles were expensive. There was much less reading and a lot more organised verbal interchange, not just in the Schools but in evening practice disputations within the colleges and hostels. Before the sixteenth century there were far fewer formal presentations of music and dramatics, although both were present. There seems to have been at least as much drinking as today, but almost no permitted contact with women. We can assume that many medieval scholars liked the place, as shown by the bequests to colleges by old boys. We have almost no personal memoirs from before 1500, but one of them indicates a certain fondness for the school. John Major was up at Godshouse for only three months in 1492–3 before moving on to Paris where he made for himself an international reputation as a logician. He chose Godshouse because it was within the parish of St Andrew, patron of Scotland, and Major was a Scot. Writing about thirty years later he recalled,[100]

---

[96] J. B. Mullinger, *St John's College* (London 1901), p. 38.
[97] J. O. Halliwell, *College Life in the Time of James the First as Illustrated by an Unpublished Diary of Sir Symonds D'Ewes* (London, 1851), pp. 14–15; S. R. Maitland, 'Original Papers Relating to Whitgift', *The British Magazine*, 32 (1847), 366, n 5
[98] *Annals*, p. 110 (1368); *Statuta Academiae Cantabrigiensis*, p. 22.
[99] CWE, *Correspondence of Erasmus*, II, no. 282, p. 265.
[100] BRUC, pp. 384–5; J. Major, *Historia majoris Britanniae tam angliae quam scotiae* (Paris, Ascensius, 1521), f. xxxviii v., trans. in H. Rackham, 'John Mair', in *Christ's College in Former Days*, p. 28; cf. H. C. Porter, in D. F. S. Thomson and H. C. Porter (eds.) *Erasmus and Cambridge* (Toronto, 1963), p. 23, 'The reminiscence, unlike the bells, rings slightly false.'

When I was a student at Cambridge I spent the greatest part of the night during the great feasts without sleep so that I might listen to the melody of the bells. The university stands on a river, and on that account the sound is sweeter from the undulations off the water.

MORE COLLEGES: 1317–1352

Peterhouse was the only college in Cambridge for thirty-three years, during which time Oxford was graced with University College, Balliol, Merton, Exeter, and the monastic colleges of Gloucester and Durham. Peterhouse was finally joined in 1317 by a unique royal enterprise that was called The King's Hall. Its origin is shadowy, the first mention being a writ of Edward II in July 1317 for the support of a clerk and twelve children whom he had sent to be educated in Cambridge. These scholars initially had an anomalous status within the university. They lived in rented premises as if members of a hostel, and were unendowed, but as in a college the King's scholars paid no rent or board themselves, their expenses being at the charge of the Exchequer.[101] Simultaneously with sending off this first group of young scholars the king sought to guarantee the international status of Cambridge. The university was already a *studium generale* by custom, but it had no document to prove that standing. So, Edward II petitioned Rome in March 1317 for such a grant, and in 1318 Cambridge received an apostolic award which acknowledged the status.[102]

Edward III inherited the role of supporter of this unique institution and took an active interest in it. In 1332 he set up a commission to examine the college with the aim of expelling those fellows who were already sufficiently beneficed, or those who were not up to the academic standards of the Schools.[103] Although the findings of this commission are not known, the king was evidently satisfied with The King's Hall. In 1336 he

[101] Cobban, *King's Hall*, pp. 9–15; *Docs.* I, nos. 66–7, pp. 349–51.
[102] A. B. Cobban, 'Edward II, Pope John XXII, and the University of Cambridge', *Bulletin of the John Rylands Library*, 47 (1964–5), 49–78.
[103] Cobban, *King's Hall*, p. 14, n. 1.

purchased a house for the society on the site of the present Trinity Great Court, and in 1337 by letters patent he endowed it. A royal society, its master appointed by the crown, it 'constitutes the first establishment of a royal "colony" of clerks in an English university setting'.[104]

The obvious question is why the two Edwards would have any desire to do this, and more particularly, why at Cambridge, then clearly inferior to Oxford in both size and reputation. The preamble to the letters patent of 1337 gives its *raison d'être* as 'the increase of learning in Cambridge University' and the service of the Church and State. These intentions, however, do not vary appreciably from those expressed by the founders of most colleges. What made The King's Hall special was its initial recruitment of scholars from the royal chapel. In this sense it was an 'extension or arm of the chapel royal set in ...Cambridge...and throughout the greater part of its history it remained a kind of physical adjunct or supplement to the court'.[105] This may well have been the Edwards' intentions, although by the next century the nexus with the royal chapel disappeared. But for over two centuries the Crown exercised direct physical control, and every fellow and warden taken onto the fellowship was individually appointed by writ of privy seal. This control by the royal household was probably particularly appealing to Edward II in 1317, as baronial control impinged on his prerogatives. The King's Hall would provide a 'reservoir of educated personnel from which the King could draw to meet his particular requirements'.[106] Although this immediate need would end with Edward's hideous death, the college members consistently specialised in law to an extent unparalleled in any other Cambridge college. The tradition was one of service.

Why a 'royal college' in Cambridge? The primary reason was probably the influence of Edward II's Chancellor of the Exchequer, the Yorkshireman John Hotham. Consecrated Bishop of Ely in 1316, Hotham was a leader among the King's official circle, which included others committed to education: Hervey

[104] Cobban, *King's Hall*, p. 12.   [105] Cobban, *King's Hall*, p. 20.
[106] Cobban, *King's Hall*, p. 23; 'The Medieval Cambridge Colleges: A Quantitative Study of Higher Degrees to *c.* 1500', *History of Education*, 9 (1980), 3–8.

de Stanton, founder of Michaelhouse; Adam de Brome, founder of Oriel College, Oxford; Walter de Stapeldon, founder of Exeter College, Oxford; and John de Salmon, benefactor of University Hall, Cambridge. Hotham surely tried to convince the king to place the royal foundation in Ely diocese.[107]

Edward II probably did not have strong feelings about the location, although he had several reasons for slighting Oxford. The clerks and burgesses of Oxford had refused to help obtain the release of Piers Gaveston when asked by Pembroke in 1312, the imprisonment which eventually led to his death. The King had also crossed swords with the university several times during quarrels with the friars, and he had insisted on the rights of the mendicants within Oxford.[108]

The King's Hall quickly became one of the most important constituent parts of medieval Cambridge. It was the first English college regularly to admit undergraduates, as were all of the original King's Hall scholars. It soon developed a graduate fellowship as well, as these boys continued into the superior faculties of theology and especially law. The minimum age for entrance by the 1380 statutes was fourteen. They could hold their fellowships almost indefinitely, and some did, often while absent from the university. At thirty-two the fellowship was enormous by medieval standards; in the fourteenth century it accounted for 40 per cent of Cambridge college fellowships.[109]

The King's Hall was the first in a series of seven colleges founded within thirty-five years. Michaelhouse was founded in 1324, a now forgotten institution that shared the same ultimate fate as The King's Hall. In Dean Rashdall's words, 'the individual existence of Michaelhouse was eventually extinguished in the great college which that munificent donor of other people's property, King Henry VIII, erected upon the ruins of more than one earlier foundation'.[110] Michaelhouse was founded by the wealthy ecclesiastic Hervey de Stanton, another Chancellor of the Exchequer, who also held prebendal stalls at both York

[107] A. C. Chibnall, *Richard de Badew and the University of Cambridge 1315–40* (Cambridge, 1963), p. 4; Cobban, *King's Hall*, pp. 24–6.
[108] Cobban, *King's Hall*, pp. 26–7.   [109] Cobban, *King's Hall*, pp. 45, 55–9.
[110] Rashdall, III, p. 302.

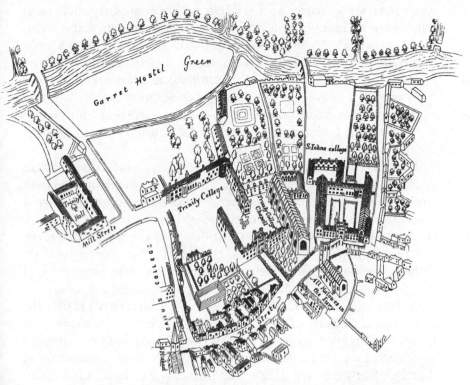

7 A view of Trinity College in 1592. The buildings of The King's Hall include the Great Gate (*c.* 1530), and King Edward's Tower (*c.* 1430). King Edward's Tower was moved to its present location next to the chapel when Great Court was built *c.* 1600.

and Wells. [111] His 'Scholars of the Holy and Undivided Trinity, the Blessed Virgin Mary, and St Michael' (the first of many Cambridge colleges at least partially dedicated to the Mother of Christ) were housed near the present site of Bishop's Hostel Gate in Trinity. They were required to serve St Michael's Church, which still stands, as Hervey rebuilt it, in Trinity Street. It was a small society primarily of theologians; all admitted to the fellowship were to be priests or at least in Holy Orders, and were to enter the faculty of theology. Provision

---

[111] Chibnall, *Richard de Badew*, p. 4.

was made for a master and six fellows (later slightly increased) who were to have 'a common table and a uniform habit in so far as possible'.[112] We know little of Michaelhouse, as only fragments of its archives have survived. An analysis of the known members shows that of graduate degrees taken, 83 per cent were in theology.[113] Among these men were William Melton and his pupil, John Fisher, who was to be so influential in the growth and internal reform of the university in the last decades before the Reformation.

The next college, known to us as Clare, was conceived in 1321 when Roger de Northburgh (another member of Edward's circle) received a licence to hold endowments to support a house of studies accommodating students in the arts and theology faculties. The next year he was promoted to the see of Coventry and Lichfield, and the project was taken up by others. John de Salmon, Bishop of Norwich, provided 100 marks in 1325, and in 1326 Richard de Badew, Chancellor of Cambridge, obtained a licence to establish the college of 'University Hall' for graduate members of the university. The endowment was meagre, however, and for a few years de Badew provided supplementary financial aid. The problems were compounded shortly afterwards by a fire that heavily damaged University Hall.[114] Help came in the person of Lady Elizabeth de Clare, widow of John de Burgh and granddaughter of Edward I. In 1336 she gave the fledgling college of ten fellows an appropriated benefice worth £20 a year, and in 1338 Richard de Badew, 'founder, patron and advocate of the house called the Hall of the University of Cambridge' granted all his rights in it to Lady Clare, 'in consideration of' the benefice that she had given.[115]

Elizabeth de Burgh was no mere titular foundress of Clare Hall; she was the first in a distinguished line of energetic women whose benevolence transformed late medieval

---

[112] Statutes in Mullinger, *Cambridge*, I, pp. 640ff.; Rashdall, III, p. 301.
[113] Cobban, 'Medieval Cambridge Colleges', p. 9.
[114] *BRUC*, pp. 229–30 and 400–1; Chibnall, *Richard de Badew*, pp. 38–41.
[115] *VCH*, III, pp. 340–1; Rashdall, III, p. 303.

Cambridge. Her active interest in the college spanned twenty-two years. After a prolonged legal process in 1346 she was able to provide it with three more appropriated benefices. In 1352, she prompted a royal commission of investigation into the college, which found that economic difficulties were causing the fellows to resort to financial irregularities.[116] With these findings in mind she promulgated a set of statutes in 1359 which served the college for nearly two hundred years. They provided for twenty fellows (when the endowment allowed), of whom six were to be priests. Of these two might study civil law and one medicine, with the remainder pursuing arts or theology. The college never had the resources for this full fellowship, and there were probably never more than ten fellows. Of the known graduates of this college, 59 per cent were theologians.[117]

Lady Clare was a friend of the French Marie de St Pol, also known as Mary de Valence, the Countess of Pembroke. Widowed at the age of twenty and immensely rich, she was influenced by Franciscan ideals. She spent her long life as a benefactress of religious institutions on both sides of the Channel, including Denny Abbey, the notable house of Franciscan nuns just outside Cambridge. Doubtless following the example of Lady Clare, she began her support of Cambridge education in 1346 by buying a piece of land on Trumpington Street to serve for a new college. On Christmas Eve 1347 Edward III signed the licence which formally established this college, called until modern times either Pembroke Hall or the Hall of Valence Marie. The Countess endowed it in the usual way, by appropriating benefices. How this foundation was initially meant to be governed is uncertain since two sets of early statutes survive. The plan that was short-lived, if ever implemented, called for Pembroke to be ruled by two annually elected rectors, who admitted the fellows that were elected by the college, and also exercised visitational powers. This scheme was more usual in the Parisian colleges and echoed the thirteenth-century statutes

[116] *VCH*, III, pp. 341.
[117] *Docs.* II, 121–46; Cobban, 'Medieval Cambridge Colleges', p. 9.

83

of Balliol College, Oxford. One of the rectors was to be a Franciscan, and the other a secular priest.[118]

Given the animosity between the seculars and the mendicants, it is not surprising that this provision is absent from the second set of statutes, specifically dated 1347. There were to be twenty-four 'major scholars' and six 'minor' ones, the latter in a probationary position. All were to study arts and then theology, except for two canon lawyers and a medical student. They originally worshipped corporatively in St Botolph's Church next door, but in 1355–66 the foundress obtained papal bulls that allowed them to include a private chapel in the college.[119] As usual, the foundation did not support the requisite number of fellows. In 1412 they numbered only twelve, with one boy.[120]

The Countess made one exceptional provision in giving preference in the election of fellows to one of French birth from Oxford or Cambridge (although few if any were elected). She alone also founded colleges in both England and France, establishing one in Paris in 1356 which remained stillborn with the vicissitudes of the Hundred Years War. The war, however, benefited Pembroke. Henry VI, regarded as the second founder, enriched it with several confiscated alien priories (religious houses in England that belonged to French mother houses).[121]

Pembroke Hall was joined shortly afterwards in 1348 by Gonville Hall. Edmund Gonville's father was a Frenchman who had settled in Norfolk and prospered. Young Edmund entered the secular clergy in that diocese and from 1320 held a series of very lucrative benefices. Why he chose to found a Cambridge college is uncertain, but he set to work in 1347 by purchasing land from St Botolph's on the present Free School Lane, in what is now the master's garden of Corpus Christi College. The next year he obtained a royal licence for his college, and in 1349 executed the deed of foundation. It provided for a master and twenty fellows to study 'in dialectics and other

---

[118] A. Attwater, *Pembroke College, Cambridge*, ed. S. C. Roberts (Cambridge, 1936), pp. 1–12. Mary de Valence's confessor was also a Franciscan.

[119] Brooke, 'Churches of Medieval Cambridge', pp. 74–5; Attwater, p. 8; Rashdall, III, pp. 305–6; *Docs.* II, pp. 189–203.

[120] Pembroke College archives, Register Aα, f. 5r.   [121] Attwater, pp. 10–11 and 17–18.

sciences'.[122] In the summer of 1351 Edmund Gonville died and the completion of his plans, with significant modifications, fell to his executor and ordinary, Bishop William Bateman of Norwich.

Bishop Bateman was already busy with his own foundation of Trinity Hall, and he dovetailed the two colleges in several ways. He exchanged with the guild of Corpus Christi and St Mary the site Gonville had purchased for land on Trinity Lane just to the east of Trinity Hall. Bateman also gave the college new statutes almost identical to those of Trinity Hall, but retained Gonville's original dedication, calling the college 'The Hall of the Annunciation of the Blessed Virgin'. In common parlance, however, it was called Gonville Hall, and is today called Caius after its Marian refounder, Dr John Caius. Bateman's statutes allowed a wider scope of studies, and the fellows could proceed in civil or canon law as well as theology. The statutory complement of twenty fellows was never filled, but varied with the college's income from five in 1426 to a mere two in 1465.[123] The usual number was about four, but the rooms were filled with paying lodgers, such as the Norwich monks mentioned above. Preference was given to potential fellows from the eastern counties, a pattern that is statutorily present at Trinity Hall and Corpus Christi.[124]

William Bateman's proper foundation was the 'College of the Scholars of the Holy Trinity of Norwich' (the dedication of Norwich Cathedral), and has always been known as Trinity Hall. Bateman was from Norwich and was a doctor of both laws of Cambridge by 1328. He was a judge at the papal court in Avignon in the 1330s and served in 1340–2 as papal pronuncio to Edward III before being promoted to the see of Norwich in 1344.[125] Serving both King and Pope, he was

---

[122] C. N. L. Brooke, *A History of Gonville and Caius College* (Woodbridge, Suffolk, 1985), pp. 1–19; *Docs.* II, p 213; Venn *et al.*, *Biographical History of Gonville and Caius College*, III, pp. 325–31.

[123] Brooke, *History of Gonville and Caius College*, p. 31, n. 49; Aston. 'Cambridge Alumni', pp. 31–2; *VCH*, III, p. 357.

[124] Brooke, *Gonville and Caius College*, pp. 16–17, demonstrates that the 'statutory provision' that the masters be from Norfolk was a fifteenth-century forgery that codified existing practice; *BRUC*, p. 44; *VCH*, III, pp. 356–8.   [125] *BRUC*, p. 44.

keenly aware of the importance of both laws in domestic and international dealings. His deed of foundation in 1350 explained that the college was for 'the increase of divine worship and of canon and civil learning and of the University of Cambridge and also for the advantage, rule, and direction of the commonwealth and especially of the church and diocese of Norwich'. There were to be twenty fellows, elected after taking the BA, who were to be divided between canonists and civilians.[126] The college in practice had only about half this number in any given year, and of the twenty-one known pre-1500 fellows, twenty were from Norwich. They were liberally provided for, with the fellows receiving six to eight marks annually, and were served by many servants.[127]

The last of these fourteenth-century foundations, 'The College of Corpus Christi and the Blessed Virgin Mary' was chartered in 1352, three years after the first wave of the Black Death. Much has been made of this coincidence, and claims have been made that Corpus, Gonville Hall, and Trinity Hall were in part an effort to replenish a diminished clergy. Unfortunately there is little evidence for this, and the express purposes of the colleges' founders were shared to a large degree by all college benefactors: to pray for their souls. What is unique about Corpus was that its founder was a corporation, the amalgamated guilds of Corpus Christi and the Blessed Virgin Mary, which were composed of townsmen, but led by the Duke of Lancaster. The college provides an example where the interests of town and university – a chantry for the citizens, and financial support for the scholars – produced a mutually agreeable solution. The guild provided the endowment and built the college's 'Old Court' in the 1350s and 60s, 'the first originally-planned closed quadrangle in Cambridge' to survive.[128] The land to the south of this court also came with the original benefaction, being bought from the fledgling Gonville Hall. Corpus had no chapel until *c.* 1500, and the neighbouring parish church of St Bene't's,

---

[126] *Docs.* II, 417–18; *VCH*, III, pp. 362–3.
[127] Aston, 'Cambridge Alumni', pp. 31–2; C. Crawley, *Trinity Hall* (Cambridge, 1976), pp. 1–27.   [128] Willis and Clark, III, pp. 256.

home of the founding guilds, served the college and gave it an alternative name.

The statutes were promulgated in 1356 and were based on those of Michaelhouse, with modifications to suit the guild's purposes. There was a master and but two fellows, priests all, who were to study theology or canon law. This tiny fellowship was augmented in later decades by further benefactions from other sources. They were to wear a common livery, pray the canonical hours (a unique requirement in an English college), and serve as chaplains to the guild and attend the funerals of all its members.[129] The college also participated in the annual Corpus Christi Day procession, one of the most splendid events in medieval Cambridge. It began with a sermon by the vice-chancellor at Great St Mary's, followed by a procession to St Bene't's, led by the guild members, then followed by the master of Corpus 'in a silk cope under a canopy' who carried the Sacrament in a gilded monstrance through the town streets. He was followed by the university officers, graduates, the mayor, and the burgesses. The sacred was succeeded by the profane, with a dinner for all provided by the college where 'good stomachs meeting with good cheer and welcome, no wonder if mirth flowed of course'.[130]

By 1352 Cambridge was well established. If not as large as Oxford, it nevertheless attracted royal patronage in a way that its mother school had not. There were now seven colleges, small graduate institutions for the most part, but influential through the seniority of their fellows. The colleges also gave a physical stability to Cambridge, for they owned land and buildings in a way that the 'University of Cambridge' did not. The days of migration, and the threat of migration, so common in the thirteenth century, were over.

But the foundation of Corpus Christi College also marks the

---

[129] R. Masters, *A History of the College of Corpus Christi and the Blessed Virgin Mary* (Cambridge, 1753), app. p. 11; *VCH*, III, p. 372.
[130] T. Fuller, *The History of the University of Cambridge*, ed. J. Nichols (London, 1840), pp. 70–1; Pope Leo X provided an indulgence of 25 years for all who attended this procession. *Annals*, I, p. 303 (1519–20).

8 The Old Court of Corpus Christi College, built *c.* 1360, although now much restored.

end of the first part of the story of medieval Cambridge. There was not to be another college founded for over eighty years. The Black Death and other plagues would return every few years, and 1381 saw a civil insurrection directed against the university, its wealth, and its privileges.

Chapter 3

TEACHING

'Gram' loquitur, 'Dia' vera docet,
'Rhet' verba colorat
'Mus' canit, 'Ar' numerat, 'Ge'
ponderat, 'Ast' colit astra.

Nicholas Dorbell

It is always a danger when describing medieval universities to tell of founders, grants, papal bulls, student life, colleges, quarrels, and great men, and to forget that the purpose of a university is to teach, and its essence is scholarship. Relatively little research has been done on the surviving Cambridge manuscripts of lectures and texts for the purpose of reconstructing the curriculum. It is difficult in many fields to say who were the favoured authors in a given generation.

Much of what will be said below about Cambridge relies on general trends and sparse evidence. Apart from the studies of the fifteenth-century faculty of liberal arts, there is little research available that closely examines the surviving library and archival evidence, or considers the textbook annotations and disputed questions. The treatment is accordingly not strictly chronological, and favours the fifteenth century, when Cambridge was larger than before and from which more evidence survives. Much work remains to be done, and the following is only a summary of the current state of the question.

In theory, the typical undergraduate began in the faculty of arts and, after taking the BA and MA, could then move into the superior faculties of theology, medicine, or the laws. The faculty of arts made up the largest part of both Oxford and Cambridge in the late middle ages. From the time of Augustine,

89

the seven liberal arts and the three philosophies were considered propaedeutic to the study of theology. The arts were only a means to this end, and at Paris there was a saying, 'one ought not to grow old in the study of the arts'.[1] The statutes of Oxford referred to the arts faculty as *fons et origo ceteris*.[2] In a sermon preached in Oxford *c.* 1412 John Shirborne, MA, elaborated on the symbolic correspondences between the human body and the university, comparing the masters of arts to the feet, which support the rest of the body.[3]

The faculty of arts could exercise its primacy in several ways. Younger and more numerous than the other faculties, its masters required that an arts degree be the necessary preparation for all of the other faculties except law. The artists also filled most of the administrative posts, including the proctorships. Their votes could dominate the congregation of regents. The arts faculty was not autonomous in the modern sense. The theologians could ultimately exercise control over what was taught in arts, although at this time there were none of the conflicts such as existed in thirteenth-century Paris or fourteenth-century Oxford, and the interests of the five faculties rarely seem to have been at odds.

The essence of the medieval master's profession was to read and dispute. Equally the case in all of the faculties, this was the basis of Christian education since St Paul defined the duties of a bishop in similar terms.[4] The scholar aspiring to the *magisterium* attended these two functions, the bachelor partially participated in them, and an inceptor (a candidate for the MA) was not fully a master until he had actually exercised the roles of lecturing and disputing.

University historians inevitably speak of the framework of

---

[1] *Non est consenescendum in artibus.* This appears in several medieval sources, including the anonymous *In hoc opusculo he continentur introductiones: In suppositiones: In predicabilia etc.* (Paris, 1496), sig. d. vi. r.–v. The sentiment is from Augustine, *De doctrina christiana*, II.

[2] S. Gibson, *Statuta antiqua Universitatis Oxoniensis* (Oxford, 1931), p. 142 (1339).

[3] BL Harleian MS 5398, f. 20v., transcribed in J. M. Fletcher, 'The Teaching and Study of Arts at Oxford, *c.* 1400–*c.* 1520', unpublished D.Phil. dissertation, Oxford, 1962, pp. 202–9. The body is also used as an institutional symbol in the Christ's College statutes of 1505. H. Rackham (ed.), *The Early Statutes of Christ's College, Cambridge, with the Statutes of the Prior Foundation of Godshouse* (Cambridge, 1927), p. 44.   [4] Titus 1:9.

the trivium (grammar, rhetoric, and logic), the quadrivium (arithmetic, music, geometry, and astronomy), and the three philosophies (natural, moral, and metaphysical). Oxford had a chest *trium philosophiarum et septem liberalium scienciarum* in the fifteenth century, and in 1456 a bachelor of arts was dispensed for not hearing 'the seven liberal arts'.[5] Although this theoretical outline, with its roots deep in antiquity, was well known and used by university men in official pronouncements, it was done so as a convention.[6] Some of the branches were predominant and others vestigial, or cultivated only by the specialist. In the fourteenth and fifteenth centuries the statutes and graces more often speak of logic, sophistry, dialectics, philosophy, and metaphysics, which were challenged in the early renaissance by mathematics, humanity, and 'Terenciana'. The first three terms all refer to logic, and philosophy was a general term for all three of its branches. Mathematics included all of the quadrivial sciences, and humanity included rhetoric, poetry, style, drama, and humanistic grammar.

There was a distinction between the theoretical and the practical arts that was common to most of the disciplines in the faculty, and had its roots in antiquity. It was popularised in the Middle Ages by Boethius' *In isagogen Porphyrii commenta*, a sixth-century introduction to Porphyry's discussion of the categories.[7] Grammar was divided between its fundamentals of reading and writing, and speculative grammar. Astronomy gave the foundation for its practical application, astrology. The two were interdependent, as the former was not useful without the latter. Medicine distinguished the diagnostician from the surgeon. Music degrees were awarded for years spent *in musica speculativa simul et in practica*.[8] The musicians, astronomers, and physicians were exposed to both practice and theory; yet these distinctions are indicative of how late-medieval men approached knowledge.

The theoretical order of study was to begin with the trivium,

---

[5] Reg. Aa, p. 117 (1452); p. 248 (1465); Gibson, *Statuta antiqua*, pp. 233–5 (1431).
[6] J. A. Weisheipl, 'Classification of the Sciences in Medieval Thought', *Mediaeval Studies*, 27 (1965), pp. 54–90.
[7] Weisheipl, 'Classification of Sciences', pp. 58–62.   [8] *GBk* B I, p. 161 (1500–1).

then the quadrivium, and finally the philosophies, finishing with metaphysics.[9] It seems unlikely that anyone followed this outline very closely, since subjects like music and astronomy were always specialist courses, and the average scholar had only a nodding acquaintance with them. Nevertheless, it was natural that some subjects should be more basic than others. The scholar's first years were spent on logic and grammar, which were then followed by two years pursuing natural philosophy. The heart of the medieval arts curriculum was this logic and natural science sequence.[10] Two codices copied at Oxford in 1490 and 1491 by the Franciscan William Vavasor illustrate this. The first contains several brief Scotist logical treatises, Bradwardine's *De proportionibus*, and disputations in logic ('Utrum est illa que distinguitur formaliter distinguitur realiter'), and then the *Physics* and *De anima*. A year later Vavasor had moved on to much longer collections of Scotus' commentaries on the *De anima* and *Meteora*, and Antonius Andreas' *De tribus principiis naturalibus*, all of which are much more sophisticated.[11]

The sources which speak the loudest, the texts, underwent a change with the growth of printing at the end of the fifteenth century. Book ownership became more widespread, books were less expensive, and they are accordingly less certain indicators of a scholar's interest in their contents. At the same time, however, the publication of a book indicates that there was a demand for it. A press was established at Oxford in 1478, and one in Cambridge in 1521. These, as well as the printers in London and St Albans, supplied books for the university trade. Even a cursory glance at their publications indicates that they were catering to established tastes, rather than leading their market.[12]

[9] Gibson, *Statuta antiqua*, pp. 233-5 (1431), 'secundum formam sequentem ascendendo gradatim'; cf. Reg. G, f. 300v. (1516), '...omnes magistri noviter creati...non teneantur legere secundum ordinem scientiarum'.   [10] See J. M. Fletcher, 'Study of Arts', p. 179.
[11] CCCO MSS, 227 and 228, deposited in the Bodleian Library, Oxford.
[12] Fletcher, 'Study of Arts', pp. 24, 178.

LECTURES FOR UNDERGRADUATES

The earliest evidence for the 'ordinary' lecture sequence in medieval Cambridge is two versions of the statute 'The way to hear the texts of Aristotle' from the late fourteenth century.[13] The breakdown of years and texts was as follows:

FIRST YEAR	*Winter*:	Porphyry, *Isagoge*; Aristotle,
(The old logic)		*Praedicamenta*
	Lent:	Aristotle, *Peri hermeneias*; Gilbert de la Porrée, *Sex principia*; Boethius, *Divisiones*
	Summer:	Aristotle, *Topica*
SECOND YEAR	*Winter*:	Aristotle, *Elenchi*
(The new logic)	*Lent*:	Aristotle, *Analytica priora*
	Summer:	Aristotle, *Analytica posteriora*
THIRD YEAR	*Winter*:	Aristotle, *Physica*
	Lent:	Aristotle, *Physica*
	Summer:	Aristotle, *De generatione* or *De anima* or *De coelo* or *Meteora* or *Ethica*
FOURTH YEAR	*Winter*:	Aristotle, *Physica* or *Metaphysica*
	Lent:	Aristotle, *Physica* or *Metaphysica*
	Summer:	Same as in the third year

In addition, another statute of the late fourteenth century added that a candidate for the BA should have heard the *Summule, De fallaciis*, and William of Heytesbury's *De insolubilibus*.[14] These are all short treatises on logic, the first three 'as used at Cambridge'. They enjoyed wide circulation until the sixteenth century, although this is the only statutory mention of them at either university.

If this was in fact the outline followed at Cambridge in the late Middle Ages, it is the starting point from which all other discussion of the curriculum must follow. An undergraduate studied almost exclusively logic and natural philosophy. But it

---

[13] Hackett, pp. 297–9.   [14] *Docs.* I, no. 139, p. 384 (by 1390).

must be remembered that by 1450 the evidence is weighted towards the autumn lectures that were not prescribed by statute, and thus allowed greater leeway for modifications. In addition, these statutes say nothing of the commentators through whom Aristotle was known. As we shall see, this was only the most general outline of the medieval curriculum at Cambridge.

The statutory course for Oxford undergraduates followed a different pattern. The determination statute of 1409 called for the *Isagoge, Sex principia*, the *Elenchi*, and Donatus' *Barbarismus* to be read in the first two years, 'by a master or bachelor in college or hall, with a recitation following'.[15] That was standard pedagogy for introductory works, 'as is the custom'. After that the scholar was to hear the *Algorismus integrorum, Compotum ecclesiasticorum*, and the *De sphera*, also read in the above manner. Following that he studied *Topica I–IV*, Priscian's *De constructione*, and Donatus, again, 'read cursorily by a bachelor in the Schools', that is, the rented rooms on Schools Street. Oxford had not yet built its own classrooms.

The outline differs sharply from that of Cambridge in its inclusion of the quadrivial studies, and its apparent exclusion of natural philosophy. What both universities had in common was that the first two years were given almost exclusively to logic before the young artist was allowed to participate in disputations.

Within three years of the promulgation of the Oxford statute there was a reaction against the strong logical component that it codified. Believing that the requirements for the BA were too burdensome, and that in the opinion of many there was too much logic, Congregation appointed four masters to rewrite the statute.[16] This never happened, however, and the scholars relied instead on graces to modify their programmes.

The graces from fifteenth-century Oxford, as well as the surviving manuscripts, show that any statutory disparity with Cambridge was not reflected in practice. Men supplicating for

---

[15] Gibson, *Statuta antiqua*, p. 200 (1409), 'secundum sufficientem exposicionem a magistro vel bachillario in collegio aut in aula...cum recitacione...subsecuta'.

[16] Gibson, *Statuta antiqua*, p. 216 (1412). See also J. M. Fletcher, 'The Faculty of Arts', in *HUO*, I, 369–99.

the BA were asked to hear and give lectures on natural philosophy as well as logic. Aristotle's *De anima* in particular is frequently mentioned.[17] John Redeler, supplicating to determine in 1453 had a typical programme: Porphyry, Gilbert, *De sphera, Computus manualis,* Burley's *De potentiis animae, Tractatus algorismus,* and Thomas of Erfurt's *De modo significandi.*[18] The statutes and graces also assume that the scholars were following hall as well as ordinary lectures.

THE BACHELOR'S COURSE

A statute from 1390 outlines the lecture course for the MA at Cambridge. The bachelor was required to hear ordinary lectures for three years after his determination, and the lectures specified included Aristotle's *Posterior Analytics* and *Physics,* and all the books of his *Ethics, Metaphysics,* and the first three books of Euclid's *Elements,* as well as *Algorismus, Compotus,* and *Tractatus de sphera.*[19] It covered the same subjects as the undergraduate course of the time and included an introduction to the quadrivium. This statute was recast in 1495 as *De incipientibus in artibus,* dropping any mention of specific texts and requiring instead three years of ordinary lectures on Aristotle. It also required three years of quadrivial lectures (see below).[20]

The Oxford statutes for bachelors wishing to incept show a general programme similar to Cambridge's. Inceptors were to have heard the trivium, quadrivium, and the three philosophies.[21] The corresponding Oxford graces from the middle of the fifteenth century indicate that the emphasis for bachelors was on the philosophies. A typical grace describes a bachelor giving one term to astronomy, three to moral philosophy, and two terms to metaphysics.[22] The graces also indicate a diversity of lectures followed by bachelors, both ordinary and extraordinary, and many requests for credit to be granted for non-statutory lectures heard, and for ordinary lectures missed.

---

[17] Reg. Aa, pp. 81, 166, 192, 247, etc. (1451–62).
[18] Reg. Aa., p. 153 (1453).   [19] Hackett, p. 277.
[20] *Docs.* 1, no. 86, pp. 360–1 (by 1495) ; see below chapter 11.
[21] Gibson, *Statuta antiqua,* p. 234 (1431).
[22] Reg. Aa, pp. 41–2 (1449).

THE UNDERGRADUATE'S ACTS

When an aspiring scholar arrived at Cambridge he was required to have his name entered on the *matricula* of a master within fifteen days, a requirement that was probably satisfied by entry on the books of a college or hostel.[23] Since no fee was paid to the university at matriculation there was no record of this kept by the proctors.

Oxford had a similar matriculation requirement, which included the provision that matriculation rolls should be read publicly at the beginning of each term.[24] In 1420 the problem of vagabond 'scholars' was so great that a royal ordinance required all scholars to matriculate and swear an oath within thirty days of entry that they would observe the university statutes.[25]

After the scholar's first two years studying grammar and the old and new logic, he reached the stage of *sophista generalis*, the midpoint between matriculation and the BA. This intermediate stage developed by the fourteenth century. Hitherto the scholar had not acted in any disputations, but now he was allowed to take a principal role. In a Cambridge statute from *c.* 1495 it was declared that:

> no one shall be admitted to respond to the question in arts [take the BA] unless he stands as a *sophista generalis* for two years, or at the very least one full year (sons of nobles excepted), hold two *sophismata generalia* at a time and place to be decided by the university, and have responded twice.[26]

As a *sophista generalis* the scholar would act as the respondent in a disputation, that is, he would respond to the arguments of the opponent(s), who would be students of the same rank. In addition to these two actors there was a third man, usually a graduate, who served as the *replicator* and summed-up the

---

[23] *Docs.* I, no. 42, p. 332 (by 1330); *GBk* A, pp. xx–xxi.
[24] Gibson, *Statuta antiqua*, p. 107 (before 1231); 60–1 (before 1275).
[25] Gibson, *Statuta antiqua*, pp. 226–7 (1420).
[26] *Docs.* I, no. 135, p. 382 (*c.* 1495), 'nisi steterit generalis sophista per biennium, seu saltem ad minus per annum integrum, exceptis filiis dominorum, et quod duo sophismata generalia pro tempore et loco ab universitate deputatis tenuerit, et quod bis responderit'.

disputation. The statute thus required four acts from the scholar in his third and fourth years, serving twice as the opponent and twice as the respondent.

Although no manuscripts survive from any Cambridge *sophismata generalia*, they no doubt served the same function as all disputations; showing the extent of the student's knowledge, and allowing him to demonstrate his command of it before an audience.[27] They were logical exercises and took place on *dies disputabiles*. The expressions *artista generalis* as well as *sophista generalis* were used at Oxford to describe this same role.[28] It was in disputing as a *sophista generalis* that a young scholar cut his teeth.

To be created a *sophista* in the late sixteenth century at Oxford was a 'sort of quasi-degree', and was attended by a ceremony and the payment of 2s to the bedells.[29] This was presaged by an entry in a ledger from St Edmund's Hall, Oxford, from 1424, which includes among a scholar's expenses 8d 'for the sophisters' gaudy'.[30] This is unmentioned in the Cambridge records, however.

The next point in a scholar's progress was responding to the question, which began the process by which he became a bachelor of arts. By the late fifteenth century it was standard for almost every student at Cambridge to seek a grace for this step, so it is possible to see how rigorous the prerequisites were. The most common element in the Cambridge records from this period is the commutation of work done in the autumn term for work in the three statutory terms. The average arts student seems to have spent three years and a term as an undergraduate, with the remaining statutory terms being excused for autumn terms. The total work done was no less than earlier in the middle ages (twelve terms) only it was done on a year-round basis. As a result of this trend, a scholar could perform the acts

[27] Fletcher, 'Study of Arts', pp. 429–30.
[28] Gibson, *Statuta antiqua*, p. 200 (1409) and pp. 485–6 (1607). This is examined in great detail in Fletcher, 'Study of Arts', pp. 114–17; see also New College MS 289, f. 18v. and *Registrum Mertonensis*, ed. Salter, I, p. 485 (1519).
[29] *Register of the University of Oxford*, ed. A. Clark, OHS 2 (Oxford, 1887), II, 22; Gibson, *Statuta antiqua*, p. 435 (1584).
[30] A. B. Emden, *An Oxford Hall in Medieval Times*, p. 194.

necessary for a BA in the late winter of his fourth year, rather than in his fifth year as prescribed by the statutes.[31] Often the only condition was that he pay for the statutory lectures in the terms he missed.[32] As ordinary lectures were not supposed to be given in the autumn, the scholar might otherwise have escaped from paying. Every few years from the 1470s to the 1490s a scholar was excused from the full course of ordinary lectures. By 1500 and later it became the rule for ordinaries to be heard 'not according to the statutory form', although some men continued to have complete courses nevertheless.

If attendance at the ordinary lectures declined, the Cambridge graces show that acts continued to be performed by candidates according to the form of the statutes. For example, Roger Wether in 1502–3 was allowed to respond to the question with nine terms of ordinary lectures and three autumn terms, together with two logical disputations (*sophismata*), provided he responded twice.[33] This total of twelve terms (four statutory years) is typical of what a student had accomplished and how long it took him to do it.

When a scholar was ready to take the BA, he had first to 'stand as a questionist', that is, complete an exercise called 'responding to the question'. The Cambridge 'questionist' was required to pay a *communa* of 12d to the university chest. The sum was never increased in the middle ages, despite the inflation in the actual cost of eating for a week in the later middle ages. The questionist was also required to give a caution to the university chest that he would perform the requisite acts. This was set at 13s 4d (one mark).

The actual act of 'responding to the question' at Cambridge is known most thoroughly through an account written by John Stokys, Esquire Bedell in the mid-sixteenth century. Although this is late evidence, it is unlikely that the form had changed significantly from the fifteenth century. The act took place before Candlemas (2 February), with the bedells on the appointed day gathering the questionists from their colleges and hostels at

---

[31] *Docs.* I, no. 140, pp. 384–5 (by 1390).   [32] *GBk* B I, p. 41 (1492).
[33] *GBk* Γ, p. 13 (1502–3).

nine o'clock in the morning, and leading them with their masters to the Schools for the ceremonies.[34] By Stokys' time this was done by college, with the master of that college leading his questionists. This collegiate grouping appears in the financial records *c.* 1500, when the colleges began to pay *communae* for their students: 'commune quinque inceptorum in aula Pembroche 8*s* 4*d*'.[35]

When the bedells, questionists, and masters reached the Schools the presiding master took the respondent seat, with the questionists lined up facing him. After the *commendaciones* (often humorous and in rhyme)[36] during which the bedells placed hoods on the students, the master of the act posed questions to the scholars, starting with the 'eldest'. This *ordo senioritatis* is the predecessor of the 'mathematical tripos' of later centuries, although there is no indication in the fifteenth or early sixteenth centuries that this was an honours list, or really anything other than a ranking of the scholars according to their age or time spent since matriculation.[37]

In Stokys' account the presiding master is called the 'father', and the questionists 'children'. The father was one of the fellows of the questionist's college or president of his hostel who asked the questions and saw that justice was done for the members of his house.[38] This role survived well into modern times, and probably existed from the thirteenth century as well.

The ceremony was a mere formality by Stokys' time, and with the questions put by a member of the scholar's college it was not a serious test. Scholars almost never failed, because they would never have been allowed to respond to the question unless the university felt that they were qualified to take the degree. Otherwise, the scholar would have been required to take further preparation before being given permission (a grace) to respond to the question.[39]

---

[34] G. Peacock, *Observations on the Statutes of the University of Cambridge* (London, 1841), App. A, pp. vi–vii.   [35] *GBk* B I, p. 169 (1500–1).

[36] *Docs.* I. no. 143, p. 385 (by 1390). In the law faculty the *commendaciones* could be no longer than a *Pater noster*.

[37] *Grace Book* Δ, ed. J. Venn (Cambridge, 1910), pp. viii–xi.   [38] *Docs.* I, p. 419 (1505).

[39] Some managed to be denied degrees anyway. See *GBk* B II, p. 147 (1527–8) and p. 150 (1528–9).

The scholars were 'questionists' after the ceremony, and the next step was the act of determination before they would be *bachalarius formatus*. By a medieval statute, revised in the late fifteenth century, no one was to determine unless he had responded to the question in the preceding year, and not before his fifth year.[40] The *Grace Books* show that this was not enforced, and the standard practice was for the two acts to be performed in the same year and even, by 1500, to count the term 'in which he is going to determine' towards the scholar's requirement for responding to the question.[41]

Separate graces and *communae* were not necessary for determining. The process began on the Monday to Thursday of the week before Quinquagesima Sunday. All the questionists were gathered in the chapel in the Divinity School, between one and five o'clock in the afternoon. There the regent masters examined them orally, with the Thursday examination reserved for 'songe and wrightynge'.[42] There was a meal between three and four o'clock, for which the scholars paid. On the Friday two regents, appointed by the university, gave orations and declared the suitability of the candidates. Those found suitable were then allowed to proceed; if the examiners found any of the candidates wanting, they could not determine that year.

On Ash Wednesday the period of determination began, giving it the alternate name, 'to stand in Lent'. There was a procession to Great St Mary's and a sermon and prayer, with the candidates swearing to determine at the will of the proctors.[43] They then processed to the Philosophy School where a solemn disputation was held between the Father and the Senior Bachelor, much later to be known as the 'bachelor of the tripos', because he sat on a three-legged stool. He propounded and disputed the two questions. This was followed by a disputation between the Father (the senior master), who acted as opponent, and the two regent masters who responded to him. The disputation ended with the proctor announcing 'We shall continue this disputation

[40] *Docs.* I, no. 140, pp. 384–5 (1300, revised by 1500).
[41] *GBk* Γ, p. 68 (1508–9).   [42] Peacock, App. A, p. xiii.
[43] Peacock, App. A, p. ix, 'ad placitum procuratorum'.

in the first hour of the Thursday after the fourth Sunday in Lent'.[44]

Each determiner, accompanied by a *sophista*, then disputed in the Schools until the Wednesday before Passion Sunday. The determiners had three questions of dialectic and philosophy written out and set before them, and acted as respondents against any scholar or bachelor who cared to argue against their positions. This was supervised by the proctors and bedells.

On the Thursday before Passion Sunday the determiners ended as they had begun, with a solemn disputation that was the continuation of the Ash Wednesday act. At the end the senior proctor announced,[45]

> By the authority which we enjoy, we decree, appoint and pronounce all the determiners of this year to have finished their determinations, and now to be bachelors of arts.

These acts of determination, whereby the new bachelor was allowed to share the role of the master ('legere et disputare') were a vital part of the medieval university programme. Every questionist was required to determine at Cambridge within two years of responding to the question or forfeit his caution of 13s 4d. The records show that between 1454 and 1500 only twenty-six scholars failed to perform this act, and only six between 1500 and 1510. As a rule, determination followed quickly after responding to the question, and it is the exceptional grace which mentions a delay of a year between the acts.[46]

The evidence from Oxford takes a slightly different form, and lacks the detail of the Cambridge records. The graces for the bachelor's degree usually state that the scholar was admitted 'to lecture on any book of the arts faculty', or more rarely, 'to determine in the arts faculty'.[47] The statutes and graces also use

---

[44] Peacock, App. A, p. xi, 'Nos continuamus hanc disputacionem in horam primam Diei Jovis post quartam Dominicam Hujus Quadragesime.'

[45] Peacock, App. A, pp. xi–xii, 'Authoritate qua fungimur, decernimus, creamus, et pronunciamus omnes hujus anni determinatores finaliter determinasse, et actualiter esse in artibus bachalaureos.'   [46] *GBk* Γ, p. 17 (1502–3).

[47] Reg. Aa, p. 16 (1450) and p. 5 (1450).

the title 'questionist' to refer to anyone taking the BA.[48] The Oxford determination statute of 1409 explains this procedure at length, and shows its similarity to Cambridge.[49]

Scholars were rarely exempted from determining, and when they were the reason is usually clear. In 1489–90 the north-countryman Hugh Dacres (the son of a nobleman) was granted that his admission stand for his determination. This was probably because he was leaving England, as he was incorporated in 1492 for an unspecified degree that he had earned 'overseas'.[50] Edward Wiggan was required in 1513–14 to be examined by two masters in lieu of determining, provided he pay the bedells and other officers the customary gifts.[51] He was already a priest and probably had duties elsewhere. The next year John Burton was excused from determination (provided he pay the customary fees) because he intended to study 'overseas'.[52] In 1525–6 two Cambridge men were excused because they were elected members of Cardinal College, Oxford.[53] In most of the other cases at both Oxford and Cambridge determination was excused because the scholar was leaving the university, was sick, or was too poor to continue his studies.

THE BACHELOR'S AND MASTER'S ACTS

The final academic act of the faculty of arts was inception, by which a bachelor became a master of arts. The Cambridge inceptor was to have determined, responded to three masters, opposed once, and to have heard lectures for three years since determining. He must also have been judged suitable 'in character and learning' (the formula, slightly altered, is still used by the university) by a panel of masters of his faculty.[54] In addition the candidate was required to have 'entered' in the *Posterior Analytics* (which involved a payment).

These exercises followed fairly rapidly one upon another.

---

[48] This is explained at length in Fletcher, 'Study of Arts', pp. 123–8, and referred to in Fletcher, 'Faculty of Arts', in *HUO*, I, pp. 380–1.

[49] Gibson, *Statuta antiqua*. pp. 199–204 (1409).

[50] *GBk* B I, p. 17 (1489–90) and p. 66 (1493).

[51] *GBk* Γ, p. 112 (1513–14). [52] *GBk* Γ, p. 124 (1514–15).

[53] *GBk* Γ, p. 221 (1525–6). [54] *Docs*. I, no. 86, p. 360–1 (by 1495).

Most bachelors heard from seven to ten terms of lectures with varying degrees of regularity. The lectures are described in the graces as either philosophical, grammatical, mathematical, humane, or metaphysical, although Cuthbert Marchall was given credit in 1512–13 for studies 'partly in philosophy, partly in sacred letters'.[55] He was clearly a member of the faculty of arts, however. Patrick Gower, MA of Paris, was incorporated in 1519–20 in that degree provided that he 'read in the Schools most of the *Secunda secundae* [of the *Summa Theologiae*] of St Thomas'.[56] That an MA from Paris was required to lecture on moral theology to be incorporated in arts indicates the flexibility of the faculties.

The most difficult part of the *forma* for most Cambridge men in the early sixteenth century was getting a third 'responsion'. It was common for the third responsion to be excused if it could not be obtained, and a 'variation' substituted. A variation occurred when a bachelor 'might choose to answer the same question as another respondent, treating it in a different way'.[57] This situation was caused when there were several men, senior to the bachelor, who had already responded to the opponent before him.

Credit was sometimes also given for terms missed due to sickness, poverty, plague, or a teaching job elsewhere.[58] A feature common to most dispensations is that the student pay as though he had attended the lectures and performed the acts anyway.

After approval by the masters, the inceptor was presented to the chancellor, or by the late middle ages, the vice-chancellor, and the candidate received his licence to incept.[59] He paid a *communa* of 20d to the university chest, and gave numerous gifts and provided meals for university officials. The bachelor also placed a caution in the university chest as security that he would incept. This varied in value between 13s 4d and £5.[60] It was

[55] *GBk* Γ, p. 104 (1512–13).   [56] *GBk* Γ, p. 181 (1519–20).
[57] *GBk* A, p. xxv; *GBk* Γ, p. 79 (1509 10).
[58] e.g. *GBk* Γ, p. 157 (1517–18) and p. 179 (1519–20).
[59] *Docs.* I, no. 126, p. 378 (by 1390).
[60] *Docs.* I, no. 127, pp. 378–9 (by 1363), nos. 133 and 134, pp. 380–2 (by 1330); e.g. *GBk* A, p. 46 (1464–5), p. 71 (1468–9).

rare for more than one bachelor a year to be fined for not incepting.

At Oxford the bachelor similarly had to study for eight terms beyond his determination, to have lectured on Aristotle, followed other prescribed lectures, and responded and opposed in disputations with other bachelors.[61] The Oxford graces indicate that inceptors had from two to six years of study after determination, although two years and one term with several vacation terms seems to have been the norm. As at Cambridge, many graces concern the need for extra responsions, and inceptors were sometimes excused terms missed because of work elsewhere.[62]

Permission to incept was controlled by eighteen regents who testified to the candidate's suitability. He then swore that he had completed his *forma*, would incept within the year at Oxford or Cambridge, not study at Stamford (a prohibition dating from when the nascent university at Stamford in 1333–5 challenged Oxford and Cambridge's monopoly), not spend more than was allowed on his inception banquet and gifts, and several other details of lesser importance. The inceptor then received his licence to incept from the chancellor (or vice-chancellor) on the payment of his 16d *communa*.[63]

The ceremony of inception at Cambridge began with a solemn disputation held in the Schools, called 'vespers' because it took place in the evening. The two questions disputed were announced publicly earlier in the day, and at the ceremony the 'father' (a master) acted as the opponent and the inceptors as respondents in turn.[64] The proctors administered an oath that the inceptors would not later take the BA at any other university. The father then read a humorous commendation to the men, placed their hoods on their heads, invested them with their insignia, and announced the end of vespers.[65]

---

[61] Gibson, *Statuta antiqua*, pp. xcv and 247 (1432).   [62] Reg. Aa, *passim*.

[63] Reg. Aa, p. xxiii; Gibson, *Statuta antiqua*, pp. xcvi–xcvii and 29–30 (before 1350).

[64] For printed examples from *c.* 1590, see CUL Sel.1.11.

[65] Peacock, App. A, pp. xx–xxiv; S. Gibson, 'The Order of Disputation', *Bodleian Quarterly Record*, 6 (1930), 107–8; Gibson, *Statuta antiqua*, p. xcviii. In the early sixteenth century bachelors wore laurel wreaths and crowns of flowers during these acts. See J. Caius, *Historia Cantabrigiensis Academiae* (1574), pp. 122–3.

The next day, the first Tuesday in July, was the Commencement or *comitia maxima*. It was held in Great Saint Mary's, although during the restoration of the church between 1479 and 1519 it was moved to the house of the Franciscans or of the Austin Friars. Stages were built for the ceremony and seating for the doctors and inceptors.[66] It began with a Mass, which was followed by the father placing a cap on the senior inceptor, who then read a philosophy text and said, 'From this text two articles will be used for the present disputation.' His *questiones*, prepared in advance, were composed in rhyme.[67] He then acted as the opponent, and was responded to by the junior regent, and the other regents and non-regents in turn.[68] The proctor then said 'ad oppositum' and the inceptor answered 'est philosophus'. The youngest doctor of the divinity faculty then gave a determination of the disputation. An oath was administered to the inceptor that he would continue his regency for at least one year, and only at Oxford or Cambridge. This same procedure was then repeated for each inceptor. The next day the new regent masters were escorted to the Schools where they read their first solemn lecture. The inception process, or *creatio* as it was sometimes called, also involved numerous gifts of gloves, hats, and meals to the university authorities.

The Oxford inception ceremony was very similar, the most significant difference being that it was not restricted to the Monday after 7 July until 1566, and was often held in late June instead.[69] It took essentially the same form, although the Oxford sources include no contemporary description with the detail of Stokys' *Diary*.

Honorary degrees, *honoris causa*, were also awarded at both schools to certain ecclesiastical and civil dignitaries. Abbots, priors, and bishops were the most frequent recipients, although John Skelton, 'poet in overseas lands' and laureate of Oxford was similarly laureated at Cambridge in 1493.[70] At Cambridge

---

[66] *GBk* B I, p. 154 (1500–1), p. 230 (1507–8); *GBk* B II, p. 2 (1511–12), p. 10 (1512–13), etc.
[67] Peacock, App. A, p. xxvi; CUL, CUA, Old Junior Proctor's Book, f. 6r; Gibson, 'Order of Disputations', pp. 107–8. [68] *GBk* Γ, p. 117 (1513–14).
[69] Gibson, *Statuta antiqua*, p. 396 (1566).
[70] *GBk* B I, p. 54 (1493), 'poeta in partibus transmarinis atque oxonie laurea ornato'.

nobles and their children were also given special consideration when seeking degrees, a practice acknowledged in the statutes and not abolished until 1825.[71] In 1458 George de Vere, son of the Earl of Oxford, was allowed to credit towards his Cambridge degree terms in which he attended only one lecture a week. His brother Richard was given a similar grace in 1470. Henry Percy, Earl of Northumberland was made an honorary MA of Cambridge in 1527–8. George Neville, son of the Earl of Salisbury, received similar preferential treatment from Oxford in 1450–2, in preparation for his election as chancellor before he was quite twenty-one.[72]

Degrees were also granted through incorporation, by which Cambridge officially recognised as equivalent a degree granted by another university. These usually involved no further work on the part of the supplicant, but payment of a fee. There are exceptions, as when Robert Wakefield, MA Louvain, was required to perform a 'variatio' within a year.[73] At Oxford in the early sixteenth century incorporations were sometimes used to obtain specific lectures which the university needed. In 1509 Bernard Pope, MA of Cambridge, was incorporated in the same degree at Oxford provided he lecture on the *Posterior Analytics*.[74] Payment was usually required for incorporation, and the Cambridge *Grace Books* from 1505 to 1506 note that those admitted to any grade beyond the MA were required to pay for the inferior grades as well.[75]

Unlike the medieval lecture system, the university-run disputations remained vital on all levels till the seventeenth century, and the exercises for determination and inception were followed by most scholars. At both universities disputations were rarely dispensed with, and additional acts were often required by graces. These acts were the simplest way of assigning extra work to supplicants who were not sufficiently prepared for degrees. The growth of statutory college disputations did not

---

[71] *Docs.* I, no. 135, p. 382 (by 1495); H. E. Peek and C. P. Hall, *The Archives of the University of Cambridge* (Cambridge, 1962), p. 34.

[72] Reg. Aa, pp. 68–9 (1450) and p. 119 (1452); G. Keir, 'The Ecclesiastical Career of George Neville, 1432–1476', Oxford B.Litt. thesis (1970), esp. chap. 2.

[73] *GBk* Γ, p. 170 (1518–19).   [74] Reg. G, f. 71v. (1509).

[75] e.g. *GBk* Γ, p. 48 (1505–6).

lessen the importance of university exercises. On the contrary, the colleges frequently insisted that their members attend them regularly, and 'they realized the value that the variety of other students would bring'.[76]

Disputations formed the cutting edge of university education from the founding of the medieval universities, and there was no significant change in this role in Tudor Oxford and Cambridge.

[76] Fletcher, 'Study of Arts', pp. 170–1.

Chapter 4

THE TRIVIUM

GRAMMAR

Grammatica quid est: ars recte scribendi recteque loquendi, poetarum enaracionem continens.

Oxford *probatio pennae, c.* 1450[1]

Grammar had three elements in medieval Cambridge and Oxford: first, the preparation of boys in Latin so they could enter the university course; secondly, the logical analysis of language and signification, called modal grammar; and thirdly, the formation of grammar masters for secondary schools. The first of these functions was that of a grammar master preparing a boy for entry into the faculty of arts; the second function, modal grammar, was that of a scholar within the faculty of arts preparing to take the BA; and the third function was that of the semi-autonomous faculties of grammar which were, essentially, medieval teacher-training colleges.

These three aspects of grammar are regularly confused by historians, who often seem unaware of modal grammar, and conflate the other two, producing the unlikely situation of apprentice grammar masters sharing classrooms with young boys with little or no proficiency in Latin. However, the distinctions were not always precise, since many masters of arts were also masters of grammar, and may have taught grammar schools before coming-up to study at either faculty. There were also masters of arts who lectured both to scholars in the arts faculty and to young boys interested only in learning the simplest parsing.

[1] Reg. Aa, p. 408.

Grammar

Latin grammar was the basis without which a student could not participate in a university community. The English schoolboy began his study of song and grammar when he was seven or eight years old, usually at a nearby grammar school or with a local teacher. A minority of boys travelled outside their region to receive this education, usually to Oxford. The grammar schools there attracted boys from all parts of England who wanted, and could afford, a superior education.[2] These Oxford grammar schools, although supervised by the university, were not part of it.[3] They declined by the late fifteenth century, and in 1466 the university wrote to the Bishop of Lincoln concerning this problem.[4] Little seems to have been done, no doubt because grammar instruction was being replaced by Bishop William Waynflete's free grammar school attached to Magdalen College, Oxford.

The statutes of Magdalen, founded in 1479, provided that 'whosoever comes to the grammar school should be informed, taught, and instructed with the greatest diligence and in the most expeditious way, freely and without charge'.[5] Needless to say, the Magdalen College School soon eliminated all competitors who charged for their tuition. The few grammar halls that still existed quickly disappeared.[6] An even broader consequence of the Magdalen College School was its role as a medium through which young arts students were exposed to classical rules and style, and were separated from the medieval grammatical tradition. The masters and students of the school before 1520 included William Lily, William Grocyn, Reginald Pole, John Stanbridge, John Anwykyll, Cardinal Wolsey, John Holt, Robert Whittington and, quite likely, Thomas More. These

---

[2] N. Orme, *Education in the West of England* (Exeter, 1976), p. 11. For Oxford grammarians, see R. W. Hunt, 'Oxford Grammar Masters in the Middle Ages', in *Oxford Studies Presented to Daniel Callus*, pp. 163–93.

[3] Reg. Aa, p. 12 (1450), 'deputati fuerunt ad supervidendum scolas gramaticales pro proximo anno...' and p. 117 (1452), etc; Gibson, *Statuta antiqua*, pp. lxxxv–lxxxvii; *Medieval Archives of Oxford*, II, pp. 278–9.

[4] *Epistolae academicae Oxon.*, ed Anstey, II, p. 381; Emden, 'Oxford Academical Halls', pp. 364–5.

[5] *Statutes of the Colleges of Oxford* (3 vols., London, 1853), II, Magdalen, p. 76.

[6] A statute of 1492 eliminated the separate supervision of the city grammar masters, since the supervisors received salaries, 'sine laboribus ad onus universitatis'. Gibson, *Statuta antiqua*, p. 300.

men, the many textbooks they wrote, and the pupils they formed, were instrumental in the dissemination of humanist Latin in Renaissance England.

When the average student matriculated at medieval Cambridge or Oxford he continued his language instruction as was necessary in his first year or two. Although basic grammar was the province of secondary schools (and by statute one could not matriculate without being learned in Latin), there was probably a wide variation in the verbal and written skills of entering undergraduates. A few academical hostels gave grammar instruction for the young artists who needed it, as well as preparation for future grammar masters in the faculty of grammar. Such a grammar hostel was taught by Thomas Chambre, MGram., in Cambridge in the late fifteenth century, a school continued by Thomas Ayera after him.[7]

The colleges provided some grammar training for a few young scholars, mostly in the form of charitable appendages, although as John Major said in 1520 of both universities, 'grammar is not studied in the colleges'.[8] The exception to this rule was his old college, Godshouse, founded in part to produce grammar masters,[9] and Jesus College which for a brief time had a grammar school attached.

Cambridge was never such a centre of grammar schools as Oxford was, and had no free grammar school to compare with Magdalen, Oxford, until the seventeenth century.[10] What collegiate instruction there was was severely curtailed later by the Elizabethan statutes which forbade the teaching of grammar in any college, with the exception of the choristers of King's, Trinity, and St John's, 'probably with a view to preventing the admission of unqualified students'.[11]

---

[7] *Michaelhouse*, p. 21; *BRUC*, p. 25; Stokes, *Hostels*, pp. 43–57; Emden, 'Oxford Academical Halls', pp. 361–2. John Rous, MA by 1444 of Oxford, listed six grammarian halls at Oxford, and none at Cambridge (with which he was less familiar). See *The Itinerary of John Leland*, II, pp. 154–7.

[8] Major, *Historia majoris Britanniae*, f. viiir.; see also Cobban, *King's Hall*, pp. 51–2, n. 4. and p. 60, n. 2; *Statutes of Oxford*, I, Merton, p. 36.

[9] Rackham, *Statutes of Christ's College*, pp. 2, 20, 24–6, 106–8, 141.

[10] Jesus College, founded in the late fifteenth century, did initially have provision for a handful of boys. A. Gray and F. Brittain, *History of Jesus College, Cambridge*, pp. 30–1.

[11] Peacock, *Observations on Statutes*, p. 4, n. 4.

As a rule grammar texts owned by members of the faculty of arts were most likely to occur in commonplace books with other introductory academic items. Extant examples include a codex of John Stampford *alias* Longe, who studied at Oxford some time before 1472. His book contains many excerpts on metrification, rhetoric, astrology, the dictamen of the Oxonian Thomas Sampson, and passages from Geoffrey of Vinsauf's *Poetria nova* and John Leland's *Distinctiones rhetorice*.[12]

Other grammatical collections were more clearly intended for the beginner. A manuscript now in the British Library contains eleven items, most of which are basic; conjugations, Stanbridge's *Sum, es, fui,* expressions translated from English to Latin, and basic letter forms all appear with heavy student annotations, along with the more advanced *Grecismus* by the thirteenth century grammarian Evrard of Béthune. The collection was written by two monks of Christ Church, Oxford, one of whom (Reginald Goldstone) studied at Oxford. Many young scholars used this codex, including Reginald Pole, who wrote his name in it in a childish hand, probably when he was a *demi* at Magdalen *c.* 1512.[13]

A thirteenth-century collection owned by Roger Marshall, MD of Peterhouse (*c.* 1450), is a typical Cambridge example. John of Garland's short *Dictionary, Accentarius,* and *Compendium grammaticae* are joined by his *De mysteriis ecclesiae.* To these are added the verse *Algorismus* of Alexander of Villa-Dei (an introduction to arithmetic), Goliardic poetry, and other items.[14] Marshall also owned far more advanced works which included Priscian's *Minor* and Peter Helias' commentary on it, part of the *De modo significandi,* bound with questions on the *Peri-hermeneias,* and Bernard Sylvester's *De proprietatibus bestiarum.*[15]

The second element of grammar was the logical analysis of language, called modal grammar, an important part of the undergraduate curriculum in the faculty of arts. It was studied primarily through the speculative grammars known as *De modo*

---

[12] *BRUO* III, 1635; Bodleian MS Bodl. 832, ff. 8r.–v.
[13] BL, Harleian MS 1587, f. 208v.; see also Bodleian MS Bodl. 487, ff. 73r.–74v.
[14] *BRUC,* pp. 392–3 (Roger Marshall); Gonville and Caius MS 385/605.
[15] Gonville and Caius MSS 593/453, 203/109, 377/597, and 417/447.

significandi, and was practised in disputations usually held on Fridays. The *De modo significandi* (falsely attributed to Albertus Magnus, Albert of Saxony, Duns Scotus, and others) was a title common to several speculative grammars, the most popular of which was Thomas of Erfurt's. Active early in the fourteenth century, Thomas was one of the last of the important *modistae*, so called because of their use of *modi significandi* (modes of signifying) to describe grammatical categories. This grammar attempted to classify 'the ways in which significant terms signify, and to give rules for possible combinations of these classes of significant terms'.[16]

Thomas' work is divided into fifty-four brief sections. His preamble begins:

> The rationale of the method. In every science understanding and knowledge derive from the knowledge of its principles, as is stated in *I Physicorum, Comment. 1*; we, therefore, wishing to know the science of grammar, insist that it is necessary first to know its principles, which are the ways of signifying.[17]

Then, he asks how a mode of signifying is divided, described, originated, and is characterised. He distinguishes *modus significandi* from *modus intelligendi (ipsa proprietas rei)* and *modus essendi (rei proprietas absolute)*. Then, *signa, dictio, pars orationis* and *terminus* are given and defined. Basically, the treatise shows how a *dictio* combines with a *modus significandi* to become a *pars orationis*, that is, 'a unit capable of functioning in a grammatical manner'.[18] These *partes orationis* are described and separated in terms of their essential and accidental modes. When combined together they produce discourse. In short, this is more a logical than a grammatical study, and is grounded in Aristotelian natural philosophy, 'the laws of which are applied to the parts of speech signifying the objects of the natural world'.[19]

The grammatical question of signification was crucial to the

---

[16] T. Heath, 'Logical Grammar, Grammatical Logic, and Humanism in Three German Universities', *Studies in the Renaissance*, 18 (1971), 5.

[17] Thomas of Erfurt, *Grammatica Speculativa*, ed. with trans. G. L. Bursill-Hall (London, 1972), pp. 34–5.

[18] Thomas of Erfurt, pp. 37, 41.   [19] Heath, p. 5.

realist/nominalist controversy of the fourteenth century. The realists followed in the tradition of Duns Scotus (and many others), while the nominalists took their inspiration from William of Ockham. What was at stake in grammar was whether words could represent, or signify, universals or only individual things. For a realist, the word 'men' represented something real. For the nominalist it was only a name (*nomen*) used for convenience to describe a grouping of individuals. There was no such thing as 'men', only individual people.

To signify meant 'to bring to mind'. What a sentence signified depended on whether you felt that the nouns signified only individual substances and their individual qualities, as nominalist ontology held, or whether the sentence could signify whatever was conventionally held by a group. The sentence could thus be true 'howsoever' it signified, rather than be true only by what its nouns signified. The realist asks, 'How does a sentence signify?' rather than 'What does it signify?'[20]

This simple excursus indicates the interpenetration that this sort of grammar had with both logic and natural philosophy. That this essentially realist analysis flourished at both Oxford and Cambridge until the sixteenth century indicates to some degree the triumph of the realist approach to logic and philosophy in England from the fourteenth century. It seems that nominalist ideas were explained primarily for the sake of refuting them.

There is no doubt that the *De modo significandi* was the fundamental work of speculative grammar at both universities. When John Argentein, MA of King's College, wrote a poem about his studies, grammar personified describes herself by saying, 'I comprehend the ways of signifying.'[21] Copies of *De modo significandi* were usually bound with other realist commentaries on logic, like those of Scotus and Antonius Andreas.[22]

[20] This is a paraphrase of P. V. Spade, 'Study', in William Heytesbury, *On 'Insoluble' Sentences* (Toronto, 1979), pp. 61–3.
[21] D. R. Leader, 'John Argentein and Learning in Medieval Cambridge', *Humanistica Lovaniensia*, 33 (1984), p. 80.
[22] e.g. copy in Peterhouse in 1418 bound with Antonius Andreas on Aristotle's *Logic* and Burley on the *Posterior Analytics*; Thomas Colyer of Michaelhouse (*BRUC*, p. 151) owned a *De modo significandi* bound with Bruni's translation of the *Ethics*; Merton College in 1452

The speculative grammar and parsing were never completely separated in the arts faculty. The *Doctrinale* of Alexander of Villa-Dei is illustrative. A standard text for schoolboys and young university scholars from the thirteenth century, it also provided an Aristotelian analysis of the correspondence of language to reality. For Alexander, grammar was ultimately based not on literary standards, but on reason, and his work engendered many commentaries that dealt with this philosophical basis.[23]

When the young scholar first came up to Cambridge he studied Donatus, Priscian, Alexander, and Thomas of Erfurt as he needed. Since a knowledge of grammar was assumed, these texts are rarely mentioned in the statutes. Priscian is the only grammar text specified in the Cambridge statutes, and it was dropped in 1488.[24] When Priscian appears in the graces, it is for the MGram., not the BA, and the pattern is similar at Oxford.[25] It seems that to say Priscian was required is only to say that arts students needed to know Latin grammar. None of the statutes at either university say anything of such ubiquitous grammarians as Thomas of Erfurt or Alexander of Villa-Dei.

The third aspect of grammar at Cambridge and Oxford was the faculty of grammar, the medieval teacher's college, which awarded the Master of Grammar degree, a kind of medieval BEd. The teaching of grammar in Christendom had been canonically controlled since the twelfth century, and no one was allowed to teach without a licence from the ordinary or his representative.[26] At Cambridge this control of the grammar schools was exercised by the Archdeacon of Ely through his appointment of a *Magister glomeriae* (Master of the Glomery), who headed the faculty of grammarians. Thus, the grammarians were simultaneously part of the university, while not being exempt from diocesan control as was the rest of the university.

purchased a copy with Scotist commentaries, and containing light annotations, Merton MS C.2.11, ff. 2r.–25r; a copy in Canterbury College, Oxford in 1501 was bound with Scotus, *Super Porphyrium*. W. A. Pantin, ed. *Canterbury College, Documents and History*, OHS n.s. 6, pt 1 (Oxford, 1947), 25.
[23] Heath, p. 12.   [24] Hackett, pp. 300–1.
[25] Gibson, *Statuta antiqua*, pp. 26 (1268); 33 (1340); 200 (1409); 378 (1565).
[26] Canon 18 of the Third Lateran Council, *CJC*, X.5.5.1.

Although the first statutes outlining the requirements for the MGram. degree did not appear before the late-fourteenth century, grammar 'masters' were being produced by the Cambridge grammarians under the supervision of the Master of the Glomery before that date. That the MGram. was awarded through the university by the late-fourteenth century indicates that the university had come to exercise practical control over the grammarians resident in Cambridge. The archdeacon continued to exercise his canonical right to appoint the *Magister glomeriae* until the mid-fifteenth century or later, and recorded the appointments in his book.[27] The continued connection of the diocese with Cambridge's grammar schools after the last entry in the Archdeacon's Book (1452) is indicated by the existence of the Master of the Glomery until 1540, when the disappearance of the office coincides with the suppression of the Ely cathedral monastic chapter.[28]

The faculty of grammar at Oxford was, in practice, similar to Cambridge's. Although the grammarians had their own faculty under the supervision of the faculty of arts, they were not, strictly speaking, part of it. Two masters of arts were picked annually to oversee the grammar schools, and the grammar masters were considered only equals of bachelors of arts.[29] The early independence of Oxford from the Bishop of Lincoln extended to the grammar schools as well, so there was no equivalent at Oxford to the Master of the Glomery.

The faculties of grammar were meant to produce qualified grammar teachers, not just instruct neophytes in Latin. What was demanded of the future grammarian in Cambridge's faculty? A statute from *c.* 1390 outlined the requirements for the MGram. The candidate had to dispute publicly on three Fridays, give thirteen lectures on Priscian's *Minor* (which deals with

---

[27] *Vetus liber archidiaconi Eliensis*, ed. C. E. Feltoe and E. H. Minns. CAS, Octavo Publications, 48 (Cambridge, 1917), esp. pp. 20–1 and 289–91.

[28] See K. Bartlett, 'The Decline and Abolition of the Master of Grammar', *History of Education*, 6 (1977), 1–8. Dr Bartlett reviews all the evidence, and follows Matthew Parker in giving the *Magister glomeriae* the role of university scribe and thus sees the new 'University Orator' of the 1520s as the eventual destroyer of the older position. I disagree: the two had little in common, since the *Magister glomeriae* was not a university letter writer or public orator. See also Stokes, *Hostels*, pp. 8 and 49–57.   [29] Gibson, *Statuta antiqua*, p. 22.

syntax), the first of which had to be solemn, that is, with a master presiding. He also had to be judged suitable in learning and morals by three masters. The candidate would then begin his inception, which involved swearing an oath that he would incept within a year, lecture for a year on Priscian's *Maior* (which deals with the parts of speech), and hold three meetings of the grammar faculty at which he would scan and parse a verse of a poet in the manner of Priscian.[30] The inception of the new Master of Grammar took place in Great St Mary's, and the master was created by receiving a rod from the vice-chancellor. The new master then took a boy and publicly beat him in the Schools. The act was then complete, and the boy was paid a groat for his suffering.[31] The programme of the MGram. took most students three or four years. The Oxford MGram. programme was very similar.[32]

The MGram. at both universities was a licence to teach, either in a school or one of the university faculties of grammar. Often the university records say nothing of 'taking a degree', but rather of allowing the candidate to be 'admitted to instructing and teaching in grammar wherever he happens to be'.

It was rare at either Cambridge or Oxford for more than two or three MGram. candidates to present themselves in any given year, and often there were none at all. The records of the Cambridge proctors indicate that in the middle of the fifteenth century most men taking the MGram. followed the statutory requirements, or were fined accordingly.

The grammar texts that appear most frequently in the college libraries and in masters' collections include the *De modo signifi-candi*, Priscian, and Alexander. Others used were Peter Helias' *Summa super Priscianum* and John Garland's *Compendium*. The most frequently consulted dictionaries were John Balbi's *Catholicon* and Hugutio of Pisa's *Derivationes*.[33]

---

[30] *Docs.* I, no. 117, p. 374.
[31] Peacock, *Observations on the Statutes*, App. A, pp. xxx–xxxvii.
[32] Gibson, *Statuta antiqua*, pp. 167–74 (*c.* 1380).
[33] See college inventories in the bibliography.

RHETORIC

Rhetoric in the medieval university meant many different things at different times, and sometimes many things simultaneously. It was, in a sense, a vestigial appendage of grammar that was difficult to isolate, and university men often did not; at Oxford *c.* 1510 the two words were interchangeable. In medieval society there was little application for the oratorical programmes of Cicero or Quintilian, although they were still read and commented on.[34] St Augustine's *De doctrina christiana* IV, 'usually seen as the *magna carta* of medieval rhetoric',[35] gave rhetoric a secure role for furthering exegesis and Christian eloquence. Nevertheless, its role was always amorphous, and at Cambridge it remained the Cinderella of the arts curriculum. It meant not only classical rhetorical theory, but also poetry and poetics, epistolary style (often overlapping with *ars dictaminis*), drama, and preaching. It took on a new life with the northern renaissance and carried a heavy humanist charge, referring to neo-classical, rather than medieval, form and style. All these elements will be examined in turn.

First, rhetoric always meant the study of the classical rhetorical texts of Cicero, Pseudo-Cicero, Aristotle, and Quintilian. These rarely appear in the early records of Oxford, and are not mentioned in the early requirements for inception (which does not mean that they were not taught). The first statutory appearance at Oxford was in 1431, when aspiring masters were required to have followed lectures for three terms in either Aristotle's *Rhetoric*, Boethius' *Topics IV*, Pseudo-Cicero's *Nova rhetorica* (*Rhetorica ad Herennium*), Ovid's *Metamorphoses*, or Virgil's poetry.[36] That was a very mixed bag, from classical theory to medieval moralising on Ovid. The rare references to rhetoric in the graces from twenty years later indicate that some

---

[34] J. O. Ward, 'From Antiquity to the Renaissance: Glosses and Commentaries on Cicero's *Rhetorica*', in *Medieval Eloquence*, ed. J. J. Murphy (Berkeley, 1978), pp. 25–6.

[35] Ward, p. 27; cf. B. Smalley, *The Study of the Bible in the Middle Ages*, 2nd edn (Oxford, 1952), p. 12, 'their programme [the Alexandrines] might be called the *Magna carta* of medieval scholars'.

[36] Gibson, *Statuta antiqua*, p. 234 (1431). Ovid's *Ars amatoria* was forbidden on moral grounds, p. 173 (by 1380).

of these were also studied by young scholars before determining.[37]

At Cambridge the archival evidence is even more scanty. The outline of studies for determination *c.* 1450 makes no mention of rhetoric; nor do the statutes for inception.[38] The first statutory move by the university in that direction seems to have been the creation of the Terence lecture in 1488, one of three salaried university lectureships (the others were in logic and philosophy). This was a general humanities lecture for scholars in their first and second years; it was not restricted to any one text, and was one of the first statutory effects of humanist influence on Cambridge studies.[39]

As the 1431 Oxford inception statute indicates, rhetoric could also mean poetry. Not only Ovid and Virgil, but many other classical and medieval poets were considered worthy of study, as well as poetic theorists like the twelfth-century Englishman Geoffrey of Vinsauf. In the library inventory of Canterbury College, Oxford of 1501, the list of *libri poetrie* included Cicero's *Rhetoric* and several copies of Geoffrey of Vinsauf's *Poetria nova* and *Tria sunt*, as well as Ovid, Boethius' *De consolatione philosophiae*, Seneca's *Epistolae*, Prudentius, Plato's *Timaeus*, and other works from Peter of Blois' *Epistolae* to Vegetius' *De re militari*. Rhetorical treatises, poetry, and more generally any classical or recent humanist work were associated together in a manner typical of the late medieval university. Poetry also took on a local meaning at Cambridge in the early sixteenth century; *poetria* was synonymous with the faculty of grammar, in the same way as *rhetorica* was at Oxford. Scholars supplicating for the MGram. claimed *forma* which included 'four years in arts and poetry', and 'one year in poetry'.[40]

Many manuscripts circulating at both Oxford and Cambridge contained poetic and rhetorical treatises. The items included

---

[37] Reg. Aa, pp. 65 (1450), 153 (1453), 160 (1453). A text from this period that was frequently annotated is New College MS 249.　　　　[38] Hackett, pp. 277, 298–9.

[39] *Docs.* I, no. 87, p. 361 (1488). There has been some confusion over who this 'Terence' was. Some consider him Terentius Varro, the encyclopaedic writer (*Docs.* I, p. 361, n. 2); others identify him with Publius Terentius Afer, the playwright. Since there were many texts of the comedian in circulation in Cambridge, and none (known) of Varro, the answer seems clear.　　　　[40] GBk Γ, pp. 70 and 91 (1508–9 and 1511–12).

indicate the introductory nature of most poetic and rhetorical studies.[41] A mid-fifteenth century compilation now in the British Library, and doubtless used in university work, included Geoffrey of Vinsauf's *Poetria nova*, Alan of Lille's *De planctu naturae*, Fulgentius' *Mythologia*, and John Garland's *Exposition on Ovid*. The *Poetria nova* is marked with many interlinear and marginal notes.[42] Written *c.* 1200 by an Englishman who had studied in Paris, the *Poetria nova* was the most popular of the *artes poeticae* in the English universities. Called 'Gaufred, der mayster soverayn' by Chaucer, his primary sources were the Pseudo-Cicero's *Rhetorica ad Herennium*, and to a lesser extent Horace's *Ars poetica*.[43] Colleges owning this text included Peterhouse (1424, two copies), and Godshouse.[44]

Poets themselves were encouraged by the universities, which laureated men such as John Skelton (Oxford 1488; Louvain 1492; Cambridge 1492–3). A tutor to the royal children, he also translated Cicero's *Epistolae* and Diodorus Siculus, 'not in rude and old language but in polished and ornate terms'.[45] Erasmus described him to Prince Henry as a 'great light and ornament of English letters', although in his poem 'Spake Parrot' Skelton attacked the trend towards Greek studies and the teaching of style before grammatical precepts.[46] In 1504 Cambridge bestowed the additional privilege on Skelton of allowing him to use a gown, granted by Prince Henry, which was white and green with the muse's name 'Calliope' embroidered on the front.[47]

A third activity which fell under 'rhetoric' was drama. There were plays performed on the collegiate level at Cambridge from 1386 at the latest.[48] The best Cambridge evidence is from the extensive surviving accounts of The King's Hall, where

---

[41] e.g. Bodleian MSS Bodl. 487 (s.c. 2067) (ff. 48v.–52v.), 832 (s.c. 2358) and 300 (s.c. 2474) (ff. 90r. 98r.). [42] BL Royal MS 12.E.xi.

[43] Geoffrey of Vinsauf, *Poetria nova*, ed. M. F. Nims (Toronto, 1967), p. 10; Chaucer, *Canterbury Tales*, Nonne Preestes Tale, 1. 4537.

[44] For Oxford examples see Digby MS 104 (s.c. 1705), Balliol MS 276, Bodley MS Bodl. 832 (s.c. 2538), BL Royal MS 12.E.xi, Sidney Sussex MS Δ.3.11.

[45] *Caxton's Eneydos*, ed. W. T. Culley and F. J. Furnivall, EETS, Extra ser. 57 (London, 1890), pp. 3–4. [46] CWE 1, no. 104, p. 197.

[47] GBk Γ, p. 37 (1504–5). See also Bernard André of Toulouse and Oxford, *BRUO*, 1, p. 33.

[48] *Annals* 1, pp. 131–2 (1386).

unnamed plays were produced in 1503–4, 1507–8, and 1508–9. The first playwright's name to appear is Terence, whose comedies were staged in 1510–11. A similar production took place in 1516–17; 'Item in regard magistro thrope |*sic*| pro ludo puerorum suorum therencii iij s. iiij. d.' Thorpe was probably the tutor of these 'boys'.[49]

The fourth element of rhetoric was homiletics, the Christian application of ancient rhetorical theory. This is well illustrated by the career of Lorenzo Guglielmo Traversagni di Savona, the first humanist who is known to have lectured on rhetoric at Cambridge. An Italian Franciscan of noble birth, he had studied and sometimes lectured in philosophy and theology at Padua, Bologna, Vienna, Avignon, and Toulouse in the middle decades of the fifteenth century. He wrote a religious treatise as well as a *modus epistolandi* (published in Cologne in 1480, and later in Paris, Leipzig, Florence, Lyon, and Cracow).[50] He came to England in 1476 and remained in Cambridge off and on until 1482, travelling several times to London, Paris, and Holland. Although he never incorporated any of his degrees at Cambridge he was styled *Doctor sacrae paginae*, and lectured on the *Rhetorica ad Herennium* and the *Ethics* in 1476–7, and on St Augustine's *De civitate dei* in 1478–9. This is another example of the flexibility of the faculty divisions; a Franciscan theologian lecturing in the faculty of arts.

In the summer of 1478 Traversagni completed his *Pearl of Essential Sacred Eloquence*, or *Nova rhetorica*, printed in 1479 by Caxton and in 1480 at St Albans. The book is part of the long tradition of oratorical manuals that give categories and topics for use in public speaking. The orator himself is described according to Cato and Quintilian: 'An orator is a good man, expert at speaking, who uses perfect eloquence in public and private matters.'[51] Traversagni's purpose, however, differed from the secular ideal promoted by Quintilian, for the *Nova rhetorica* is a learned manual for preaching with large doses of

[49] Cobban, *King's Hall*, p. 228.
[50] J. Ruysschaert, 'Lorenzo Guglielmo Traversagni de Savone', *Archivum Franciscanum Historicum*, 46 (1953), 200 1; *BRUC*, pp. 593 4.
[51] L. G. Traversagni, *In novam rhetoricam* (St Albans, 1480), p. 15 (STC 241190).

Christian moralising included. The categories are classical, but the examples are usually Christian. For example: '*Complexio* is when two embellishing phrases are connected, such as "Blessed be the Lord of the lord angel; Blessed be the Lord of heaven; Blessed equally...".'[52] His list of orators includes Moses, Gregory, Bernard, Hugh of St Victor, Chrysostom, Basil, and Nicholas of Lyra, among others. It is clear that there is no sense of antagonism between the old and the new learning, and little between pagan and classical antiquity. Traversagni taught classical rhetoric at Cambridge, but with an effective Christian purpose. There was no distinction in his mind between rhetoric as a liberal art, and rhetoric as preaching. The *explicit* of this book describes him as a 'professor of theology', but he describes the book as a 'work of the rhetoric faculty'.

A fifth element of rhetoric in the faculty of arts was epistolary style (this was in addition to the purely practical application of the *artes dictaminis*). 'The collecting of epistolaries has a long tradition dating from the classical times, but it never proved as popular as in the middle ages.'[53] Collections of letters had circulated in the English universities from the thirteenth century, and in 1400 the libraries of Oxford and Cambridge often had the popular collections of Peter of Blois, Peter of Vineis, and Thomas of Capua, as well as Seneca. When the first contacts with the Italians were made in the early fifteenth century, there was no sense of conflict between humanist forms and the medieval curriculum.[54] When, from Petrarch onward, the leading stylists of Italy published their letters, they were accepted as worthy and useful additions to the English formularies. The works of Poggio, Guarino, Bruni, Aeneas Silvius, and others were included. There are many examples of epistolaries that were owned by masters of arts.[55]

---

[52] Traversagni, p. 258.
[53] R. Weiss, *Humanism in England during the Fifteenth Century*, 3rd edn (Oxford, 1967), p. 29; see also G. Constable, *Letters and Letter Collections*. Typologie des sources du moyen âge occidental, fasc. 17 (Turnhout, 1976).
[54] *Letter Book of William Joseph*, ed. W. A. Pantin, OHS n.s. 19 (Oxford, 1964), p. xxxv.
[55] e.g. Bodleian MS lat. misc. d. 34, (s.c. 36217); Oriel MS 54; New College MS 127, BL Royal MS 14.c.iv, Magdalen MS 166, and Balliol MS 310.

LOGIC

Logic gave structure to nearly all university study in medieval England, and English logic was esteemed throughout Europe from the fourteenth until the sixteenth century.[56] The Oxford statutes for determination of 1409 speak of 'the faculty of arts, honoured many times, and the remarkable subtlety of logic, by which our university is still celebrated over all the universities of the world'.[57]

The official curricula of both universities were dominated by logic in the first two years of study, before a scholar could become a sophister and act in disputations. But logic did not tyrannise the arts curricula.[58] Rather, it complemented the speculative grammar, realist natural philosophy, and metaphysics of the faculty.[59] The handbooks used in the instruction of logic included tracts on natural philosophy as the normal ground for using the dialectics the scholar learned. And, of course, logic was the bedrock of scholastic theology and law. The arts curriculum of the later middle ages was not haphazard, but a synthetic whole.[60]

The unity of the studies is seen in the statutes (two years of logic, two years of philosophy), the graces that reflect this structure, and the manuscripts that the undergraduates used. This is very clear if the manuscripts are viewed in their entirety, rather than looking at individual texts. When logic, grammar,

[56] L. M. de Rijk, 'The Place of Billingham's *Speculum puerorum* in 14th and 15th Century Logical Tradition', *Studia Mediewistyczne*, 16 (1975), 99.

[57] Gibson, *Statuta antiqua*, p. 199 (1409), 'ipsa arcium facultas, multipliciter honoratur, ac mira sciencie logicalis subtilitas, qua prefata mater nostra super cetera mundi studia dinoscitur actenus claruisse'; cf. Thomas More in 1518, 'humanistic education is the chief, almost the sole reason why men come to Oxford'. *Thomas More: Selected Letters*, ed. E. F. Rogers (New Haven, 1961), no. 60/19, p. 98.

[58] Cf. Fletcher, 'Study of Arts', p. 50, 'The fame of Oxford as a centre for the study of logic was only achieved by enforcing a rigid and intensive training in this one branch at the expense of the others'.

[59] E. J. Ashworth, *Language and Logic in the Post Medieval Period* (Dordrecht, 1974), pp. 30–3.

[60] Cf. E. J. Ashworth, 'The *Libelli Sophistarum* and the Use of Medieval Logic Texts at Oxford and Cambridge in the Early Sixteenth Century', *Vivarium*, 17 (1979), 136. '[They] are unstructured, haphazard collections of anonymous tracts on logical topics with a generous admixture of tracts on natural science, and the reader is at a loss to know how they might have been presented to the undergraduates for whom they were surely intended.'

and theology were modified by sixteenth-century attitudes, all these disciplines interacted with the changes, and the programme of studies that resulted was more heterogeneous.[61]

At Cambridge *c.* 1450 the first year of the scholar's programme covered the 'old logic' of Aristotle, using Porphyry's *Isagoge* and Gilbert de la Porrée's *Sex principia*, Boethius' *Divisiones*, and Aristotle's *Praedicamenta*, *Perihermeneias*, and the *Topica* (although this last is usually considered part of the new logic). The second year was given to Aristotle's 'new logic', using his *Elenchi*, and *Analytica priora* and *posteriora*.[62]

These books were the basis of medieval scholarship, and the foundation of scholastic philosophy and theology. The 'old logic' was known throughout the early middle ages. Porphyry's commentary dates from the fifth century, and Gilbert's from the twelfth. The 'new logic' entered northern Europe in the twelfth and thirteenth centuries in translations from Arabic and Greek, and provided a fuller understanding of the syllogism. By 1260 they were an integral part of the studies of all universities, and many religious houses as well. Commentaries were written on them by countless masters from the thirteenth century onward. They were surely required texts at Cambridge from its earliest decades.

A statute from the late fourteenth century added some non-Aristotelian *logica moderna* to this *logica antiqua*: 'nobody shall be admitted to responding to the question in arts unless he first publicly and properly hears the lectures on the *Summule*, *De fallaciis*, and *Abstractiones* according to the current use in the Schools for dealing with insoluble questions'.[63]

The short tracts were all part of the *Logica Cantabrigiensis*, and were practical introductions to the medieval formal logic of the disputations. They were supplements to Aristotelian logic, not condensations of it.[64] The *Summule* was a short explanation of terms, modes, and figures in syllogisms; *De fallaciis* was on sophistic disputations; *Abstractiones* might have been the compendium of Heytesbury's *Sophismata* by Robert Stonham

---

[61] Heath, pp. 9–64.   [62] Hackett, p. 299.
[63] *Docs.* I, no. 139, p. 384 (by 1390).
[64] See Fletcher, 'Study of Arts', p. 180, for the opposite view.

of Merton College, Oxford; and the *Tractatus insolubilium* was Heytesbury's popular work on logical paradoxes.

Bachelors at Cambridge were also required to follow a lecture on the *Posterior Analytics*. Known as 'the entry to the *Posterior Analytics*', most of our knowledge of these lectures is from widespread graces after 1470 excusing bachelors from hearing them or regents from giving them.[65] They are also mentioned in a statute from *c.* 1500 which abolished them, although they were still on a schedule of fees drawn up in the mid-sixteenth century.[66]

The statutory requirements at Oxford show a similar if less specific pattern. For determination in 1409 the scholar had to hear the *logica vetus* (twice), Boethius (once), the *Prior Analytics*, *Topics*, and *Elenchi* (twice), and the *Posterior Analytics* (once).[67] For inception in 1431 the course included three terms of the *Perihermeneias* or the *Prior Analytics*, or the *Topics*, or Boethius' *Topica I–III*.[68] There is no mention in any of the Oxford statutes of the *logica moderna*, the medieval logic. Yet these statutes provided only a sketch of the logical studies. As an examination of surviving manuscripts at both Cambridge and Oxford shows, logic was as largely concerned with medieval logic as with Aristotle, and had finished its creative period by 1420. Fifteenth-century scholars at both universities studied fourteenth-century logicians, and made few if any contributions to them. No contemporary logical works were printed in England from 1475 to 1530.[69] If the English universities made their reputations on logic, they were resting on their laurels by the later middle ages.

The philosophical dispute between realists and nominalists dominated logical writings at Oxford and Cambridge during the fourteenth and first decades of the fifteenth centuries. The

---

[65] *GBk* A, pp. 141–3 (1479–80), 184 (1483–4); *Docs.* I, no. 136, pp. 382–3 (by 1500).
[66] 'Item Baccalaureus in artibus volens incipere in eisdem solvet Bedellis 5s. 4d. pro introitu libros posteriorum.' CUL, CUA, *Old Junior Proctor's Book*, p. 27.
[67] Gibson, *Statuta antiqua*, pp. 200–1 (1409).
[68] Gibson, *Statuta antiqua*, pp. 234–5 (1431).
[69] Ashworth, 'Libelli Sophistarum', p. 137; Ashworth, 'The Eclipse of Medieval Logic', in *The Cambridge History of Later Medieval Philosophy*, pp. 787–96.

discussion of universals and whether they were 'real', an argument with roots in antiquity, was rekindled in the early fourteenth century when the nominalist William of Ockham challenged the realism associated with Duns Scotus and other masters. Ockham found many supporters on the Continent and, for a few decades, in the English universities, but also served as a catalyst for distinguished English realists like Walter Burley and John Wyclif. Although the discussion of universals was, strictly speaking, the province of metaphysics (an advanced subject read by bachelors), the basis of the contest was familiar even to first-year scholars due to the presence of the question of universals in the 'old logic', particularly in the first book, Porphyry's *Isagoge*.

The *Isagoge* is an introduction to the basic terms of Aristotle's philosophy, the 'predicables'.[70] It is aimed to teach beginners the meanings of genus, species, difference, property, and accident (Porphyry altered Aristotle by including species and difference, and eliminating definition). In this way the *Isagoge* covers more than formal logic; by discussing what is predicable of a being, it implies a certain reality to the larger categories to which that individual belongs. Fourteenth-century commentaries on Porphyry used this handbook as a forum for discussing universals, and their commentaries circulated widely at Oxford and Cambridge. An examination of several of these collections from the early part of the fifteenth century shows this continuing preoccupation.

A good example of these now forgotten later medieval logicians is William Penbegyll, rector of Exeter College 1406–7, MA, BTh. by 1417, who died in Oxford in 1420.[71] Penbegyll wrote three realist logical tracts: *Universalia*, *Divisio entis*, and *Super Porphyrii Isagogen*. A contemporary copy of these was made by Richard Calne, an Austin Canon and fellow west-countryman, who was a scholar at Oxford from 1413 until at least 1421.[72] While in Oxford Calne also purchased works of Walter Burley, William of Ockham, Giles of Rome, and several

---

[70] Porphyry, *Isagoge*, trans. with intro. E. W. Warren (Toronto, 1975), pp. 11–21.
[71] *BRUO*, III, p. 1455. [72] Lambeth Palace MS 393, f. 243v.

theological items, all of which he gave to the priory of Lanthony by Gloucester.[73]

Calne's logical collection includes eight short items, all widely known at Cambridge and Oxford:

1. William Penbegyll, *Universalia* (Lambeth Palace MS 393, ff. 1r.–11r.). This is a commentary on Porphyry. Calne's marginal notes indicate it was written in the light of the realist controversy, e.g. '1. opinio Ocham; 2. opinio Burley; 3. opinio Wyclyff'. (Although Wyclif's writings had been proscribed *de jure*, that great champion of realism continued to be read in the first half of the fifteenth century.)[74]

2. Penbegyll, *Divisio entis* (ff. 11v.–12v.). A commentary on Aristotle's *Categories*.

3. Penbegyll, *Super Porphyrii Isagogen* (ff. 13r.–30r.). This is a more complete treatment of item 1 above, and includes an illustration of Porphyry's famous tree.[75]

4. John Sharpe, *Universalia* (ff. 30v.–68v.). A German fellow of Queen's College 1391–1404, BTh. 1396–7, he was a prolific Aristotelian commentator.[76] His other works include a well-known commentary on the *De anima*, the *Physics*, and several anti-Wyclif tracts. This *Universalia*, which survives in at least three manuscripts,[77] also rehearses the fourteenth-century writers: Burley, Wyclif, and *argumenta contra Ockham*.[78]

5. Robert Alyngton, *Super Praedicamenta* (ff. 69r.–143r.). Another fellow of Queen's, MA, DTh. by 1393 and chancellor of Oxford in that same year, Alyngton was a colleague of Wyclif who (like Sharpe) was to write extensively as a logician in agreement with Wyclif, and as a theologian against him.[79] His commentaries on the *Praedicamenta*, *Sex principia*, and his *Suppositiones* all survive in several manuscripts, and were formerly in the libraries of Clare and Corpus Christi College, Cambridge, and Balliol and All Souls, Oxford. The fifteenth-century marginal

---

[73] Lambeth Palace MSS 70, 74, 83, 97, 111, 141, 145, 370, 393 and 396; cf. N. R. Ker, ed. *Medieval Libraries of Great Britain*, 2nd edn (London, 1964), pp. 109–11, 273.
[74] e.g. Magdalen MSS 47 and 92; CCCO MS 116; Fletcher, 'Study of Arts', p. 187.
[75] Lambeth Palace MS 393, f. 30r. [76] *BRUO*, III, p. 1680.
[77] BL Harleian MS 2178; New College MS 238.
[78] Lambeth Palace MS 393, f. 50v. [79] *BRUO*, I, pp. 30–1.

glosses in this copy (in three or four hands) refer to Boethius, Aquinas' *De ente et essentia*, Anselm, Grosseteste, and Burley.

6. William Milverley, *Super sex principia* (ff. 143r.–184r.). An MA of Oxford, little is known of this man. He was probably a contemporary (or slightly older) of Penbegyll, Sharpe, and Alyngton. His bibliography includes the same kinds of things: *Sophismata, Universalia, Super sex principia, De inceptione, De differentia, De scientia.*[80] This particular commentary includes marginal references to Aquinas' *Super physicam II*, as well as tables of signs, humours, planets, the zodiac, etc.[81]

7. John Tarteys, *Problemata in Porphyrii Isagogen* (ff. 184r.–238v.). An MA of Oxford, he might have been a Balliol man.[82] Like the men above, he was a late-fourteenth-century realist logician; this particular item is another concordance of realist logic and physics.

8. John Tarteys, *De figuris* (ff. 239r.–243v.).

Penbegyll, Sharpe, Alyngton, Milverley, and Tarteys were all active during the last productive period in the English medieval universities. There were others during this time who wrote similar short works sparked by the nominalist controversy, among them Roger Whelpdale, fellow of Balliol and later Provost of Queen's, who wrote a *De universalibus* and a commentary on the *Posterior Analytics*.[83] A disputation by him in natural philosophy 'given…in Schools Street' also survives.[84] John Chilmark of Merton (fellow 1384–93), MA, was another member of this group. The author of seven treatises on logic and natural philosophy, they are found in many university manuscripts.[85] Chilmark was more sympathetic to nominalism than most of his contemporaries.

A later contemporary of these men was William Russell, OSA, DTh. in 1430 of either Cambridge or Oxford.[86] Russell wrote a *Super Porphyrii universalia* and a commentary on the

---

[80] *BRUO*, II, p. 1284.
[81] Lambeth Palace MS 393, f. 146v.
[82] *BRUO*, III, p. 1849.
[83] *BRUO*, III, p. 2031.
[84] CCCO MS 116, f. 68v.
[85] e.g. Bodleian MS 676 (s.c. 2593), CCCO MS 116, New College MS 289, BL Royal MS 12 B.xix, Oxford Magdalen MS 92, Bodl. MS Laud misc. 706, (s.c. 809), CCCO MS 103.
[86] *BRUO*, III, p. 1612.

Praedicamenta. Both of these were included in a codex with Antonius Andreas' *Questiones super metaphysicam* and Thomas Penketh's autograph of his *Questiones logicales* and *Questiones naturales.*[87] Penketh was an Oxford Franciscan, BTh. who was incorporated DTh. at Cambridge in 1468.[88] He also taught at Padua 1474–9 and edited Scotus' *Opera omnia* (Padua 1474, Venice 1477). This champion realist annotated the codex, probably while at Oxford in the 1450s, as did many other users in the later fifteenth century. The marginal notes follow the usual pattern, 'contra hockam, contra hockham' (as well as the very understandable 'non intelligo').[89] There are several schematic breakdowns, and the impression is that Russell's work is a primer for beginners in logic. Penketh's own *Questiones* are more sophisticated, e.g. 'Whether transcendence is said univocally of God?'[90] Since metaphysics was for more advanced students, Antonius' text was consequently the least used item in the codex. Among the few marginal notes in it is a reference to Russell's fellow Augustinian, Giles of Rome.[91]

The original contributions from Cambridge are very limited in this area. John Thorpe, DTh. *c.* 1410 wrote a now lost work,[92] as did John Barker of King's, MA 1479. Barker's *Scutum inexpugnabile* was used as a set text within his college, and the vice-provost, Bryan Rowe, wrote a preface for it in 1499. Unfortunately no copy has survived.[93] There were transcribers, however, like Thomas Water, MA 1482, DTh. 1505 who copied the *Logica Cantabrigiensis.*[94] John Beuten, a Franciscan from Cambridge *c.* 1480 transcribed Antonius Andreas' *Questiones in Praedicamenta* and *Questiones in Porphyrii librum Isagogen.*[95]

None of these men from Oxford or Cambridge were as innovative as their fourteenth-century predecessors of the school of Merton College: Walter Burley, Richard Swineshead, William Heytesbury, Simon Bredon, or Thomas Bradward-

[87] CCCO MS 126.
[88] *BRUC*, p. 448.
[89] CCCO MS 126, ff. 7v., 8v., and 10r.
[90] CCCO MS 126, f. 13v.
[91] f. 67v.
[92] *BRUC*, p. 586.
[93] *BRUC*, p. 37; *DNB*, I, p. 1122; King's College Archives, *Allen's Catalogue*, pp. 147–8.
[94] Gonville and Caius MS 182/215; *BRUC*, p. 621.
[95] Gdansk, Bibl. Civ. MS 2370; *BRUC*, p. 59.

ine.[96] They form a group that, although well known at Cambridge, received little inspiration from the younger university.

There are many manuscripts that contain the late-fourteenth- and early fifteenth-century logicians, with commentaries on the *Organon* and *Posterior Analytics*, together with natural philosophy texts. None of these were copied after *c.* 1450, and, although they circulated and were annotated until *c.* 1500, their popularity waned as logical studies returned to less polemical concerns. Among texts from the early fifteenth century is one owned by Richard Calne. It contained seventeen logical items attributed to Walter Burley, and William of Ockham's *Expositio in duos libros Elenchorum*[97] – a rare case of Ockham himself being read rather than his disciples. William Exton, a Benedictine from Peterborough and BTh. of Oxford by 1435, had a similar collection of Whelpdale, Burley, Milverley, Sharpe, and Alyngton, as well as John of Sacrobosco's *De sphera*, Grosseteste's *De statu causarum*, and notes on palmistry. A well-used and annotated text, the marginal notes on Alyngton's *Praedicamenta* refer to the Scotist Antonius Andreas' *Super metaphysicam*, Robert Cowton's *Sentences I*, Grosseteste, Albert, Ockham ('contra ocham; derisio ockham'), as well as the *Posterior Analytics*.[98] Burley's *Super I*^{m} *Posteriorum* includes marginal notes referring to Grosseteste, Albert, and Al-Farabi, and a discussion of the subalternation of sciences and a breakdown of 'scientiae mathematicales' and 'sermonicales' added marginally.[99]

Cambridge manuscripts are nearly identical. John Hall, DTh. *c.* 1450 gave to St Mary's Hostel a complete *logica vetus et nova*, and Robert Hayles of Gonville Hall, MA 1456–7, BTh. 1480, gave that college the *Topics*, *Sophistic Refutations*, and *Posterior Analytics* in 1497.[100] The Cambridge manuscripts show the same sort of use as those from Oxford, although not nearly as many examples survive.

[96] For a bibliography of these men, see J. A. Weisheipl, 'Repertorium Mertonense', *Mediaeval Studies*, 31 (1969), 174–224.   [97] Lambeth Palace MS 70.

[98] Bodleian Library, Rawlinson MS C.677 (s.c. 12521), esp. ff. 24r.–64v.

[99] ff. 143v.–144v.; ff. 146r.–149v. This is treated in *Posterior Analytics*, I.7.

[100] Gonville and Caius MSS 466/573 and 469/576; *BRUC*, pp. 281, 294–5.

William Kyrkgarth and Thomas Loughtburgh were both secular masters of Oxford *c.* 1430–40, and both owned a well-glossed book that included Tartey's *In Porphyrii Isagogen*, Milverley's *Universalia* and *Sex principia*, Burley's *Super Porphyrium* and *De potentiis animae*, and Whelpdale's *Super Posteriorum I.*[101] The marginalia are typical, although a note contrasting Wyclif and Burley's positions on universals is of particular interest.[102] Another manuscript of Kyrkgarth's contains natural philosophy disputations, along with a *questio*, 'Whether logic is a science'.[103] A similar text from Oxford includes notes taken by an artist *c.* 1400, and logic and natural philosophy works by masters who included Wyclif and Edward Upton, yet another logician from *c.* 1400.[104] There are many other like examples.[105]

By the fifteenth century the nominalist position was known primarily through compendiums such as these. In effect, nominalism in the strong Ockhamist form was a straw man for most young artists at Cambridge and Oxford. There are few copies of Ockham that survive from the English universities, and they are mostly of his political works.[106] Several of his theological works did circulate. Pembroke College, Cambridge had the *Dialogus* and some logical commentaries, and Peterhouse in 1424 had a codex which included the *Defensorium* and *Summa logicae* of Ockham, Swineshead's *De insolubilibus*, Heytesbury's *Sophismata*, and seventy-eight *conclusiones* on Aristotle's *Metaphysics*. Only the Ockham was annotated, in the early fifteenth century.[107] But this is an exceptional text; in the century after his death, the *Venerabilis inceptor* was known primarily through his detractors, or his lesser followers.

The most 'popular' nominalists of late medieval Cambridge

---

[101] Magdalen MS 47.
[102] Printed in H. O. Coxe, *Catalogus codicum MSS qui in collegiis aulisque Oxoniensibus hodie adservantur* (2 vols., Oxford, 1852), II, p. 28.
[103] Magdalen MS 38, ff. 92v.–93r. and MS 92, f. 8r. This is also the first *questio* of Duns Scotus, *Super porphyrium*.   [104] CCCO MS 116.
[105] e.g. Magdalen MSS 92 and 162.
[106] e.g. *Dialogus* in Queens' College Cambridge in 1472, and the 'Defensorium', given by Thomas Gascoigne to Lincoln College.   [107] Peterhouse MS 102.

and Oxford were the Merton fellows (*c.* 1340) William Heytesbury and John Dumbleton. The former wrote *Regulae solvendi
sophismata* which he directed to 'you young men in your first
year of logical studies', although he goes on to state that it
is to help sophisters responding in disputations.[108] Primarily a
logical work, many questions arise in the later chapters, and
the last chapter is 'devoted entirely to questions of physical
motion'.[109] Heytesbury was a nominalist, 'although never
outspoken in his defence of Ockham's doctrines'.[110] He believed
that 'there exists nothing besides individual occurrences of
sentences to serve as the bearers of truth or falsehood'.[111]

Heytesbury was known primarily through his short tract on
Insolubilia (Chapter One of the *Regulae*), and the *De relativis*,
both of which circulated in the *Logica Cantabrigiensis* and
Oxoniensis collections which will be discussed shortly. The
Insolubilia was owned by the Cambridge University Library in
1424 and Clare College in 1440, and probably appeared in other
collections where it was not specifically identified. His circulation in England was minimal when compared with his very
favourable reception in Italy and elsewhere on the Continent.[112]
An abbreviation of his *Regulae* was written by Robert Stonham,
a Merton fellow 1387–97, who died at the Council of Pisa.
This, however, had a very limited circulation.[113] Stonham also
owned two manuscripts by Wyclif, showing his interest in both
sides of the controversy.[114]

John Dumbleton was a more open exponent of Ockham's
doctrines, 'although he never quoted Ockham once by
name'[115]—the impression is gained that even Ockham's followers
realised his name was poison to most English university men.

---

[108] W. Heytesbury, *On 'Insoluble' Sentences*, ed. P. V. Spade (Toronto, 1979), pp. 7 and 15.
[109] J. A. Weisheipl, 'Ockham and Some Mertonians', *Mediaeval Studies*, 30 (1968), 197.
[110] Weisheipl, 'Ockham and Some Mertonians', p. 198.   [111] Heytesbury, p. 61.
[112] See C. B. Schmitt, 'Philosophy and Science in 16th Century Universities: Some Preliminary
Comments', in *The Cultural Context of Medieval Learning*, ed. J. E. Murdoch and E. D. Sylla
(Dordrecht, 1975), p. 493.
[113] Worcester Cathedral MS F 118, ff. 101r.–107v.   [114] *BRUO*, III, pp. 1789–90.
[115] Weisheipl, 'Ockham and Some Mertonians', p. 199. A more complete view of his work
can be found in J. A. Weisheipl, 'The Place of John Dumbleton in the Merton School',
Isis, 50 (1959), 439–54.

From Worcestershire, Dumbleton was a fellow of Merton from 1338 until his death in 1349; like Ockham, he probably died of the Plague. His unique work is the *Summa logicae et philosophiae naturalis*. Part I is similar to Heytesbury's work in that it deals with *insolubilia*, and the intention and remission of certitude and doubt. Parts II–X deal with the *Physics*, *De coelo*, *Meteora*, *De generatione*, and *De anima*.

Dumbleton enjoyed wider circulation in England than Heytesbury. Merton College had two fourteenth-century copies, and single copies were in All Souls *c.* 1440, Peterhouse in 1424 (which was annotated by an anonymous scholar *c.* 1400), and the Cambridge University Library.[116] John Chilmark, mentioned above, was a follower of Dumbleton's natural philosophy. All these nominalists and fellow travellers were read less and less in the fifteenth century, and they never achieved the popularity of even the now-forgotten fourteenth-century realists.

The question of universals, although very important at both universities in the fourteenth and fifteenth centuries did not dominate logical studies completely. The actual texts of Aristotle continued to be read both alone and with commentaries. Among the best known commentators was Walter Burley of Merton College (*c.* 1274–1344). His commentaries on the *ars vetus* include several early versions, as well as a later one that is directed against Ockham. This last is the version that circulated and was later printed.[117] He also commented on the *Posterior Analytics* (always the capstone of logic), using Albert and Grosseteste as his guides.

At Cambridge at least one of Burley's logical commentaries appears at Peterhouse in 1424, Clare in 1440, King's in 1452, and the University Library in 1424 and 1473. They are also listed in four private collections and appear on caution lists twice. They were equally popular at Oxford. Burley continued to be read into the sixteenth century, and his commentary on

---

[116] Now Peterhouse MS 272.
[117] Weisheipl, 'Ockham and Some Mertonians', p. 178; C. Martin, 'Walter Burley', in *Oxford Studies Presented to Daniel Callus*, pp. 194–230.

the *Posterior Analytics* was printed in Oxford in 1517.[118] The Oxford stationer John Dorne records frequent sales of Burley's *Super logicam* and *Super posteriorum* in 1520.[119]

The college libraries of both universities had logical commentaries in addition to Burley, by Antonius Andreas and, to a lesser extent, his master Scotus. Albert and Aquinas were also present.

It is worth noting that there is little evidence at either university of the *Summulae logicales* of Peter of Spain. From its composition in the late thirteenth century it served as a fundamental logical text throughout Europe. Erasmus, writing in 1516, claimed that all that was taught at Cambridge thirty years earlier was the *Parva logicalia*.[120] This usually refers to the seventh and last part of the *Summulae*, which contained the medieval analysis of terms, and did not correspond to any part of the Aristotelian *Organon*. It seems that Peter of Spain was not an oft-read logician at either school, at least not in his original form. Erasmus probably meant the *logica moderna* in general when he referred to the *Parva logicalia*.

Along with the commentaries of Aristotle, the *logica moderna*, and those treatises dealing specifically with the questions raised by the *Categories* and the *Isagoge*, there were general logical primers which were available to the undergraduate student. Known as the *Logica Cantabrigiensis* and *Logica Oxoniensis*, these were collections of seven to ten short items on medieval logic, and each collection usually contained slightly different sets of items.

Both these collections had their origins in manuscripts that were compiled *c.* 1400. They were introductory works in the *logica moderna*, and were not just simplifications of Aristotelian logic. They also lacked the emphasis on universals found in the codices mentioned above. One of these *Logica Oxoniensis* collections from New College, Oxford (used by member fellows) calls itself a 'common book for a sophister, not having four

[118] W. Burley, *Super libros posteriorum Aristotelis* (Oxford, 1517). *STC* 4122.
[119] J. Dorne, 'The Daily Ledger of John Dorne', ed. F. Madan in *Collectanea*, I, OHS 5 (Oxford, 1885), 73–177. [120] *CWE*, IV, no. 456, p. 52 (1516).

years in the university'.[121] In other words, not a beginner, but someone less than a bachelor.

L. M. de Rijk has analysed the manuscripts of the two traditions, and it is not necessary to rehearse his work.[122] In general, the *Logica Cantabrigiensis* included the following tracts:[123]

1 *Summule secundum usum Cantabrigiensium.* A short explanation of terms, modes, and figures of the *logica moderna*. The overlap of this introduction with tracts on speculative grammar is clear.

2 *De suppositionibus.* An anonymous description of what a *suppositio* is, and which terms serve that role.

3 *De consequentiis.* A tract by William Heytesbury, this describes in simple terms what a *consequentia* is in a proposition, and which are valid consequences, such as, 'Man runs; therefore an animal runs'.

4 *De expositione terminorum.* Again anonymous, this explains the role of a *terminus* in a syllogism, and what roles it can have (*mediatus* and *immediatus*, etc.).

5 *Obligationes.* An anonymous explanation of what an *obligatio* is, and the three species it has (*positio*, *impositio*, and *depositio*).[124]

6 *De insolubilibus.* By William Heytesbury, this deals with logical paradoxes and the validity of syllogisms. Another *insolubilia*, specifically for sophisters' disputations, was printed in Oxford in 1517 and 1520.[125]

7 *De fallaciis secundum usum Cantabrigiensium.* An anonymous treatise on sophistic disputation.

8 Thomas Bradwardine, *Proportiones breves.* A treatise on mathematical physics by the celebrated fourteenth-century Merton fellow who died as Archbishop of

---

[121] New College MS 289, f. 18v. This MS shows signs of heavy use, and includes *ex libris* marks by Richard Clere, fellow 1464–6; Thomas Chaundler, fellow 1437–50, Warden 1454–75; John Dobbes, fellow 1488–98; and Andrew Bensted, fellow 1474–84.

[122] L. M. de Rijk, 'Logica Cantabrigiensis', *Revue Internationale de Philosophie*, 29 (1975), 297–315; 'Logica Oxoniensis', *Medioevo*, 3 (1977), 121–64.

[123] de Rijk, 'Logica Cantabrigiensis', p. 309.

[124] For 'Obligationes' from Oxford in the 1390s, see A. Perreiah, 'Logic Examinations in Padua *c.* 1400', *History of Education*, 13 (1984), 89–92.   [125] *STC* 18833 and 18833a.

Canterbury. It explains the basics of proportions found in physics.

9 Thomas Walsingham, *Introductorium naturalium*. A short but very compact collection of about fifty paragraphs and four diagrams explaining the essentials of Aristotelian physics (nature and motion), the predicables, number speech ('Note that speech is spoken of in three ways: in voice, in mind, and in writing'), bodies (simple and mixed), mathematics (fractions), the four elements, and the four kinds of cause. The basic facts are all stated simply, and the interrelationship of Aristotle's logic and natural philosophy is clear.

As was mentioned above, several of these tracts were mentioned specifically in the Cambridge determination statutes from just before 1400.

The *Logica Oxoniensis* circulated in much the same form.[126] No two manuscripts seem to have exactly the same contents. There was no rigid statutory outline of the logical curriculum at either school, despite the mention of several of these tracts in the Cambridge statutes. These collections from both universities included the *logica moderna* along with basic Mertonian and Aristotelian physics, but there was considerable diversity without that framework.[127]

The differences between the Cambridge and Oxford logical traditions should not be overemphasised. What can be said is that the collections identified as being *ad usum Oxoniensium* include more Oxford writers, and the Cambridge texts have more anonymous tracts. Cambridge lacked the fourteenth-century flowering of logicians and scientists found at Oxford – there was no Cambridge equivalent of the remarkable Merton school – and the Cambridge texts were probably derived from Oxford scholarship.

At both schools these collections were used to introduce

---

[126] This is not the view of de Rijk in 'Logica Cantabrigiensis' and 'Logica Oxoniensis'.
[127] Two very complete examples are Worcester Cathedral MS F 118 and New College MS 289, both fully described in de Rijk, 'Logica Oxoniensis'.

young scholars to logical subtleties and vocabularies different from the *Organon,* and they were more general than the tracts devoted to the controversy on universals (although they often included these things as well). The *logica* manuscripts complemented the Aristotelian logic. Although some of the authors included were nominalists, the collections are essentially realist in tone, and they always related the logic to natural philosophy, and included natural philosophy texts as well.

These English treatises were copied and circulated widely in Europe, particularly in Spain and Italy.[128] They are today found in libraries in Toledo, Salamanca, Venice, Vicenza, Padua, Florence, Rome (including one copied in Worms), Erfurt, and Wrocław.[129] It was the immense renown of these primers that led Oxford to claim in 1409 that the faculty of arts, and especially 'the amazing subtlety of logic', caused the university to be everywhere honoured over all other schools of the world.[130]

England lost its logical primacy during the fifteenth century. No master at either university wrote anything original in the field, and the manuscript evidence shows the continuing dominance of the fourteenth-century Mertonians. The contrast with the Continent is striking. Following the introduction of printing, continental publishers produced many editions of Burley, Buridan, Heytesbury, and Ralph Strode of Merton (by then almost unknown in the English universities), as well as Thomas Aquinas, Antonius Andreas, and many contemporary logicians.[131] The presses of England, however, were less and less interested in logic, and printed nothing by any contemporary logician. Andreas's commentary on the *Ars vetus* was printed in St Albans in 1483,[132] and Burley's commentary on the *Posterior Analytics* came out in Oxford in 1517,[133] as did an *Opusculum insolubilium* based on Richard Swineshead's *Insolu-*

---

[128] de Rijk, 'Logica Cantabrigiensis', pp. 310–11, 315; 'Logica Oxoniensis', pp. 150 and 156–7.
[129] Paul Strode's *Quaestiones* and Heytesbury's *Regulae* were in the statutes of Padua in 1496. Schmitt, 'Philosophy and Science in the 16th Century Universities', p. 493.
[130] Gibson, *Statuta antiqua*, p. 199 (1409).
[131] W. Risse, *Bibliographica Logica* (Hildesheim, 1965), I. This comparison is taken from Ashworth, 'Libelli Sophistarum', pp. 135–6.   [132] *STC* 582.   [133] *STC* 4122.

bilia.[134] A very short *Libellus secundarum intentionum* was printed in London in 1498, *c.* 1505, and 1527.[135]

All these were for the university market, as was the *Libellus sophistarum ad usum Cantabrigiensium*, published four times in London between 1497 and 1524,[136] and its counterpart for Oxford, printed seven times between 1499 and 1530.[137] These were printed editions of the *logicae* discussed above, and their frequent reprinting indicates their continuing use in the early decades of the sixteenth century.

Like the *logicae* manuscripts, the printed *libelli* do not seriously differ in content. The Cambridge handbook, 128 pages in black-letter, has a frontispiece illustrating a master, rod in hand, lecturing to scholars. The elementary nature of the work is clear, and the foundational role of logic is explicit in the first page.[138] The introduction to the Oxford version admits that logic is very difficult, but states that it is necessary to achieve the sweeter fruits of higher studies: 'he does not deserve sweet things who has not tasted the bitter'.[139] The text then goes on to explain propositions, consequences, insoluble sentences, and like material. Both *libelli* included Walsingham's *Introductorium naturalium* and Bradwardine's *Proportiones breves*.

The annotations on the surviving copies shows that they were not read straight through by scholars, or lectured on by masters, but rather the various tracts were studied and annotated by the scholar as needed, alone or in conjunction with his tutor in a college or hostel. The *libelli* were companions for *sophistae*, students with only a few terms in university; not exactly beginners, but not advanced students either. These *libelli* helped

---

[134] *STC* 18833.   [135] *STC* 15572–4.

[136] *STC* 15574.5, 15575.5, 15576, and 15576.4.

[137] *STC* 15576.6, 15576.8, 15577, 15578, 15578.3, 15578.5, 15578.7.

[138] 'Et quamcumque sciencia quis excellere mavult, principio opus est (si ad altas structuras progredi voluerit) logicalia principia in animo suo prostabili iaciat fundamento ad omnem namque logica viam habet'. *Libellus sophistarum ad usum Oxoniensium* (London, 1499), p. 1. This passage is noted with a hand in the margin of Bodleian Library 4°.S.38 Art. Seld.

[139] cf. with the late 16th-century handbooks of logic that claim to have eliminated the difficulties, 'omissis intricatis et spinosis omnibus'. I. Thomas, 'Medieval Aftermath: Oxford Logic and Logicians of the Seventeenth Century', in *Oxford Studies Presented to Daniel Callus*, p. 297.

them to master specific logical and sophistical problems, and to relate them to basic natural philosophy. They made no effort to give an outline of the *Organon*, or a survey of the *logica moderna* in all its subtlety. They had an effective purpose: to help the scholar perform more capably in disputations. As is clear in the surviving Merton College disputations from 1490 onwards, and from the Cambridge and Oxford university disputation records of the late sixteenth and early seventeenth centuries, the subjects of the disputations among the more advanced students were overwhelmingly taken from natural philosophy.[140] Logic's role was to prepare scholars to serve in those disputations.

[140] CUL Sel. 1.11; *Reg. Mert.*, ed. Salter, I, II, and III *passim*; Clark, *Register of Oxford*, II.

Chapter 5

THE QUADRIVIUM

The quadrivial studies, or *artes mathematicales* (arithmetic, music, geometry, astronomy), were not a very important part of the arts curricula in the middle ages. Most scholars had only a sketchy knowledge of astronomy and perspective, and even less familiarity with music.

Before determining, the average scholar was acquainted with little beyond the three basic quadrivial texts: *Compotus*, for determining ecclesiastical feasts; *Algorismus*, which explained the basics of mathematics; and *De sphera*, which was a simple cosmology, often supplemented with the *Theorica planetarum*. These texts came in several versions, often anonymous, and form a distinct manuscript tradition which was reflected in the statutes of both universities and their colleges.[1] Bachelors were required to study astronomy further, but not much beyond the basic works.

Nothing really new was contributed by the English to these disciplines in the fourteenth and fifteenth centuries. The only continuous activity was the composition of astronomical tables, based on the Alfonsine tables of the thirteenth century. This relatively low interest in the mathematical sciences continued into the sixteenth century. William Harrison, after visiting Oxford and Cambridge about 1570, described the lectures in the 'quadrivials' at both universities as being 'smally regarded'.[2]

The quadrivial sciences, and especially astronomy, were the

---

[1] Hackett, p. 277 (1390); Gibson, *Statuta antiqua*, p. 200 (1409); *Statutes of Oxford*, Magdalen, p. 35; e.g. Gonville and Caius MS 141/174; BL Royal MS 12.C.xvii; BL Egerton MS 2622; Bodleian Library, Ashmole MS 1522; Digby MSS 15, 48, 147.

[2] W. Harrison, *Description of England*, ed. G. Edelen (Ithaca, NY, 1968), p. 72. The interest was growing, however. See M. Feingold, *The Mathematician's Apprenticeship* (Cambridge, 1984).

province of the specialist in the medieval English universities. A graduate usually owned several works in this area, or none at all. Although astronomy was not detached from the arts faculty, and the astronomers were required to follow the same studies as other artists, they were clearly a species apart, and were allowed as bachelors to concentrate on astronomy. When they disputed for their degrees, it was often on their speciality.[3]

Similarly, colleges were either centres of quadrivial studies and had many manuscripts in this area, or almost none at all. At Cambridge the University Library and Queens' College had no quadrivial works, and of the other well-recorded college libraries only Peterhouse, King's, and Clare had any real holdings in this area. Of these, Peterhouse was by far the strongest, owning over seventy treatises in their catalogue of 1424. A systematic study of the fellowships of these colleges shows that Peterhouse and King's also had (relatively) large numbers of medical graduates, a profession that was heavily grounded in astronomy.[4]

The Oxford collegiate records show a similar pattern. The catalogues of Canterbury and Lincoln Colleges show no quadrivial works at the end of the fifteenth century. All Souls, however, had over thirty such manuscripts. Merton, not surprisingly, exceeded even that richness, and also produced many scientific writers and a large number of physicians.

In each manuscript of quadrivial texts there were usually a dozen or more items, which were often catalogued only by the first item, or by general category (e.g. *liber astronomie*). It is thus nearly impossible to know the comparative popularity of many individual texts, or variants of treatises with the same name.

ARITHMETIC

Although a basic skill for any work in the quadrivium, and the propaedeutic for music, arithmetic was a minor subject in the universities. The only text required at Oxford in the deter-

---

[3] e.g. *Reg. Mert.*, ed. Salter, I, p. 444 (1514).
[4] Cobban, 'Cambridge Medieval Colleges', pp. 9–10.

mination statute of 1409 was John of Sacrobosco's *Algorismus integrorum*, and in the inception statute of 1431 Boethius' *Ars metrica*. The Cambridge statutes of 1390 required arithmetic only on the bachelor's level, and specified the *Algorismus*.[5]

The English masters produced few arithmetical works, and all of them seem to have been at Oxford. John Killingworth, MA, a Mertonian from 1432 until his death in 1445, was recorded by his college as a 'noble astronomer who drew-up many tables'.[6] He also wrote an *Algorismus*, or introduction to arithmetic, that survives in a manuscript of Lewis Caerlyon, a Cambridge astronomer on whom more later.[7] Killingworth's *Algorismus* is notable primarily for its conservatism. It is one of the last treatises written in England that uses column-reckoning of the abacus type to perform operations more easily handled by Arabic numerals.[8] Another Mertonian, Thomas Thurlby, MA 1462, wrote a *Novus modus computandi*, a two-page diagram which uses the same method to illustrate basic arithmetic functions.[9] A last Oxford mathematician was John Norfolk, MA and fellow of All Souls between 1438 and 1467. Although his private library was primarily theological, he wrote a *Summula in artem progressionis*, a basic work on numerical progressions and sequences. From its dedication it is likely that this was taught in college.[10]

The average student in arts spent relatively little time on arithmetic, which was just a skill necessary for work in the other branches of science. An examination of the manuscripts shows that even in the large and well-used collections of quadrivial works, arithmetic was usually restricted to the following works:

    1. John of Sacrobosco, *Algorismus*.[11] Required by the statutes of both universities, this was a short work divided into sections on counting in Arabic numerals, the four arithmetical operations,

---

[5] Gibson, *Statuta antiqua*, pp. 200 (1409) and 234 (1431); Hackett, p. 277.
[6] *BRUO*, II, pp. 1049–50.   [7] CUL, MS Ee.III.61, ff. 28v.–39r.
[8] L. C. Karpinski, 'The Algorism of John Killingworth', *English Historical Review*, 29 (1914), 707–17.   [9] BL Egerton MS 2622, ff. 82v.–83r.
[10] J. O. Halliwell, *Rara mathematica* (London, 1841), pp. 94–106.
[11] Halliwell, pp. 1–26.

and extracting square and cube roots. It is very elementary, was in college libraries in both universities, and is found in many manuscripts owned by masters.[12] Fourteen editions appeared in the fifteenth and sixteenth centuries. The name *Algorismus* was generic for any text that explained how to reckon with nine digits and zero, and included those of John of Lineriis and John Killingworth.[13]

2. Alexander of Villa-Dei, *Carmen de algorismo*.[14] Written by the early thirteenth century Norman better known for his grammar, this poem of about 280 lines covers the same material as the previous text. The use of verse to teach introductory material was common medieval pedagogy. A passage from the poem conveys its style:[15]

> Seven are the parts, not more, of this art
> To add, subtract, double and half
> And six is to divide, but five is to multiply
> To extract roots is said to be the seventh part.

This *Carmen de algorismo* circulated almost as widely as Sacrobosco's work.

3. Boethius, *Ars metrica*. Although not specified by the statutes, this was a standard introductory work. At Cambridge Peterhouse had two copies, Clare one, as did three known graduates.

4. Euclid, *Elementa*. Books VII–X deal with the properties of numbers. As a classical work, its popularity increased in the sixteenth century, and it was often printed.[16] The most common translation was Adelard of Bath's, and it was often accompanied by the commentary by Campanus.

---

[12] e.g. Gonville and Caius MS 385/605 (John Marshall); Ashmole MS 1522 (John Gisborne); Merton MS, C.2.12 (Thomas Bloxhart).
[13] e.g. CUL MS Ee.III.61.   [14] Halliwell, pp. 73–85.
[15] ll. 26–9.
[16] Printed copies owned by Oxford artists include Merton 39.H.18 (Richard Rawlyns) and Brasenose S.1.32 (William Smith).

MUSIC

Music, like most of the arts, consisted of both theory and practice. The music in the faculty of arts meant the theory of harmonic proportion, and had very little to do with chapel choirs.[17] It was a subject not read statutorily at Cambridge until *c.* 1500, although the Oxford inception statute of 1431 does assign Boethius' *De musica*.[18]

In the late fifteenth century separate music degrees were granted by Cambridge and Oxford. A bachelor or doctor of music appears in the Cambridge *Grace Books* every second or third year, although there seems to have been no statute regulating this degree. No specific *forma*, acts, or lectures were required for it. The first such musician was Henry Abynton, BMus. 1464 and MMus. 1465, who was required to remain at Cambridge for a year after taking the master's degree, although his regency is not described.[19] Since his ecclesiastical career stretched back fifteen years before his graduation, it seems likely that the degree was as much an acknowledgement of an established reputation as of university study. This was probably true of most of the musicians recorded in the graces.

Since there were no statutes governing music degrees, everyone who took a degree needed a grace to do so. Music degree graces refer to time spent 'in the study and theory of music as well as in practice', or 'both in music theory and practice'.[20] The most specific evidence of classroom work is in John Parker's grace for his MMus. in 1502–3, with three and a half years, 'in this university in the art of music' as his only *forma*.[21] He was evidently a scholar in the faculty of arts who chose to be honoured for his musical ability rather than take an arts degree. Unfortunately, we do not know specifically what he studied.

In the late fifteenth century there is mention of cautions

[17] N. C. Carpenter. *Music in Medieval and Renaissance Universities* (Norman, Oklahoma, 1958). This work does not adequately distinguish the music theory of the artist from degrees in music. [18] Gibson, *Statuta antiqua*, p. 234 (1431).

[19] *GBk* A, pp. 41 and 45 (1463–4).

[20] *GBk* A, p. 86 (1471); *GBk* B, I, p. 161 (1500–1). [21] *GBk* Γ, p. 16 (1502–3).

deposited in the common chest for those taking music degrees, implying that there was some sort of act involved, although it is never described. In 1501–2 Robert Fairfax, one of the greatest Tudor musicians, was allowed that 'his erudition stand for the requirements of inception in music'.[22] Graduates in music paid no *communa*.[23] By 1515 and later musicians were sometimes required to compose a mass and antiphon to stand for their *forma*.[24] Perhaps the degrees were only a method of obtaining suitable music for academic exercises without having to pay for it. The situation was similar at Oxford.[25]

The more common music texts in medieval Cambridge libraries were:

Boethius, *De musica*
Guido of Arezzo, *Regulae de arte musica*

In addition to these, Augustine's *De musica* was known. Probably the most frequent exposure to musical theory was through encyclopaedic works like Isidore of Seville's *Etymologiae* or Bartholomeus Anglicus' *De rerum natura*. Moreover, Vitruvius' *De architectura* includes some musical material.

GEOMETRY

Geometry was a diverse discipline and included, besides geometry itself, optics, statics, and the mechanical arts. In its basic Euclidean form it was propaedeutic to astronomy; in its practical form it taught measuring and surveying.[26]

At Cambridge the inception statute of 1390 specified *de geometria tres primos libros Euclidis*.[27] In the Oxford inception statute of 1431, two years were to be spent on Euclid's *Elementa*, among other subjects.[28]

There are few records of lectures in geometry at either university. Edmund Bekyngham, MA, MD 1405 of Merton

---

[22] *GBk* Γ, p. 4 (1501–2), 'sua erudicio potest stare pro forma ad incipiendum in musica'.
[23] *GBk* B, I, p. 229 (1507–8).
[24] *GBk* Γ, p. 132 (1515–16).
[25] e.g. Reg. Aa, p. 153 (1453) and 277 (1457); Reg. G, f. 34r. (1507) and f. 65v. (1508).
[26] See Digby MS 147, f. 35r., 'Geometrie due sunt partes principales, theorica et practica'.
[27] Hackett, p. 277.   [28] Gibson, *Statuta antiqua*, p. 234 (1431).

College, and John Westcote, MA, BTh. 1389, are mentioned in a marginal note as having given such lectures: Bekyngham on *Euclid II* and Boethius' *Ars metrica I*, and Westcote on *Euclid III*.[29] Geometry is only mentioned four times in the graces from mid-fifteenth century Oxford, to dispense scholars from reading *Euclid I* and *II*, and to substitute logic and grammar lectures for geometry.[30] As with music, it was always a subject of the trivium which was substituted for one of the quadrivium.

At Cambridge a William Malleveray was created a 'bachelor in geometry' in 1492, after two years study at Oxford and Cambridge.[31] No other like degree was ever given, and nothing else is ever heard of Malleveray. There is no other mention of geometry in the Cambridge graces.

Like all the quadrivial subjects, the tracts on geometry are usually brief (except for Euclid's *Elementa*), and are collected into manuscripts with a dozen or more scientific items in them.[32] The usual texts were:

1. Euclid, *Elementa*. Although only the first three books seem to have been read, Books IV to VI all deal with geometry.

2. *Tractatus de quadrante*. This title was shared by several practical treatises, the most common usually ascribed to Robertus Anglicus. A quadrant is an instrument containing an arc of 90°, used for measuring altitudes. Some manuscripts contained more than one of these works.[33]

3. Jordanes of Nemur, *De ponderibus*. This work of a thirteenth-century French scientist was the most popular introduction to statics in the middle ages.

PERSPECTIVE

Although this was not, in classical terms, a separate science, it was often treated that way in the English universities. It deals with the behaviour of light rays. In 1470 John Argentein gave perspective a separate *cantus* in his poem on the arts studies.[34]

---

29 F. M. Powicke, *Medieval Books of Merton* (Oxford, 1931), p. 34, n. 1.
30 Reg. Aa, pp. 31, 115, 153, 168 (1449–54).
31 *GBk* B, I, p. 38 (1492).   32 e.g. CCCO MS 251.
33 e.g. Ashmole MS 1522 (John Gisborne, OSAE, BCL Oxford).
34 Leader, 'John Argentein', pp. 82–3.

At Oxford, two years of Euclid's *Elementa* could be replaced by 'Alhazen or Witelo on perspective'.[35] Alhazen was Ali ibn Hasan al-Haitham, an eleventh-century Arab who wrote a *Perspectiva*, translated by Gerard of Cremona. Witelo was a thirteenth-century Polish philosopher and scientist who wrote a *Perspectiva* as well. Witelo shared an interest in the 'metaphysics of light' with Robert Grosseteste.

No one text dominated this field. In addition to the two above, other works in circulation included John Pecham's *Perspectiva*, John of Pisa's *Perspectiva*, Euclid's *Optica* and *Catoptrica*, Hero of Alexandria's (Ps-Ptolemy) *Catoptrica*, and Roger Bacon's *Perspectiva*. There are also several works of Grosseteste's which touch on perspective.

ASTRONOMY

Astronomy was the most important of the quadrivial studies, and was required of all artists at both universities. At Cambridge the incepting masters were to hear for a term the *Tractatus de sphera* and the *Compotus*.[36] At Oxford the 1409 determination statute also required the *De sphera* and *Compotus*, and the incepting masters in 1431 were to spend two years on astronomy, reading the *Theorica planetarum* or Ptolemy's *Almagest*.[37] The Oxford graces from about 1450 confirm that this was what was being lectured on.[38]

The principal aim of astronomy in Christendom since late antiquity had been to calculate the variable feast days of the ecclesiastical year.[39] Known as *Compotus*, this was one of the basic astronomical skills. There are dozens of extant manuscripts from Cambridge and Oxford that contain treatises on *Compotus*, one in particular which describes itself as *Compotus manualis secundum usum Cantebrigiensium*, and a version *ad usum Oxonien-*

[35] Gibson, *Statuta antiqua*, p. 234 (1431).
[36] Hackett, p. 277 (c. 1390).
[37] Gibson, *Statuta antiqua*, p. 234 (1431) and 200 (1409).
[38] e.g. Reg. Aa, pp. 101, 129, 153, 224 (1452–6).
[39] J. A. Weisheipl, 'Curriculum of the Faculty of Arts at Oxford in the Early Fourteenth Century', *Mediaeval Studies*, 28 (1966), p. 172.

sium was printed there in 1519.[40] Attributed to one 'Anianus', it was printed in Europe at least thirty times before 1529. It had a text of 250 hexameters which treated the solar and lunar cycles, the moveable and immoveable feasts, and the seasons. It gave a mnemonic for remembering a letter for each knuckle of the hand, and then a poem for the feasts of each month which began with the letters represented by the parts of the hand.

The other statutory texts had been popular throughout Europe since the thirteenth century. Ptolemy's *Almagest* was the cornerstone of all other Arabic and medieval astronomy. His *Quadripartitum* and pseudonymous *Centiloquium* were astrological works that circulated even more widely than the *Almagest*, often with commentary by Haly Abenragel (Ali ibn abi'r-rijal). Since the *Almagest* was too advanced a work for most scholars, the anonymous *Theorica planetarum* served as the introductory manual to the same information. Often ascribed to Gerard of Cremona, it is a 'technical presentation of celestial mechanics, usually in the form of definitions of terms and rules for computing planetary movements'.[41] Derived from Arabic sources, it was often bound with Sacrobosco's *De sphera*, a *Compotus*, and an *Algorismus*, a collection known as the *Corpus astronomicum*. The *De sphera* was a simple cosmology whose four chapters defined what a sphere is, the circles of spheres, the rising and setting of signs, and the motions of the planets. In general, astronomy at both Oxford and Cambridge was little changed after the thirteenth century.

Although a standard, if minor part of the arts curriculum, astronomy also attracted a small group at both universities who specialised in both its theoretical and practical aspects. These men were often physicians who applied their knowledge of celestial influences to the care of the body. The special nature

---

[40] *STC* 5613, reprinted in *The Ancient Calendar of the University of Oxford*, ed. C. Wordsworth, OHS 65 (Oxford, 1904), and in facsimile in *Le Comput Manuel de Magister Anianus*, ed. D. Smith (Paris, 1928). The Cambridge example is in Digby MS 15, ff. 1r.–11r. For other examples see Gonville and Caius MS 141/174; Bodleian MSS Bodl. 487 and 507, BL Royal MS 12 C. xvii, and Digby MSS 15, 29, 48, 104.

[41] J. F. Carmody, *Arabic Astronomical and Astrological Science in Translation* (Berkeley, 1956), p. 169.

of astronomy within the faculty of arts was recognised in college statutes at both universities, and in some colleges fellowships were set aside for astronomers. King's College in the statutes of 1443 allowed two fellows who had completed their regencies in arts to study *in sciencia astrorum*; following this they were to transfer to either theology or medicine.[42] King's also had internal lectures in both astronomy and medicine.[43]

The medieval astronomer expressed the practical side of his art not only through astrology, but also by producing tables. Based on the *Almagest*, astronomical tables could be used to predict the rising and setting of stars, planets, eclipses, etc., and were popularised in Europe in a late-thirteenth-century version attributed to Alfonso X of Castile. With modifications, these Alfonsine Tables and their introductory canons became a standard university text throughout Europe for three hundred years.[44] Although not required by statute, they are omnipresent in the quadrivial manuscripts of English scholars, and usually show evidence of use and correction. Lectures on the Alfonsine Tables are also mentioned in the graces of Oxford.[45]

To verify these tables the astronomer had to make observations at his own latitude. Astrolabes were not uncommon among the scholars interested in astronomy, as Chaucer noted.[46] Three questionists in the Cambridge arts faculty, and one BCn.L used them as cautions between 1484 and 1514, which also indicates an extra-statutory interest, as astronomy was only required on the bachelor's level.[47] One of these instruments was described as 'silver and gilded'.[48] Peterhouse also had an astrolabe and three volvelles (for determining the movement of the stars) in its library. Gonville Hall had at least one astrolabe, probably given by Walter de Elveden in the middle of the fourteenth century. At Oxford, although no caution lists survive, there is frequent enough mention of astrolabes and other

[42] *Docs.* II, 483–4.
[43] King's College Archives, *Mundum Books*, III, ff. 81v.–100v. (1457–9).
[44] E. Grant, *A Source Book in Medieval Science* (Cambridge, Mass., 1974), p. 465.
[45] Reg. Aa, p. 32 (1449).
[46] Chaucer, *Canterbury Tales*, Miller's Tale, 1. 3207.
[47] *GBk* A, pp. 181–2 (1483–4), *GBk* B, I, p. 127 (1499–1500), *GBk* B, II, p. 18 (1514).
[48] *GBk* B, I, p. 207 (1505–6), 'argenteum et deauratum'. For what follows, see M. R. James, *Catalogue of Peterhouse* (Cambridge, 1899), p. 26, and *BRUC*, pp. 210–11.

instruments in the records of Merton. Their inventory included an astrolabe, a quadrant, a planisphere, various spheres, and globes of both wood and brass.[49] There were also several tracts in circulation on how to use an astrolabe.[50] Some of these had been composed in Oxford in the fourteenth century, and several include elaborate parchment models of astrolabes.[51]

Astronomy also had practical application in astrology, as it could be believed even by the orthodox that the position of the stars was able to influence, although not dictate, the free actions of men. Physicians had to know these celestial influences and how they affected their patients' health. Some manuscripts included diagrams of the body with the signs of the zodiac superimposed over the parts that they controlled.[52]

Astrology was both practised and suspect in the English universities. Thomas Gascoigne, the chancellor of Oxford, writing around 1450 spoke of the 'false astrologers' who predicted many things that did not happen.[53] This seems to have been relatively common. John Stacey, MA and fellow of Merton 1463–77, and Thomas Blake, a priest of Oxford, were described in the Merton records as 'a notable astronomer' and 'rather more accomplished' respectively. They were both accused of practising the black arts on behalf of the wife of John, Lord Beauchamp, to kill her husband, and of later trying to kill Edward IV and the Prince of Wales 'by art, magic, necromancy, and astronomy', specifically through the use of horoscopes and leaden images. Stacey was executed for high treason in 1477, while Blake was pardoned.[54]

Others at Merton shared their interests. Richard Fitzjames, DTh. 1481, warden of Merton 1483–1507 and described by Erasmus as 'superstitious', also indulged in astrology.[55] He calculated by the stars what was the best time to lay the foundation stone for a college building, and he also conducted

---

49 *Reg. Mert.*, ed. Salter, I, p. 195 (1496); *Reg. Mert.* II, pp. 42–3 (1529). See also reference to an astrolabe of Robert Dobbys of Merton in S. Gibson, 'Order of Disputations', pp. 107–8.
50 e.g. CUL MS Ee.III.61, Gonville and Caius MS 35/141, Ashmole MS 1522 (s.c. 6750), Bodleian MS 300 (s.c. 2474), Digby MSS 29 and 57 (s.c. 1630 and 1658), Laud MS misc. 674 (s.c. 504), BL Royal MS 12.C.xvii.   51 e.g. Digby MS 48 (s.c. 1649), f. 113r.
52 Digby MS 48 (s.c. 1649), ff. 15v. and 16r.   53 Gascoigne, p. 7.
54 C. L. Scofield, *The Life and Reign of Edward IV* (2 vols., London, 1923), II, 188–90.
55 Erasmus, *Opus epistolarum*, IV, no. 1211, 523 (1521).

a search for lost college property 'by dice and cards'.[56] This, however, was forbidden by canon law.[57]

None of these activities was unique to Merton. The Oxonian Thomas Southwell, BA and MB, and Roger Bollynbroke, MA, were both convicted in 1441 of practising necromancy with Eleanor Cobham, Duchess of Gloucester. Southwell died in the Tower, but Bollynbroke was hanged, drawn, and quartered after being exhibited at St Paul's Cross with the 'instruments' of his trade.[58] The fellows of Magdalen in 1502 made several payments to have astrologers from Westminster determine who had robbed the bursary of £112.[59] Five years later, during a college visitation, John Stokesley of Magdalen was accused of many crimes, including baptising a cat at its native place with the object of finding treasure by magical means.[60] None of the charges was substantiated.

The sources for Cambridge, though sadly less rich in anecdote, are not entirely silent. John Metham, who described himself as a 'sympyl scoler of philosophye' at Cambridge in the 1440s, wrote several vernacular treatises on astrology and prognostications, as well as books on physiognomy and palmistry.[61] The Carmelite William Blakeney, DTh. 1462, was described as a necromancer capable of effecting 'many incredible portents'.[62] The death of the protestant George Stafford was caused in 1529 by visiting a sick scholar reputed to dabble in the black arts. Stafford got him to recant and burn his conjuring books, but not before he had caught the Plague from him.[63]

Vernacular treatises on astronomy were common in fifteenth-century England, and there were also Latin works on chiromancy, palmistry, and geomancy circulating in the

---

[56] Digby MS 57, ff. 184v.–185v. 'per talos et cartas'.   [57] *CJC*, x, 5.21.283.

[58] C. L. Kingsford, *English Historical Literature in the Fifteenth Century* (Oxford, 1913), p. 340; Fletcher, 'Study of Arts', p. 62.

[59] R. Chaundler, *The Life of William Waynflete* (London, 1811), p. 278, 'Solutum cuidam scholastico quatenus misso ad quendam astrologum consulendum pro bonis coll' ablatis superiori anno xvi d. In regardis 2bus astrologis calculantibus pro eisdem bonis coll' xx s. Pro vino dato astrologis variis vicibus per billam xii d. Uni astrologo de Westmynstre pro furto recuperando xiii s. 4 d.'   [60] *BRUO*, III, pp. 1785–6.

[61] *The Works of John Metham*, ed. H. Craig (London, 1916), p. 45, 'Quod Jon Metham, skolere off Cambryg amen'.   [62] *BRUC*, p. 65.

[63] J. Foxe, *Acts and Monuments*, ed. G. Townsend (London, 1846), IV, p. 656.

universities, both privately and in the libraries. [64] A prognostication book was printed in Oxford in 1518. [65]

As has been emphasised, astronomy was a field for specialists. The following seven men, four of them from Peterhouse, collected astronomical texts and did some practical work in the field themselves.

John Holbroke, from the diocese of Chichester, was a fellow of Peterhouse from 1393 until 1421. [66] A mathematician and astronomer as well as DTh. and chancellor of Cambridge (1429–30), he wrote a *Tabulae mediorum motuum*, and gave to Peterhouse copies of Haly Abenragel's *De iudiciis stellarum* (trans. Aegidius de Tebaldis), [67] and John Ashinden's *Summa iudicialis de accidentibus mundi*, which are both astrological works. The best indications of his interests are in the 'Codex Holbrookensis', written in his own hand and given to Peterhouse in 1426. [68] It includes two short works of his own, one of them a set of tables for Cambridge which he computed along with five other men in 1406. The manuscript was lightly annotated by subsequent users in the Peterhouse library. It includes:

1 *Tabulae astronomicae*
2 A horoscope for the birth of Henry VI
3 *Theorica planetarum* (with the commentary of Campanus)
4 Simon Bredon, *Tabula declinationis solis*
5 *Tabulae variae*
6 John Walter, *Canones et tabulae*
7 Alfonso X, *Tabulae*
8 John Holbroke, *Ars inveniendi figuram conceptionis nati*
9 William Reed, *Canones tabularum cum tabulis eiusdem*
10 John of Wallingford, *De corda recta et versa*
11 *Tabulae Cantabrigienses*

---

[64] A Munby, *History and Bibliography of Science in England* (Berkeley, 1968). For Latin works, see London, Society of Antiquaries MS 39 (owned by John Argentein of King's); New College MS 162 (which includes Argentein's works); Bodleian Library, Laud MS misc. 594 (s.c. 1030). For library copies see catalogues of All Souls Library and New College Library; John Dorne sold three books on chiromancy in 1520.
[65] *STC* 470.3.　　　　　[66] *BRUC*, p. 309.　　　　　[67] CCCO MS 151.
[68] BL Egerton MS 889. Another copy of the Cambridge tables is in BL Royal MS 12.D.vi, ff. 7r.–50r., esp. f. 43v.

Holbroke also owned a manuscript of his tables, computed from the longitudes of Norwich and Cambridge.[69]

Roger Marshall entered Peterhouse in 1437, the year of Holbroke's death, and remained there through his studies for the MA and MD, which he completed by 1453–4. Physician to Edward IV, he married and practised in London until his death in 1477. He owned a large scientific library, which he divided between King's College, Gonville Hall, and Peterhouse, settling his books where he thought they were needed. It included:[70]

1   Witelo, *Perspectiva*
2   *Expositio super theoricam planetarum*
3   *Tabulae equacionum planetarum magnae*
4   Jordanes, *Arithmetica*
5   Sacrobosco, *Algorismus*
6   John de Lineriis, *Algorismus*
7   Campanus, Commentary on the *Theorica planetarum*
8   Nicholas Oresme, *De proportionibus proporcionum*
9   Jordanes, *De commensuratione celestium*
10 *Algorismus proporcionum*
11 *Demonstrationes astrolabii*
12 Alfonso X, *Tabulae*
13 John Danekow of Saxony, *Canones tabularum Alfonsi*
14 John de Lineriis, *Canones tabularum* with Marshall's own tables
15 Campanus, *Compotus*
16 Roger Bacon, *Ars metrica*

Marshall's library shows an interest not only in astronomy, but in the developments of Oresme in physics of the preceding century.

John Steke studied at Cambridge in the 1460s, and entered Syon monastery in 1489. He gave over seventy books to Syon when he entered, which included items he might have used at Cambridge. They include arithmetic, perspective, Ptolemy with

---

[69] Peterhouse MS 267.
[70] *BRUC*, pp. 392–3; M. R. James, *A Descriptive Catalogue of the Manuscripts in the Library of Peterhouse* (Cambridge, 1899), pp. 354–6; M. R. James, *A Catalogue of Manuscripts in the Library of Gonville and Caius College, Cambridge* (2 vols., Cambridge, 1907–8), has the largest surviving number of Marshall's books. See Brooke, *Gonville and Caius*, p. 36.

Arab commentaries, and astrological items.[71] Steke also used a Gonville Hall scientific manuscript while a scholar.[72]

William Gedge, yet another Peterhouse fellow, took his MA in 1481 and DTh. in 1493–4. He lived in Cambridge until his death in 1500, and left to his college a copy of Guido de Forlevio's *Tabulae*, Aristotle with the commentary of Averroes, two astrolabes, and all of his medical books, both printed and written.[73] As was usually the case, there was a connection between his interests in medicine and astronomy, although he never matriculated in medicine.

A last Peterhouse fellow was Thomas Deynman, MA 1473. He took his MB abroad before returning to Cambridge for his MD in 1485–6 and serving as physician to Henry VII and Lady Margaret Beaufort by 1494. He succeeded a fellow physician, John Warkworth, as Master of Peterhouse in 1500. He died in 1501, and his surviving books include an astronomical and astrological collection.[74]

John Argentein was associated off and on with King's College between 1458 and his death fifty years later. The poem he wrote for his inception shows his familiarity, while in the faculty of arts, with both medicine and astronomy. His surviving library includes these fields.[75]

Perhaps the most celebrated Cambridge astronomer in his own time was Lewis Caerlyon, MD by 1481. He served as physician to both Henry VII and Lady Margaret, and was briefly imprisoned in the Tower in 1485 by Richard III for these sympathies; he spent his time in prison making astronomical observations.[76] Academically, his astronomical interests outdistanced his medical, and he composed a number of tables, corrected others, and wrote several short tracts.[77] He annotated the works of the fourteenth-century Mertonian astronomers Richard of Wallingford, John Walter, and Simon Bredon, of

[71] *BRUC*, pp. 552–3.
[72] Gonville and Caius MS 35/141, esp. f. 21r.
[73] *BRUC*, p. 255.   [74] *BRUC*, p. 187; Peterhouse MS 250.
[75] *BRUC*, pp. 15–16; D. E. Rhodes, *John Argentein, Provost of King's: His Life and Library* (Amsterdam, 1967).
[76] BL Royal MS 12.G.i., P. Kibre, 'Lewis of Caerleon: Doctor of Medicine, Astronomer, and Mathematician', *Isis*, 43 (1952), 100–8; *BRUC*, pp. 116–17.
[77] P. Kibre, 'Lewis of Caerleon', pp. 104–8.

the fifteenth-century Oxonians John Pray and John Killing-worth,[78] and the tables of Humphrey, Duke of Gloucester.[79] Lewis Caerlyon was also familiar with contemporary Merton College, and in 1490 he gave a chained astronomical volume to the college library, 'for the use of students in that field'.[80] The Merton records describe him as a 'doctor of medicine and learned in astronomy'.[81]

Caerlyon was an admirer of his Cambridge predecessor John Holbroke, and transcribed Holbroke's works into one of his own collections. Preserved in this collection is a horoscope for Henry VI, cast by Roger and John Southwell and sent 18 July, 1441 to Holbroke, John Somerset, and John Langton, who were all with the royal family at Sheen (Thomas Southwell had died in the Tower eight days before, while condemned for necromancy).[82] Holbroke described Somerset and Langton as *magistris meis specialibus*.[83] Somerset was a royal physician from Cambridge; Langton, BCn.L, MA 1428, was chancellor of Cambridge from 1436 until his death in 1447.[84] In addition to his university duties Langton was chaplain to the King in 1445; his library includes many works of law and theology. The links between astronomy, medicine, and royal patronage are clear in all of these men's lives.

As is evident from the libraries that have been itemised, there was much diversity in the astronomical texts and tables available to the specialist. However, only the *corpus astronomicum* consistently appears in statutes, graces, libraries and surviving manuscripts: Sacrobosco's *De sphera* and *Compotus*; the anonymous *Theorica planetarum*; and the works of Ptolemy and those ascribed to him. For astrology, the *De iudiciis astrorum* was an omnibus title for many different works on prognostication, the most popular of which was by John Ashinden of Merton College.

---

[78] CUL MS Ee.III.61; Bodleian Library, Savile MS 38 (s.c. 6584).
[79] BL Sloane MS 407; BL Arundel MS 66; CUL MS Ee.III.61.
[80] *Reg. Mert.*, ed. Salter, I, 139 (1490), 'ad usum et profectum studencium in eadem'.
[81] In Latin there is a play on *doctor* and *doctus*.
[82] CUL MS Ee.III.61.   [83] CUL MS Ee.III.61, f. 171r.
[84] *BRUC*, pp. 351–2 and 540–1.

Chapter 6

THE PHILOSOPHIES

The important place given to the three philosophies in the university curricula in the middle ages is beyond dispute. Natural philosophy, moral philosophy, and metaphysics were studied not only for their own sake, but as a propaedeutic to scholastic theology. Oxford and Cambridge both put strong emphasis on the philosophies, and from the founding of Cambridge *c.* 1209 its philosophy was integrated into and reflected the current ideas of European learning.

Cambridge philosophy was 'scholastic' in that the scholars studied the texts – almost exclusively Aristotle or Aristotelian – by the scholastic method. Scholasticism had matured in the eleventh and twelfth centuries, and was the accepted method of European academic enquiry when the Cambridge schools opened. Questions were drawn from a text, like Aristotle's *Physics*, and analysed by marshalling the interpretations of earlier masters, comparing them, and reaching conclusions. That was how most university philosophers wrote, and it was how they disputed in the Schools. 'Is the world eternal?' or 'Can there be motion in a void?' are typical examples from the *Physics*.

The authorities relied upon included Aristotle's ancient commentators like Simplicius, the arabic translators and inter-preters such as Avicenna and Averroes ('The Commentator'), and the more recent Christian masters from Boethius to St Bonaventure, St Thomas Aquinas, Robert Grosseteste, Duns Scotus, and William of Ockham. That list is by no means inclusive; there were hundreds of medieval thinkers who were cited in manuscripts used in the Cambridge philosophical schools.

To these authorities must be added Sacred Scripture and the Church Fathers for, to many medieval thinkers, philosophy and theology were inseparable. There were many tensions. The questions where Aristotle and others seemed to contradict Christian doctrine, like whether the world is eternal, caused celebrated disputes. Intellectual propositions were condemned by bishops in Paris in 1270 and 1277, and at Oxford in 1277. 'Latin Averroists' like Siger of Brabant and Boethius of Dacia were thought heterodox for following Aristotle when he parted ways with the Bible.[1] These thirteenth-century debates surely had repercussions among Cambridge philosophers, but there is scant evidence, and we know of no action by ecclesiastical authorities against anyone in the university.[2]

The primary conduits of international thought for Cambridge philosophy were the religious orders. From the university's earliest days the friars had houses of study where philosophy gave form to theological enquiry. Although the friars were not members of the faculty of arts, they pursued similar investigations. Their members moved between Oxford, Cambridge, and the continental universities, and the English friaries housed confreres from provinces across the Channel. Through the friars Cambridge was in touch with what was being taught elsewhere. The friars often followed the philosophical traditions of their orders, but there were many exceptions.

The early growth of Cambridge coincided with the flowering of scholastic philosophy. Aristotle's *Physics* and *Metaphysics* became accessible in the middle of the thirteenth century, and Aquinas, Bonaventure, and others were producing commentaries shortly afterwards. By 1300 Duns Scotus was well into his prolific career, multiplying distinctions and categories to produce a subtle, but impressive, synthesis of nature and the divine. Between 1319, when he incepted at Oxford, and 1346–9 when he died, possibly of the Plague, William of Ockham caused considerable controversy with his 'nominalist' philosophy, which severely limited the scope of what was knowable through the intellect. He held that words could refer only to

[1] J. I. Catto, 'Theology and Theologians 1220–1320', in *HUO*, I., pp. 498–9; J. A. Weisheipl, 'Science in the Thirteenth Century', in *HUO*, I., pp. 467–8.
[2] P. O. Lewry, 'Grammar, Logic, and Rhetoric' in *HUO*, I., p. 423.

individuals, not to groups, and he divided those things which can be understood by reason from the Christian mysteries, which could not be subject to philosophical investigation. This bifurcation of faith from reason had a political dimension as well. Ockham supported a division between the spiritual realm of the Church and the temporal realm of civil authority, with each supreme in its own sphere.

It is difficult to put Cambridge philosophy into clear focus between its founding *c.* 1209 and the later fourteenth century. There are few exclusively Cambridge masters to examine, and there is no evidence of any distinct 'Cambridge school'. Philosophy at Cambridge shared much with Oxford, Paris, and the other universities.

By the late fourteenth century the English universities began to contrast sharply with the continental universities. Cambridge and Oxford lacked the diverse philosophical schools which co-existed across the Channel in the later middle ages. There were chairs simultaneously in the *viae Thomae, Scoti,* and Ockham at many German, Italian, and Spanish universities in the fifteenth century, but not at Oxford and Cambridge.[3] William of Ockham was little read in English universities after the late fourteenth century. The logical works of William Heytesbury, John Dumbleton, and others who held nominalist positions were known, but their philosophy was not read ordinarily at either university, and their surviving manuscripts were rarely used except for the sections on logic. Both universities were dominated by the followers of Scotus. But dozens of other realist Aristotelian commentators besides Duns Scotus and his followers were also used, and there are many exceptions to any generalisation.

The student of philosophy in late medieval England knew Scotism primarily through the writings of the Subtle Doctor's fourteenth-century Catalonian followers Joannes Canonicus (or Marbres), and Antonius Andreas. The former was a canon of Tortosa and MA of Toulouse whose best known work was

[3] D. R. Leader, 'Philosophy at Oxford and Cambridge in the Fifteenth Century', *History of Universities*, 4 (1984), pp. 37–9.

Questiones on the *Physics*, written in 1321–3.[4] The latter, known as *Doctor dulcifluus* or *Scotellus*, was a Franciscan who studied under Scotus at Paris and taught there himself from 1304 to 1307. Andreas wrote several philosophical works, the most widely diffused of which was the *Questiones* on the *Metaphysics*.[5] Both Canonicus and Andreas agreed with Scotus on all essential points of doctrine.[6] The agreement was so close that Andreas did not even comment on *Metaphysics XIII–XIV* since, 'I followed the doctrine of Master John Duns'.[7]

Another general characteristic of philosophy at both Oxford and Cambridge was that subjects were approached through textbooks organised in *questiones* that were adapted from and useful for disputations in the Schools. The texts of Aristotle were rarely studied alone, and the manuscripts of even such popular commentators as Aquinas and Averroes were less frequently used than those of their now obscure successors such as Canonicus and Andreas. The use of this format was found in the study of the seven liberal arts as well.[8]

A third characteristic was the interpenetration of logic and philosophy, which was particularly evident in the polemical tracts of the nominalist controversy. As was described above, the logical commentaries on Porphyry's *Isagoge* were a springboard to philosophical foundations.

---

[4] This work survives in some thirty manuscripts, ten of which are in English libraries. There are also seven early printed editions, the earliest being that of Padua in 1475. It was printed in St Albans in 1481. See C. H. Lohr, 'Medieval Latin Aristotle Commentaries, Authors Jacobus – Johannes Juff', *Traditio*, 26 (1970), 183–4.

[5] This survives in over forty manuscripts, thirteen of which are in English libraries. There are also seven early printed editions, the earliest being Bologna in 1471. It was printed in London in 1480, and is also included in the *Opera omnia* of Duns Scotus, ed. by L. Wadding (Lyons, 1639), V, pp. 440–725, VI, pp. 1–600. See C. H. Lohr, 'Medieval Aristotle Commentaries, Authors A–F', *Traditio*, 23 (1967), 364–5.

[6] J. A. Weisheipl, 'John Canonicus' in *NCE*, VII, p. 1038. These included the univocity of being, the plurality of forms, denial of the real distinction between essence and existence, *haecceitas* as the principle of individuation, the quantification of matter prior to form and quantity, and actual formal distinctions.

[7] Gonville and Caius MS 368/590, f. 228r., 'Notandum quod in 13° et in 14° libris...secutus sum doctrinam...magistri Johannis duns...'

[8] e.g. Magdalen College MS 38, ff. 10v.–13v., owned by William Kirkgarth in the mid-fifteenth century, includes a *Tractatus de fallaciis pro parte respondentis* and *pro parte opponentis*. The humanist commentaries eschewed this approach for more literal notes. See E. F. Rice. 'Humanist Aristotelianism in France', in *Humanism in France*, ed. A. H. T. Levi (Manchester, 1970), pp. 136–9.

The university statutes say nothing about Scotism, *questiones*, or realist logic, but insist only on the central position of Aristotle. At Cambridge the late-fourteenth-century statute for taking the MA required three years of reading or hearing the *Physics* and shorter natural philosophy works, the *Metaphysics*, and the *Ethics*.[9] For the Cambridge undergraduate in the later middle ages the first two years were given to Aristotle's logic and the *logica moderna*, and the third and fourth years to the three philosophies, but primarily natural philosophy using the *Physics*.[10] The *Physics* was given pride of place as the *sine qua non* for everything else in Aristotelian natural philosophy.

At Oxford philosophy was studied along the same lines. Although the 1409 statute for the BA says nothing about natural philosophy,[11] the mid-fifteenth-century graces provide many examples of undergraduates who were required to hear lectures on natural philosophy: on the *De anima I–II, Meteora I–III, De coelo et mundo I–IV*, Burley's *De potentiis animae*, or other works of Aristotle.[12] The early sixteenth-century graces follow the same pattern regarding natural philosophy, and even specify Canonicus' commentary on the *Physics*.[13] Thus, despite the statutory differences between Oxford and Cambridge, they seem to have been similar in practice in the fifteenth century. Philosophy, and especially natural philosophy, was the heart of the advanced undergraduate and bachelor's course.

NATURAL PHILOSOPHY

Manuscripts used in the Schools show that scholars were first introduced to natural philosophy through short elementary tracts that were included in collections of introductory logical works. Many of these circulated anonymously, including one often attributed to Thomas Walsingham that was printed in all the editions of the *Libelli sophistarum* for both Oxford and Cambridge between 1497 and 1530.[14] This *Introductorium natur-*

[9] Hackett, p. 277.
[10] Hackett, p. 299.
[11] Gibson, *Statuta antiqua*, p. 200.
[12] Reg. Aa, pp. 76, 153 and 247–9 (1451–3).
[13] Reg. G, f. 21r. (1505).
[14] *STC* 15574.5 – 15578.7; see also Chapter IV, pt c.

alium is a short and very concise collection meant for beginners, and contains only the essentials of natural philosophy.

After being exposed to the rudiments of natural philosophy in his first two years, the scholar moved on to more sophisticated works, but still studied them along with logic. A good example from Oxford is the collection owned by William Kyrkgarth (*c.* 1440): along with Burley's *De potentiis animae* it has short works on the *logica vetus* and *nova* by the late-fourteenth-century masters John Tartys, William Milverley, and Roger Whelpdale, as well as Burley's exposition on Porphyry.[15] A similar but larger codex was owned by the Benedictine William Exton, BTh. by 1434. Again there are short works on the *logica vetus*, Burley on the *Posterior Analytics* and *De anima*, John Sharp's *Questio de anima*, Sacrobosco's *De sphera*, and the *Theorica planetarum*.[16] Both of these books were well used in fifteenth-century Oxford, and there are others like them.[17]

The general pattern at Cambridge was one of diversity of authorities, with Canonicus dominant among the commentators on the *Physics*. Aquinas' parallel work was read as well, but not as much as his commentary on the *De anima*. A last work that must be mentioned is Thomas Bradwardine's *Proportiones breves*. A short tract, it deals with the mean-speed theorem, a mathematical analysis of the movement of bodies in space. Perhaps the most important work on gravity between the ancient world and Galileo, it was one of the achievements of the fourteenth-century Mertonian school of physics.[18] It was often bound in the *Libelli sophistarum* for both Oxford and Cambridge. It was, however, never a subject of disputation to the extent of Aristotle's work.

Despite its central position in the faculty of arts, Aristotelian natural philosophy was the subject of little creative scholarship in England after the mid-fourteenth century. There were transcribers and compilers of tables, but only one man at either

[15] Magdalen College, Oxford, MS 47.
[16] Rawlinson MS C. 677 (s.c. 12521).
[17] e.g. BL Royal MS 12.B.xix; New College MS 289; Lambeth Palace MS 675.
[18] The *Proportiones breves* is the *Tractatus de Proportionibus* without the *Proemium* and the last four chapters. See *Thomas Bradwardine, His Tractatus de Proportionibus*, ed. H. I. Crosby (Madison, Wisconsin, 1955), p. 184, n. 46.

university produced work that circulated widely, and he was not a Cambridge man.

John Sharpe, a priest from Westphalia, was a fellow of Queen's College Oxford from 1391, provost in 1403, and MA and BTh. [19] His surviving work includes a typical *Universalia* that uses the arguments of Burley and Wyclif to refute Ockham, [20] as well as *Questio de anima* in four articles and *Questiones* on the *Physics*. Sharpe wrote these latter collections for disputations; the last was 'collected in the manner in which they are normally disputed in the philosophical schools of Oxford'. [21] The reliance on authorities in the realist tradition is evident throughout, particularly in the discussion of place and void in *Physics IV*. The text rehearses the opinions of Aquinas, Burley, and Wyclif, and also includes refutations of their positions. [22] These two works of Sharpe were often copied along with the texts of Scotus, Burley, Milverley, Alyngton, and other realists. [23]

Cambridge reared no important philosophers in the middle ages, save possibly Duns Scotus, who rapidly passed to a wider world; but it left many manuscripts which can be read. There we find much Scotism by the late fourteenth century, although not unchallenged by other realists. It was a situation that was paralleled in the theology faculty.

Among the transcribers of philosophy texts was William Gedge, MA 1482, who copied Canonicus on the *Physics*, a copy he passed on to William Worthington, MA 1503 and fellow of Godshouse and Clare. [24] Thomas Penketh, BTh. Oxford and DTh. Cambridge by 1468, went to Padua to teach metaphysics and theology, and there edited Scotus' *Opera omnia* (Padua 1474 and Venice 1477). [25] William Wyckys of Clare Hall, BCL c. 1440, owned and annotated Canonicus' *Questiones* on the

---

[19] *BRUO*, III, p. 1680.
[20] Lambeth Palace MS 393, f. 50v.; see Lohr, 'Medieval Aristotle Commentaries, Authors: Johannes de Kanthi – Myngodus', *Traditio*, 27 (1971), 279–80.
[21] Balliol MS 93, f. 91v. 'superficialiter collecte modo quo in scholis philosophicis Oxoniae disputari consuerant'.
[22] Balliol MS 93, ff. 65r.–67r. The best survey of the motion in a void controversy is E. Grant, *Much Ado About Nothing* (Cambridge, 1981). John Sharpe's work is not mentioned.
[23] e.g. Balliol MS 93; Oriel MS 35; Bodleian Library, Rawlinson MS C. 677 (s.c. 12521).
[24] *BRUC*, p. 652.   [25] *BRUC*, p. 448; *BRUO*, III, p. 1457.

Physics.[26] John Brystow, MA 1470, gave Peterhouse a copy of Canonicus transcribed in Cambridge in 1450 by the Swedish scribe Tydeman or Tielman. The manuscript also includes Grosseteste on the *Physics*, Albertus Magnus, *Questiones* on the *De coelo et mundo*, and anonymous introductory *Termini naturales*. It is lightly annotated, and was placed in caution twice in the fifteenth century.[27] John Warkworth, MA of Merton but DTh. of Cambridge and master of Peterhouse 1475–1500 owned Antonius' *Super Porphyrium* and Canonicus on the *Physics*. The latter contains notes in several fifteenth-century hands of the positions of Aquinas, Scotus, Aureolus, Averroes, Ockham, Giles of Rome, Bacon, and Burley on points raised in the text. The text itself is organised like a disputation, with conclusions and distinctions, for example, 'therefore the opinion of the Thomists and Peter of Alvernia...is false'. The last item in the codex is a short 'Exposition on the use of certain terms in the schools' – words such as *essentialiter* and *formaliter*.[28]

The Scotists were not unchallenged, however. William Goldston, MA by 1414 of Peterhouse, owned Giles of Rome on the *Physics*, placed it in caution in the 1420s, and annotated the questions on place, void, and motion in a void in Book IV.[29] In 1406 Nicholas Butler, OP, bought Albertus Magnus' *De naturis rerum* from another friar.[30] Thomas Lavenham of Pembroke, DCn.L by 1427, owned Averroes on the *Physics*.[31] William More, MA of Peterhouse and later DTh., owned a mixed collection of natural philosophy: Alexander of Hales, Scotus, Aquinas on the *De anima*, and many shorter works by Peter of Alvernia, Aquinas, Giles of Rome, John Danekow of Saxony, Avicenna, and Richard Killington.[32]

Among the better known commentaries on the *Physics* was Walter Burley's. Although a realist, he is clearly not a follower

[26] *BRUC*, p. 656; Gonville and Caius MS 368/590 (incorrectly attributed to Antonius Andreas); see also Gonville and Caius MS 167/88 for another fifteenth-century copy of this.
[27] Peterhouse MS 188; *BRUC*, p. 103.
[28] Peterhouse MS 240; *BRUC*, pp. 618–19.
[29] Peterhouse MS 183; *BRUC*, p. 262.
[30] Gonville & Caius MS 414/631.   [31] *BRUC*, p. 356.
[32] Peterhouse MSS 143, 157, 195, and 239. Roger Marshall also owned Albertus Magnus, Gonville and Caius MS 507/385. For similar Oxford texts from the fifteenth century, see Oriel MS 48; CCCO MS 225; Lambeth Palace MS 97.

of Scotus, and relies heavily on the opinions of Averroes, Avicenna, Albertus Magnus, and Grosseteste. His work has more in common with the commentary of Aquinas than those of any of the Scotists.[33] Burley also wrote a *De potentiis animae* that relies on the same authorities, excepting Grosseteste.[34] The popularity of Burley's work shows that a plurality of philosophical positions within the realist tradition peacefully co-existed.

MORAL PHILOSOPHY

Aristotle divided moral philosophy into ethics, economics, and politics. A small but important part of the bachelor's preparation for inception, it was stressed equally at both English universities, and changed little during the later middle ages. Besides the texts of Aristotle, some attention was also given to Boethius' *De consolatione philosophiae*, a non-statutory work that was universally known and accessible. Nearly every library and dozens of masters are known to have owned it. Moral philosophy also impinged on the study of theology, and Aristotelian tracts were sometimes bound with theological and parochial works.[35] Finally, many classical and humanist items, particularly works of Seneca, Ovid, Cicero, Boccaccio, and Petrarch could fall within this branch of philosophy.

The graces only occasionally speak of lectures and disputations 'in moral philosophy'.[36] One from mid-fifteenth-century Oxford shows that a candidate did hear the requisite three terms in moral philosophy, although only one grace ever mentions the *Ethics*.[37] Moral philosophy was sometimes disputed by the masters of Merton College, Oxford (I have found none in moral philosophy from Cambridge), usually using topics taken from the *Ethics*. In some of the Merton examples the position taken by the disputant was recorded as well:

---

[33] Weisheipl, 'Ockham and Some Mertonians', p. 181.
[34] M. J. Kitchel, 'The "De potentiis animae" of Walter Burley', *Mediaeval Studies*, 33 (1971), 85–113.
[35] e.g. Royal MS 6.B.v; Gregory, *Homeliae*, Giles of Rome, *De regimine principum*, etc. This 15th-century codex shows signs of frequent use.
[36] Reg. G, f. p. 177r. (1513).
[37] Reg. Aa, pp. 41 (1449) and 121 (1452).

Whether happiness consists in an act of the will or in an act of the intellect (will) [38]

Whether happiness consists in works of virtue (denied) [39]

Whether anyone can be called happy in this life (denied) [40]

Whether the moral virtues are in the will as in its subject [41]

Whether the contemplative life is preferable to the active [42]

As with natural philosophy and metaphysics, these questions are not very different from those disputed at Cambridge and Oxford one hundred years later. [43]

Among the medieval university men interested in moral philosophy was the eclectic fifteenth-century lay scholar William of Worcester, who visited Cambridge but is unlikely to have studied there. He wrote a *Saiengis of Philosophres* for his patron Sir John Fastolf, which is known only through its presentation copy. [44] Worcester elsewhere referred to Aristotle's *Ethics* and Cicero's *De amicitia* when writing on friendship. [45] Thomas Hoccleve, who is not certain to have attended university, wrote an English *De regimine principum* c. 1410–12. [46] Hoccleve shows a broad knowledge of the subject, citing extensively from Giles of Rome, the pseudo-Aristotle's *Secretum secretorum*, Cicero, Virgil, Quintilian, Sallust, and Burley's *Super politicam*, all marshalled into a critique of contemporary society and politics. This work was transcribed by William Wylflete, MA, DTh. of Clare Hall, Cambridge, chancellor of the university in 1458,

---

[38] *Reg. Mert.*, ed. Salter, I, p. 443 (1514), 'Utrum felicitas consistit in actu voluntatis vel in actu intellectus. (voluntatis)'.

[39] *Reg. Mert.* I, p. 443 (1514), 'Utrum felicitas consistit in operibus virtutis. (non)'.

[40] *Reg. Mert.* I, p. 443 (1514), 'Utrum aliquis potest dici felix in hac vita. (non)'.

[41] *Reg. Mert.* II, p. 31 (1527), 'Utrum virtutes morales sint in voluntate ut in substantivo'.

[42] *Reg. Mert.* II, p. 31 (1527), 'Utrum vita contemplativa sit activa preferenda'.

[43] *Register of the University of Oxford*, II, 170–9.

[44] *BRUO*, III, pp. 2086–7; CUL MS Gg.I.34, pt 2. For William of Worcester, see K. B. McFarlane, 'William Worcester' in *Studies Presented to Sir Hilary Jenkinson*, ed. J. C. Davies (London, 1957), pp. 196–221, and W. Worcestre, *Itineraries*, ed. J. H. Harvey, Oxford Medieval Texts, Oxford, 1969.

[45] *The Paston Letters*, ed. N. Davis (Oxford, 1976), II, p. 203.

[46] T. Hoccleve, *De Regimine principum*, ed. T. Wright, The Roxburghe Club, 79 (London, 1860).

and described by a contemporary as a 'very industrious and cultured man'.[47]

The most popular work arising from Aristotle's moral philosophy in later medieval England was Giles of Rome's *De regimine principum*. It appears in nearly every library with any holdings in philosophy at both universities, and was owned by many masters. It is mentioned in the prologue of an inception disputation at Oxford in 1420, which touched on the foreign policy of Henry V.[48] The use of such contemporary political examples, if rare, was not unknown in the medieval universities. Edward II in 1326 sent a roll to the universities explaining his quarrel with the King of France, and asking them to vindicate his conduct publicly.[49]

Other than Giles' *De regimine principum*, the best known texts of moral philosophy at Cambridge were the commentaries of Aquinas and Burley on the *Ethics* and *Politics*. In the fifteenth century there was a complement to these, the *Questiones* on the *Ethics* by John Dedicus. Possibly of Portuguese origin, he studied at Oxford in the late fourteenth century.[50] Although this rather long text (the printed edition is 153 pages in highly abbreviated black-letter) never enjoyed the popularity of the texts above, its *questiones* format made it a valued item well into the sixteenth century.

Not many Cambridge masters have left evidence of their interest in moral philosophy. John Howson of St Edmund's Hostel transcribed Dedicus' *Questiones* while preparing to take the MA in 1467.[51] John Argentein of Eton and King's College, MA 1467 showed familiarity with the *Ethics* and *Politics* on graduating.[52] Robert Hacumblen, also of King's College, MA 1480, copied the *Ethics* along with a brief commentary.[53]

---

[47] J. Harryson, *Abbreviata chronica*, ed. J. Smith, CAS, 1, n. 2 (Cambridge, 1840); *BRUC*, p. 657; CCCC MS 496.
[48] Magdalen MS 38, f. 17v. and Gibson, *Statuta antiqua*, p. 644, '...qui mortiferis nimis architenensium suorum totam Galliam precipitat in ruinam iuxta famosissimum consilium Egidii de regimine principum plerisque capitulis in ultima parte libri'.
[49] *Annals*, 1, 81 (1325–6).   [50] *BRUO*, 1. p. 555.
[51] *BRUC*, p. 318; Gonville and Caius MS 369/591. This also contains Antonius Andreas on the *Metaphysics*.   [52] Leader, 'John Argentein', pp. 84–5.
[53] *BRUC*, p. 278; King's College MS 11.

There are many manuscripts that show how the medieval masters approached moral philosophy. Among the more interesting is a text of the *Ethics* in Bruni's translation, together with a commentary by Aquinas. It was copied by William Reynoldson, MA 1457, BTh. 1464, while he was at Michaelhouse, Cambridge.[54] During his lifetime Reynoldson lent it to John Gunthorpe, the early English humanist, and on his death left it to Michaelhouse.[55] The codex includes a schema of the three branches of moral philosophy and is marginally annotated in several fifteenth- and sixteenth-century hands, including that of Thomas Cranmer.[56] Copied on slightly irregular parchment in a clear hand with little ornamentation, it is a typical school textbook.

Other well-used manuscripts include an Oxford text with Giles of Rome's *De regimine principum* and commentary on the *De anima*, and Aquinas' *Super ethicam*.[57] It was placed in caution by three different men. As was often the case, this was heavily annotated in several hands in the margins of Giles' treatment of the *Ethics* in the *De regimine principum*, but the rest of that text and the other items in the codex are almost spotless. This same pattern of study occurs in the repeatedly used text of Burley on the *Ethics* and *Politics* given to New College, Oxford, by Thomas Chaundler, DTh. in 1455 and sometime warden and chancellor of the university,[58] and in a copy of Bruni's translations of the *Ethics* and *Politics* transcribed by John Gold of Magdalen College, Oxford, MA 1464.[59] As frequently happens today, the lectures rarely got beyond the first set book; in this case, it was usually the *Ethics*.

Cambridge manuscripts show similar patterns of use. Thomas Lavenham, DCn.L by 1430 gave Pembroke Hall his copy of Burley on the *Politics* and Giles' *De regimine principum*.[60] The *Politics* has marginal notes throughout, while the *De regimine principum* was given less attention. A Pembroke manuscript with

[54] *BRUC*, p. 479; BL Royal MS 9.E.i. This Bruni translation of the *Ethics* was printed in Oxford in 1479 (*STC* 752).   [55] *BRUC*, pp. 275–6.

[56] Royal MS 9.E.i, f. lv; Cranmer's signature on f. 2r.

[57] Bodleian Library, Hatton MS 15 (s.c. 4121).   [58] *BRUO*, I. pp. 398–9.

[59] *BRUO*, II, pp. 780–1; New College MS 242 and Magdalen MS 49.

[60] Pembroke MS 158; *BRUC*, p. 356.

Burley on the *Ethics* and *Politics* with a list of *questiones* after each, was possibly owned by the Scots' fellow Gavin Blenkynsop, MA 1459 and DTh. by 1475.[61] The *Ethics* is annotated only on the first folios, while the rest of the codex shows few signs of use.

More revealing is a book owned by Thomas Wryght of Pembroke, MA 1463, DTh. 1480, who died in 1488. His library included Grosseteste on the *Ethics*, the *Vita Jesu*, printed copies of Nicholas of Lyra's biblical commentaries, and William Durand's *Rationale*. Wryght also owned a codex of Aristotle's *Metaphysics*, *Ethics*, *Politics*, *Rhetoric*, *Magna moralia*, and the pseudonymous *Secreta secretorum*, annotated in several fourteenth- and fifteenth-century hands.[62] The *Ethics* shows heavy use, especially books VI and VII, which concern the intellectual virtues, continence, incontinence, and pleasure, with fifteenth century marginalia on Aquinas' opinions. The *Politics* is similarly annotated on books VI–VIII, the discussions of the types of constitutions, democracies and oligarchies, and revolutions. Perhaps this last part was read with reference to the dynastic struggles of that century.

Platonism, as known through St Augustine and others, was profoundly influential in medieval thought, but Plato's own texts were little known before the Renaissance. There were few copies in the libraries of anything other than the *Timaeus*, even in the early sixteenth century. Duke Humphrey gave a copy of Bruni's version of the *Phaedrus* to Oxford in 1439, which he borrowed back in 1445,[63] and he also gave King's College Pier Candido di Decembrio's translation of *Republic I–V* (dedicated to Duke Humphrey).[64] John Doket, a fellow of that college, wrote a commentary on the *Phaedo*, but it survives only in the presentation copy.[65] Plato could not challenge Aristotle in university studies during this time.

---

[61] Pembroke MS 157; *BRUC*, p. 66.
[62] Pembroke MS 130; *BRUC*, pp. 653–4.
[63] *Epistolae Academicae*, ed. Anstey, I, pp. 181 (1439) and 246 (1445); see also *BRUO*, II. pp. 983–5, with a list of manuscripts given to Oxford and a bibliography of Duke Humphrey's contacts with Pier Candido di Decembrio and other Italian humanist scholars.
[64] BL Harleian MS 1705.
[65] BL Add. MS 10344; *BRUC*, p. 191 (which incorrectly has BL Add. MS 10334).

METAPHYSICS

Metaphysics, the third of the philosophies, was a very difficult subject and was studied almost exclusively by BAs. Aristotle's *Metaphysics* was the primary text, studied through *questiones* or commentaries. At Cambridge it was an optional text to be read in the autumn and lent terms of the fourth year, but was required *pro forma* for taking the MA.[66] At Oxford there is no mention of metaphysics before the bachelor's level, at which point three terms were to be devoted to it.[67] The graces from both schools confirm that only advanced students studied metaphysics.[68]

The *Questiones super metaphysicam* of the Scotist Antonius Andreas was the overwhelming favourite in this field. Organised for ready adaptation to disputations, it was virtually unchallenged by the later middle ages. Aquinas' commentary ran a poor second, followed by Averroes and Duns Scotus.

As with most of the arts studies in late medieval England, the original contribution was minimal. There were a few Oxford masters who compiled *tabulae* on Andreas' *questiones*.[69] At Cambridge nothing beyond transcriptions survive. William More, MA of Peterhouse, copied Andreas in the early fifteenth century,[70] as did John Howson of St Edmund's Hostel while preparing to take the MA in 1467,[71] and William Gedge of Peterhouse, MA 1482, a copy which he bequeathed to William Worthington of Godshouse, MA 1503.[72]

A secondary text for the study of metaphysics was the *Liber de causis*, derived from Proclus but thought to be by Aristotle in the middle ages. Although this brief text was found in many libraries in medieval Cambridge and Oxford, there appeared to

---

[66] Hackett, pp. 277 and 299.
[67] Gibson, *Statuta antiqua*, pp. 200 (1409) and 235 (1431).
[68] e.g *GBk* Γ, p. 72 (1508–9); Reg. Aa, pp. 41–2 (1449).
[69] e.g. Thomas Derham (*BRUO*, I, pp. 572–3); Thomas Appulby (*BRUO*, IV, p. 10).
[70] Peterhouse MS 239; *BRUC*, p. 410.
[71] *BRUC*, p. 318; Gonville and Caius MS 369/591.
[72] *BRUC*, pp. 255 and 652. See also Pembroke MS 130, owned by Thomas Wryght (*BRUC*, pp. 653–4), a text of the *Metaphysics* with many fourteenth-century notes.

be little interest in it. What is striking about almost all metaphysical manuscripts is how little evidence of use they bear. This was a study for only the most committed scholars, and even they produced nothing in this field at Cambridge after the early fourteenth century.

Chapter 7

THEOLOGY

'Whatever fame Cambridge achieved in the middle ages was due to its theology faculty.'[1] Developing in the first decades of the university's existence, the faculty, though small, put Cambridge in an exclusive company that included only Paris and Oxford until well into the fourteenth century. When Bologna founded its theology faculty in 1365, it recognised only those three as having prior status. It was the theology faculty that brought the great friar-scholars to study and teach in Cambridge, and the mendicants even went so far as to claim that they were the founders of the faculty.

Theology, the 'Queen of Sciences' in medieval universities, was primarily studied through the Bible and the *Sentences* of Peter Lombard. The Bible was the paramount authority. Lombard's *Sentences* provided the framework through which the contentious points of theology, where Scripture, the Fathers, the councils, and the popes were at variance, could be examined and resolved by the scholastic method. As in other faculties, theologians followed lectures and sharpened their learning in disputations.

Perhaps one third of the 600 or 700 scholars in fourteenth-century Cambridge were friars. Of the remaining secular scholars, roughly 50 per cent were in the arts faculty, 40 per cent in law, and only 10 per cent in theology. Thus, theology in some years could have been the largest faculty with some 40 per cent of the total scholars. If these figures are anything like

---

[1] Hackett, *Statutes*, pp. 131–2. If Duns Scotus studied in Cambridge (*BRUC* pp. 198–201), he was perhaps the most prestigious theologian ever to do so. But the evidence is very slight, and there is no evidence he studied *theology* there.

Theology

correct, the arts faculty would have been slightly smaller, about 33 per cent, with the remaining 27 per cent in legal studies.[2] However, given the fluid nature of the arts faculty, with many secular clerks coming up for only a few terms of grammar or basic logic and leaving no trace, it is likely the arts faculty was always at least as large as theology. From 1400 the mendicant vocations fell off in England while Cambridge expanded, the difference being made up mostly of seculars in arts and law. In the fifteenth century the relative size of the theology faculty diminished considerably.

Friars normally followed their preparatory classes in the arts within their orders' *studia* before becoming members of the university. This exemption from the MA requirement for entry into theology was a hard-won privilege and applied at both Oxford and Cambridge, although only Cambridge extended it to monks as well.[3] But they had to know what was taught in the arts faculty, for it was the necessary formation that was presupposed in the theology classes. As Augustine wrote in the *De doctrina christiana*, the arts and philosophies served to unlock the full understanding of Sacred Scripture.[4] In 1506 William Ramsey, a monk in Cambridge, supplicated for his DTh. and recorded nine years of study in the university and two 'in the cloister in arts and theology'. At Oxford John Yoxford, a Cistercian monk, supplicated for his BTh. in 1449, claiming eight years in philosophy, four in theology, and three 'in theology in the cloister, partly in moral theology and partly in scholastic theology'. In this grace the distinction between university and monastic study is clear, as well as the two types

[2] Aston *et al.*, 'Cambridge Alumni', pp. 58–62.
[3] See above chapter II, Convents. A statute from 1438 at Oxford (Gibson, *Statuta*, pp. 258–9) shows that *religiosi possessionati* had certain exemptions concerning arts requirements but, like seculars, were still required to incept. Accordingly, graces were required of monks who lacked this formation and wanted to incept in theology, *non obstante quod non rexit in artibus* (Reg. Aa, p. 42 (1449); p. 74 (1451)). At Oxford and Cambridge both monks and mendicants were usually excused from most fees, and the financial accounts from the fifteenth century show that they maintained these exemptions. See Aston *et al.*, 'Cambridge Alumni', pp. 60–1 and *GBk* A, p. 189 (1484).
[4] Augustine, *De doctrina christiana*, II.xl: J. A. Weisheipl, 'The Structure of the Arts Faculty in the Medieval University', *British Journal of Educational Studies*, 19 (1971), 163–71.

of theology. Both were counted towards the degree; both Abelard and Bernard were placated.[5]

Although theology attracted only about 10 per cent of the secular members of Cambridge in the middle ages, theological texts enjoyed wide circulation among members of the faculty of arts. These artists were primarily composed of men destined for careers in the Church, and they accordingly had an interest in theology even if they did not enter that faculty.[6] A good individual example is Robert Barker, MA 1487 and later vicar of Godmanchester. He was never in the theology faculty. On his death in 1504 he carefully bequeathed his varied books to many institutions. Of his theology codices The King's Hall received John Gerson's *Opera* in four volumes; Michaelhouse the *Glossa communa* on Job and a sermon collection; Corpus Christi an *Apocalypse*; King's College Scotus on the *Sentences*; St Bernard's Hostel Augustine's *Opuscula*; Trumpington Church a *Liber de virtutibus et viciis*; Bridlington Abbey in Yorkshire Gregory's *Moralia* and Augustine's *Sermones*; and a certain canon of that abbey Nicholas Lyra's biblical commentary and Ludolph of Saxony's *Vita Jesu*.[7] This series reflects an inquisitive mind restricted to no school, with scholastic, biblical, pastoral, and homiletic theology equally represented. As a vicar there was practical application to his study.

The interplay between the arts and theology was also due to the nature of scholastic speculative theology, the propaedeutic role of most logical study, and the unity of Christian philosophy during the middle ages. This can be seen in the *questiones* used for arts disputations within Merton College, Oxford. 'Whether the intellective soul is incorruptible?' and 'Whether anyone can

---

[5] *GBk* Γ, p. 47 (1505–6). A similar grace was given Alexander Bell in *GBk* Γ, p. 64 (1507–8); Reg. Aa, p. 47 (1449); see also p. 134 (1452), p. 154 (1453), p. 231 (1456), and *passim*.

[6] For examples of theology texts placed in caution by artists, see *GBk* A, p. 169 (1482–3) and *passim* to *GBk* B I, p. 79 (1495–6). One particular work, the *Liber de tabula septem custodiarum* (a list of biblical commentaries and the monastic libraries where they could be found), was placed in caution by successive artists in 1483, 1484, 1485, 1488, 1493, and 1496, indicating if nothing else a certain degree of accessibility. It was originally copied in 1452 by Richard Bottesham of Gonville Hall, BA *c.* 1456, and bequeathed to the Franciscan friary in Lichfield in 1521 by Ralph Collyngwode of Queens', MA 1487, DTh. 1498. It is now BL Royal MS 3 D. i. For Bottesham and Collyngwode see *BRUC*, pp. 81 and 149.   [7] *BRUC*, p. 38.

be called happy in this life?' were both from Aristotelian natural philosophy, but their theological ramifications are also obvious.[8] When one compares the disputed questions 'Whether happiness consists in virtuous deeds?' (faculty of arts) and 'Whether human providence is praiseworthy in all states?' (faculty of theology), it is easy to see the overlap.[9] Theological texts also could be used to explain logical ones. William Exton, OSB and BTh. of Oxford by 1435 owned William Milverley's commentary on the *Sex principia*, and in the margins he cross-referenced a discussion on quality to Robert Cowton's popular commentary on *Sentences I*.[10] Similar marginalia appear in Cambridge manuscripts. John Botelsham, MA and DC and Cn.L by 1400, gave Pembroke College his copy of Aquinas on *Sentences I*. It is annotated in several fourteenth- and fifteenth-century hands, which note the ramifications of creation on natural philosophy and metaphysics, and ask the question, 'In what manner does metaphysical speech contain truth?'[11]

The intimacy between logic and theology is spoken of in Richard Flemyng's statutes for Lincoln College, Oxford, in 1427,[12]

> Since, as Gregory says, nothing is known completely by the human senses unless it is first broken by the teeth of disputation, so too the honeycomb of the sweeter theologians is not able to be broken open except by the teeth of disputation, the principles of which are taught by the faculty of logic and philosophy.

A century later Hugh Millyng, MA of Lincoln College, was required to lecture on an arts text (Sacrobosco, *De sphera mundi*) for his grace to incept DTh. Thomas Barton, OSB included a lecture on Aristotle's *De longitudine et brevitate vite* in his *forma*

---

[8] *Registrum Merton.*, ed. Salter, I, 443 (1514), 'Utrum aliquis potest dici felix in hac vita', and p. 487 (1519), 'Utrum anima intellectiva sit incorruptilis'.

[9] *Registrum Merton.* I, 443 (1514), 'Utrum felicitas consistit in operibus virtutis', and pp. 230–1 (1499), 'Utrum providencia humana sit in omni statu laudabilis'.

[10] Oxford, Bodleian Library, Rawlinson MS C. 677, f. 128r., 'vide in Cowtone li⁰ pᵒ ad tale signum ✗'.   [11] Pembroke MS 125 (unfoliated); *BRUC*, p. 76.

[12] *Statutes of Oxford*, Lincoln, p. 8, 'Nam cum ex Gregorio nihil in humanis sensibus perfecte cognoscitur, nisi prius dente disputationis frangatur, theologici dulcioris favum malleum frangi nequit nisi disputationis dente, quam logicae et philosophiae facultas principiis suis edocet...'

for his BTh. [13] At Cambridge, Patrick Gower, an MA of Paris, was incorporated in 1519, 'provided he lecture on most of Saint Thomas' *Secunda secunde*', the part of the *Summa* that deals with moral theology. [14]

The statutes of the Cambridge faculty of theology required experience in three areas: lectures, both attended and given by the candidate; disputations acted in; and sermons preached. A late-thirteenth-century statute in force until the Reformation itemised these stages and demands. It began by prohibiting anyone from taking the doctorate in theology unless he had first served as a regent in arts. This was the anti-mendicant provision, mentioned earlier, from which the friars were exempted by 1366. The candidate must have had at least ten years' study in theology. He began by hearing lectures on the Bible for two years, lectures on the *Sentences* of Peter Lombard for two years, and giving cursory lectures on any of the books of the Bible for a year. In his fifth to seventh years he had to 'oppose' for a year, which involved participation by the fifteenth century in at least sixteen disputations, and acting as respondent in an act with his master and the other regents in theology. [15]

With this completed, the candidate obtained a deposition concerning his learning from his master and the other regents. At this stage he became a full bachelor of theology, and was admitted 'to entering the *Sentences*'. The road to the doctorate then required giving cursory lectures on the *Sentences* for two years, followed by a course of lectures on the Bible. By the fifteenth century the candidate was also required to preach publicly (in English) at St Paul's Cross in London to whomsoever came to listen at that outdoor site. Then came another series of disputations to be acted, depositions to be obtained, and a Latin sermon 'to the clergy' in Great Saint Mary's to be delivered. Three full years after he finished the lectures on the *Sentences*, and after the required oaths and depositions were given, the candidate was licensed by the chancellor to incept in theology.

[13] OUA, Reg. G, f. 65v. (1509). He was excused this obligation later, f. 86v; Reg. G, f. 67 (1509).

[14] *GBk* Γ, p. 181 (1519–20), 'in scolis publicis secundam secunde Sancti Thome pro maiori parte'.

[15] *Docs.* I, no. 124, p. 377, no. 107, pp. 369–70; *GBk* A, pp. xxvi–xxvii and p. 62.

As in the arts, the inceptor began his course of lectures and had a two-year regency before fully earning the doctorate.[16]

Thus, the studies in theology were much more protracted than in arts, but contained the same essential components of lectures and disputations, as well as the sermons. The Oxford theology faculty followed a similar programme. At both universities the disputations were organised in the same manner as in arts, and the lectures were similarly divided into ordinary, extraordinary, and cursory.[17]

We are fortunate in having a manuscript collection of theological disputations from the 1280s which allow us to know the content of some of these acts. The manuscript was compiled by a scholar who was first at Cambridge in the years preceding 1285, and then at Oxford in the latter half of the decade. Still later he included *questiones* from the University of Paris, probably copied from another manuscript or, less likely, while he was a student there as well. Our scribe might have been a friar, which would explain his movement between Oxford and Cambridge.[18]

The disputed questions show the breadth of theological interests and the unity of enquiry at both Oxford and Cambridge. An unknown master disputed 'Whether the idea in God has reason (understanding) of everything universally or particularly or integrally?'[19] Master Grenesby, possibly a Dominican, asked 'Whether essence and person are the same thing according to the thing?' and 'Whether person is that thing itself according to the thing which is essence, and whether relation constitutes essence?'[20]

Other topics included Christology. 'Whether the body of Christ was immediately after the resurrection in its glorified

---

[16] For a list of *sermones ad clerum* see *GBk* B, II, p. 77 (1519–20) and p. 140 (1527–8). For an English university sermon, see *GBk* B, I, p. 65 (1493). This was for William Atkynson, who later translated the *Imitatio Christi* for Lady Margaret Beaufort (*BRUC*, p. 22).

[17] Gibson, *Statuta*, pp. cix–cxii; A. G. Little and F. Pelster, *Oxford Theology and Theologians c. AD 1282–1302*, OHS 96 (Oxford, 1934), pp. 29–52; Reg. Aa, p. 28 (1449) and p. 227 (1457).

[18] A. G. Little and F. Pelster, *Oxford Theologians*, pp. 10–18.

[19] Little and Pelster, *Oxford Theologians*, p. 112, 'Queritur utrum idea in Deo habet racionem alicuius tocius universalis vel particularis vel integralis'.

[20] Little and Pelster, *Oxford Theologians*, p. 112, 'Queritur utrum essencia et persona sint idem secundum rem' and 'Queritur [utrum] persona sit id ipsum secundum rem quod essencia et utrum relacio constituat essenciam'. For Grenesby, see *BRUC*, p. 270.

form? Whether one person is nobler than the others in the Godhead, as Arius posited? Whether, the soul being separated from the body of Christ, the body of Christ was the same flesh as before?' and 'Whether the body of Christ by the quality of glory was incapable of suffering after the resurrection?' This last was by Ralph of Walpole, then Archdeacon of Ely and later Bishop of Norwich and Ely.[21]

Mariology and the Immaculate Conception were debated: 'Whether when the angel announced and the Holy Spirit overshadowed the Virgin, she was cleansed from sin, and whether this occurred at the time of conception or before, in such a way that she was not bound to sin afterward? Whether the virgin conceived without male seed and whether she gave birth while remaining intact?' The Albigensian heresy was recalled when the Franciscan Thomas of Bungay disputed 'Whether God made the world or some creature?' and angelology was represented by 'Whether angels seeing God see all things which are in him?'[22]

Unlike the disputations, we have no certain evidence for Cambridge lectures in the thirteenth century. The statutes speak only of the Bible and the *Sentences* of Peter Lombard, the two standard works in all of the theology faculties of Christendom. Peter Lombard lived *c.* 1100 to 1160 and studied first at Bologna and later at Reims and Paris, where in the last year of his life he became bishop. His *Sentences* were very much a product of that turbulent and fertile period in theology, philosophy, and law. A contemporary of Peter Abelard, the Lombard was one

---

[21] Little and Pelster, *Oxford Theologians*, p. 114, 'Queritur an corpus Christi fuit simul post resurrecionem in sua forma gloriosa', p. 107, 'Queritur an una persona sit nobilior alia divinis, sicut ponit Arrius', p. 106, 'Queritur utrum anima separata a carne Christi fuit caro univoce que prius', and p. 114, 'Queritur an corpus Christi post resurreccionem per dotem glorie fuit impassibilis'. For Walpole, see *BRUC*, p. 612.

[22] Little and Pelster, *Oxford Theologians*, p. 106, 'Queritur utrum angelo nunciante et spiritu sancto obumbrante virginem, fuit mundata a fomite peccati et hoc sive in tempore concepcionis sive ante, ita quod non habuit post necesse peccare. Queritur an virgo conceperit absque virili semine et utrum peperit manente integritate', p. 105, 'Queritur utrum Deus fecit mundum an aliqua creatura', p. 114 'Questio est utrum angeli videntes Deum vident omnia que in eo sunt'. For Bungay see *BRUC*, p. 106. The Carmelite Thomas Maldon, prior in Cambridge *c.* 1370, also held for the Immaculate Conception. J. H. P. Clark, 'Thomas Maldon, O. Carm: A Cambridge Theologian of the Fourteenth Century', *Carmelus*, 29 (1982), 224.

of the early exponents of the scholastic method, whereby issues were treated by marshalling the teachings of Scripture, the Church Fathers, councils, and theologians in a systematic way that took into account the role of reason. Lombard set forth the problems and opinions and presented what by the thirteenth century were, for the most part, uncontroversial resolutions. The *Sentences* is organised into four books: the first treats the Trinity, providence, predestination, and evil; the second deals with angels, demons, the Fall, and the roles of grace and sin; the third treats Christ's incarnation, the redemption, and the Decalogue; and the fourth discusses the sacraments and the 'four last things', death, judgement, heaven and hell.

Generally dispassionate, the *Sentences* was clearly written, organised, and documented, and provided a ready plan for theological discussion on the contentious points of Christian Doctrine. It quickly became a popular text and was widely glossed in the twelfth century, and in the thirteenth was the subject of numerous commentaries. With its statutory use in all theology faculties, which in effect required every doctor of theology to have written his own commentary, the copies of the text and commentaries are legion. In 1518 Erasmus observed quite correctly that 'there be almost as many commentaries upon the Master of Sentences as be names of divines'.[23] By the late thirteenth century these commentaries followed the Lombard less closely, but used his organisation and authorities as their *point de départ* while concentrating on the many theological writings of the years following 1160.

There are few commentaries on the *Sentences* that we can positively attribute to the Cambridge faculty. Bishop Bale, a sixteenth-century antiquary and former Carmelite, records the existence of many that have since been lost. Others were written by friars with other university affiliations, making it difficult to say what if anything is distinctly Cantabrigian. The Augustinian John Godwick took his BTh. at Cambridge in 1359, but his DTh. was from Oxford. To which do his *Disceptiones theologiae*

---

[23] The best edition of the Lombard's *Sentences* is in the *Spicilegium Bonaventurianum* (Grotta-ferrata, Rome, 1971); CWE, *Correspondence of Erasmus*, VI, no. 858, p. 74; F. Stegmüller, *Repertorium Commentariorum in Sententias P. Lombardi* (2 vols., Würzburg, 1947).

belong?[24] Nicholas Bottlesham, a Carmelite, is a similar case: prior of the Cambridge house, but BTh. of Oxford and DTh. of Paris. His commentary (now lost) on the *Sentences* could show a diversity of sources and influences.[25] His coreligionist John Baconthorpe had nearly identical credentials and lectures in the three universities.[26]

In general the Cambridge friars, an international group, followed the theological traditions of their orders. Franciscans worked in the Augustinian–Bonaventurian–Scotist traditions, the Dominicans were usually devotees of Thomas Aquinas, and the Augustinians followed Giles of Rome.[27] Everybody, of whatever order, read the Fathers of the Church. Roger Marston, OFM and Cambridge lector *c.* 1269–71 was typical of his order in this Augustinian and Bonaventurian bent.[28] Giovanni di Casali, OFM and Cambridge lector in 1340–1 dealt with the questions of grace and predestination in the same tradition.[29] William Morys, OFM, at Cambridge *c.* 1407, owned the commentaries on the *Sentences* by his confrères William of Ockham and Gregory of Rimini.[30]

But there were exceptions, and the friars were only slightly less eclectic in their readings than the secular theologians. Robert Orford, a Franciscan at Cambridge *c.* 1284–6 was an early follower of Aquinas.[31] The Carmelites and Augustinians showed particularly diverse tendencies. Thomas Maldon of Essex was prior of the Carmelite house in 1369–72 and held the DTh. of Cambridge. A close examination of his *Lectura* on Psalm 118 shows him to have been of the Augustinian school, but with a reliance on the Dominican Thomas Aquinas. His sources, however, were even more varied: the Fathers and a host of pre-fourteenth-century authorities, along with Aristotle, and to a lesser extent Ovid, Pliny, Seneca, and Valerius Maximus.[32] Of the Augustinians, John de Clare, prior in 1304, owned

[24] *BRUC*, p. 261.   [25] *BRUC*, p. 80.   [26] *BRUC*, pp. 669–70.

[27] N. R. Ker, 'Cardinal Cervini's Manuscripts from the Cambridge Friars', *Xenia Medii Aevi Historiam Illustrantia oblata Thomae Kaeppeli, OP*, I, ed. R. Creytens and P. Künzle, Storia et Letteratura, Raccolta di Studi e Testi 141 (Rome, 1978), pp. 51–71.

[28] *BRUC*, pp. 393–4.   [29] *BRUC*, p. 125.

[30] *BRUC*, p. 414; Ker, 'Cervini MSS', pp. 62–3. Vatican Library MSS Ott. Lat. 69 and 2088.

[31] *BRUC*, p. 435.   [32] Clark, 'Thomas Maldon'.

Aquinas' *Sentences III, Prima secundae, Contra gentiles,* and Gregory's *Moralia in Job.* His confrère, Thomas Penketh, a BTh. of Oxford, incepted in theology at Cambridge in 1468. After returning to Oxford to lecture, he went to Padua in 1474 and became successively professor of metaphysics and, in 1476, professor of theology. He returned to England in 1480 and died in London in 1487. One of the greatest Scotists of his era, Penketh edited the *Opera omnia* of the Subtle Doctor (sojourns in Italy were not reserved for budding English humanists). He was also the author of commentaries on the *Sentences* and *Metaphysics,* as well as a *de arte sermocinandi.* [33]

Another very active Augustinian was John Capgrave, who took his DTh. in the 1420s, and was later a prior provincial of the order and confessor to Humphrey, Duke of Gloucester. After leaving Cambridge he wrote several vernacular saints' lives and spiritual treatises and royal biographies. His surviving theological works also date from after his Cambridge years: commentaries on *Genesis, Exodus, Kings,* and *Acts.* [34]

Secular masters have left even fewer commentaries on the *Sentences*; the best sources for their studies are the private library inventories and those of the colleges to which they belonged. The records of fellows' gifts to Pembroke College show the diversity of authorities that ran through theological study among the seculars. John de Tynmouth gave *c.* 1380 Peter Comestor's *Historia,* a glossed Psalter, a book of sermons, several works of canon law and logic, Averroes' and Aquinas' commentaries on the *Physics,* and Augustine's *De trinitate* with other works. [35] The variety of enquiry and its unity with the liberal arts and law is evident. John Botelsham, MA, DC and Cn.L *c.* 1400, master of Peterhouse and Bishop of Rochester showed more specific taste in giving Aquinas' *Summa* and Gregory's *Pastoralia.* [36] His contemporary John Norwich gave Aquinas as well, with Grosseteste's *Dicta,* Gregory's *Homilies, Dialogues,* and

---

[33] *BRUC,* p. 136; Ker, 'Cervini MSS', pp. 67–8, Vatican Library MSS Ott. Lat. 196, 202, 211, 229, the latter annotated by his confrère John Toneys *c.* 1500 (*BRUC,* p. 590). For Penketh, see *BRUC,* p. 448 and Corpus Christi College, Cambridge, MS 423, pt II, ff. 1r.–13r.

[34] *BRUC,* pp. 121–2; *DNB,* III, 929–31; P. Lucas, 'John Capgrave, OSA (1393–1464), Scribe and Publisher', *TCBS,* 5 (1969), 1–35.

[35] *BRUC,* p. 601.   [36] *BRUC,* p. 76; Pembroke MSS 122–4.

Pastoralia, and a sermon collection.[37] Michael de Causton, DTh.
by 1361, took a more Franciscan line with Scotus on *Sentences
I* and *IV*, as did John Spencer, MA by 1409, with Bonaventure
on *Sentences I* and *II*.[38] In the middle of the fifteenth century
Nicholas Stokesley, BCn.L and Richard Grene, BTh., gave
Scotus on *Sentences III* and Ludolph on *Sentences IV*, respectively.[39] Pembroke College purchases were equally diverse. In
1438 they bought Aquinas on *Sentences I–II*, in 1471 his *Sentences*
and *Secunda secundae*, and in 1473 the Scotist Francis de Meyronibus' *Sentences II–IV*.[40]

Other libraries show the same lack of pattern. Peterhouse in
1418 chained the Lombard and the commentaries of de Meyron-
ibus, Robert Cowton, OFM (who had studied at Oxford under
Scotus himself), Thomas Bokyngham, DTh. of Oxford and a
secular master of Merton College, and Aquinas himself. The
University Library in 1424 had the commentaries of Lombard,
Tarantarius, Aquinas, Bonaventure, and John Baconthorpe, a
Carmelite of Oxford, Paris and Cambridge who rejected many
of the doctrines of Aquinas.[41] Clare College received gifts of
Aquinas from Robert Scolys, and Scotus from John
Millyngton.[42] In the 1440s Clare bought Scotus' *Sentences II*
and *IV*, and by the end of the century possessed Sutton's and
Cowton's as well. Thomas of Sutton was a Mertonian who
later joined the Dominicans. He was a strong Thomist, and the
first three books of his commentary defend Aquinas against
Cowton's attacks; the fourth book takes the offensive against
Scotus himself.[43] King's College's inventory in 1452 shares this
eclecticism, as does that of Queens' in 1472. St Catharine's
benefaction from its founder Robert Wodelarke differs in having
a whole shelf of Aquinas, and only Scotus on *Sentences I* and
IV.

A codex written by the secular Gerald Skypwith of Pembroke
contains a selection characteristic of the books found in one of

[37] *BRUC*, p. 428; Pembroke MSS 175, 223, 230, 242, and 245.
[38] *BRUC*, p. 128; Pembroke MS 201; *BRUC*, p. 544.
[39] *BRUC*, pp. 559 and 269.
[40] See the college library catalogues in the bibliography.
[41] *BRUC*, pp. 669–70.
[42] *BRUC*, pp. 512–13 and 417.   [43] *BRUO*, III, pp. 1824–5.

these medieval college libraries. Written before he took his BTh. in 1463–4, his dated transcripts show the progress of his studies during the years for which the statutes prescribed the study of the *Sentences*: in 1459 Giles of Rome's *De peccato originali*, in 1460 de Meyronibus' *De indulgentiis*, and in 1461 Scotus on *Sentences II* and de Meyronibus' *Questiones de ente*. Skypwith included in the margins an excellent series of notes for finding and organising the material, and at the end of each tract *questiones* for use in disputations. As in the manuscripts of the arts faculty, *questiones* for ready use in the Schools were included in countless theological manuscripts. [44]

A secular theologian less interested in scholastic disputations was John Clynt, DTh. of Gonville Hall *c.* 1425–53, and later vicar of Saffron Walden in Essex. Clynt owned Albertus' *Super ethica*, Aquinas' *Secunda secundae* and *De veritate*, William de Montibus' *Sermones*, a collection of the mystic Richard Rolle, Bernard, Augustine, Gregory and other works. [45] Clynt gave the Albertus to Gonville Hall, but on his death in 1462 many of his books passed onto the market and were bought by John Warkworth of Peterhouse.

Warkworth was an MA and BTh. of Oxford who came to Cambridge *c.* 1460 and took his DTh. in 1463. He was master of Peterhouse from 1473 until his death in 1500, leaving his large library to the college where it remains today. His books reflect his forty years in Cambridge, and include. Aquinas on the *Sentences*; the *Summa*; Lombard himself; Scotist commentaries on Aristotle; Anselm, Augustine, Origen, and Gregory; many commentaries on Scripture by fourteenth-century writers; Bernard of Clairvaux; several sermon collections; many texts for the liberal arts; and Augustine of Ancona's polemic against Marsilius of Padua (with a table of *questiones* at the end). [46] Warkworth read his books carefully, correcting scribal errors, and in some of them included extensive marginal notes of his own. In his copy of Aquinas on the *Sentences* he annotated the sections on clerical tonsures, indulgences, purgatory and the

---

[44] *BRUC*, p. 532; Pembroke MS 255.   [45] *BRUC*, pp. 141–2.
[46] *BRUC*, pp. 618–19.

anointing of the dead. [47] His collection of Anselm's writings shows a particular interest in the Christological and Mariological questions, and his Augustine *De trinitate* was closely read. [48]

A contemporary of Warkworth was the Scotsman Gavin Blenkynsop of Pembroke, MA 1459 and DTh. 1475. His library included Fitzralph's attacks on the mendicants along with Scotus, Aquinas, Boethius, Lombard, Augustine, Burley, Seneca, and a Bible, among other items. These manuscripts, and the signs of use they contain, are not very different from those of Thomas de Lisle, OP and Bishop of Ely a century before. [49]

The scholastic theology disputed by Warkworth and others relied on the Lombard, Scotus, Aquinas, and a host of earlier medieval authorities. They were universally familiar with the Fathers, especially Augustine and Gregory. There is little evidence that nominalist theology was read. Scotism was very popular and dovetailed neatly into the Aristotelian commentators Andreas and Canonicus who were so widely read in the faculty of arts. This popularity seems to have become more marked in the mid- and late-fifteenth-century libraries and personal collections. Men like William Chubbes, fellow of Pembroke and first master of Jesus College wrote a *Declaracio super Scotum in secundo*, [50] and John Colyns of Queens', MA 1497, bought from his college Scotus on *Sentences I–IV*. [51] King's College paid an unnamed Franciscan doctor of theology for an internal lecture on Scotus, from 1499 to 1503. [52] But even in these same years Queens' established a college lectureship that was specifically to deal with Aquinas' commentary on the *Sentences*. [53]

Cambridge theologians were aware of the great controversies of their age, as they showed in their thirteenth-century dispu-

---

[47] Peterhouse MS 49, esp. ff. 192r.–v, 290r., 284r., 290v., and 291r. This manuscript was written for Richard de Ykeworth of the Ipswich convent, and was later bought by Henry Totil of Gonville Hall *c.* 1425–34 for £2, and was used as a caution in 1440.

[48] Peterhouse MS 246, esp. ff. 43r.–52r.

[49] *BRUC*, p. 66; Peterhouse MS 239; for Lisle, see *BRUC*, pp. 370–1 and Peterhouse MSS 38, 46, 58, and 117.   [50] *BRUC*, p. 136; CUL MS Kk. I. 18.

[51] *BRUC*, p. 152; Queens' College Archives, Bursar's Roll (Bd. 42).

[52] King's College Muniments, *Mundum Book* 9, f. 38r., 39r., etc. (1499–1503).

[53] Queens' College Archives, *Journale*, I, f. 23r. (1484–5), *Item magistro songar pro lectura sancti thome*, 33/4 (*BRUC*, p. 542).

tations. Their opinion was sought by the papacy during the Avignon schism.[54] The mendicant controversies that had such immediate consequences on the university were also reflected in the texts that were studied. The Franciscan Thomas of York, lector in the Cambridge *studium* in 1255–7, wrote against William of St Amour's attacks on the friars.[55] The University Library and Pembroke College had Richard Fitzralph's anti-mendicant polemics. Queens' in 1472 owned the attacks by William Woodford, OFM, on Fitzralph, and the University Library had the rejoinder of William Myllyngton, DTh. and first provost of King's, to Bishop Reginald Pecock.[56] Pembroke had seven tracts by Wyclif, and Queens' had Woodford's and John Welles' (the 'Hammer of Heretics') attacks on him. John Deveros, an Irishman of Corpus Christi College and DTh. 1399 was a particularly active opponent of Wyclif's heresy,[57] although Thomas Markaunt of the same college owned several of Wyclif's logical works.[58] John Warkworth, reading St Bernard in the 1460s, took care to note in the margins material in the text that could be used to refute the Lollards.[59] Adam de Stockton, the Augustinian lector *c.* 1375, copied Wyclif's *Determinatio* in 1379–80 and described the author as *venerabilis doctor*. Later, Stockton altered it to read *execrabilis seductor*.[60]

Along with systematic theology, the theologian studied the Bible. The distinction here was not sharp, since Scripture provided the grist of scholastic theology and points of exegesis were often disputed questions. But the Bible itself was read and lectured on as the foundation of the aspiring doctor's curriculum. This cannot be overemphasised given the continued strength of the Reformation historiographical tradition. What humanists like More and Erasmus said about the blindness towards Scripture in the universities was directed against the

---

[54] W. Ullmann, 'The University of Cambridge and the Great Schism', *Journal of Theological Studies*, n.s. 9 (1958), 53–77.

[55] BRUC, p. 666.   [56] BRUC, pp. 417–18.

[57] BRUC, p. 186.   [58] BRUC, pp. 390–1.

[59] Peterhouse MS 166, purchased in 1462, ff. 11r. and 48v.

[60] BRUC, p. 557; Trinity College, Dublin MS A.5.3., which also contains a commentary on Ovid, Walley's *Breviloquium*, Fulgentius' *Mythologia*, and Grosseteste's *De oculo morali* (copied in Cambridge in 1377).

methods used by scholastic commentators, the importance of
the scholastic disputation, and the ignorance of the Greek and
Hebrew originals. It was the approach to Scripture that was
their target, not the lack of Scriptural study. These polemics
were popularised in a blunt form by Frederic Seebohm in his
The Oxford Reformers (1867), a book that continues to be read
and continues to mislead its readers. [61]

The problem turns on what is understood by the 'literal'
interpretation of Scripture, and what authority Church tradition
has in exegesis. The western tradition of the medieval Cambridge
theologians came from the teachings and example of the early
Church Fathers Jerome, Augustine, and Gregory. Despite all
the developments of the twelfth and thirteenth centuries, these
three Fathers were still widely read in the primary texts in
medieval Cambridge. Augustine's *De doctrina christiana* was
especially important for the medieval exegetes, as it was for the
humanists, for it set out the application of the liberal arts and
philosophies for Scriptural study. In biblical interpretation
Augustine insisted on the sufficiency of Scripture as read and
interpreted in and by the Church Universal. This reliance on
traditio – the councils, popes, and early Fathers – was, and remains,
the shibboleth separating Catholic and reformed hermeneutics.
These differing ideas of just what *sola scriptura* included were to
cause many problems. Both sides always insisted that they were
giving primacy to the 'literal' interpretation of the Word. [62]

For Augustine, the literal was distinguished from the spiritual
meanings by being concrete and historical. However, it also
encompassed metaphor, while the purely allegorical levels
involved gradations of meaning which lead the reader to a
fuller understanding of God's teaching. As John Warkworth
noted on his copy of Augustine, the Trinity can be understood
'through metaphor'. [63] Within these boundaries Augustine as
neo-platonist put the spiritual sense above the literal, while
steering a middle course between them. They were both neces-

[61] Frederic Seebohm, *The Oxford Reformers* (London, 1914).
[62] The best introduction to medieval exegesis is still B. Smalley, *The Study of the Bible in the Middle Ages*, 2nd edn (Oxford, 1952).   [63] Peterhouse MS 246, f. 77r.

sary, both 'real', and the literal meaning was the foundation from which you proceeded.

As late antique theology developed the spiritual levels were specified to include the allegorical (the hidden meanings for understanding faith), the moral (how it applies to daily life), and the anagogical (how it relates to Christ's saving work). By the thirteenth century both Bonaventure and Aquinas acknowledged the legitimacy of all of these levels, while assigning priority to the literal. Aquinas in the *Summa* elaborated that by the literal sense words signified things, but by the other senses these things signified other things in turn. In Aquinas' terms, the late medieval theologians were much concerned with the literal interpretation of the Bible. To those who came later like Latimer, Ridley, Bilney, and Barnes, such a definition of 'literal' was nonsense. They brought a new grammar to the discussion, and did not admit much of the post-Apostolic tradition. When Ridley and Cardinal Pole said 'literal' in 1550, they were no longer speaking the same language.

The Bible was studied in several ways in the universities; first, through glosses (either interlinear or marginal), and from the twelfth century through commentaries. The glosses, usually anonymous, continued in use throughout the middle ages, and at Cambridge appear in nearly all the surviving library inventories and among the books of many masters. They range from those on specific books, like the *Glossa super epistolas Pauli* given to The King's Hall in 1435 by Henry VI, to the four volumes of the *Glossa ordinaria* (a twelfth-century work with much earlier antecedents) given to Pembroke by its master John Sudbury, BTh. by 1419, who died in 1436.[64]

The biblical commentaries differed in being more extended discussions of each verse. These included the works of the four Latin Fathers, as well as more contemporary approaches. Aquinas' *Cathena aurea* remained popular, as did the late-twelfth-century commentary of Stephen Langton, subsequently Archbishop of Canterbury (1207–28). Nicholas Gorran, a Parisian Dominican of the later thirteenth century also wrote

[64] *BRUC*, p. 565.

on the whole Bible, a work that was even more widely circulated among the libraries and masters of late medieval Cambridge.

The thirteenth century saw an evolution of the simple glosses into the *postilla literalis*, a more complete treatment. The earliest and one of the most enduring was that of the French Dominican Hugh of St Cher and his colleagues.[65] A BTh. of Paris and later a cardinal, his *Postilla* contained exegetical notes on both the literal and spiritual senses. This Hugh, also called 'of Vienna', was an ubiquitous authority in late medieval Cambridge, but even he took second place to the Franciscan Nicholas of Lyra or Lyre, a Frenchman who died of the Plague in 1349.[66] Lyra knew Hebrew and was familiar with the Jewish commentators, especially Rashi, and in spite of being a Franciscan relied heavily on Thomas Aquinas. Lyra treated the literal meaning as the most important and decisive, the basis of any mystical interpretation. His influence in late medieval Cambridge was unparalleled. Every library lists him, usually several copies of his multi-volume work, and he appears regularly among Cambridge scholars' books until the Reformation, including several printed editions.

Other exegetes included Robert Holcot, OP, who also died in the Plague of 1349.[67] An Oxford DTh., he wrote his *Postillae super librum Sapientiae* while teaching in Cambridge. Although some of his works were condemned for Ockhamist tendencies, this Scriptural commentary shows more Thomist leanings. Holcot had many Cambridge readers. There were many other biblical works in circulation, but none of them enjoyed the influence of Lyra, Hugh of St Cher, Gorran, or Holcot, except perhaps the Church Fathers themselves.

Sadly, little has survived to show more fully the exegetical

[65] C. Jerman, 'Hugh of St Cher', *Dominicana*, 44 (1959), 338–47; R. G. Lerner, 'Poverty, Preaching, and Eschatology in the Revelation Commentaries of "Hugh of St Cher"', in *The Bible in the Medieval World, Essays in Memory of Beryl Smalley*, ed. K. Walsh and D. Wood (SCH Subsidia 4, London, 1985), pp. 157–89.

[66] C. V. Langlois, 'Nicholas de Lyre, frère mineur', *Histoire littéraire de la France*, 36 (1927), 355–400.

[67] *BRUC*, 309–10; *DNB*, IX, pp. 1007–9.

work of the Cambridge theology faculty. Thomas Maldon's *Lectura* on Psalm 118, mentioned above, worked in the Augustinian tradition, and he gave full scope to both the literal and spiritual senses of his text.[68] We know of two Austin Friars, John Godwick, BTh. by 1359, and John Capgrave, DTh. *c.* 1430, who wrote biblical commentaries now lost.[69] Pierre Barrière and Thomas Gasele, Augustinians from the Toulouse province compiled a table in Cambridge *c.* 1420 for Albert of Padua's *Postilla super evangelia quadragesimalia.*[70] William d'Eyncourt, a Dominican at Cambridge *c.* 1331–44 composed a *Lectura super Ecclesiasten* that cites by name over fifty authors, including Vitruvius, Livy, Adelard of Bath, and Aristotle's *Poetics.* An Englishman in spite of his name, d'Eyncourt took a firm stand against vivisection through an appeal to experience.[71]

Surviving manuscripts include Thomas de Lisle's glossed copy of John's gospel. Lisle, a Dominican and Bishop of Ely in the 1340s, noted the meaning of the Greek ΛΟΓΟΣ, written in an untrained hand.[72] John Argentein of King's in the late fifteenth century had a copy of the *New Testament* for which he wrote an 'Interpretations of Difficult Hebrew Words', a Latin glossary of transcribed Hebrew words.[73] But these are exceptional; it seems that there was little study of Greek or Hebrew before the arrival of Erasmus.

Biblical commentaries written outside Cambridge survive in abundance. John Warkworth bought John Lathbury on *Lamentations* in 1462, possibly from the estate of John Clynt. A large, fifteenth-century English book, it has frequent annotations in at least two hands. The text is largely concerned with the allegorical and moral aspects of Jeremiah,[74] and the sections on the Blessed Virgin have continuous notes, concluding with the pious observation, 'England is the dowry of the Most Blessed

[68] J. H. P. Clark, 'Thomas Maldon, O.Carm., a Cambridge Theologian of the Fourteenth Century', *Carmelus,* 29 (1982), pp. 205–6.   [69] *BRUC,* pp. 261 and 121–2.

[70] *BRUC,* pp. 41 and 253; Bordeaux, Bibliothèque municipale MS 44.

[71] Balliol College, Oxford, MS 27(2). See R. A. B. Mynors, *Catalogue of the Manuscripts of Balliol College, Oxford* (Oxford, 1963), pp. 19–20; *BRUC,* p. 187.

[72] Pembroke MS 38, f. 1r. See also Pembroke MSS 141–2.

[73] Oxford, Bodleian Library, Rawlinson MS G. 25 (s.c. 14758).

[74] Peterhouse MS 23; cf. f. 48r., 'nota exposicionem literalem'.

Mary.'[75] In another place Warkworth particularly noted the definitions of comedy and tragedy, and then jotted down as a possible disputation topic 'Whether a theologian is licitly able to use poems and philosophical writings for his ends?'[76] Warkworth also owned Holcot's popular commentary on *Wisdom*, bound with Peter Comestor's *Allegoriae historiarum veteris testamenti*, a well-known history of pre-Christian times.[77]

Hugh Damlett, DTh. and master of Pembroke 1447–50, gave his college a copy of Hugh of St Cher on St Paul's *Epistles*, a text with fifteenth-century annotations on the parts that refer to what makes a good preacher and priest.[78] The same commentary was owned by Thomas Westhaugh, DTh. by 1448, who later joined the Sheen Charterhouse in 1459 and the Bridgettines at Syon in 1472. This codex also contains Gorran on the *Epistles* and a list of *questiones*, and was annotated in at least three hands.[79]

Preaching was the third requirement for degrees in theology, both *ad clerum* and at St Paul's Cross in London. Homiletic literature came in several forms. There were treatises *De arte praedicandi*; collections of sermons for the liturgical year by established preachers, either in full or in outline; *distinctiones*, which were *florilegia* of biblical and patristic passages; and *exempla*, illustrative stories for particular points of doctrine.[80]

Very few volumes of *De arte praedicandi* were produced in medieval Cambridge, and only one significant text survives, Guillermo Traversagni di Savona's *Rhetorica nova*, the classically based oratorical handbook designed for and illustrated by Christian homiletics.[81] The Irish Austin Friar Geoffrey Schale, DTh.

---

[75] Peterhouse MS 23, ff. 67r.–101v., esp. f. 68v. for symbolic correspondence of Mary and fire, ff. 99v.–101r. of Mary and the zodiacal signs, and f. 77r.–v. for Mary's knowledge of geometry and astronomy. [76] Peterhouse MS 23, ff. 111v.–112v.

[77] Peterhouse MS 99. See also Pembroke MS 181 of Holcot, with marginalia in several fifteenth-century hands.

[78] *BRUC*, p. 176; Pembroke MS 186. [79] *BRUC*, pp. 630–1; Pembroke MS 173.

[80] S. L. Forte, 'A Cambridge Dominican Collector of *Exempla* in the Thirteenth Century', *Archivum Fratrum Praedicatorum*, 38 (1958), 115–48.

[81] See pp. 120–1. Several Oxford manuscripts show the relationships of rhetoric, the arts, and preaching. Thomas Eborall, DTh. of Oxford, owned by 1443 a large, well-used codex written in several hands, containing a collection of philosophical and theological extracts for use in preaching (BL Royal MS 5.C.iii). Propositions from the *Metaphysics*, *Physics*, *De anima*, *Ethics*, *Politics*, and *Rhetoric* are included. In addition to several theological texts, there

c. 1422, copied Thomas Walley's *De modo sermocinandi*, bound with a sermon on Matthew, a treatise on the virtues and vices, and a glossary. It was a book for practical use.[82] John Warkworth also bought a copy of Walley's work in 1462.[83]

Sermon collections were found in abundance in the college libraries, and among the masters the great collections of the twelfth- and thirteenth-century preachers retained their appeal until the Reformation. John Irby, DCn.L 1479–80, had Nicholas of Aquavilla's *Sermones dominicales*, with schemata of points of doctrine included in the lower margin by the scribe. This codex is well annotated in several fifteenth- and sixteenth-century hands, and includes a note of a certain Dr Penkey's opinion on consanguinity, something of interest to a canon lawyer.[84] John Warkworth had several collections of sermons, including those of the early-thirteenth-century Frenchmen John of Abbeville and Philip the Chancellor.[85] The sermons of the Fathers were read throughout Cambridge's medieval history, both in full and excerpted in *florilegia*.

By the fifteenth and sixteenth centuries other preachers gained wide circulation as well, like the English Dominican John Bromyard, and the Italian Hugh de Florido Prato. William Scalys of King's, DTh. 1506, owned Hugh's *Sermones dominicales*, and John Sampson of King's, who earned his DTh. in 1517 and died the same year, left his college Bromyard, Hugh, and the sermons of Jacobus de Voragine and Nicholas de Blony.[86]

One last sermon collection is noteworthy for being on the watershed of the new learning. Robert Ridley of Pembroke, MA, DTh. 1517–18, and uncle of the celebrated reformer, was

---

is Giles of Rome's *De regimine principum*, (with many marginal notes), an abbreviation of Boethius' *De consolatione philosophiae*, and two treatises on preaching. A similar collection was given in 1478 to Thomas Stevenson, MA of Oxford, by the estate of William Gray, Bishop of Ely and humanist diplomat. It contains three preaching manuals, Eusebius' *Homelia*, Coluccio Salutati's *De saeculo et religione*, and two of his rhetorical treatises (BL Royal MS 8.E. xii. *Ex libris* on f. 218r.).

[82] *BRUC*, pp. 510–11; CUL MS Gg.6.20, ff. 107r.–111v.; N. Toner, 'Augustinian Spiritual Writers of the English Province of the Fifteenth and Sixteenth Centuries', *Sanctus Augustinus* (*Analecta Augustiniana*), II, 520–1.

[83] Peterhouse MS 200.   [84] *BRUC*, p. 327; Pembroke MS 263, f. 33r.

[85] Peterhouse MSS 174 and 135. MS 135 was probably bought while he was at Oxford.

[86] *BRUC*, pp. 509–10 and 505.

of the circle of humanist scholars of the early sixteenth century, and was one of the university men licensed in 1513–14 by papal bull for preaching throughout England. While a young theologian he copied the cycle of sermons of the eleventh-century Benedictine monk William of Merula.[87] The sermons are fairly easy, but with a heavy allegorical content. At the end of the codex Ridley copied short pieces by John Chrysostom and Laurentius Valla's sermon *De mysterio eucharistie*. The old and the new were peacefully meeting, as they usually did before the 1520s.

Books of *exempla* and *florilegia* were also popular, like the Oxford Dominican Simon de Boraston's *Distinctiones pro sermonibus faciendis*, and John Lathbury's *Distinctiones*.[88] William Rawson of Pembroke, DTh. 1490, gave the college on his death unbound 'materials for sermons' (and 'scholastic and disputation material together with scholastic lectures'), and books that included John Bromyard and the more recent Leon de Utino's *Sermones*.[89] The earliest and best surviving collection of *exempla* from Cambridge was compiled by an anonymous Dominican in the 1260s. It contains 315 brief stories for use in sermons. The collection is of special interest for its mention of events in and around Cambridge, including several apparitions that took place within Blackfriars Cambridge.[90]

Other examples of Cambridge sermon literature are known only from references, like the Carmelites William Coxford, a DTh. *c.* 1376, and Nicholas Kenton, DTh. *c.* 1440, who wrote out their required 'sermons to the clergy'.[91] A surviving reference from late in our period is the sermon at St Paul's Cross of John Chapman, DTh. of Queens' in 1480.[92] John Sowle, a Carmelite who took his doctorate in 1483, was a friend of John Colet and preached many sermons at St Paul's Cross, which are unfortunately lost.[93]

[87] *BRUC*, pp. 480–1; CUL MS Dd. 5.27, f. 1r., 'exscripsi hunc librum ab alio in pergameno scripto, in bibliotheca maiori universitate Cantabrigie latere aquilonari', which is a very rare detail.

[88] Both were owned by Warkworth, Peterhouse MSS 91 and 160.

[89] *BRUC*, pp. 473–4.

[90] BL Royal MS 7.D.1 selections printed in S. L. Forte, 'A Cambridge Dominican Collector of *Exempla* in the Thirteenth Century', *Archivum Fratrum Praedicatorum*, 38 (1985), 115–48.

[91] *BRUC*, pp. 165 and 336.   [92] *BRUC*, p. 131.   [93] *BRUC*, p. 542.

Other elements of theological study were more peripheral and do not appear in the statutes, but were quite familiar to the medieval master. Peter Comestor's *Historia scholastica*, a twelfth-century universal history with special reference to salvation history, was known to all. Cassiodorus' and Eusebius' histories circulated to a much lesser extent. Ludolph of Saxony's *Vita Jesu* also had a large readership in late medieval Cambridge, as it did on the Continent. Written in the mid-fourteenth century, it relied heavily on the allegorical and moral interpretations of Scripture.[94] Pious biographies were also written by Cambridge men, like Osbern Bokenham, DTh. who wrote a *Legendys of Holy Wummen*, and Henry Hornby, master of Peterhouse in 1501 and chancellor of Lady Margaret Beaufort, who wrote Latin lives of Jesus and Mary.[95] Concordances and indices of the Bible were also readily available.

This, then, gives an outline of theological enquiry in medieval Cambridge. Much more that was written remains to be properly identified, and careful research into the use, transcription, and marginalia of Cambridge theological manuscripts would focus this sketchy view. But the outline is there, in the balance between the speculative theology of the Scotists and Thomists, the biblical scholarship, and the practical application that both streams of theology found in the preaching of the theologians outside of the university.

[94] M. I. Bodenstedt, *The Vita Christi of Ludolphus the Carthusian* (Washington, 1944).
[95] *BRUC*, pp. 69–70 and 313–14.

Chapter 8

LAW

There were two faculties of law in medieval Cambridge, canon and civil. The first was the scientific study of the law of the Roman Church as found in Gratian's *Decretum (c.* 1140), and succeeding collections promulgated by the papal curia. Gratian compiled the mass of biblical passages, conciliar documents, papal bulls, patristic opinions, and theological authorities dealing with Church law and, by applying the scholastic method, organised them into a *summa*. It was soon complemented by many glosses and commentaries by lawyers, known as 'decretists'. In the following decades more opinions were added to these through the growing activity of the papacy and councils. In 1234 Pope Gregory IX issued a definitive collection of these post-Gratian materials, called the *Decretals* or *Liber Extra*. The process was continued by Pope Boniface VIII in 1298 with his *Liber Sextus*, and by John XXII in 1317 with the *Clementinae*. [1]

The faculty of civil law studied Roman law as it was rediscovered by Italian lawyers in the eleventh and twelfth centuries. The texts of the *Corpus juris civilis* included the Code of Justinian (529; 534), a collection of laws; the *Digest* (533), the opinions of many Roman jurists; the *Institutes*, a textbook for students in four parts; and the *Novellae*, the legislation of Justinian after 534. In the middle ages the *Code* and the *Digest* were the principal texts used.

In the earliest Cambridge statutes of *c.* 1250 the only legal

---

[1] The most accessible introductions in English to canon law are the entries in the *NCE*: 'History of Canon Law', III, pp. 34–47; L. E. Boyle, 'Decretals', IV, pp. 705–7 and 'Decretists', IV, 711–13; and C. Duggan, 'Decretals', IV, pp. 707–9 and 'Collections and Decretals', IV, 709–11. For Oxford see J. L. Barton, 'The Study of Civil Law before 1380' and L. E. Boyle, 'Canon Law before 1380' in *HUO*, I, pp. 519–64.

faculty mentioned is 'Decrees', or canon law. But the faculty of civil law was probably already forming in that year, for by *c.* 1255 Simon de Asceles was a DCL of Cambridge, having previously taken his BA at Oxford.[2]

None of the Cambridge civil law statutes appears to date from before the late thirteenth century. To proceed to the bachelor's degree the scholar had to have spent five years in the faculty (or seven if he was not first a regent in arts) of which three years were to be spent hearing lectures on the *Digestum novum* (the last part of the *Digest*). The baccalaureate also involved being licensed and required lecturing on at least four books of the *Institutes*, both the text and glosses, and then the *Digestum novum*. For the doctorate a total of eight years in civil law was required, or ten years if one had not first been a regent in arts. The candidate should have heard the course of ordinary books twice and extraordinary once, that is, the *Digestum novum*, and have given cursory lectures on both that work and the *Institutes*. He had to oppose and respond, and oaths were to be given by the doctors concerning the candidate's learning and behaviour.[3]

The faculty of canon law is mentioned in the statutes of *c.* 1250, but nothing is said of the curriculum.[4] The course of study changed in the early fourteenth century as more authoritative collections were promulgated by the papal curia. In the thirteenth century the course was based on Gratian's *Decretum* and the commentaries by the Decretists, and on the 1234 *Decretals* of Gregory IX and his commentators, the Decretalists. With the increase of authoritative texts in the following years the relation of the ordinary and extraordinary lectures (in the case of law, the afternoon lectures) changed. In the thirteenth century the *Decretum* was read ordinarily in the morning, and the *Decretals* extraordinarily in the afternoon. The *Decretals* achieved ordinary status by the early fourteenth century when the *Liber sextus* and the *Clementinae* were introduced into the

[2] Hackett, pp. 29–33; *BRUC*, p. 17.
[3] *Docs.* I, no. 93, pp. 363; no. 96, pp. 364–5; no. 120, pp. 375–6.
[4] Hackett, p. 202.

afternoon, extraordinary lectures. This was the case in other European universities as well.[5]

By the late fourteenth century the requirements demanded that a bachelor hear three years of civil law lectures, or five if he had not been a regent in arts, and hear lectures on the *Decretals* for three years and the *Decretum* for two. If he were a priest, monk, or beneficed clerk (and thus forbidden to study civil law by the bull *Super specula* of Honorius III in 1219) he could be exempted from the civil law requirement by dispensation. The statutes accordingly make allowances for years of civil law study to be commuted into canon law study.[6]

The bachelor then gave cursory lectures while preparing for the doctorate, which required five years of civil law study, another three hearing the *Decretum*, including two courses on the tracts *De simonia, De matrimonio, De poenitentia*, and *De consecratione* (all sections of the *Decretum*), and two years hearing cursory lectures on the Bible. The candidate also had to give cursory lectures on any of these above mentioned tracts, as well as on the *Decretals*. As in arts and theology, oaths were required from the masters as to the suitability of his morals and learning, and he had to oppose and respond in disputations. These disputations had only a small role in legal studies, and were not required of bachelors. The incepting doctor also swore that he would, during his regency, give a carefully prescribed course of lectures which included ordinary lectures on the *Liber sextus*, *Decretals 'Antiquae'* and *Clementinae*, and extraordinary ones on the *Decretals*.[7]

[5] L. E. Boyle, 'The Curriculum of the Faculty of Canon Law at Oxford in the First Half of the Fourteenth Century', in *Oxford Studies Presented to Daniel Callus*, OHS, n.s. 16 (Oxford 1964), pp. 147–9.

[6] *Docs.* I, nos. 100–1, pp. 365–6. For *Super specula*, see *CJC*, II: X.50.10.

[7] *Docs.* I, no. 104, pp. 367–9 and no. 122, pp. 376–7; Boyle, 'Curriculum', pp. 143–50. The *Antiquae* were the five books of the *Decretals* of Gregory IX (1234). Thus the full list of texts, as contained in the *Corpus Iuris Canonici*, ed. E. Friedberg (Leipzig, 1879–81), comprised:

  1 The *Decretum*, originally the *Concordia canonum discordantium*, of Master Gratian of Bologna (*c.* 1140), Friedberg, I.

  2 The *Decretals*, or Liber Extra(vagantium), hence 'X', Friedberg, II, in five books.

  3 The sixth book, the *Liber Sextus*, of Pope Boniface VIII, 1298.

  4 The *Clementis papae V. Constitutiones*, the *Clementinae*, named after Clement V but promulgated by John XXII in 1317.

  5 The *Extravagantes* of John XXII, published after his death in 1334.

Law

In the later fourteenth century about 40 per cent of the recorded secular scholars were in law, and almost no friars, who were prohibited from studying civil law, and chose to avoid canon law. In the fifteenth century the documented percentage in civil law dropped, and between 1450 and 1500 lawyers seem to have comprised about one third of the university, with canonists outnumbering *civilistae* two to one.[8]

The university faculties were interdependent, with some study of liberal arts expected of lawyers (although from the beginning exceptions were made), and biblical studies required of all canon lawyers. The law faculties were in one sense undergraduate, since no previous degree was absolutely required. But earning an MA made the statutory demands lighter, and many law students who never took a degree in arts had some experience in them. The graces from 1458 onwards record lawyers who list, as a rule, two years study of arts towards their *forma* in either civil or canon law. In 1467 eight of twelve lawyers mentioned in graces did so, and in 1502 fifteen of eighteen bachelors of civil or canon law had some exposure to the arts, usually about two years. This meant they left the arts faculty just before they would normally become sophisters, and participate in disputations. The Oxford graces from the same period tell the same story. These fifteenth-century statistics are very different from what we know about the entire period 1200–1500, when only 18 per cent (282 of 1587) of the Cambridge lawyers are known to have studied the arts.[9] That low figure is probably due to the scanty evidence of the thirteenth and fourteenth centuries.

These students may have entered the universities with the intention of moving on to law, or they may have chosen this more lucrative field having initially planned to complete the programme in arts. The celebrated Paston family provides two examples. John Paston went up to Trinity Hall as a pensioner in the late 1430s, was married by 1440, and then moved to Peterhouse. On taking his BA he went to the Inner Temple in

[8] Aston *et al.*, 'Cambridge Alumni', pp. 58–61.
[9] *GBks* A, B I and II, and I *passim*; Reg. Aa and G, *passim*; Aston, 'Oxford Alumni', p. 58, n. 134. The fellows of King's College were forbidden to enter law until after their MA and necessary regency. *Docs.* II, 483.

1443 to read common law. His son Walter went to Oxford in the late 1470s, and when he found that he was not immediately eligible for ordination, went no further than the BA, before going to the Inns in London as well.[10] Although these men went on to common law, there were doubtless many who made the easier transfer from arts to law within the university. Nobody seems to have graduated in civil law and then become a common law practitioner, however.[11]

When arts studies are mentioned in lawyers' graces, it is to transfer credit towards law degrees. At Cambridge Richard Thornton in 1458 was given permission to count two years in arts as one in civil law; William Hornby in 1460 was given entry as a BCn.L with five years' study in civil and canon law and four in arts, all done at Oxford; in 1476 one student entered as BCn.L with four years' study of arts and an equal time in canon law, while others of the same year recorded no arts study at all; Thomas Ormeston in 1494 entered BCn.L with five years of arts and three of civil law; and the list could go on. Similarly mixed graces are found at Oxford for this time.[12] Many students in the arts faculty had access to law texts while at Cambridge, or owned their own copies. They were frequently used as cautions for artists taking arts degrees, and also appear in the private libraries of many masters of arts.

The relationship between the arts and law seems to have been the same at Oxford and Cambridge. Several years in arts provided the grammatical and logical tools useful in the higher faculties, and many lawyers had at least this minimal background. The graces survive only from the middle of the fifteenth century; nearly half the lawyers mentioned in them had some terms in the arts faculty.

The faculties of civil and canon law were in theory and practice twinned, although they voted separately in congrega-

---

[10] *Paston Letters,* ed. N. Davis, I, 21 and 215–16; II, 365–7. See also H. S. Bennett, *The Pastons and their England* (Cambridge, 1951), pp. 106–7.

[11] J. L. Barton, *Roman Law in Britain,* Ius Romanum Medii Aevi, Pars V, 13a (Milan, 1971), pp. 27–8.

[12] *GBk* A, pp. 15 (1458–9), 29 (1460–1), 118–19 (1476–7), and *GBk* B I, p. 70 (1494). For Oxford, see Reg. Aa, pp. 151 (1453), 153–4 (1453), and Reg. G, f. 108v. (1 Feb. 1511) and f. 113r (11 March 1511).

tion. Some took both doctorates simultaneously, *in utroque jure*, and most of the canonists had those statutory years in civil law as well to provide instruction in procedure. The unity of purpose of the two was ultimately due to the vocational nature of both. As a then current adage had it, 'the canonist ignorant of the civil law is worth little; the civilian ignorant of canon law is worth nothing at all'.[13] Most law students were preparing for careers in the Church (not necessarily as priests) whether practising canon law or in administration; that is where the money and jobs were. The *civilistae* who entered royal service seem to have been in the minority. The convocation of the province of Canterbury in 1417 tried to help in the promotion of university graduates to benefices, but the decree never took effect because the universities refused to accede to the stipulation that scholars could earn the BCn.L in seven years with no study of civil law. A similar decree by the province in 1438, without that stipulation, required all patrons for ten years to confer benefices only on graduates, and 'vicars-general, commissaries, and officials should be chosen from graduates in civil and canon law'.[14]

This careerism, which drew qualified secular scholars away from the study of theology, was a concern from the fourteenth century on. The preachers John Bromyard, Thomas Wimbleton, and John Wyclif deplored this development, as did Thomas Gascoigne, the mid-fifteenth-century Oxford chancellor.[15] The lawyers also made enemies within the university by not paying the bedells regularly for their ordinary lectures, and usurping the prerogatives of doctors while only bachelors.[16] Royal intervention attempted to check these abuses. Similar problems arose at Oxford when the lawyers assumed the title 'magister' for those with bachelor's degrees. The arts men, holding a majority

[13] 'Canonista sine legibus parum valet, legista sine canonibus nihil', P. Hughes, *The Reformation in England* (London, 1950–4), I, p. 73.
[14] Cooper, *Annals,* I, pp. 159 and 187.
[15] G. R. Owst, *Preaching in Medieval England* (Cambridge, 1926), pp. 32–3; J. Wyclif, *Sermons,* ed. J. Loserth. Wyclif Society, IV (London, 1890), p. 172; Gascoigne, p. 220; for the opposite view, that theologians were favoured in papal promotion *c.* 1320, see H. E. Salter, *Snappe's Formulary,* OHS 80 (Oxford, 1923), pp. 303–5.
[16] *Docs.* I, no. 76, p. 356 (1415), no. 105, p. 369 (by 1390), and no. 176, p. 402 (1414).

in congregation, eventually forced the lawyers to abandon their pretensions.[17]

Both canonists and *civilistae* did well among Cambridge men appointed to prebendaries. In the Court of Arches (the provincial court of the Archbishop of Canterbury that sat in St Mary-le-Bow in London) Cambridge lawyers provided five medieval deans, Oxford sixteen. In general, promotion was less certain for Cambridge men than for their Oxford counterparts. Cambridge lawyers did much better in the late fifteenth and early sixteenth century, however.[18] During that period time spent in the courts frequently counted towards a supplicant's degree requirements. At Oxford in 1456 Thomas Eggecombe, BCL, was admitted BCn.L with only one year 'in this university in canon law', but with six years 'in study and practice in the Court of Arches'. A master R. Berde, licensed in civil law, took his doctorate in canon law at Cambridge 'with private study and long practice' in 1473, and in 1517 John Thomas had six years study of civil law 'with practice in the Court of Arches' counted towards his baccalaureate in civil law.[19] If there is any doubt as to the canonical purpose of civil law studies, this grace, along with many others, is a corrective.

The great centre of medieval law study was Bologna, to which a number of English students had travelled in the twelfth century. There was always some intercourse between English and Italian lawyers, but less than between theologians. The most frequent travellers were the friars, who avoided law by preference and profession. Such English connections as there were with Bologna in the thirteenth century seem to have been through Oxford men. There were a few Cambridge men, like Gilbert de Yarwell, who became rector of the ultramontane 'nation' in Bologna in the 1340s, and William Comyn (1298–9) who may have taken a doctorate there before coming to Cambridge.[20] The graces from the fifteenth century show a scattering of Englishmen who returned from Bologna and

---

[17] *Epistolae academicae Oxon.*, ed. Anstey, I, 218–19, 243–4, and *passim*.
[18] Aston *et al.*, 'Cambridge Alumni', pp. 75–7.
[19] Reg. Aa, pp. 259–60 (1456); *GBk* A, p. 97 (1472–3); *GBk* Γ, p. 159 (1517–18).
[20] Hackett, pp. 93–4; *BRUC*, p. 664 (Gilbert de Yarwell); pp. 153–4 (William Comyn).

incorporated their degrees in Cambridge, as did a lawyer from Cologne in 1468 and Orleans in 1473.[21] There are no Oxonians known to have been in Bologna during those years, although there were Oxford lawyers who studied at Padua and at the papal curia.[22] The early sixteenth century shows a great increase in these continental connections at both universities.[23]

Neither English university produced a lawyer of international reputation during the middle ages.[24] In nearly 300 years before the abolition of canon law at the Reformation (which also effectively de-emphasised civil law), Cambridge had only a handful of noteworthy legal writers. John de Acton, DCL Oxford and DCn.L of Cambridge by 1350, engaged in a *questio disputata* in the form of a fictitious suit between two Cambridge friars, and also wrote a gloss on the Legatine Constitutions of Otto and Ottobuono.[25] Walter de Elveden, DCL by 1350 and benefactor of Gonville Hall, was Acton's opponent in the fictitious suit, and also wrote a *tabula* on the *Decretals*. Elveden was also known for his astronomy, and his private library included civil and canon law, medicine, logic, and a Bible.[26]

Gonville Hall was not a haven for lawyers, but an impressive collection of legal texts survives in its library. It was also the home of the most influential medieval Cambridge lawyer, William Lyndwood, who was a pensioner, a paying resident, possibly after completing his degrees. Doctor of both laws by 1407, lawyer, clerk, and diplomat, Lyndwood wrote the *Provinciale seu constitutiones Angliae* (1422–30), a digest of synodal constitutions and the like down to Henry Chichele, that was used throughout England until the Reformation.[27]

Legal studies were accommodated in nearly all the Cambridge

---

[21] *GBk* A, pp. 67 (1467–8), 97 (1472–3), and 209 (1468–87); *GBk* B, I, pp. 54, 70, 124, and 133 (1493–1500).

[22] Aston, 'Oxford Alumni', p. 26; Reg. Aa, pp. 72–3, 75, 93, and 116.

[23] *GBk* Γ, pp. xxvi–xxvii.

[24] Boyle, 'Canon Law at Oxford', pp. 161–2; Aston *et al.*, 'Cambridge Alumni', p. 64.

[25] *BRUC*, p. 2 (John de Acton); *DNB*, I, p. 67; Gonville and Caius MS 483/479, ff. 275r.–v., and end flyleaf.

[26] *BRUC*, pp. 210–11 (Walter Elveden); BL Royal MS 9.E.II, ff. 156v.–157v.

[27] *BRUC*, pp. 379–81 (William Lyndwood); C. R. Cheney, *Medieval Texts and Studies* (Oxford, 1973), pp. 158–84; *DNB*, XII, pp. 340–2. 'The two canonists with the most importance for the study of English practice are John de Acton and William Lyndwood', Barton, *Roman Law in Britain*, pp. 79–80, n. 294; Brooke, *Gonville and Caius*, pp. 26, 33–7.

colleges, but were particularly important in Trinity Hall and The King's Hall. The former was founded exclusively for law by Bishop Bateman in 1350, and so it remained in spirit for many centuries. The King's Hall, one of Trinity College's predecessors, was a special centre of civil law studies, although it is not so described in its statutes. Its bias is not surprising, however, since 'one of its chief aims was the provision of a reservoir of educated personnel for royal service'.[28] King's College, from its foundation in the 1440s, was also a haven for lawyers. The important Oxford colleges for legal studies were New College (1379) and All Souls (1441).[29]

The studies themselves turned on the *Corpus juris civilis*, the *Corpus juris canonici*, and the many canon law commentaries and auxiliary texts that thorough study demanded. There are few surprises, and except for specifically English collections like Lyndwood's and the texts of English constitutions, they would be familiar to any continental lawyer; Hostiensis, Johannes Andreas, Hugutio, Raymund of Peñafort, Azo, and Odefredus all recur in the library inventories.

There was also widespread reading of extra-statutory pastoral manuals that included canon law material. Elucidating both theological and legal points, these were practical guides for anyone in parish work and, 'the plain fact is that most of those who attended university in the thirteenth and fourteenth centuries ended up with *cura animarum* of one sort or another'.[30] Among the more popular pastoral manuals was the Cambridge master Richard de Leycestria's *Qui bene praesunt* (c. 1215), the fourteenth-century *Oculus sacerdotis* of William of Pagula (Oxford DCn.L 1321), and its 'second edition', the *Pupilla oculi* ('Apple of the Eye') by the Cambridge chancellor John de Burgh in 1384.[31] Many of these books were in college and

---

[28] A. B. Cobban, 'Theology and Law in the Medieval Colleges of Oxford and Cambridge', *Bulletin of the John Rylands Library*, 65 (1982), 68–9.

[29] Cobban, *The King's Hall*, intro. and chapter 1.

[30] L. E. Boyle, 'Aspects of Clerical Education in Fourteenth Century England', *The Fourteenth Century*, *Acta*, 4 (1977), 20–1.

[31] *BRUC*, III, pp. 1436–7 (William of Pagula); *BRUC*, p. 367 (Richard de Leycestria), and p. 107 (John de Burgh); L. E. Boyle, 'The *Oculus Sacerdotis* and Some Other Works of William of Pagula', *Royal Historical Society Transactions*, 5th series, V, 1955, pp. 81–110; W. A. Pantin, *The English Church in the Fourteenth Century* (Cambridge, 1955), pp. 195–202.

private libraries. Richard Dunmow gave Pembroke College in 1390 his civil law books and the *Pupilla oculi*. The large collection Robert Wodelarke gave on founding Catharine Hall in 1472 included the *Pupilla oculi*, Grosseteste's *De oculo morali*, and an anonymous *Confessionale*. The 1472 inventory of Queens' shows a *Pupilla oculi*. John Warkworth, MA of Oxford and DTh. of Cambridge (1463) and later master of Peterhouse was not a lawyer and possessed no legal texts, but his library of fifty-four books (and an astrolabe) included the *Pupilla oculi* (with tables), and anonymous tracts entitled '*Summa penitencie, Forma penitentis, Speculum Penitentie*, and *Manuale sacerdotis*'.[32]

The law faculties continued to attract young men until the Reformation. It was considered excellent training for those hoping for advancement within both the Church and in royal service. Others, with no intention of taking a degree in law, found it useful for parochial work, and a valuable complement to theology. Although law never had the prestige of theology or the arts within the university, its practical value assured its appeal.

[32] *BRUC*, p. 198 (Richard Dunmow), 645–6 (Robert Wodelarke), 618–19 (John Warkworth, many of whose manuscripts survive in the Peterhouse library). Peterhouse MS 120, the *Pupilla oculi*, includes an 18th-century note attacking Aquinas, 'Maledictus Thos. omnes eius asseli...' f. 76v.

Chapter 9

MEDICINE

Medieval European medicine was based almost entirely on Greek and Arab authorities. Galen and Hippocrates were translated and commented on by Arab and Jewish physicians in the early middle ages, and these works entered Europe in Latin translations from the areas where the Arab and Latin cultures met. By the twelfth century the great Latin medical schools were in Salerno and Montpellier. Medicine was acknowledged as a superior faculty in the northern European universities in the thirteenth century, but it attracted few scholars in England.

Medicine was by far the smallest of the superior faculties at Cambridge. We know of only 59 physicians at Cambridge before 1500, and only 157 at Oxford. They were almost exclusively seculars.[1] The small number made for a continuing problem of insufficient regent physicians at both universities. The Oxford statutes from the fourteenth century include a clause, 'since there are few teachers in medicine', and in 1450 congregation elected as scrutator for the medical faculty William Lambton, a scholar in theology, because there were no MDs in the university that year.[2]

At Cambridge the statutes assume a shortage, and graces excusing lectures missed are common. William Skelton, MA, was excused from part of his *forma* when incepting MD 'because there are not enough doctors teaching'. The situation was exacerbated by the widespread graces between 1462 and 1500

[1] Aston *et al.*, 'Cambridge Alumni', p. 62, n. 147; Aston, 'Oxford Alumni', pp. 10–11; see also V. Bullough, 'The Mediaeval Medical School at Cambridge', *Mediaeval Studies*, 24 (1962), 160–8, and G. Lewis, 'The Faculty of Medicine', in *HUO*, III, 213–56.

[2] Gibson, *Statuta antiqua*, p. 42 (by 1350); Reg. Aa, p. 13 (1450).

excusing graduates from their regency lectures in medicine. The new physicians were eager to leave the university and start practising as soon as they took their degrees; some had already practised before they came up. The locations of Cambridge and Oxford did not help the problem, since they could not compete with London for potentially lucrative practices.[3]

There was no Cambridge medical faculty when the first statutes were promulgated *c.* 1250, but by 1270–80 the first mentions of physicians appear, and the earliest medical statutes date from this time. The bachelor of medicine was required to have heard lectures for three years on the whole of the *corpus medicinae*, or five if he had not been a regent in arts, and to have obtained the usual depositions from his masters. The bachelor could then lecture cursorily.[4]

The doctorate in medicine demanded graduation in arts and at least five years' study 'here or elsewhere', and hearing once Honeien ben Ishak's *Isagoge in artem parvam Galeni*, Philaretus' *De pulsibus*, Theophilus' *De urinis*, and one of the books of Isaac Iudaeus (*Liber urinarum, De dietis particularibus, Liber febrium,* or *Liber viatici*) and Nicholas' *Antidotarium*. Galen's *Tegni*, the *Prognostica,* the *Aphorismi*, and *De regimine acutorum* were to be heard twice with commentaries. The candidate also had to read cursorily at least one book on theory and one on practice, oppose and respond in the Schools, obtain depositions on his character and his learning, both in theory and practice, from his masters, and have two years of medical practice. The required texts were frequently read in the Continental universities also, although the absence of Hippocrates and Dioscorides is surprising. However, the university library and Peterhouse both had the works of both men, along with those of Avicenna, Averroes, and Razi.[5]

Medical science was divided between surgery and medicine, and medicine in turn was divided at both universities into

---

[3] *GBk* A, p. 77 (1469–70); J. M. Fletcher, 'Linacre's Lands and Lectureships', in *Linacre Studies: Essays on the Life and Works of Thomas Linacre c. 1460–1524,* F. Maddison, M. Pelling, and C. Webster, eds. (Oxford, 1977), pp. 118–19; Hackett, pp. 123n. and 130n.

[4] Hackett, pp. 29–30; cf. Bullough, p. 164; *Docs.* I, no. 90, p. 362.

[5] *Docs.* I, no. 119, p. 375; Bullough, p. 165.

theory and practice by the statutes and graces.[6] Cambridge gave licences to practise surgery, but had no prescribed course for surgeons. No student would have gone to university expressly to study it, and those who took the licence in surgery usually had few years of study.[7] Surgery was not open to those in major orders, since cautery and incision were prohibited to them by a canon of the Fourth Lateran Council of 1215.[8]

Although the connection between the arts and medicine was not as strong in the English universities as in Italy, it was genuine. Medicine was taught as a philosophy that relied on established authority and put little emphasis on observation and experimentation.[9] Most physicians seem to have had less than an MA, and a Cambridge grace of 1473 called for all medical students to attend a course in the arts in addition to these lectures in medicine. James Barkley incepted MD in 1503 with only two years' study of arts, although others, like Thomas Hall in 1507 and William Butts in 1518 have very complete *formae*. At Oxford the impression is similar; most physicians had less than an MA.[10]

The strongest link between medicine and the arts was the study of astronomy. Astronomy (or astrology, its 'practical' side) was seen as the handmaid of medicine, and Chaucer's doctor of physic was well-versed in the quadrivium. This, as we have seen, was evident in the personal libraries of many medieval university physicians, as well as in the graces. In 1462 William Philipps claimed that he spent 'four years in medicine and astronomy in the university' in his grace for an MB at Oxford, and a Merton fellow who disputed on the bipartite

---

[6] Gibson, *Statuta antiqua*, p. 41 (by 1350). See the disputed questions in *Reg. Mert.*, ed. Salter, I, 441 (1513): (1) medical science is not well-divided into speculative and practical; (2) one's disposition ought to be kept midway between health and sickness; (3) a coleric complexion is the most noble. The disputant, John Blysse, studied medicine in the faculty.

[7] C. H. Talbot, *Medicine in Medieval England* (London, 1967), p. 20.

[8] *CJC*, x.3.1.50; Talbot, *Medicine*, pp. 20 and 206–8.

[9] C. H. Talbot and E. A. Hammond, *The Medical Practitioners of Medieval England – A Biographical Register* (London, 1965), p. ix; cf. N. G. Siraisi, *The Arts and Sciences at Padua: The Studium of Padua before 1350* (Toronto, 1973), p. 9.

[10] *GBk* A, p. 97 (1473); *GBk* Γ, p. 13 (1503), 58 (1507), and 163 (1518); Aston, 'Oxford Alumni', p. 10.

division of medicine was described as 'learned in both astronomy and medicine.[11]

The study of medicine was provided for in the statutes of Peterhouse, King's College, Clare Hall, Pembroke, Gonville Hall, and Queens' College. At Peterhouse this interest was particularly strong, with holders of medical degrees appearing regularly from the college's foundation through to the end of the middle ages, more so than at any other Cambridge college.[12] The library catalogue of 1418 included fifteen chained medical codices, and three that were allowed to circulate among the fellows. Among its successful physicians was Roger Marshall, MD by 1454, who was also an astronomer. He later moved to London, married, and served as physician to Edward IV. In 1472, five years before his death, he gave books to Peterhouse, Gonville Hall, and King's College, collections heavy with medical and astronomical books, but also including some natural philosophy and grammar. He composed tables of contents in several other medical manuscripts, and was the author of the *Lanterne of fisicians and of surgeons*, perhaps the earliest English vernacular medical work by a university man.[13]

Clare Hall listed only four medical works in its short inventory of *c.* 1440, although it produced Robert Yaxley, one of the more illustrious graduates of Cambridge from that period. BA 1477, MA 1482, and MB 1486–7, he was admitted as a fellow of Clare in 1489 and received his MD in 1497–8, as well as a DCL the following year. He was a founding fellow of the College of Physicians in 1518 and, never having taken major orders, was married. His name appeared on a grace granted to

---

[11] Reg. Aa, p. 366 (1462); *BRUO*, IV, 53. There are several other men so described; G. Chaucer, *Canterbury Tales*, General Prologue, 411–14:

> With us ther was a Doctour of Phisik
> In al this world ne was ther noon hym like
> To speke of phisick and of surgerie
> For he was grounded in astronomye.

[12] *Docs.* II, 22 (Peterhouse), 483 (King's College), 132 (Clare Hall), 226 (Gonville Hall); Attwater, *Pembroke*, p. 10; A. B. Cobban, 'Medieval Cambridge Colleges', pp. 9–10.
[13] *BRUC*, pp. 392–3 and 679; New York Academy of Medicine Library, formerly Phillips MS 9418; Brooke, *Gonville and Caius College*, p. 36.

Thomas Harwood in 1520–1, another fellow of Clare, who had studied 'medicine here and in London with Doctor Yaxley'.[14]

At Oxford, New College, Balliol, and Magdalen all had provision in their statutes for fellows to study medicine, but it was at Merton that the link between the arts and medicine was most apparent.[15] The statutes included no mention of physicians; Archbishop Pecham complained of their presence during his visitation in 1284. Yet throughout the middle ages Merton outshone any other English college in number of medical graduates. It was a natural concomitant of Merton's strong scientific tradition.

There was some interchange of medical students between Cambridge, Oxford, and the Continent in the late fifteenth and early sixteenth centuries. The Peterhouse fellow and astronomer Thomas Deynman, MA 1473–4, took his MB overseas and then returned to Cambridge for his MD in 1485–6. Another royal physician, on his death in 1501 he left a bequest of medical texts to Peterhouse, eight of which survive.[16]

The astronomer John Somerset studied arts at Oxford ('apud nos trivialibus intendentem') in the first years of the fifteenth century. After becoming a *sophista generalis* there he, 'fleeing the Plague', removed to Cambridge where he was described in 1418 as a 'teacher of arts and grammar and a bachelor of medicine' and an MD by 1428. He claimed to have studied medicine in London, Paris, and Rouen as well. He served Humphrey, Duke of Gloucester, and Henry VI. His astrological knowledge is demonstrated by his co-authorship of the 1441 horoscope of the nativity of Henry VI.

Somerset was closely connected with the affairs of both universities. Oxford sought his aid in 1447, 1450, and 1452 to secure the library promised them by the late Duke Humphrey, and Oxford also wrote to thank him for his own gifts. He gave a copy of the *Isagoge* of Honeien ben Ishak to Merton College. The author of several (lost) medical treatises, he was a benefactor

[14] *BRUC*, pp. 664–5; *GBk* Γ, pp. 191 (1520–1) and 245–6 (1529–30).
[15] G. Louis, 'Faculty of Medicine', *HUO*, III, 215–16.
[16] *BRUC*, p. 187.

of Pembroke Hall (Avicenna's *Canon* and Almanasor)[17] and Peterhouse (medicine and theology). He helped to write the foundation statutes of King's College. At the end of his life he became embittered towards Cambridge, and particularly King's College, for their ingratitude after all he had done to help them (the problem was over ownership of land). In a massive outpouring of self-pity, he wrote an autobiographical lamentation of eighty-three hexameters, his 'Complaint...concerning the ingratitude of Cambridge University', which he begins like a latter-day Jeremiah, 'What did I do to you Cambridge, once so sweet? / Oh! You turn your face away'.[18]

Twice married, Somerset exemplifies the diverse concerns in politics and academics open to the physician. Like most university men, the physicians were from the 'middling classes' who saw in medicine a potentially lucrative profession that was increasingly prestigious in the fifteenth century.[19] They were more worldly than most scholars, and were more likely to marry. Although there was not a single medieval English physician of European reputation, they did very well at home, regularly filling the office of royal physician by the fifteenth century. The Cambridge physicians wrote little, and that was mostly derivative from other sources. Oxford and Cambridge had a monopoly on medical practice in England by authority of Parliament in 1421. This remained unchanged until 1523, when the recently founded College of Physicians in London was given the privilege of licensing physicians within seven miles of the City.[20]

One last noteworthy Cambridge physician was John Argentein, the author of the poem on the arts studies. Born in Cambridgeshire in 1442, he came up to King's College from

---

[17] Pembroke MS 137.
[18] Somerset's 'Queremonia' is printed in Thomas de Elmham, *Vita et gesta Henrici Quinti*, ed. T. Hearne (Oxford, 1727), app. iv, pp. 347–50; for Somerset see *BRUC*, pp. 540–1;

> Quid tibi, Cantabrigia, dudum dulcissima, feci?
> Vultum divertis O!

Epistolae academicae Oxon., ed. Anstey, II, pp. 253–4, 285–7, 313–14; CUL MS Ee.III.61, ff. 155r.–171r.
[19] Talbot and Hammond, p. ix; Nicholas Carr, regius professor of Greek in the 1550s, took up medicine because it paid better. *DNB*, III, 1080–1.   [20] *Annals*, I, 166–7 and 220.

Eton in Michaelmas term 1458.[21] King's provided an extensive programme of college lectures, and Argentein was one of four scholars put under the supervision of William Wyche, a fellow then twenty-six years old. Like many, he seems to have been an Aristotelian of the Scotist school.[22] Argentein took his BA in 1462 and MA in 1466, and in 1467–8 was a paid lecturer in the liberal arts within King's.[23] He shortly afterwards composed the poem of 154 lines in twelve cantos on the 'eight' liberal arts (he separates perspective from geometry), the three philosophies, and medicine.[24] Medical study while in the faculty of arts was not unprecedented, and Argentein pursued it within his own college under William Ordew, a King's fellow, MA 1457 and MB 1462. Ordew was paid to teach both medicine and astronomy in 1457–8, and possibly until he left in 1467.[25] Argentein's training also included 'clinical' observations. In a *Loci communes* he compiled in the 1470s he gives examples of cures he witnessed in Cambridgeshire, including one performed by William Ordew. In the medical canto Argentein speaks in general terms of the Hippocratic and Galenic theories of the balancing of humours and the importance of diet.[26]

On finishing his arts studies Argentein entered the theology faculty, took his BTh. in 1472–3 and was senior proctor of the university in the same year. From 1473 to 1476 he almost certainly went to Padua to study medicine, where he compiled for his own use a collection of medical and astronomical works.[27] Argentein returned to Cambridge from 1476 to 1478 before entering the medical service of Edward IV. He served the young Edward V in the Tower shortly before his murder, and later Richard III, Henry VII (who made him dean of St George's Chapel at Windsor), and Prince Arthur, indicating

[21] Rhodes, *John Argentein*; 'Provost Argentein of King's and His Books', *Transactions of the Cambridge Bibliographical Society*, 2 (1954), 205–12; *idem*, 'The Princes in the Tower and Their Doctor', *English Historical Review*, 77 (1962), 304–6; Leader, 'John Argentein'.

[22] King's College Muniments, *Mundum Books*, III, f. 80v. There is a gap in these records from 1459 to 1467; *BRUC*, p. 654.

[23] *Mundum Books*, V, f. 67v., 'Item Mr. Argentyne lecturis suis infra collegio hoc anno...40s'.

[24] Leader, 'John Argentein', pp. 80–5.

[25] *Mundum Books*, III, f. 81v.; *BRUC*, p. 435.

[26] Bodleian Library, Ashmole MS 1437 (s.c. 8342) item 15 (the pagination is confused). The dated cases are 1471, 1476, and 1477.   [27] New College MS 162.

9 Provost John Argentein's brass in his chantry chapel in
King's College Chapel.

that his political skills equalled his medical. He returned to Cambridge as provost of King's in 1501, became a doctor of theology in 1504 at the age of sixty-two, and died in 1508. His brass survives in the college chapel. Argentein, as a priest, physician, and theologian demonstrates the possibilities of promotion and travel available to a man of modest upbringing but with skill and determination. And he did all of this without ever actually matriculating in medicine at Cambridge, or necessarily taking any medical degree while studying in Padua.

Chapter 10

INTERLUDE AND EXPANSION

THE PLAGUE

In 1348–9 England was ravaged by the first wave of the Black Death. Up to 40 per cent of the population died – a striking percentage no matter how frequently we are reminded of it. Cambridge University was not spared, although curiously there are no contemporary accounts left to us by this literate society, nor are there for Oxford. Scholars suffered and died, but in what numbers we can not be sure. Of the townsmen, the Castle side of the river was almost totally depopulated, and of the other bank perhaps half died.[1]

The enrolment figures for the universities are guesswork before the later sixteenth century. However, the mortality rate at Oxford was far below the national norm, and perhaps the Cambridge scholars too did not suffer a radical drop in absolute numbers. The university population was fluid in the best of times, and scholars had the advantage of being younger (and presumably more resilient) than the average citizen, as well as being more able to flee to the less rat-infested countryside during outbreaks. We have no evidence that the university was suspended during the first killing wave (although it is almost certain that it was for a time) but rather that colleges continued to be founded in the next few years. There was a continuous supply of young men willing and able to begin academic work in the years that followed.[2]

Although the cataclysm of 1348–9 did not cripple Cambridge,

[1] R. R. Williamson, 'The Plague in Medieval Cambridge', *Medical History*, 1 (1957), 51.
[2] W. J. Courtenay, 'The Effect of the Black Death on English Higher Education', *Speculum*, 55 (1980), 697–703.

disease was a continuous problem in the late medieval university. The Plague returned every few years until 1666, as did other contagious diseases such as cholera, influenza, and 'sweating sickness'. The normal mortality rate was perhaps as much as 10 per cent for the first four years of residence.[3] Cambridge shared the problems of all medieval towns: open sewers, rats, filthy streets, drafty rooms, floors strewn with soiled straw, and shared, flea-infested beds. These were compounded by the surrounding stagnant waters of the King's Ditch, and its location near the as yet undrained Fens. There was legislation from the thirteenth century onward that attempted to make the town healthier by prohibiting throwing filth into the streets and waterways. In 1502 the masters of Buckingham College, Trinity Hall, and Clement Hostel were singled out before the town court for having privies which overhung the river. These problems continued into the seventeenth century before being partially alleviated by cleansing the King's Ditch with the flow of water from Hobson's Conduit.[4] The symptoms still persist in vestigial form, and on any warm summer day swarms of mosquitos rise up from the dank standing water in the ditches which lace the otherwise lovely Backs. 'Even by medieval standards, Cambridge was notorious both for the insalubrity of the air and the unhealthiness of the climate.'[5]

As the university records become more complete in the fifteenth century, so do the mentions of plague. Henry VI cancelled a visit in 1441 due to 'the pestilence that hath long reigned'.[6] As in the Oxford records, the omnibus term was *pestis*, and meant any of a panoply of contagious diseases.[7] Sometimes the distinction is made between 'fever' and 'plague'. The former included outbreaks of 'sweating sickness' which occurred at both universities every few years from 1485 to

---

[3] Aston *et al.*, 'Cambridge Alumni', pp. 24–5.
[4] Williamson, 'Plague in Cambridge', pp. 51–8, citing *Annals*, I, *passim*. In the 1580s the question, 'An pestis communicatur proximis' was disputed at Cambridge. CUL Sel.I.II, p. 15.
[5] Cobban, *King's Hall*, p. 220.   [6] *Annals*, I, pp. 199 (1441).
[7] J. F. D. Shrewsbury, *A History of the Bubonic Plague in the British Isles* (Cambridge, 1970), p. 127.

1551. The latter, *pestis*, was sometimes specified, as in a Cambridge grace of 1520–1 which refers to absence caused by 'fear of the bubonic plague'.[8]

A chronicle from Ely shows the deep awareness of this fear in Cambridge. An entry for 1462 tells how an eleven-year-old boy, walking at dusk in the street between King's College and Clare Hall encountered an old man with a long beard and shabby clothes. The boy, unable to flee, was told by the man to come back the next night, when he would tell him 'some news'. This was repeated the next night, and on the third night the old man ordered the boy to tell everyone that there would be an unparalleled plague and famine within two years. The prophecy must have seemed reasonable, for the boy was examined afterwards by William Myllington, DTh. and first provost of King's, who concluded that the child had spoken with a ghost.[9]

The early sixteenth century was particularly unhealthy in both Oxford and Cambridge. In 1506 the Cambridge chancellor John Fisher preached before Henry VII and attributed 'the weariness of study and learning in Cambridge' in the 1490s partially to the Plague.[10] 1506 was the year in which the fewest degrees were conferred in the decade. The problem only increased in the next decade. The outbreak of 1513, which drove Erasmus first to nearby Landbeach and finally from Cambridge altogether, was severe enough to cause the postponement of Michaelmas term until 6 November. Study done elsewhere sufficed for students' requirements, 'provided

---

[8] *GBk* Γ, p. 188 (1520–1), 'ob metum morbi inguinarii'; see also J. A. H. Wylie and L. H. Collier, "The English Sweating Sickness (*Sudor Anglicus*): A Reappraisal', *Journal of the History of Medicine and Allied Sciences*, 35 (1981), 425–45.

[9] *Three Fifteenth Century Chronicles*, ed. J. Gairdner (Westminster, 1880), p. 163. For Dr Myllington, see *BRUC*, pp. 417–18, and G. Williams, 'Notices of William Millington', CAS, *Proceedings*, 1 (1859), 287–328. He was a fellow of Clare Hall in 1462. There were several other apparitions in medieval Cambridge. The glorified ghost of a lector of Blackfriars appeared *c.* 1250 (*The Lives of Brethren of the Order of Preachers*, trans. P. Conway, ed. B. Jarrett (London, 1924), pp. 49 and 257). In 1389 a miracle which occurred during a eucharistic procession next to Austin Friars was followed by a Plague, and a causal link was noted (Thomas Walsingham, *Historia Anglicana*, II, ed. H. T. Riley, Rolls Series 28, I, pt 2 (London, 1864), pp. 185–6.

[10] J. Lewis, *Life of Dr John Fisher* (London, 1855), II, 269.

that they pay the accustomed amount especially for their ordinary lectures'.[11] Michaelmas term was adjourned on 12 November 1518 for the same reason. In 1519 the Queen sent a pursuivant to Cambridge to determine whether the city was infected before she passed through it on her way to Walsingham.[12]

As a rule the outbreaks of contagious disease were worse in summer and autumn.[13] Although the graces at both universities indicate widespread removal to the countryside during these times, there is usually the implication that work was carried on there. Colleges were often particularly well suited for these peregrinations. Walter de Merton's statutes of 1274 provided for continuity should his college be forced to move for any reason, and the college *Register* shows that they frequently availed themselves of this clause: in September 1486, August 1487, October 1487, and every few years after that. The college moved *en masse* to Islip in 1493, where both lectures and disputations were carried out. In 1512 the warden proposed rebuilding a college-owned building in Hampton Poyle, 'for the fellows during plague times'.[14]

Merton was not alone in its wanderings among either Oxford or Cambridge colleges, although the detail is lacking from the Cambridge records. Queens' College had provision in its statutes of 1448 for continuing in exile, King's had a plaguehouse in Grantchester (used as a retreat from possible German air-raids in the Second World War), St John's had a place in the country as did Christ's at Malton, which was given to them by Lady Margaret Beaufort.[15]

The congregations of both universities were very understanding about these absences, and hardly a year went by in which an exemption was not given for time spent 'in the countryside in the time of plague'. In mid-fifteenth-century

---

[11] *GBk* Γ, p. 110 (1513–14), 'ita quod solvantur consueta solvenda maxime pro ordinariis'.
[12] W. G. Searle, *Queens' College*, I, p. 163.
[13] The Oxford statutes of 1549 are specific about the danger during the summer term. Gibson, *Statuta antiqua*, p. 355 (1549).
[14] *Statutes of Oxford*, Merton College, pp. 35–6, 'causis aliquibus emergentibus quae facile numerari non possunt', *Registrum Merton.*, ed. Salter, I, pp. 173 (1493) and 429–30 (1512).
[15] *Docs.* III, 36–7; King's College Archives, *Mundum Books*, 9 (1500–1), f. 28r.;. *VCH*, III, 430.

Oxford these dispensations were as frequent as at Cambridge, as in 1458 when 'all scholars of the arts faculty' were dispensed with twelve ordinary lectures missed the previous Trinity term 'because of fear of the Plague'.[16] In 1519 all members of Oxford's *Aula cervus* were allowed to disperse following the death from plague of one of their members.[17] Sometimes the scholars fled to the other university, as in an Oxford grace from 1449 for an artist who spent two terms and a long vacation in Cambridge 'during the Plague'.[18]

The graces imply that students had access to lectures while elsewhere. When William Browne supplicated for his MA at Oxford in 1453, he offered a year 'outside the city because of the Plague in which he studied in the same faculty'.[19] Richard Reynolds, later a fellow of Corpus Christi College, Cambridge, and a Syon martyr of 1535, mentioned frequent lectures he had given 'in the countryside' when supplicating for his MA in 1508–9.[20] Some Cambridge scholars claimed entire terms, like the priest Richard Wether who, in 1503, was granted permission to take the BA with three terms spent in the countryside (provided he pay the fees for the lectures he never took).[21] That frequent rustication was an impediment to a scholar's progress is certain, but to what extent it caused a decline in standards is difficult to say. Removal from the university was usually a matter of personal choice for all but college fellows. But the death threat was there, and it was a cause for concern throughout late medieval Cambridge.

POPULAR INSURRECTION

The town and university always had an ambivalent relationship, a marriage marked simultaneously by economic advantage, pride, and resentment. The university gave the town rents, clients, jobs, spiritual support, and made Cambridge more than an East Anglian market town. Many scholars were yeomen's sons from the region, and spoke with the same accent. The

---

[16] Reg. Aa, p. 327 (1458).   [17] Reg. H, f. 18r.   [18] Reg. Aa, p. 44 (1449).
[19] Reg. Aa, p. 159 (1453), 'extra villam causa pestis in quo studuit in eadem facultate'.
[20] *GBk* Γ, p. 72 (1508–9).   [21] *GBk* Γ, p. 11 (1502–3).

townsmen founded Corpus Christi College, and collaborated with the university in several parish churches. There were years of tranquil prosperity between the moments of strife.

The tension was always there, and though it usually erupted over specific grievances, it was fuelled by more general divisions: the antipathy of the local for the outsider, the labourer and tradesman for those who do not work with their hands, the layman for the clerk, and the unschooled man for the academician. Cambridge University was born out of such a clash at Oxford in 1209. It was not really a financial division, for most of the scholars were penurious and the town leaders relatively prosperous. After the 1381 riots the Cambridge citizens tried to claim the trouble was caused by the lower classes and outside agitators from Essex, Hertford, and Kent; it was proved, however, that the mayor and bailiffs were actively involved as well.[22]

The fourteenth century shows a pattern of these town–gown fights which led up to the local expression of the popular revolt of John Ball. In 1305 the townsmen broke into several hostels and assaulted masters and scholars. By the new university charter of 1317 the mayor and bailiffs were required to swear to maintain the privileges of the university, which they were not happy to do. 1322 saw a greater outburst, with one scholar killed, several hostels attacked, walls scaled, doors and windows broken, and books carried off. When the university presented the mayor with a writ of their liberties, the rioters threw it in the mud. The King intervened on the side of the university, and the mayor, bailiffs and 319 others (a fantastic number) were tried for crimes against the scholars. In all of these incidents both sides could be guilty of provocation, as in 1371 when scholars were indicted for breaking into houses, assaulting their owners, and stealing fowling nets. When the bailiffs attempted to arrest the malefactors, they were beaten by a gang led by a parish rector and other clerks.[23]

These were the preludes to 1381. On 1 May that year a contingent of townsmen forced the chancellor to execute deeds

[22] *Annals*, I, p. 123 (1381).
[23] *Annals*, I, p. 70 (1304–5), p. 76 (1317), p. 79 (1322), pp. 110–11 (1371); *VCH*, III, pp. 8–12.

under the common seal of the university and the seals of all the colleges renouncing all their privileges. In the future, the university was to be governed by the laws and customs of the borough. On Saturday 15 June a mob gathered, elected captains, and proclaimed that they should destroy the house of William de Wykmer, the university bedell and cut off his head. As the agent of the university with whom they had most dealings, the bedell had evidently had many occasions to earn the hatred of the townsmen. They did not catch him, but they did pillage and destroy his house. The next target was Corpus Christi College, founded by townsmen only twenty-nine years earlier. Perhaps the animosity towards this small college was due to its extensive endowments within the city. For whatever reason, they looted the Old Court and destroyed all the books, charters, and endowments they could find. [24]

The action continued on Sunday with assaults and looting of scholars' properties as well as burgesses who were out of favour. Many old scores were settled. [25] The mob went to Great St Mary's during Mass, where the common chest of the university was kept. Its contents of bulls, charters, and other muniments were burned before an appreciative crowd, that then moved on to the Carmelite friary where another university chest was seized. Then the citizens took all the old university and college documents that remained and made a bonfire of them in Market Square. These intemperate actions indicate both a belief in the ultimate victory of the revolt throughout the kingdom (for surely they knew that the forcibly obtained concessions were meaningless if civil and ecclesiastical authority were restored?), as well as a naive sense of the power of the written word. New deeds made for new law. The sense of pent-up hatred and resentment, and the thrill of apparent victory were exemplified by an old townswoman who threw the ashes of the seized charters into the air and shouted, 'Away with the learning of the clerks! Away with it!'

Authority was not long in reacting. The Bishop of Norwich marched on the city with an armed band and defeated the

---

[24] *Annals*, I, 120–5 (1381), from which the narrative is taken; T. Fuller, *History of Cambridge*, pp. 82–5; *BRUC*, p. 656 (William de Wykmer).   [25] *VCH*, III, 8–12.

rebels, with some deaths and imprisonments. An excommunication of unrepentant rebels was declared by the Bishop of Ely,
and in August the King began an enquiry to punish them.
Parliament was petitioned by the university in November, and
a further enquiry was held. The townsmen submitted. The
coerced deeds were delivered up and declared null and void.
By the final settlement of February 1382 the university was
restored to all its former privileges. It was also given custody
of the assizes of bread, wine, and beer, the oversight of weights
and measures in the town, control of the victuallers, and other
privileges previously belonging to the town. The town did not
have its remaining privileges restored until May. The townsmen
were clearly beaten, and the university was stronger and more
secure than ever. But the quarrels and occasional riots continued
into the present century.[26]

NEW GROWTH

By the last decade of the fourteenth century the university was
growing in size and faculties. From an approximate population
of 400 to 700 scholars and masters (nearly half of them mendicant friars) in the 1370s, it rose by 1450 to 1,300 or so, roughly
double in seventy-five years. During the same period Oxford
increased only from about 1,500 to 1,700.[27] There were several
possible reasons for this expansion. The Black Death told heavily
on the secular clergy of England, killing between 20 and 40 per
cent. Thus there were many openings for university men. This
was William of Wykeham's thought in founding New College,
Oxford, and a variation on it was used by the founder of
Godshouse, Cambridge in the 1430s when he spoke of a severe
shortage of grammar masters throughout the countryside.[28]

Placing university men in ecclesiastical livings was a preoccupation throughout this period. The statutes of Provisors (1351/
1390) and Praemunire (1353/1365/1393) prohibited appeals to
the papal court for appointments to benefices and advowsons.

[26] There was another riot in 1484. *Annals*, I, pp. 128–9.
[27] Aston *et al.*, 'Cambridge Alumni', pp. 26–7.
[28] Courtenay, 'Black Death', pp. 703–4; *Statutes of Oxford*, New College, p. 2; *Docs.* III, 155.

The universities were constant in their pleas for exemption. In 1392 Parliament gave the King power to moderate these acts for the benefit of university men. This petition was repeated in 1400, and in 1403 the King granted letters patent to Oxford and Cambridge that allowed their graduates to procure ecclesiastical dignities and benefices from the Pope. Similar exemptions were repeated in 1415 and 1417. This theme was continued in 1437 when Cambridge sent a complaint to the King for promotions to fulfil the needs of graduates.[29] A similar appeal in more melodramatic terms was sent by Oxford to the Archbishop of Canterbury in 1438: 'Our dear university is like Rachel mourning her lost children...alas!'[30]

Whether there was truly a 'crisis in patronage' is difficult to prove. Certainly university men were given more preference in some decades than in others, but the overall picture was not bleak. Bishops' registers indicate priests were frequently being given licences to study, and former scholars and graduates were a noticeable element in English dioceses. The percentage of graduates is more striking when viewing men who served in administrative positions, and even more so in diocesan administration. Law graduates were particularly successful in securing promotion. The appeals of the universities on behalf of their graduates were more an effort to improve their career possibilities than to correct a critical situation.[31]

This was also the period when Cambridge escaped from the control of the Bishop of Ely, who from the earliest years had the right to confirm the chancellor who was elected biennially by congregation. The first chancellor to attempt to avoid this duty was John de Donewich, who on his re-election in 1374 refused to take the oath to the bishop. His appeal went to the Court of Arches, where he lost.[32] In 1379 Ivo de la Zouch was

[29] *Annals*, I, p. 141 (1392), p. 146 (1400), p. 149 (1403), p. 158 (1415), p. 159 (1417), p. 187 (1437–8). The 1423 University Library catalogue lists the practical text. *Forma appellandi in beneficialibus secundum stilum curie Romane.*

[30] *Epistolae academicae Oxon.*, ed. Anstey, I, 154–7. 'Universitas mater nostra clamat cum Rachel, plorans filios suos et noluit consolari...Sed heu!'

[31] J. Dunbabin, 'Careers and Vocations' in *HUO*, I, pp. 565–605; Aston *et al.*, 'Cambridge Alumni' pp. 68–70; cf. G. F. Lytle, 'Patronage Patterns and Oxford Colleges, c. 1300–1530' in L. Stone, ed. *The University in Society* (2 vols., Princeton and London, 1975), I, 111–49.

[32] John de Donewich had been elected 'anti-chancellor' in 1362. *BRUC*, pp. 191–2.

elected, but was exempted from the oath because he was a nobleman. The exemption made the rule uncertain, and in 1400 Dr Richard Billingford was the last chancellor to be confirmed by the Bishop of Ely. In 1401 Pope Boniface IX exempted the chancellor-elect from this obligation. [33]

In the same year Cambridge was subject to a visitation by Archbishop Arundel of Canterbury. With due advance notice, the archbishop and his entourage arrived in September. He received canonical obeisance from the senior members of the university gathered in the new Regent House, and then questioned the chancellor on ten articles, of which all but one dealt with the administration of the university and colleges. Were the statutes followed? Were the common chests carefully kept? Were college fellowships complete according to the founders' wills? Were any of the scholars notorious criminals? Arundel then examined the doctors individually, and appointed commissioners to visit the colleges, St John's Hospital, and St Radegund's nunnery. Nothing was found to be seriously out of order. [34]

The more general question of spiritual and ecclesiastical jurisdiction remained unsettled until the Barnwell Process of 1430. The university had petitioned Pope Martin V and claimed it was accustomed to exercise autonomy from diocesan control. The university cited recently-produced copies of spurious bulls of Honorius I (624) and Sergius I (689) to substantiate this claim. It would be charitable to assume the university believed that these bulls reflected authentic papal decisions made 750 years earlier, for Cambridge was convinced of its great antiquity.

Pope Martin delegated the authority to settle this matter to the prior of Barnwell, and to a canon of Lincoln. The canon did not participate, so in 1430 the prior alone heard this case, called the Barnwell Process. The university produced six articles to prove their independence, as well as bringing witnesses aged twenty-six to seventy-nine who swore to the chancellor's

---

[33] *VCH*, II, pp. 155 and 164; *Calendar of Papal Registers*, V, pp. 370–1.
[34] *Annals*, I, p. 147 (1401). The King's Hall and Corpus Christi were not visited.

independence in their own experience. Later they produced the authentic bulls of John XXII (1317) and Boniface IX (1401) which supported their position, as well as the documents purported to be by Popes Honorius and Sergius. The prior was convinced, and settled that no archbishops or bishops should interfere with the university, or excommunicate or put under interdict any of its members.[35]

During Archbishop Arundel's visitation in 1401, the one question he asked which did not concern administrative practice was 'Whether there were any suspected of Lollardy or any other heretical pravity?'. The teaching associated with John Wyclif, DTh. of Balliol College, Oxford, a realist scholar of great reputation in Oxford, had been condemned in 1377, seven years before his death. Both in learned and popular form Lollardy lingered, and proved well adapted to the anti-clerical strain in late medieval popular culture. It included a rejection of papal authority, clerical celibacy, Transubstantiation, the veneration of relics and included other proto-protestant points.

Wyclif in his own life had many supporters in Oxford, where in 1381 his anti-sacramental theses were publicly maintained in the theology school. The following year William Courtney, the Archbishop of Canterbury, ordered that the university officially condemn these positions. The chancellor refused, claiming jurisdictional exemption, and when forced into submission later, said that he had not dared to condemn Wyclif in the face of his numerous Oxford supporters. The archbishop replied, 'Then is Oxford the university of heresies, if she will not allow orthodox truths to be published?'[36]

The dispute flared again in 1397 when some Oxford theologians complained that Lollardy was still being taught in the Schools. Archbishop Arundel now entered the fight with Oxford over jurisdiction, although Oxford was, by a bull of Boniface IX in 1395, exempt from Canterbury's control. Oxford was

---

[35] *Annals*, I, pp. 182–3 (1430); *VCH*, III, p. 164.
[36] Rashdall, III, pp. 126–7; *Fasciculi zizaniorum*, ed. W. W. Shirley. Rolls Series 5 (London, 1858), p. 311; A. Hudson, 'Wycliffism in Oxford 1381 – 1411', in *Wyclif in His Times*, ed. A. Kenny (Oxford, 1986), pp. 67–84.

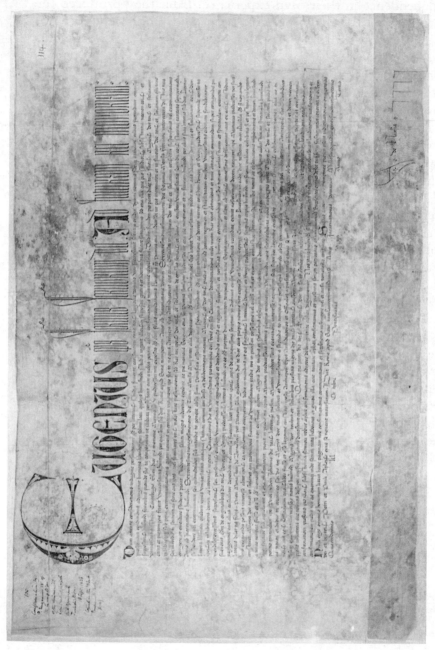

10 Pope Eugenius IV's bull of 1433 confirming the university's exemption from diocesan control.

obstinate in both its rights and its heresy. In 1411 Arundel tried to make a visitation, but the university refused to allow him to enter. Eventually the King came in on the archbishop's side, the Pope revoked the bull of 1395, and Oxford suffered the visitation late in 1411.[37]

Cambridge's experience was quite different. In 1384 there was an inspection of some books by the chancellor and some heretical ones were burnt.[38] But the evidence throughout the fifteenth century shows only isolated figures involved in heresy, and no widespread support for Wyclif. In 1412 Peter Irford, BA, recanted his Wycliffite opinions before the chancellor, the only scholar so indicted in the entire century.[39] Cambridge's orthodoxy was a popular assumption. John Lydgate wrote, '...of heresie Cambridge bare never blame'.[40] As late as 1527 Archbishop William Warham of Canterbury looked in sorrow at the zeal of the Lutherans in Cambridge, a university that had 'afore now taken upon her praise that she never was defiled'.[41]

The stability and permanence of Cambridge were secured in a physical way in the late fourteenth century when the masters began expressing their corporate existence in stone. The days of migration were over. Previously the university had used Great St Mary's for gatherings of congregation, and rented houses (the 'Schools') to the west of the church for statutory disputations and acts. About 1359 it was decided that a more worthy and commodious house was needed for the theology faculty, to be paid for by members and friends of the university. Construction began on this building, now the north side of the 'Old Schools Court' but proceeded very slowly for lack of money. Then in 1365 Sir Robert Thorp got things moving through his generosity. On his death in 1372 while Royal Chancellor he left further bequests. The new school was not completed, however, until the 1390s, through the contributions of Sir William Thorp

[37] Shadwell, *Enactments*, pp. 7–14.
[38] *Annals*, I, p. 128 (1384).
[39] *BRUC*, p. 328.
[40] Quoted in Mullinger, *Cambridge*, I, p. 637.
[41] Quoted in H. C. Maxwell-Lyte, *A History of the University of Oxford* (London, 1886), pp. 457–9.

(Robert's brother) and his wife Lady Grace. A licence was obtained for a chapel to be included, and the new building was in use by 1400.[42]

It has two storeys, the lower originally used as the theology school, and the upper, now the University Combination Room, doubled as the university chapel and regent house, or 'Senate House', as it came to be called in sixteenth-century Latin. Described in 1438 as being of 'surpassing beauty', it was paved, glazed, had an altar at the east end, and stalls and masters' chairs for more secular uses.[43] Of the central university buildings of Oxford and Cambridge, specifically built by and for university use, it is the oldest. Oxford did not begin its albeit far more splendid Divinity School until 1427. The Cambridge structure is the first university example of the 'academic gothic' style that would have so many descendants around the world. It was given a Palladian facade in the eighteenth century which masks its true character; at the same time the gothic east gate which was added later in the fifteenth century was sold and moved to Madingley Hall, where it can still be seen.

The theology school and regent house were joined in the 1430s by a western range, with a school of canon law below and a library above, and on the south side by the philosophy school with another library, between 1458 and 1471. These were paid for by fees from scholars.[44] The quadrangle was completed when the east wing was built between 1470 and 1473 with a gift from Thomas Rotherham, the university chancellor and later Archbishop of York, with yet a third library and a university courtroom below. At the university's initiative the reconstruction of Great St Mary's was begun in 1478. While the work was in progress the university used the Franciscan Church for its larger assemblies. Contributions for this remarkable project were obtained through various fees: on

---

[42] H. P. Stokes, *The Chaplains and the Chapel of the University of Cambridge*, CAS, Octavo Publications, 41 (Cambridge, 1906), esp. chapters V and VI; Willis and Clark, III, pp. 19–20; RCHM, Cambridge, II, 14–15.

[43] Stokes, *Chaplains*, p. 50.

[44] *GBk* A, p. xli; J. C. T. Oates. *Cambridge University Library: A History* (Cambridge, 1986), pp. 1–97.

masters taking chairs in either of the laws, on religious foundations, and on students entering the advanced faculties.[45]

NEW COLLEGES

The acceleration of population growth and building was matched in the fifteenth century by a renewal in the foundation of colleges. Following Corpus Christi in 1352 there was an interval of eighty-four years before the next was begun by William Bingham, rector of St John Zachary in London. The story of Godshouse is complex, as it underwent several changes in purpose, place, and structure in its early years. Bingham was the first of a breed usually associated with the English Renaissance: an educational reformer who used the influence and wealth of his enlightened London connections to further his plans. Among those friends and acquaintances were John Carpenter, MP and founder of the City of London School; William Lychfeld, rector of All Hallows the More and author of 3,083 sermons; Sir John Frey, second Baron of the Exchequer; the London clerks Gilbert Worthington, DTh. and John Cotes, both described by a contemporary chronicler as 'grete prechours'; the prosperous John Brokeley, Master of the Worshipful Company of Drapers and possibly the primary source of Bingham's financial strength; and finally, King Henry VI. It was just such combinations of royal and lay patronage which united to found several colleges in sixteenth-century Oxford and Cambridge.[46]

Bingham began his efforts in 1436 by purchasing land for a new college on Milne Street near Clare Hall (now Clare College), and in 1439 he received a royal licence for the new foundation of Godshouse. Bingham's express motive was the low standing of grammar teaching in England, and the petition

[45] Mullinger, *Cambridge*, I, p. 301. An example is found in *GBk* A, p. 41 (1463–4); *VCH*, III, p. 130; W. D. Bushell, *The Church of St Mary the Great* (Cambridge, 1948), pp. 33–43, esp. 34–6.

[46] A. H. Lloyd, *The Early History of Christ's College* (Cambridge, 1934), pp. 10–11, 72–3, and 82–3; C. L. Kingsford, 'A London Chronicle, 1446–50', *English Historical Review*, 29 (1914), 505–15.

to Henry VI described how on his travels eastward between Hampton and Coventry and north to Ripon, he saw seventy grammar schools empty for want of teachers. His new college would be unique in that it was to produce exclusively grammar masters who, after taking the MGram. degree were to accept any teaching post with an adequate stipend at a school built within the previous forty years.[47] The college was also exceptional in being a dependency of Clare Hall: Bingham was possibly a Clare man.

This licence was never acted upon, and Bingham obtained two further royal licences in 1442, which broke the Clare connection, and widened the scope of permissible studies from grammar alone to all the liberal arts.[48] A further royal licence followed in 1446, and finally in 1448 yet a fifth and final licence was obtained which can properly be called the foundation charter. The college had to vacate its original site, which was acquired by the King for his new royal foundation (King's Chapel now occupies the spot), and Godshouse was moved just outside the Barnwell Gate where it was renamed Christ's College in the early sixteenth century. More importantly, this final licence names Henry VI as the founder, since he provided the ground for the college and increased the endowment with several recently-seized alien priories.[49]

Godshouse was on the small side with only four fellows, while in the same century Corpus had seven, Gonville five, Queens' four, and St Catharine's three. But the numbers in Godshouse were swelled by pensioners renting rooms. The statutes (not sealed until 1495) detailed that undergraduate members begin with two or three years of sophistry and logic in the arts faculty, and then return to grammar, and specifically to the study of the books of 'Priscian, Virgil, and other poets, metrification, versification', and similar studies. When the master and fellows decided that the scholar was properly prepared, he was to take the master of grammar degree and incept as the statutes required, and keep his required *convenite* (grammar

[47] *Docs.* II, 153; Lloyd, *Christ's*, pp. 35–40 and 356–7.   [48] Lloyd, *Christ's*, p. 52.
[49] Lloyd, *Christ's*, pp. 86–8 and 289.

acts).[50] To assist the fellows and pensioners in their studies there was a salaried college lector, the first at Oxford or Cambridge.

We know of forty-four scholars who were probably fellows or pensioners of Godshouse, and they seem as varied as those from any other college. In spite of the statutory provisions of the founders, the attraction of the higher degrees and the career opportunities which they provided proved too strong; Godshouse was less 'the first secondary school training-college' than the founder would have wished.[51] Only eight of the men are certain to have taken the MGram., and four of these had at least a BA and two of them the BTh. as well. For example, John Hurt, BTh., the master in the 1450s, had a personal library of arts, theology, medicine, and astronomy.[52] John Scott incepted in grammar in 1501 with a grace that mentions lectures on Priscian's *Maior*. He then stayed on at Godshouse and, later, Christ's to take a BA, MA, and BTh. by 1517, and served as junior proctor and university preacher.[53] Thomas Nunne was a fellow from 1500, receiving his BA and MGram. in 1504. His supplication to the university included Priscian's *Maior* and *Minor*, and he was excused one grammar responsion, 'because of the lack of masters in that faculty', provided he respond the next year in either grammar or philosophy.[54] This dual concentration seems to have been the rule at Godshouse.

Lancastrian aid to Cambridge was expressed on a more extravagant scale in King's College. It was the religious orthodoxy of Cambridge that doubtless made it rather than Oxford the recipient of so much royal favour. At King's College every member was required to take an oath against the teachings of Wyclif (and the eccentric Bishop Reginald Pecock).[55] A more immediate cause of this aid might have been the king's agents John Langton, chancellor of Cambridge, and John Somerset, Chancellor of the Exchequer and MD of Cambridge.[56]

---

[50] H. Rackham, *The Early Statutes of Christ's College, Cambridge* (Cambridge, 1927), p. 22.
[51] A. F. Leach, *The Schools of Medieval England* (London, 1915), p. 257. Biographical details are from Lloyd, *Christ's*, corrected with *BRUC*.
[52] *BRUC*, p. 322.   [53] *BRUC*, p. 513.
[54] *BRUC*, p. 429 (Thomas Nunne); *GBk* Γ, pp. 3, 23–4, and 52 (1501–7).
[55] The first provost, William Myllington, wrote a polemic against Pecock. *BRUC*, pp. 417–18.
[56] *VCH*, III, pp. 376–7.

The college, called St Nicholas' in 1441 – St Nicholas' Day, 6 December, was Henry VI's birthday – was to have a rector and twelve scholars. This plan was enlarged in 1443 and again in 1445 into the 'College of the Blessed Virgin Mary and St Nicholas, called King's College', with a provost and seventy scholars, and an immense endowment. Nine papal bulls were obtained which made the college and its members immune not only from external control, but even from the chancellor's. This latter point was contested by the university and after a riotous attack on King's in 1454, the foundation withdrew the claim, but Kingsmen were exempt from university examinations until the nineteenth century. More significantly, Henry tied the college to his 1440 foundation of Eton College, with the fellowships at King's open exclusively to Old Etonians. It was a nexus modelled on William of Wykeham's New College and his school at Winchester. The full complement of King's fellowships was filled by 1451, exceptional at any college, and by 1460 college revenues were over £1,000 a year. A large, dilapidated section of the city between High Street and the river was cleared for his monumental college, and plans were drawn up for the enormous chapel, a large court and cloister, towers, etc., to supplement the small court built for the original King's foundation. [57]

This privileged situation was dependent on Henry VI, and with his deposition in 1460 the college feared total ruin. It lost much of its endowed property, but Edward IV left something. Its revenues in 1464 were £500, which was still substantial, but its fellowship had fallen to twenty-three. [58] Recovery was slow. Nothing was ever done about the extensive building that had been planned, and the fellows contented themselves until the eighteenth century with the original small court, which is now the University Registry. The great chapel stood unfinished until the Tudors, and the large part of the city that was levelled to make way for the anticipated complex of courts remained open. The lovely green lawn that rolls down to the Cam today remains as a reminder of thwarted Lancastrian benevolence.

[57] Willis and Clark, IV, plan no. 13 (Henry VI's plans for King's).
[58] *VCH*, III, p. 379–80.

While the King was making sumptuous plans for his new college, Andrew Docket was planning a much more modest foundation. Docket was the rector of St Botolph's in Trumpington Street and principal of St Bernard's Hostel across the road. Besides these qualifications, he had a singular and very useful ability to get other people to underwrite the costs of his dreams. In 1446 Docket obtained a licence from Henry VI to found a college of St Bernard for a president and four fellows, on the site of his present hostel. The following year he obtained another licence from the King to refound it on the present site of Queens'. At this point Docket approached the Queen, Margaret of Anjou, for help. She then petitioned the King to license the college yet again, with her as foundress and patroness of the 'Queen's College of St Margaret and St Bernard'. This was granted on 30 March 1448, and by 14 April Docket had already made the contract for the new building, now the elegant First Court. Built of Dutch brick and probably designed by his friend and parishioner Reginald Ely, the costs were paid in part by the King and Marmaduke Lumley, Bishop of Lincoln. [59]

The fall of the Lancastrians would have been a crippling blow to a less resourceful man than Andrew Docket. He was able to convince the new queen, Elizabeth Woodville, to refound the college for a fourth time. Thus it became the college of two royal foundresses, not the Queen's, but Queens' College.

The initial charter of the foundation claimed that the college was for the 'extirpation of heresies and errors and the increase of the faith'. The latter purpose was standard with nearly all college founders, while the former reflects a special interest of Henry VI. Elizabeth Woodville's statutes provided for a president, twelve fellows, and three young Bible clerks. The fellows were to study in the arts or theology faculties, unless they had special permission to turn to law, medicine, or letters. The Bible clerks were poor undergraduates in the arts faculty. [60]

Queens' was joined by Catharine Hall, now St Catharine's College, in 1473. Founded by Robert Wodelarke, provost of

[59] Searle, *Queens' College*, I, pp. 1–17; *VCH*, III, pp. 408–9.
[60] For the early history and organization of Queens' College see Searle, *Queens' College*, I.

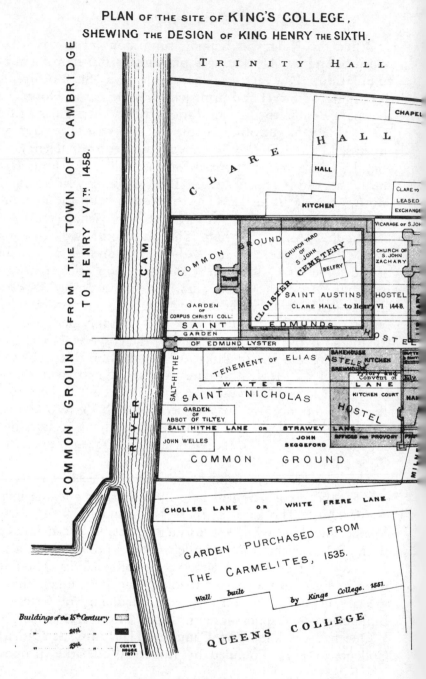

PLAN OF THE SITE OF KING'S COLLEGE,
SHEWING THE DESIGN OF KING HENRY THE SIXTH.

COMMON GROUND FROM THE TOWN OF CAMBRIDGE TO HENRY VI.ᵗʰ 1458.

TRINITY HALL

CLARE HALL

CHAPEL

HALL

CLARE TO
LEASED
EXCHANGE

KITCHEN

CAM

COMMON GROUND

VICARAGE OF S.JOHN

CLOISTER

CHURCH YARD
OF
S. JOHN

CEMETERY

BELFRY

CHURCH OF
S. JOHN
ZACHARY

GARDEN
OF
CORPUS CHRISTI COLL:

SAINT
GARDEN

EDMUNDs

SAINT AUSTINS HOSTEL

CLARE HALL to Henry VI 1448.

HOSTEL

OF EDMUND LYSTER

SALT-HITHE

TENEMENT OF ELIAS ASTELE

BAKEHOUSE
BREWHOUSE

KITCHEN

Convent of

BUTTS
HILL

RIVER

SAINT

WATER

NICHOLAS

LANE

KITCHEN COURT

GARDEN
OF
ABBOT OF TILTEY

HOSTEL

SALT HITHE LANE OR STRAWEY LANE

JOHN WELLES

JOHN
SEGGEFORD

OFFICES FOR PROVOST

COMMON   GROUND

MILN

CHOLLES LANE OR WHITE FRERE LANE

GARDEN PURCHASED FROM
THE CARMELITES, 1535.

Wall built   by King's College. 1551.

Buildings of the 15ᵗʰ Century
„   18ᵗʰ   „
„   19ᵗʰ   „

CORVS
HOUSE
1871

QUEENS COLLEGE

11 A plan showing what King Henry VI demolished between the High
Street and the river, and what he planned to build in its place. To the
north is the Schools quadrangle, with the Old Court of King's (now

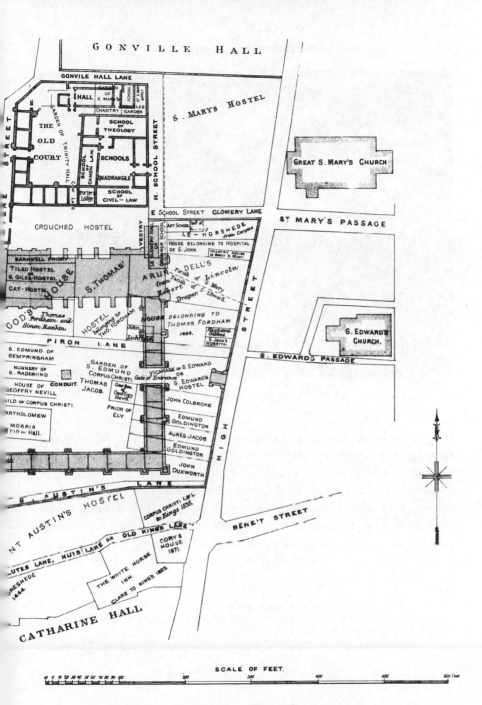

the site of the University Registry), one of the few parts of the proposed college that King Henry actually built (from Willis and Clark, IV, no. 13).

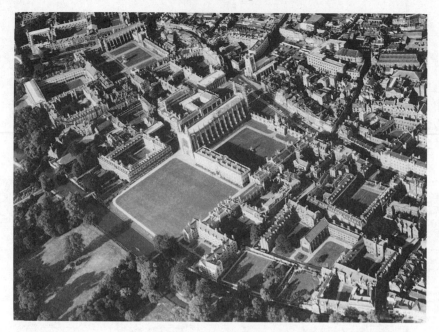

12 The lawn of King's College.

King's, it was adjacent to King's to the south. Wodelarke envisaged a small society of a master and three fellows, all priests. They were to study only philosophy and theology, although in fact they had three canon lawyers in their first thirty years. Catharine Hall's size and purpose put it outside the mainstream of collegiate foundations of this period, for it had no undergraduate pensioners or internal lectures, the hallmarks of the new roles the colleges were coming to play in the fifteenth century.[61]

[61] A. B. Cobban, 'Origins: Robert Wodelarke and St Catharine's', in *St Catharine's College, 1473–1973*, ed. E. E. Rich (Leeds, 1973); *Documents Relating to St Catharine's College, Cambridge*, ed. H. Philpott (Cambridge, 1861).

Chapter 11

INTERNAL REFORM

The fifteenth century is not considered a very productive or prosperous time in northern Europe. The 'Fifteenth Century' conjures up an interim period of plague, the Hundred Years War, and the exhaustion of scholasticism, yet preceding the classicism of the northern renaissance; a very different image from that evoked by 'quattrocento'. The medievalist tends to use the adjective 'late' to refer to its art, philosophy, and theology, and the historian of northern humanism similarly employs 'early' when finding expressions of humanism. The master of fifteenth-century Cambridge knew nothing of these later constructs. Did he feel himself part of a dying world, or an awakening one?

The contemporary authorities present Cambridge and Oxford in depressed conditions: 'Rachel mourning her lost children' and the promotion problems of graduates. Bishop Fisher while addressing the visiting Henry VII in 1506 claimed that before the King showed interest in helping the university in the 1490s, learning had been in decline, a situation Fisher attributed to the quarrels with the townsmen, the frequent plagues, and the lack of patrons.[1]

These were all indeed problems; but one must not take panegyrics and soliciting letters at face value. A shrewder test for judging the condition of any institution is its size and resources. Is its population growing? Is it building? Is it attracting new endowments? The answer to all of these questions

---

[1] Lewis, *Fisher*, II, p. 269.

for fifteenth-century Cambridge is in the affirmative. Jurisdictional independence was fully recognised in 1430. Six new colleges were founded between the 1430s and 1496. The colleges attracted lay patronage both large and small.[2] The number of scholars rose throughout the century both in absolute numbers and relative to Oxford, and the percentage of higher Church offices they filled also rose at the end of the century.[3]

Confidence in the future of Cambridge and the value of its mission is clear in nearly all areas. Royal assistance was continuous. Lancastrian generosity built King's College and helped Godshouse and Queens'. Yorkist aid was also secured for Queens' and the university showed itself skilful in bending with the wind. It courted Richard III before he came to power, and later wrote to remind him of it, but also celebrated Masses for his predecessor.[4] The assistance they later obtained from the Tudors overshadowed even the Lancastrian benefactions. The frequent dynastic wars had no real ill effects on Cambridge, except for King's College.

The university had a growing sense of its own importance, and consequently its own past. The Carmelite friar Nicholas Cantelow, DTh. (d. 1441) and an acquaintance of Humphrey, Duke of Gloucester, wrote the *De antiquitate et origine universitatis Cantabrigiensis*. Cantelow took the story only up to AD 924: through Anaximander, Anaxagoras, the early theology faculty founded by Damianus, and King Alfred's foundation of Oxford, assisted by a Cambridge man. It is the earliest of the long series of English university histories, and a product of pride and loyalty.[5] The Cambridge congregation shared this spirit, and paid to have it copied out in 1471.[6]

This optimistic estimate must be balanced, however, by the absence of creative genius among the Cambridge men of the

---

[2] In addition to those examples mentioned in the previous chapter, see the smaller benefactors in Searle, *Queens' College*, I, p. 66, and *Annals*, I, pp. 235 (1489), 243 (1493), and 275 (1505).

[3] Aston *et al.*, 'Cambridge Alumni', pp. 26–7 and 71–6.

[4] *GBk* A, pp. xviii–xix, pp. 158–9, 170–2, 174, and 185.

[5] *BRUC*, p. 120; N. Cantelow, 'De antiquitate', in Thomas Sprott, *Chronica*, ed. T. Hearne (Oxford, 1719), pp. 221–80.

[6] *GBk* A, p. 90 (1471–2). For a curious early manuscript of Cantelow, with 1465 *Questiones contra Wyclif*, and a letter from an English prelate to Oxford University promoting a young Cordovan scholar, see BL Royal MS 8.E.vii.

he. Nothing new was being done in the Schools, and there
no indications of intellectual ferment, or even heresies. The
iars no longer brought to the university theologians of international reputation. The logic of the sophister was unchanged
for a century, and Aristotle was still read through the fourteenth-
century commentaries.

The masters were serious men, though. They delivered their
lectures, acted in disputations, produced competent if unexciting
work, and earned positions of national distinction. John Argentein, MD, DTh., studied in Italy, was a royal physician, and
died as provost of King's.[7] William Myllington, DTh. and first
provost of King's, showed himself a principled man by refusing
to violate his university oaths, an action which cost him his
office in 1447.[8] The Austin Friar Thomas Penketh left for Padua
with his DTh., where he lectured on metaphysics and edited
Scotus, the closest to an internationally celebrated scholar that
Cambridge produced.[9] There were other men like these, hard-
working but not very memorable. There is no answer as to
why Cambridge had no great scholars then; no more so than
why there are no Russells, Moores, or Wittgensteins in the
philosophy faculty today. But without the growth, foundations,
and patronage of that century Erasmus would never have come
in the next, nor would royal favour necessarily have given St
John's and Trinity Colleges to the smaller of the ancient
universities.

EARLY HUMANISM

Against the background of medieval continuity are found the
first examples of humanism. In fifteenth-century Cambridge
documents *humanitas* was synonymous with *rhetorica, poetria,
Terenciana,* and *oratoria*. It meant the classical literary form that
something took, and it also meant classical learning in general.
Libri poetrie on a library inventory meant anything classical or
dealing with epistolary style, and a lecture in *humanitate* could
cover anything from Virgil to Sallust to Vegetius. If this

---

[7] *BRUC*, pp. 15–16 (John Argentein); Leader, 'John Argentein', pp. 71–4.
[8] *BRUC*, pp. 417–18 (William Myllington).
[9] *BRUC*, p. 448 (Thomas Penketh).

definition is vague, it is because the concept was vague to
late medieval schoolmen. They sometimes divided the classi
and renaissance Italian from other disciplines by virtue of sty
irrespective of content, and other times organised their studie
by content; Plato was included with Scotus, and Alexander oi
Villa-Dei with Perotus. [10]

The great rhetorical works of antiquity were available in
medieval Cambridge. Cicero's *De oratore*, the pseudo-Cicero's
Rhetorica ad Herennium, Aristotle's *Rhetorica*, Quintilian's *Institutiones*, Virgil, Terence, and Ovid could be found in the
libraries. Some colleges were better equipped with classical
works than others. Peterhouse had most of these works in the
fifteenth century, in addition to several codices of Seneca, Pliny,
Macrobius, Martianus Capella, Lucian, Sallust, Martial, and
Statius. Among medieval sources for epistolary style there were
the collections of Peter of Blois, Peter of Vineis, and Thomas
of Capua to accompany Petrarch. The library of King's College,
although smaller than Peterhouse's, had the same kind of
classical section, in part through the generosity of Humphrey,
Duke of Gloucester, the apostle of the early renaissance in
England. [11] Cicero, Seneca, Sallust, Quintilian, Ovid, Virgil,
Caesar, Statius, and Horace were all there, along with several
medieval poets and Poggio's *De avaricia*. By contrast, Queens'
College in 1472 had only three texts for rhetoric: Plutarch's *De
virtutibus*, Peter of Vineis' *Epistolae*, and the *Rhetorica ad Herennium*, and Gonville Hall was also ill provided.

In spite of the medieval access to classical texts, there was a
real change with the coming of Italianate fashions. The change
was not initially polemical, and coexisted with the scholastic
studies that all Cambridge men continued to pursue. But it had
its consequences. The appreciation of classical style led to the
decline of the medieval grammarians. There was a gradual
movement away from medieval logic as the primary study of
the undergraduate, and a growing emphasis on classical litera-

[10] See also R. Weiss, *Humanism in England during the Fifteenth Century*, 3rd edn. (Oxford, 1967),
p. 22; K. B. McFarlane, 'William Worcester: A Preliminary Survey', p. 214: 'He [Worcester]
is less interested in their manner than their content. The ancients possessed knowledge he
was anxious to learn; it never occurred to him to alter his Latin prose in imitation of theirs.'
[11] For Humphrey, see A. Sammut, *Umfredo duca di Gloucester e gli umanisti italiani* (Padua, 1982).

ture that was codified by statute in 1488. These linguistic studies provided the groundwork for the Erasmian theology with its reliance on scriptural and patristic studies in the original tongues, as well as the eloquence to preach the Word clearly.

A reasonably complete discussion of fifteenth-century humanism in Oxford and Cambridge (and there was much interpenetration) lies outside the scope of this work, and several important studies have already been made. In brief, humanism, or the interest in classical authors and style, first appeared in the universities in the 1430s and 1440s. The first proponents merely had an interest in the fashions from Italy, and were not concerned with restructuring learning to serve a reformed Christianity, as would happen later. This early interest is often identified with the large gifts of books given by Duke Humphrey *c.* 1440 to Oxford and King's College. But, as even a cursory glance at this bequest shows, traditional medieval works outnumber the classical texts, most of which were accessible to Cambridge scholars anyway.[12] Although a great patron of Italian learning and enthusiast of classicism, the duke, like most fifteenth-century Englishmen, did not consider these cultures to be in conflict.

The scholars associated with early humanism had little impact on the teaching of the universities. Those interested in the new learning left England for Italy; after returning they had little direct contact with their old schools. William Gray, a Balliol man, MA 1434, left England in 1442 and studied in Cologne, Florence, Padua (DTh. 1445), Ferrara (where he followed the classes of Guarino da Verona and supported Nicholas Perotus), and Rome. After returning to England he became Bishop of Ely, and on his death in 1478 left a large humanist library to Balliol. Most of the humanist and classical works saw little use, but the medieval items often seem to have done yeoman service.[13]

---

[12] H. Craster, 'An Index to Duke Humphrey's Gifts to the Old Library', *Bodleian Quarterly Review*, 1 (1914–16), pp. 131–5; M. R. James, *A Descriptive Catalogue of the Manuscripts other than Oriental in the Library of King's College, Cambridge* (Cambridge, 1895), pp. 72–83.

[13] See Balliol MS 93, works of Burley, John Sharp, and Antonius Andreas. Similarly, Richard Fox's humanist donations to Corpus Christi College, Oxford, have been barely touched up to the present. Fletcher, 'Teaching and Study of Arts', p. 54.

Robert Flemyng, MA of Oxford by 1437–8, and nephew of the founder of Lincoln College, followed Gray to Cologne and Italy, had an important diplomatic and ecclesiastical career, and wrote *Lucubratiunculae* (Rome, 1477), an encomium to Pope Sixtus IV. One of the earliest Englishmen to know Greek, he left an impressive library to Lincoln College. Like Gray's humanist books at Balliol, they show either no signs of use, or very light indications.[14]

There are several important exceptions to this pattern. Perhaps the first Cambridge master with strong classical rhetorical interests was John Gunthorpe, MA by 1452 and BTh. 1468. After his MA he went to study classics in Italy, and is known to have attended the rhetorical lectures of Guarino da Verona in Ferrara by 1460. He also learned Greek on that visit, and returned to England by 1460, after which he became warden of The King's Hall. Gunthorpe served the crown as a diplomat, secretary, and chaplain to the Queen, and keeper of the privy seal before his death in 1498.[15]

While in Ferrara Gunthorpe met John Free, MA 1454 of Oxford, who had spent many years in Ferrara and Padua at the expense of William Gray.[16] Free gave Gunthorpe his notebook, which Gunthorpe added to. It includes copies of the *Rhetoric* of Chirius Consultus Fortunatianus (also copied by Perotus while he was in Gray's household),[17] a *Dialectica*, medical treatises, an anonymous *Liber de transformationibus*, lecture notes on Virgil and others, a Greek vocabulary, notes on perspective and refraction, and diplomatic speeches.[18] Clearly, he was a man of varied interests. The notebook seems to date from the 1460s, the time he spent in Italy and Cambridge.

Whether Gunthorpe ever taught Greek or rhetoric at The King's Hall during his years as warden (1467–72) can not be known, but he could well have, or encouraged others to do so. His diverse library included copies of St Augustine, St Jerome, Einhard, Ranulph Higden, Bede, Gerald of Wales, Albertus

---

[14] e.g. Lincoln MSS 21 (Bruni's trans. of Aristotle's *Ethics*), 60 (Plutarch and Valla), and 93 (Suetonius).　　[15] *BRUC*, pp. 275–7 and 677.
[16] R. J. Mitchell, *John Free* (London, 1955).　　[17] Vatican MS Urb. Lat. 1180.
[18] Bodley MS 587 (s.c. 2359)

Magnus, Homer (in Latin), Isocrates, Cicero, Suetonius, Pliny, Macrobius, Chalcidius, and T. Livius Frulovisius' *Comoediae*. As with so many early English humanists, he shows 'no sense of conflict between the old and new learning, no suggestion of unorthodoxy attached to humanism.'[19]

Another man who returned to Cambridge after visiting Italy was John Doket, an Etonian and King's College fellow from 1454–9, and BTh. by 1463. He went to Padua the next year and later to Bologna, where he was DCn.L by 1469. He then returned to Cambridge and took his DTh. in 471–2. Doket's career in the next thirty years included a string of benefices, diplomatic appointments, and incorporations of his doctorates at Oxford, and concluded with the provostship of King's from 1499–1501.[20] Doket, like Gunthorpe, was one of the few Englishmen to study in Italy and return to his old college in a position to influence others. He perhaps encouraged John Argentein, also of King's and later his successor as provost, to go to Padua for his medical studies.

Doket wrote a commentary on Plato's *Phaedo* some time after his return from Italy. Surviving only in its dedication copy to his uncle Cardinal Bourgchier (chancellor of Oxford 1434–7), it is written in Doket's beautiful humanist hand.[21] Dependent on Bruni's translation of the *Phaedo* with references to Decembrio's *Republic*, Doket cites Plotinus, Porphyry, Apuleius, and Pseudo-Dionysius.[22] The commentary is an interpretation of Plato in the light of Christian neo-Platonism, and is thus in the spirit of both medieval exegesis and Bruni and Ficino.[23] This copy soon fell into the possession of Robert Sherborn of New College, BA 1477, MA, MB, Oxford University scribe 1480–6, and later diplomat and Bishop of Chichester.[24] The manuscript shows little sign of use, and Doket's work had no influence.

---

[19] W. A. Pantin, *Letter Book of Robert Joseph*, OHS n.s. 19 (Oxford, 1964), p. xxxv.
[20] *BRUC*, pp. 190–1.   [21] BL Add. MS 10344.
[22] Weiss, *Humanism*, pp. 164–7.
[23] '...the main interest of Doket's commentary is the handling of antique materials with scholastic methods towards the fulfilment of a scholastic ideal, for in this he embodied the compromise between medieval and modern learning which was typical of the earlier stages of English humanism'. Weiss, pp. 167–8.
[24] *BRUO*, III, pp. 1685–7 (Robert Sherborn).

But there were other men, more important to Cambridge, who aided the coming of the new learning through their sympathy, if not actual scholarship. None of the three Rotherham brothers was ever in Italy. Thomas, of Eton and King's, was an MA and DTh. by 1463 (aged forty), and rose to be successively Bishop of Lincoln and Archbishop of York, as well as chancellor of England under Edward IV. He was an archetypal late-medieval ecclesiastical careerist. But he was also chancellor of Cambridge 1469–71 and 1473–92, and master of Pembroke 1480–8 (although usually absent from both posts). As we will see, his chancellorship covered a period of revolutionary curricular changes. Rotherham himself built the eastern front of the Cambridge library, thus closing the 'Old Schools' court, contributed to the restoration of Great St Mary's, and gave over 200 volumes to the University Library.[25] Although mostly law books, his bequests include Paduan editions of Aristotle, and manuscripts of Aulus Gellius, Apuleius, and Macrobius. There are few items that could be called scholastic. Thomas Rotherham also received a printed presentation copy of Flemyng's *Lucubratiunculae* from the author.[26]

Thomas' younger brother, Roger, DCL by 1471, had a much less prominent career as Archdeacon of Leicester. But like John Gunthorpe he was warden of The King's Hall from 1473 until his death in 1477, and gave the Hall a copy of Frontinus' *De re militari* that had been copied in Bologna in 1458.[27] A third brother, John, of King's College 1448–56, chose a lay career, married, was clerk of the receipt of the duchy of Lancaster, controller of customs at Sandwich, an alderman of Canterbury, guildmaster of Luton, and member of parliament for Canterbury (1472–5) and Bedfordshire (1477–8).[28] The three Rotherham brothers indicate the variety of careers available for talented late medieval university men; and Thomas and Roger, although not visitors to Italy, were clearly sympathetic to the Italian trends.

[25] *BRUC*, pp. 489–91. He was also a benefactor of Lincoln College, Oxford.
[26] Bodleian Library, BB.19.Art.Seld. (4); The Aulus Gellius is now Pembroke, Cambridge, MS 168. Like Robert Flemyng's gifts to Lincoln College, Oxford, it shows little sign of use, except for the illuminated initials, which have been razored-out.
[27] BL Royal MS 12.C.xxi.   [28] *BRUC*, p. 489.

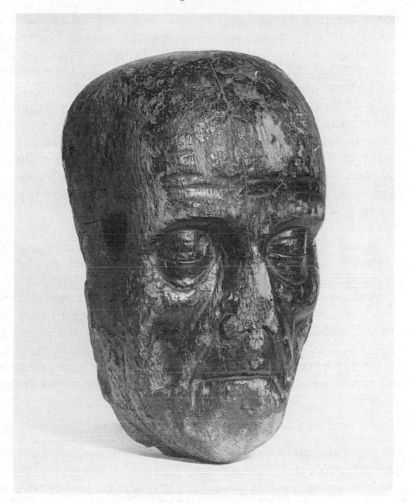

13 A wooden head of Archbishop Rotherham, carved for his funeral
services and subsequently left in his tomb in York Minster.

More direct but less documented conduits of Italian thought
were the foreign teachers, such as Lorenzo Traversagni and
Stephano Surigone. Surigone was from Milan, and taught
rhetoric at Oxford from 1454 to 1464, and possibly until 1471.
Among his pupils were William Sellyng, a Benedictine from
Canterbury who would later study in Italy and return to

promote Greek studies in England. Surigone matriculated at Cologne in 1471–2, where he met Caxton, was at Louvain in 1472, taught at Augsburg and Strasbourg, and incepted DCn.L at Cambridge in 1475–6.[29] A humanist, he wrote *De institutionibus boni viri libellus*,[30] composed for Caxton the Latin elegy in praise of Chaucer which was engraved on Chaucer's tomb in Westminster Abbey, and wrote a collection of Latin poems.[31] Lorenzo Traversagni was a widely travelled Franciscan. The author of several rhetorical works, he was in Cambridge off and on from 1472 to 1482, lecturing on the *Rhetorica ad Herennium* and *Ethics* and writing in 1478 his *Nova rhetorica*, the first such work published in England.[32]

It was probably to visiting teachers like Traversagni, Surigone, Caius Auberinus and others whose visits were briefer and left no traces, that the popularisation of renaissance ideals and the revivification of classical style should be credited. The influence of graduates who, after sojourns in Italy and careers in the service of Church and State donated their libraries to their old colleges, should not be overestimated. The sympathy of the mighty is always important. But Traversagni earning his living teaching rhetoric in Cambridge for several years was a far more influential factor in leading young scholars to the new learning.

UNIVERSITY PROFESSORSHIPS

The growing interest in classical and humanist form and content between 1460 and 1488 gradually caused the university as a whole to recognise that the curriculum was no longer stressing the proper studies. The watershed was reached in 1488 when the regents voted in congregation to change the statutory requirements for undergraduates in arts, requiring them to follow a four-year sequence of lectures: the first two in humane letters, the third in logic, and the fourth in philosophy. These lectures were to be given by salaried professors, the beginning of the system of university 'chairs' that replaced the medieval

---

[29] *BRUC*, pp. 566–7.
[30] Trinity College, Cambridge, MS 330 (B.14.47).
[31] BL Arundel MS 249, ff. 94r.–117v.
[32] *BRUC*, pp. 593–4.

system of necessary regency.[33] To understand this change one must first look at the gradual decline in necessary regency lectures through the fifteenth century, a phenomenon equally apparent in Oxford.

The ordinary lecture was the primary method of instruction in the medieval university, and it was the sworn duty of the master to give them and of the scholar to attend them. At the beginning of the fifteenth century this system was still vital, and the incepting master spent at least one year reading ordinary lectures for his regency. By 1520 this system had fossilised, with masters frequently excused from giving any lectures beyond their *principium*. The change was never absolute, as neither Oxford or Cambridge passed statutes eliminating necessary regency. The change occurred through the congregations exercising their dispensing powers and, in the case of Cambridge, instituting these new, salaried professorships. It was further propelled at both universities by the growth of internal collegiate lectureships.

The dispensing powers of congregation were not always directed towards improved instruction. Chancellor Thomas Gascoigne of Oxford frequently complained of congregation selling graces (and the office of bedell) as a form of fundraising.[34] In particular he accused the heretical Bishop Reginald Pecock of having obtained his theology degree this way in 1444, and thus avoiding all academic acts.[35] There seems to have been some truth in these observations, since Oxford graces *c*. 1450 sometimes did require contributions towards the new Divinity Schools or to the rebuilding of St Mary the Virgin.[36] However, it was not common at this time to supplicate for a grace unless one had an irregular programme. Most students were within the limits of the statutes, and thus never had to ask for graces. There is a remarkable diversity in the programmes

---

[33] There was no consistent use of the words professor, praelector, lector, or reader in the Tudor university. For the sake of clarity, I use 'professor' only to mean those men appointed and salaried by the university to deliver lectures that were required of scholars in their respective disciplines, and which were without direct charge to the auditors.

[34] Gascoigne, pp. 3, 20, and 215.   [35] Gascoigne, p. 215.

[36] e.g. Reg. Aa, pp. 37, 44, and 58 (1449–50).

of those who did supplicate, but their programmes always included at least some ordinary lectures.

There were already signs of a move away from ordinary lectures, however. At Oxford a term was defined in 1431 as having at least thirty legible days.[37] By the middle of the century it was not unusual for common graces to be given which allowed all students in all faculties to count 26, 20, 18, 16, or sometimes as few as 12 legible days as a full term.[38] Sometimes this was because of the Plague, but often no reason was given and the only condition was that the scholars had remained in the city.[39]

The Oxford graces after 1505 show that these dispensations developed into the rule rather than the exception. Bachelors were always required to incept, but not to lecture for long afterwards. Instead, the usual requirement was to say a Mass of the Holy Spirit or of the Five Wounds, to say the psalter of the Blessed Virgin, or several Pater Nosters or Ave Marias: this substitution of devotional exercises for lectures did not happen at Cambridge.[40] Often the Oxford congregation gave a simple grace for a specific reason: the inceptor had collegiate duties;[41] his father was at death's door;[42] he was a resident of Whittington's College in London;[43] he was required at his benefice;[44] he taught grammar elsewhere;[45] or he was not able to be admitted as a fellow of Queen's College while still a regent.[46]

More telling than these individual exemptions were the general graces which excused whole classes of inceptors from lecturing. In October 1506 'all doctors and masters recently created' were not held to their lectures.[47] This grace meant that their regency lasted only from July until October. In May 1509 all masters created in the last act were dispensed with their regency immediately after the next act, provided that they pray a *Deus laudem* for the health of the proctors.[48] The regents were

[37] Gibson, *Statuta antiqua*, p. 234 (1431).
[38] e.g. Reg. Aa, pp. 35, 58, 102, 146, 150 (1449–53).
[39] e.g. Reg. Aa, p. 182 (1454).
[40] e.g. OUA Reg. G, ff. 2r.–6v. (1505).
[41] OUA Reg. G, f. 10v. (1506).
[42] OUA Reg. G, f. 218v. (1514).
[43] OUA Reg. G, f. 173v. (1513).
[44] OUA Reg. G, f. 21r. (1506) and f. 164r. (1513).
[45] OUA Reg. G, ff. 66r. and 67r. (1509).
[46] OUA Reg. G, f. 19v. (1506).
[47] OUA Reg. G, f. 24r. (1506).
[48] OUA Reg. G, f. 76r. (1509).

being excused as soon as more were created. In February 1511 all masters created the previous July were not required to lecture 'for the greater part of the hour nor to reconcile textual ambiguities' (the phrasing was from the statutory definition of an ordinary lecture), provided that they lecture for fifteen minutes.[49] This was taken to its logical conclusion in 1518 when all masters were excused their regencies 'because nobody attends those lecturing'.[50] This is not surprising if the lectures were only fifteen minutes long.

Despite this fossilisation, necessary regency survived in a vestigial form, since an inceptor only became a master by the act of lecturing. The Elizabethan statutes of Oxford and Cambridge continued to require a regency period; at Cambridge it was even lengthened to five years. But by then it was a distinction that served only to define voting rights in the Senate (congregation).[51]

Oxford and Cambridge differed in the ways in which they replaced the regency lectures. The senior university dealt with the need for appropriate lectures by selectively demanding them from new degree holders. Accompanying the exemptions from regency after 1510 are numerous graces requiring lectures on specific subjects and books, often to be read 'publicly and freely'. *Belles-lettres* were served by demanding of inceptors in the grammar faculty (or 'rhetoric faculty' as it was coming to be called) lectures on Cicero's *De officiis* and *Epistolae*, Terence, or Sallust. Thus, the same instruction was given as at Cambridge, but through grace requirements rather than by professors.[52] These university efforts were supplemented by the free public lectures offered in Oxford by Magdalen College (1459) in many subjects, by Corpus Christi (1517) in Greek and the humanities, and by Cardinal Wolsey's lectureships in the humanities, first given in the autumn of 1518.[53]

---

[49] Gibson, *Statuta antiqua*, p. 194 (1407) and Reg. G, f. 111v. (1511).
[50] OUA Reg. H, f. 6v. (1518).   [51] *Docs*. I, p. 459 (1570).
[52] e.g. Reg. G, ff. 134r. (1511), 70v. (1509), 124v. (1511), 232r. (1514), 92v. (1510), 145v. (1512), and 183v. (1513).
[53] *Statutes of Oxford*, II, Magdalen College, p. 47; Corpus Christi, pp. 48–54; *Epistolae Academicae Oxon. 1508–1596*, ed. W. T. Mitchell, OHS n.s. 26 (Oxford, 1980), pp. 74–7, 81, 83–4, 90–1, 95–6, 105–6, 116–19, 154–6, 165–8, 174–5, 188–9, and 234–7.

The regency lectures were also in decline at Cambridge, and the statutes from the late fifteenth century show that many students admitted to not having followed the ordinary lectures according to the statutory form.[54] The statute instituting the new Cambridge mathematics lecture in 1500 spoke of how the regency system of lectures had fallen out of use 'either through age or carelessness', and was now 'inane, burdensome, and useless'.[55] Congregation saw the problem, and was eager to rectify it through the novel expedient of salaried professorships. It was a situation of evolution as much as decline, and Cambridge as a university had no wish for teaching to be left entirely to the colleges and hostels. By the middle of the fifteenth century instruction in arts and law was extensively offered by the colleges and hostels. Theology had, of course, always been taught within the friars' houses of study as well.

The decline of regency lectures must also be seen in the light of the introduction of inexpensive printed books. They eliminated the need for cursory lectures, and also lessened the importance of all lectures. Knowledge could be transmitted through private reading, and then form the basis of disputations.

This evolution in the method by which the universities obtained lectures did not necessarily change the nature of the teaching. Whether a scholar followed a lecture on the *De sphera* that was paid for by King's College, or by the university, was a question of financial, not intellectual interest. The method of lecturing, and indeed the masters delivering the lectures, were probably the same as for those ordinary lectures traditionally given early in the morning in the Schools. If there was an intellectual difference, it was that the endowed lectureships in the humanities, Greek, and mathematics at Cambridge were indicative in their content of a changing emphasis within the curriculum.

Almost without exception, the new Cambridge professorships were established, endowed, and delivered by members of the reforming, humanist circles that desired a redirection in studies,

---

[54] e.g. *GBk* B, I, p. 30 (1491) and *passim*.   [55] *Docs.* I, no. 136, p. 382.

including humanist Latin, Greek, and science, to serve a more scripturally based theology. The seminal figures in this renaissance were Lady Margaret Beaufort and her confessor, Bishop John Fisher, university chancellor and guiding light of Christ's College, Queens', and St John's College. But others, less well known, were involved: a generation of young scholars, many of whom were affiliated with these colleges, and lay lawyers in the royal service who patronised the new learning at Cambridge and elsewhere. All these men (and women) reoriented both the content and form of the studies, so that the Royal Injunctions of 1535 and the first regius professorships were less a real change than an apparent one.

The idea of salaried professors appeared first in several stillborn efforts at Oxford. In 1432 John, Duke of Bedford, told Gilbert Kymer, MD and then chancellor of Oxford, of his intention to endow a lecture in 'the seven liberal arts and three philosophies'. The Oxford congregation quickly followed this up with several letters urging him to carry out his plan.[56] Although Bedford never did, the university seems to have persuaded his brother, Humphrey, Duke of Gloucester, to fulfil the promise.[57] In spite of the Duke Humphrey's other bequests to Oxford, he never implemented this request.

This idea appeared in another form in 1453 when the Oxford congregation considered 'whether it would seem expedient for the university to hire five or fewer regents to lecture on the arts which are not being given by the necessary regents'.[58] But this idea bore no fruit, and which arts were being neglected was not specified.

Oxford's third unrealised attempt occurred in March 1482 when Edward IV founded a professorship in theology. Oxford wrote the king a letter of thanks, promising that a special prayer would be included for him in the annual Mass at the beginning of the year.[59] Edward died the next year, and nothing more is heard of this professorship.

[56] *Epistolae Academicae*, ed. Anstey, I, pp. 81–3, 94–5, and 106–7.
[57] *Epistolae Academicae*, ed. Anstey, I, pp. 107–8 and 139–40. See also the letter to Henry VI in 1442, pp. 210–11, where Oxford claimed that all arts lectures were delivered without fee, a statement contradicted by many other university records.   [58] Reg. Aa, p. 153 (1453).
[59] *Epistolae Academicae*, ed. Anstey, II, pp. 478–9.

No such false starts at endowed professorships are known at Cambridge. The statutory change of 1488 codified a development that began in 1486 when the first of these professors was paid for his lecturing. It is instructive to see who might have been the leading figures in congregation when this change was discussed. The incoming senior proctor was Thomas Metcalf of Peterhouse, MA and scholar in theology. He later went to Ferrara for his doctorate, and died in Rome while at the English Hospice.[60] Thomas Rotherham was probably still the chancellor, and had in April resigned the mastership of Pembroke.[61] His nephew, John Blythe, DCL, had just been named warden of The King's Hall. Christopher Urswick, DCn.L, left the wardenship in the same month to serve as a royal envoy to France and Spain. His humanist credentials are striking; he had visited Italy several times earlier in the decade, was a chaplain to Lady Margaret and agent in her dynastic plotting, and in later life was a friend of Erasmus and John Colet. Urswick commissioned a number of humanist books, including in 1488 William Sellyng's translation of Chrysostom for presentation to both the Greek scholar Thomas Goldstone of Canterbury and Archbishop Morton, Thomas More's patron.[62]

Other senior members of the university included John Yolton, DTh. and master of Michaelhouse, whose piety was expressed by bequests to Lichfield's library, and for the maintenance of 'a priest to preach the gospel without charge in the neighbouring parishes or to plead for poor litigants in the bishop's consistory without fee'.[63] Ralph Barton, proctor of Godshouse, had himself lectured freely and publicly in the Schools forty years earlier (salaried by his college). Thomas Cosyn, BTh. and master of Corpus was the second Lady Margaret Professor of Theology from 1504 to 1506.[64] So, from the beginning the reform of the teaching was accomplished from within, by men who were

---

[60] *BRUC*, pp. 403 and 680. At least thirty-five Cambridge men were associated with this hospice between 1450 and 1520. See *BRUC*, pp. 669–87, and *The English Hospice in Rome: Venerabile Sexcentenary Issue* 21 (May 1962).

[61] *BRUC*, pp. 489–91; cf. Brooke, 'John Fisher', Appendix 1.

[62] *BRUC*, p. 685; J. K. McConica, *English Humanists and Reformation Politics* (Oxford, 1965), pp. 70–2; BL Add. MS 15673.   [63] *BRUC*, p. 667.

[64] *BRUC*, pp. 161–2.

connected with the wider political and intellectual currents of their day. There is absolutely no evidence of any resistance to the new learning until twenty-five years after this date.

The new statute authorised that three regent masters in arts be chosen annually at the end of each summer term to lecture ordinarily in the Schools. The first of the three masters covered unspecified 'humanity books' for scholars in their first two years, the second logic for third year students, and the third philosophy for men in their fourth year and bachelors. These three lectures were to last an hour, and each professor was to receive 26s 8d per term, payable by the masters of colleges and the principals of hostels.[65]

Previously the Cambridge undergraduate had spent his first two years on Aristotle's *Organon* and medieval terminist logic, and his third and fourth years were then given to natural philosophy (and to a lesser extent moral philosophy and metaphysics).[66] With this new statute the emphasis moved away from logic as the foundation study and towards the hazily defined 'humanity books', to which the young scholar was to devote his first years. This was not a blanket condemnation of scholasticism, but rather a redirection of young artists towards more humanistic goals within an increasingly eclectic academic environment.

This new curricular emphasis was reiterated by another statute passed in 1495 which listed the requirements for the BA.[67] It was the same plan of study as in the 1488 statute, but the word 'Terence' is substituted for *libros humanitatis*. The comedian Publius Terentius Afer was widely known in the middle ages, but also enjoyed a reputation during the English renaissance as a cornucopia of the nice points of Latin grammar.[68] Unfortunately, there is no clear evidence for the content of this lecture other than that Terence was a frequent text; it seems

---

[65] *Docs.* I, no. 87, p. 361. For an example of these payments, see Queens' College Archives, *Journale*, I, f. 49r. and *passim*.

[66] *Docs.* I, no. 139, p. 384 (by 1390) and Hackett, pp. 297-9.

[67] *Docs.* I, no. 140, pp. 384-5.

[68] e.g. John Anwykyll used Terence in his *Compendium totius grammaticae* (Oxford, 1483) and John Colet prescribed Terence in his statutes for St Paul's School. J. H. Lupton, *A Life of John Colet, D.D.* 2nd edn (London, 1909), p. 279.

that many other humanist and classical texts were used as well.
What is clear is that Cambridge as a corporate body was giving
its assent to the new learning, and doing it in a more permanent
manner than Oxford.

The payments by the proctors listed in the *Grace Books*
establish that the first Terence professor was Caius Auberinus.
Of Auberinus we know very little.[69] Styled *poeta* he was an
Italian resident in Cambridge by 1483, when he was first
employed by the university to compose letters, occasional work
which he did until 1504. That his letters were directed to the
more important royal and ecclesiastical officials indicates an
appreciation by congregation of Italianate style. Unfortunately,
none of these letters survive. Of Auberinus' learning we know
only that he was a master of an unknown foreign university,
and was so incorporated at Cambridge in 1490–1.[70] He does
not seem to appear in any other English records, or in the
letters and literary documents of the period; he bequeathed no
books and was patronised by no other institution. In spite of
this anonymity and the probable modesty of his achievements,
his influence in teaching a generation of Cambridge scholars
should not be underestimated.

Auberinus, who doubtless supported himself by teaching
after his arrival in 1483, was given special attention by the
university in April 1486 when he was voted four marks (2 ×
26s 8d) by congregation for lecturing.[71] No records of disburse-
ments exist for 1486–7, but in 1487–8 Caius was paid 26s 8d
for each of the three terms.[72] At the end of that year the new
statute was passed, and Auberinus henceforth needed to be paid
by the proctors only if he lectured out of term. That happened
in 1491–2, 1492–3 (*pro lectura puplica*) and 1499–1504.[73] After
that year he disappears from the university records.

During these years other men were occasionally paid for
lectures given in vacation, men who probably held one of the

[69] *BRUC*, p. 23.   [70] *GBk* A, p. 202 (1485–6); *GBk* B, I, p. 30 (1490–1).
[71] *GBk* A, p. 202 (1485–6).   [72] *GBk* A, pp. 219–20 (1487–8).
[73] *GBk* B, I, pp. 44, 51, 138, and *passim* (1491–1504). In 1499 he received 20s for lecturing
during feast days in Michaelmas term and during the long vacation, p. 138.

three public professorships. In 1496 John Fisher, MA and then fellow of Michaelhouse, was paid 8*d* for lecturing in the long vacation and 26*s* 8*d* for lecturing in Christmas term.[74] He was probably the humanities professor, or even possibly the Lady Margaret Professor, which was in an inchoate form during that term. In 1499–1500 John Fawne, MA 1497, fellow of Queens' College, future vice-chancellor (1512–14) and Lady Margaret Preacher (1515), was paid 10*s* 'for his ordinary lectures'.[75] He was later to become a friend of Erasmus and was patronised by Richard Fox, Bishop of Winchester and founder of Corpus Christi College, Oxford.[76] The following vacation Thomas Patenson of Pembroke, then junior proctor, received 2*s* 4*d* for his lectures. He later founded a scholarship at Christ's College and donated several books to Pembroke, including the *Epistolae* of Pico della Mirandola.[77] During the next few years the restructured undergraduate course was reflected in the graces of students taking their BA. Scholars described their programmes as four years of lectures 'in humanity and logic', or 'in Terence and dialectic', or having at least two years 'in humane arts'.[78]

The next certain Terence professor after Auberinus was John Philippe, who in 1507 was paid by the proctors 'for the Terence lecture' for the previous two years.[79] Philippe, MA 1500, senior proctor and university preacher 1507–8, was a fellow of Queens' along with Fawne and under Fisher's presidency. His Latin credentials were well known to congregation since he had composed letters for them since 1500.[80] Philippe reappears in 1518–19 when the proctors reimbursed John Vawen (another Queensman and friend of Erasmus)[81] for £3 13*s* 4*d* paid through him to Philippe for unknown services.[82] Another Terence professor was Robert Ridley, MA 1500, who was paid from 1508 to 1510.[83] Although not a reformer of the same

[74] *GBk* B, I, pp. 104–5 (1496–7). [75] *GBk* B, I, p. 138 (1499–1500).

[76] *BRUC*, p. 221. *Opus Epistolarum Erasmi*, VI, no. 1656, p. 244 and no. 1766, p. 436.

[77] *BRUC*, p. 444. [78] *GBk* Γ, pp. 2, 12, and 49 (1501–7).

[79] *GBk* B, I, p. 232 (1507–8). [80] *GBk* B, I, pp. 158–242 (1500–9).

[81] *CWE*, II, no. 283, p. 271 and V, no. 777, p. 304 and no. 826, p. 398.

[82] *GBk* B, II, pp. 68–9 (1518–19).

[83] *GBk* B, I, pp. 237, 239, and 245 (1508–10); *BRUC*, pp. 480–1.

stamp as his nephew Nicholas, Robert Ridley was, with the other university professors, a supporter of the new learning and clerical reform.

These lectures were clearly an important element in the faculty of arts, yet they remained on an uncertain footing until an independent endowment could be found. To this end Cambridge sought the patronage of a great man of the realm, as Oxford had unsuccessfully done in the previous century. They found such a man in the London lawyer Sir Robert Rede. Rede was a justice of the King's Bench in 1495 and chief justice from 1509 until his death in 1519. He was a regular recipient of gifts from Cambridge, probably for his help in the chronic litigation with the town. [84]

Rede's connections with the humanist circles of London were many and varied. In addition to his cultivation by Cambridge, he knew Thomas More through their common profession, was speaker of the House of Commons in 1514–15, and was an executor of Henry VII along with Richard Fox. These connections are particularly apparent in his will: he requested burial in the London Charterhouse and founded a chantry there, and left other bequests to King's College, the Bridgettines at Syon, and the nunnery of Malling, Kent, where his daughter was professed (Elizabeth Barton, the 'Holy Maid of Kent' joined a few years later). [85]

Rede's largest benefaction, made no doubt at Bishop Fisher's suggestion, was to establish an assured annual stipend for the three professorships that had hitherto been funded through the heads of houses. [86] Rede died in 1519, but the endowment was not finalised until December 1524, after several years of effort by the university. [87] The final indenture specified that every May Day 20 marks be paid by Waltham Abbey, Holy Cross, to the master of Jesus College, who in turn paid the three men 26s 8d on the last day of each term (i.e. £4 per annum) for the lectures in the Schools, 'one lecture in humanitye the seconde

---

[84] *GBk* B, I, pp. 120, 136–7, and *passim*; *GBk* B II, pp. 2, 5, and *passim* (1511–19).
[85] *DNB*, XVI, pp. 816–17.
[86] This continuity is not noticed by Mullinger, *Cambridge*, I, p. 518.
[87] *GBk* B, II, pp. 102 and 114 (1521–4).

in logicke and the third in philosophie naturall or morall'.[88]
The professors were to be chosen on the day before the Feast
of St Barnabas, 11 June, thus giving them the later name
'Barnaby Lectures'. As a proviso the men chosen were required
to have their pupils pray for Rede once a term.[89] The Rede
professorships are one of several examples of a layman,
sympathetic to humanism and Erasmian reform, furthering
those ideals through his patronage of education. The Rede
Lectures have proved a permanent feature of the university.[90]

A salaried professorship was also founded for the quadrivial
sciences (arithmetic, music, geometry, and astronomy), collec-
tively called 'mathematics'.[91] Congregation passed two statutes
c. 1500 that restructured the bachelors' programme. In addition
to the traditional demand that students spend three years studying
'books of Aristotle's philosophy' they were to divide that time
with new lectures 'in mathematics'.[92] This was outlined more
clearly in the second statute, which begins by rehearsing the old
sequence which led to the MA: dialectics, the *Posterior Analytics*,
and the philosophy of Aristotle.[93] However, since that
programme of regency lectures had fallen out of use, and since
mathematics was 'not unworthy', congregation established a
three-year sequence in that field.

The first year of the lectures was to cover arithmetic and
music, the second geometry and perspective, and the third
astronomy. They were to be read in term, except during Lent.
The six weeks missed during Lent were to be read in the long
vacation instead. As with the Terence lectures, the university
was regularly offering instruction outside the medieval *dies
legibiles*. The mathematics professor was to be chosen by a vote
of the regent masters and be paid a stipend of 26s 8d per term.
The money was to be gathered from fees collected from students

---

[88] CUA, Black Parchment Book, pp. 190–1. After the suppression this was paid by the rents
of the abbey's former estate at Babraham.
[89] CUA, Black Parchment Book, p. 196.
[90] They were abbreviated to an annual lecture in 1858.
[91] For this distinction, see Weisheipl, 'Nature, Scope, and Classification of the Sciences', pp.
85–101.   [92] *Docs.* I, no. 86, pp. 360–1.
[93] Bachelors had frequently been excused these lectures on the *Posterior Analytics* in the previous
30 years. They last appear in graces in 1494 (*GBk* B, I, pp. 70–1).

taking any degree, and the university accounts after 1500 show that this was regularly done.[94]

The first mathematics professor was Roger Collyngwode, MA 1499, student of canon law at Paris and fellow of Queens' College, who held the post in 1501–3, 1504–7, and 1514–17. Under the name *Carbo in ligno* he wrote a long but incomplete treatise entitled *Arithmetria experimentalis* which he dedicated to Richard Fox. In the dedication Collyngwode states that Cambridge 'imposed on me, although unworthy, the task of teaching the youths the quadrivial studies'.[95] Collyngwode wrote in an italic hand and in a humanist style, and his work is essentially the arithmetic of Euclid and Campanus explained in detail; numbers, proportions, the four operations, square and cube roots, and quadratic equations are all explained, with tables and diagrams included.

Collyngwode was followed by a succession of men with strong ties to the new learning, most of whom were fellows of Queens' or St John's, colleges strongly influenced by Fisher. William Peyto, Henry Bullock, and Humphrey Walkden were all fellows of Queens' during Erasmus' stay from 1511–13, and this tradition of humanistic scientists who served as mathematics professor continued well into the sixteenth century.[96]

COLLEGE AND HOSTEL TEACHING

The founding of university professorships was paralleled by the establishment of salaried lectors in the colleges, something which did not exist in early Cambridge. The formalisation of collegiate instruction was a gradual and natural evolution, which began as both hostels and the handful of colleges had their members instruct each other and practise disputations before presenting themselves for the statutory exercises in the Schools. This movement accelerated with the influx of undergraduates from the hostels into the colleges between 1450 and 1540, and was formalised in the statutes of the newer colleges, which made

---

[94] *GBk* B, I, pp. 163, 171, and *passim*.   [95] *BRUC*, p. 149; CCCO MS 102, f. iv.
[96] P. L. Rose, 'Erasmians and Mathematicians at Cambridge in the Early Sixteenth Century', *Sixteenth Century Journal*, 8 (1977), 47–59.

provision for salaried deans and lectors to be responsible for this teaching. This was never meant to replace disputation or lecture attendance in the Public Schools, which was required of any candidate presenting himself for a degree, although the increase in college teaching lessened (and by the seventeenth century eliminated) the need to attend university lectures regularly. There is no contemporary evidence whatever to show that collegiate and university instruction were considered to be in 'competition'.[97] The lecturing techniques were the same and, from the foundation of the first professorships in 1488, these posts were held, almost to the man, by college fellows, sometimes while simultaneously serving as college lectors.[98] For the college member attendance at both was required.[99]

Several kinds of teaching took place in medieval colleges, convents, and hostels. The friars' convents were also the *studia* for their orders, and had programmes of disputations and lectures in the arts studies to prepare their brothers for entrance into the theological faculty. They also had their own course of theology studies.[100] With the founding of the first colleges, the seculars within them followed this natural practice of scholars to rehearse their studies privately before being tested on them publicly. Peterhouse, Cambridge's proto-college, in its statutes of 1344 called for two deans to supervise these internal acts.[101] Colleges also gradually took on the moral, financial, and intellectual supervision of the younger scholars by their superiors, a practice mentioned in the Peterhouse statutes. This only occurred on a widespread basis when the college had more than a few undergraduates in residence.

The King's Hall, founded in 1317, was unique among the early Cambridge colleges in accepting undergraduates in its fellowship. Thus, a scholar could 'pass through the entire educational gamut within the walls of the same institution'.[102]

---

[97] cf. Cobban, 'Decentralized Teaching', p. 202.
[98] e.g. William Bill was regius professor of Greek, 1540–1, the same year that he was Greek lector in St John's College. St John's College Archives, Bursar's Accounts SB3.15.
[99] e.g. J. E. B. Mayor, *Early Statutes of St John's College*, pp. 39–41.
[100] For the 1438 regulations of the Cambridge Austin Friars, see F. Roth, *The English Austin Friars 1249–1538* (New York, 1966), I, 32–3.   [101] *Docs.* II, 17.
[102] Cobban, *King's Hall*, p. 303.

This mixture of undergraduates and more mature students allowed the college to develop a tutorial system whereby the senior members took over the financial and educational supervision of their juniors. By the 1430s these younger pupils included *extranei*, undergraduates who were not on the fellowship but who lived within the college paying their own way, much as they would have had they lived in a hostel. [103]

Before the late fourteenth century only The King's Hall had a significant undergraduate population. But from the 1380s at the latest, the other colleges began to accept men who were not on the fellowship into residence – 'pensioners' (or *extranei, perhendinantes*, etc.) who paid weekly for their room and board, accepting the discipline of the college and often the supervision of a particular master on the fellowship. The attractions for the pensioners were obvious: a stable community and perhaps better food and drink, as well as the teaching and hope of eventually being elected into the fellowship. For the college, it was more lucrative to fill rooms with fee paying men than to stretch their endowment by electing the statutory number of fellows. [104]

Pensioners lived in college for other reasons, however, and they were by no means all young scholars seeking teaching. Senior members of the university are often found as well as former fellows and the occasional son of a nobleman. There were also monks and canons who rented rooms in the colleges. It has been widely held that in the late sixteenth century the well-born sons of the gentry were pushing the poor clerks out of the colleges. This may have been true to some extent, but the apparatus for the change dates from far earlier in the middle ages. The well-born in the late medieval university were also sometimes pensioners in the colleges. [105] Pensioners in the medieval colleges are ill-documented, and may have been far more numerous than we know. The extensive archives of The King's Hall show the extent of the pensioner system. Admitted

[103] Cobban, *King's Hall*, pp. 66–77.
[104] Cobban, *King's Hall*, p. 272, claims there was no financial gain received from renting to pensioners. But cf. his n. 1 and J. K. McConica, 'Undergraduate College', in *HUO*, III, 51–64.
[105] cf. M. Curtis, *Oxford and Cambridge in Transition, 1558–1642* (Oxford, 1959). See also J. K. McConica, 'Elizabethan Oxford: The Collegiate Society', in *HUO*, III, 666–93.

to pay either the full commons or half commons (and accordingly enjoying a lower standard of fare), they appear in the records from 1364 onward, and included many ex-fellows who had returned from their benefices for further studies under *Cum ex eo* or *Licet canon* licences. Some pensioners stayed for only a few days while others remained for many years.[106] By the 1430s many of the younger pensioners were involved in extra-statutory tutorial arrangements with fellows of the Hall, and 'those fellows who served in the capacity of tutors to pupils of this kind were also responsible to the college for the expenses incurred by their private charges'.[107] Although The King's Hall never had a salaried tutorial system similar to the one at New College, Oxford, this amounted to the same thing. It was a small step from these informal arrangements to the statutory tutorial arrangements found in the sixteenth-century Cambridge colleges.[108]

Other colleges were doing the same as The King's Hall in this period. There were two pensioners in Peterhouse in 1388–9; one of them, Henry Beaufort, natural son of John of Gaunt and later cardinal and chancellor of England, left the next year to become a pensioner of Queen's College, Oxford.[109] By the 1460s Peterhouse was regularly taking in pensioners. At Godshouse in the 1440s the community was described in a petition to the king as being fifty persons 'communaly logged therein', far more than the statutes describe, and a document of 1451 refers to the 'fellows, scholars, and others residing in same'.[110] If the records survived we would probably find examples of the tutorial system for the undergraduate pensioners in most of the colleges in the fifteenth century. In a rare archival survival at Oxford's St Edmund's Hall we find the same phenomenon *c.* 1412.[111] At Pembroke College, the few medieval records tell of masters, like John Camberton in 1476, paying for the pensions of their pupils.[112]

---

[106] Cobban, *King's Hall*, pp. 259–79.   [107] Cobban, *King's Hall*, p. 67.

[108] J. Venn, *Biographical History of Gonville and Caius College*, III (Cambridge, 1901), 251–2; W. W. Rouse Ball, *Cambridge Papers* (London, 1918), pp. 26–47.

[109] *BRUC*, pp. 46–9; *First Report of the Royal Commission on Historical Manuscripts* (London, 1874), p. 79.   [110] Lloyd, *Early Christ's*, pp. 133 and 146.

[111] Emden, *An Oxford Hall in Medieval Times*, p. 193; Salter, 'Oxford Hall in 1424', pp. 421–33.   [112] Pembroke College Archives, Reg. Aα, f. 5r.–v.

The growth in college pensioners was directly tied to the acquisition of hostels in the later middle ages. The scholars in some of these hostels then fell into an anomalous position, being still members of the hostel, while simultaneously pensioners of the college. Their governance was often split between an 'outer principal' appointed by the college, and an 'inner principal' chosen by the residents. Queens' College and St Bernard's Hostel, Corpus Christi and St Mary's Hostel, and Gonville Hall and Physwick Hostel all enjoyed this relationship, arrangements which usually led to outright incorporation in the sixteenth century.[113] Some, like Physwick Hostel which belonged to Gonville Hall from the start, were always dependencies. At Oxford it was observed in 1526 that halls (hostels) suffered from rising food prices which, being unendowed, they passed directly onto their members.[114]

In hostels owned by colleges the hostel members were often recorded as college pensioners. For example, St Thomas' Hostel was acquired by Pembroke College in 1451. In the college accounts of 1457 (the first that survive in that decade) the thirty-four hostel members are recorded as pensioners of Pembroke.[115]

This absorption of hostels by colleges is particularly hard to document. The hostels have left us almost no records, and the college account books rarely record pensioners as college members, or itemise their payments. A good example is Queens' College in 1522. The bursar's accounts list the master, fifteen fellows, and four bible clerks, for a total of twenty members. However, a tax audit of Cambridge, made college by college in the same year, lists approximately forty Queens' College members, including about nineteen 'scholastici' who are unmentioned in the bursar's accounts. The same is true for the other colleges. Trinity Hall had statutory provision for twenty fellows, but probably only had ten in 1522. But the tax assessment lists about thirty *scholastici* in addition to these. Michaelhouse never had more than seventeen fellows, but has

---

[113] Stokes, *Hostels,* pp. 34–8.   [114] Emden, 'Oxford Academical Halls', p. 358.
[115] Pembroke College Archives, Reg. Aα, f. 5r.–v.; Attwater, *Pembroke,* p. 22. In 1477 there were twenty-eight members of St Thomas' Hostel.

thirty members on this roll, probably filled out by pensioners from St Gregory's Hostel, which it owned.[116]

As a result of these and perhaps other factors, the hostels were fast disappearing. By a 1514 university statute the independent Cambridge hostels were to have only one turn in eight in the nomination of the proctors, the other seven belonging to the colleges.[117] This may have reflected the proportion of hostel students to collegians, about 14 per cent of the university. In the 1522 census members of colleges comprised 90 per cent of the university.[118] Since legal studies were under-represented among most of the college fellowships, the lawyers' hostels were the most persistent in maintaining their independence and activity. Borden Hostel, jointly owned by Clare and Peterhouse, was occupied by members of the grammar faculty until the faculty's demise in the 1480s, when the hostel became filled with lawyers. The lawyers continued undiminished into the sixteenth century. In 1529 the university even deposited twenty-six law books in the hostel for the members' use. Borden Hostel, however, could not survive the suppression of canon law studies by the Royal Injunctions of 1535. It shortly disappeared, as did the last of the other independent Cambridge hostels.[119]

The growth of the undergraduate population of the colleges in the fifteenth century led to the founding of college lectureships, the reading and expounding of texts given under the auspices of a college lector, a man appointed by the college and paid, if not always by the foundation, at least through the college. The first instance of a statutory college lector is found at Godshouse, created by William Bingham in 1439 specifically to produce grammar teachers but later widened to allow for other studies as well. The Godshouse statutes required the lector

[116] Queens' College Archives, *Journale*, II, f. 38r., and Public Record Office, S.P. I, vol. 233, f. 154, 'The book of the view, valuation, and tax of the University of Cambridge'. This comprises twenty-one very mutilated folios. The modern restoration has rendered it less legible than it was 50 years ago when catalogued in *LP* Addenda vol. I, part I, pp. 105–10. I am indebted to Dr H. C. Porter for drawing this to my attention.
[117] *Docs.* I, pp. 425–8.   [118] See note 116 above.
[119] CUA, Coll. Admin. 2, f. 153v.; Stokes, *Hostels*, pp. 16–21.

to lecture on 'every day on which lectures were usually read in the hostels' as well as in the long vacation. He was to give three or four lectures, depending on the number of auditors present: in sophistry, logic, and philosophy, and on the *De modo significandi* or 'some other grammatical, poetical, or rhetorical work'.[120] The first three subjects were, of course, part of the arts curriculum, and the *De modo significandi* is a speculative grammar that is more properly the province of the faculty of arts than grammar. The lector was also to hear two or three disputations a week, in logic, philosophy, or grammar.[121]

A clearer picture is seen in an indenture *c.* 1451 between the founder Bingham and Ralph Barton, BA, appointing Barton to this college post.[122] His duties included those specified by statute, but with interesting elaborations; the three lectures in arts were to be the norm, but could be changed to grammar, rhetoric, or oratory if the needs of the scholars warranted. In addition, after Barton took his MA he was to deliver his regent lectures in the Schools according to the university custom to all comers, but to do it 'freely and apart from any monetary payment'. Barton's salary was £2 per annum plus livery.[123]

Godshouse honoured Henry VI as its co-founder in gratitude for his early benefactions. Henry followed this patronage of Godshouse by shortly afterwards founding King's College. By its statutes of 1453 there was to be a provost and seventy fellows, recruited from among Eton scholars between the ages of fifteen and twenty, who could pass from matriculation to the DTh. while remaining within the college. The undergraduates in their first three years were taught by advanced undergraduates, bachelors were taught by masters, and MAs attended internal lectures by graduates in law or theology. Provision was made for disputations both in term and during the vacations. Three deans were appointed (two in arts and one in theology) to oversee these acts, as well as superintend the

[120] Rackham, *Early Statutes of Christ's*, pp. 28–9.
[121] Rackham, *Early Statutes of Christ's*, pp. 28–9.
[122] Lloyd, *Early Christ's College*, pp. 134–6 and 275–6; *BRUC*, p. 42.
[123] cf. *Docs.* I, no. 155, p. 391, 'De magistris qui gratis legunt' (pre-1390), which prohibits this.

students 'in scholastic study and honest behaviour'.[124] The tutorial system was further based on *informatores*, who delivered lectures to the members of the college at their several levels.

The King's College accounts from 1456 give detailed information of payments for these lectures, and the fees collected from the members of each class. Separate lecture sections appear for the arts, theology, civil and canon law, medicine, and astronomy.[125] An edict of 1483 further required the lectors to be in hall from six to eight a.m. and that they conduct *repetitiones* of the preceding day's lectures before the new lecture was given. In addition, all bachelors and undergraduates had to give the vice-provost or one of the deans at the end of each week a written summary of all the lectures, and each day in the lecture hall give a report on one chapter of a logical or philosophical text, and submit these reports in writing at the end of each week.[126] As at Godshouse, the King's lectures regularly took place during the non-statutory autumn term, which allowed undergraduates to complete their studies in less time than the earlier university statutes allowed.[127]

The lectures in King's College were not open to all members of the university, nor were they without supplementary charge to the Kingsmen who attended them. The first college lecture that was permanent, public, and free was due to another partly Lancastrian foundation, Queens' College. In Margaret of Anjou's petition to found Queens' in 1447 she began by stating the usual reforming intentions, 'the conservacion of our faith and the augmentacion of pure clergie'. To this end she included provision for 'plain lecture and exposicion' in theology to be performed twice daily[128]

> by two docteurs notable and well advised upon the bible aforenoone and maistre of the Sentences afternoon to the publique audience of alle men frely bothe seculiers and religious to the

[124] *Docs.* II, 524–5, 548–9, and 551–4.
[125] e.g. King's College Archives, *Mundum Books*, 3, ff. 22r., 81r., and 100v. (1456).
[126] College Order of June 14, 1483. J. E. Thorold Rogers, *History of Agriculture and Prices in England,* III (Oxford, 1882), p. 741.
[127] *VCH*, III, p. 384; Lloyd, *Early Christ's*, p. 375.
[128] Searle, *Queens' College*, I, pp. 15–16.

magnificence of denominacion of suche a Queens college and to laud and honneure of sexe femenine.

No evidence survives from the confusion of the next twenty-five years to indicate whether this programme was implemented, but an external source of endowment appeared in 1472. Dame Alice Wyche made provision in her will for both a chantry and an annual dirge for herself and her husband, and also included two bequests more generally associated with reformation piety. There was to be an annual sermon preached in London on Easter Sunday, and a 'lecture of divinity to be read according to the statutes and ordinances of the college' with a salary of £2 per annum. [129] The earliest extant accounts of Queens', in 1484–5, show the payments for these lectures, called for by Queen Margaret and endowed by Dame Alice. [130] They continued from at least that date, and other lectures for the arts faculty were added in the early sixteenth century and were regularly given by men associated with the new learning. [131]

The King's Hall obtained an endowed lectureship in canon law in 1492, the legacy of a former fellow, Robert Bellamy, DCn.L. It was of a 'semi-public' nature, open and free to fellows of the college and poor clerks outside of the college, but closed to outsiders who had sufficient exhibition. The first known Bellamy lector served in 1501–2. [132] Peterhouse also established a lectureship sometime in these years. [133]

The fifteenth-century hostels had no corporatively salaried lectors, but they did offer internal lectures and disputations. Bingham's provisions of the Godshouse lector charge him to lecture on the same days as the hostel lectures were given. In 1460–1 the graces for David Blodwell and William Woode to incept as doctors of canon law both refer to hostel lectures they have given. [134] At Physwick Hostel, an appendage of Gonville

[129] Searle, *Queens' College*, I, pp. 80–1.
[130] Queens' College Archives, *Journale*, I, ff. 23r., 24v., 35v., and *passim*. The lectures were given in the chapel. Searle, *Queens' College*, I, p. 66.
[131] See D. Leader, 'Teaching in Tudor Cambridge', *History of Education*, 13 (1984), 115.
[132] Cobban, *King's Hall*, pp. 77–9; BRUC, pp. 53 and 330–1; GBk Γ, p. 9 (1501–2).
[133] BRUC, pp. 313–14 (Henry Hornby).
[134] BRUC, pp. 66 and 650; GBk A, p. 29 (1460–1), 'in lectura in aula pro scolaribus'.

Hall, both the external and internal principals lectured in the hostel and presided over disputations, for which they divided the 16*d* that each resident paid quarterly.[135]

By 1500 Cambridge had significantly changed from its medieval form. The hostels were fast disappearing and the colleges were growing in number, size, and in the instruction which they offered their members. On the university level the teaching had been restructured: regency lectures were falling out of use and being replaced in the arts faculty by salaried professors chosen by congregation. And the emphasis had changed as well, with *libri humanitatis* taking the first two years of the scholar's programme and a strong mathematical component being required of bachelors. Medieval logic, philosophy, and theology were still the backbone of the curriculum, but soon the implications of the new grammar and languages were to change logic and theology into something quite different from what the medieval schoolmen had known.

John Fisher has been mentioned at several points when discussing these internal reforms. The full blossoming of these movements in the sixteenth century was in large part due to his actions and irenic influence, and it is to Fisher that we look next.

[135] J. Caius, *Annals*, p. 9.

Chapter 12

JOHN FISHER AND LADY MARGARET

ORTHODOX REFORMERS

In 1483 Caius Auberinus received the first recorded payment for writing Italianate letters for congregation. In that year or soon after John Fisher began the arts programme in Cambridge. He was perhaps about fifteen, a mercer's son from Beverley in Yorkshire, where he had learned his grammar at the minster school. He became a pensioner of Michaelhouse where his tutor was his fellow townsman William Melton, about eight years his senior.[1] Fisher took his BA in 1488, the year the arts curriculum changed, and his MA in 1490–1, was elected to a Michaelhouse fellowship, and entered the theology faculty. He was senior proctor 1494–5, and was paid by congregation for lecturing in 1496–7. Shortly afterwards the mathematics professorship was begun, no doubt with Fisher's support, since he would later prove to be a great proponent of the quadrivial arts in the colleges he helped found.[2] His talents led to still higher posts : vice-chancellor and DTh. in 1501, first Lady Margaret Professor of Divinity in 1502, chancellor of the university and Bishop of Rochester in 1504, Queens' College president in 1505, and chancellor of the university for life in 1514.

Fisher's earthly success was a rare example of virtue triumphant. He was a grave, ascetic man, while no drudge. He appreciated and encouraged Erasmus' humour, loved learning

---

[1] *BRUC*, pp. 229–30; Fisher was also a classmate of John Bonge, who in 1535 recalled how at Michaelhouse, 'I myght speke to hym out off my chambyr wyndow in to his chamber wyndow', J. Gairdner, 'A Letter Concerning Bishop Fisher and Thomas More', *English Historical Review*, 7 (1892), 714.

[2] F. van Ortroy, 'Vie du Bienheureux Martyr Jean Fisher, Cardinal Evêque de Rochester (d. 1535)', *Analecta Bollandiana*, 10 (1891), 207.

in general, lacked avarice, and tended his flock carefully. That this man with no benefices or court offices would be given a bishopric, even poor Rochester, astonished his contemporaries.[3] Fisher attributed the promotion to the King and former Cambridge chancellor Richard Fox. The encouragement of the King by his mother, Lady Margaret was surely a factor, as was a possible desire by Henry VII for a 'kind of reparation for the many unsuitable men he had promoted'.[4] Henry VIII had no similar qualms, and Fisher never made the usual climb up the *valor ecclesiasticus*, remaining in Rochester until his death thirty-one years later.

John Fisher's career spans the most dynamic period in pre-modern Cambridge. The university went from a provincial status to one of international reputation. It became influential in the politics of the Tudor State and Church. He brought Erasmus to teach in Cambridge, and he oversaw the reform of its curriculum. He was the conduit of Lady Margaret's substantial aid: two large colleges, a professorship, and a preachership.

These years have been called the 'Catholic Reformation' of Cambridge, part of an international awakening in late-medieval piety that was expressed by such varied people as Thomas à Kempis, Savonarola, and Erasmus. Erasmus' ideal was the *philosophia Christi*, an unsacramental, lay piety which focused on the ethical Christ. It repudiated the 'dead' theology of the universities and the language that expressed it. The way to Christian improvement was through the reading of Scripture and the Patristic Fathers in their original tongues, acting upon them, and preaching the message clearly. The necessary educational reform was clear: a familiarity with classical Latin and Greek, and the concomitant reading of the best pagan authors wherein that grammatical knowledge (and much more) could be found. John Fisher as teacher and later chancellor saw the complete implementation of this Erasmian programme by 1520. The purpose was not disinterested admiration of classicism, but the reformation of English spiritual life through the education of the secular clergy. These humanist priests would lead the

---

[3] Lewis, *Life of Fisher*, II, p. 270.
[4] P. Hughes, *The Reformation in England*, rev. edn, 3 vols. in 1 (London, 1963), I, p. 78.

14 A bust by Pietro Torrigiano, traditionally believed to be John Fisher.

people back to true religion.[5] Fisher's involvement was not necessarily always causal, but he always seems to have been very near, encouraging, directing, financing. He knew all the central characters.

Dr H. C. Porter has written, 'the chancellorship of Fisher marked the Spring of Renaissance Cambridge, no less surely than it witnessed the Indian Summer of the medieval university'.[6] As with all times, there was both change and continuity. Fisher was a friend of Erasmus but an admirer of Scotus. To try to separate Cambridge men of this time into 'humanists' and 'scholastics' is a futile task; few fit entirely into

[5] McConica, *English Humanists*, p. 78.
[6] H. C. Porter, *Reformation and Reaction in Tudor Cambridge* (Cambridge, 1958), pp. 6–7.

one party or the other. Nobody in the Cambridge of 1517 would have guessed that the lines would be so cruelly drawn in the coming decades. That royal authority would condemn specific scholastic authorities in 1535 would have been thought preposterous. Why would the crown care which logicians were used in the universities? It never had before. But with printing and the subsequent spread of political and religious polemics in the 1530s, a new battleground opened up. The new learning was conscripted for far less gentle ends than the *philosophia Christi* had intended.[7] Reform became a proper noun and the middle ground disappeared, along with the lives of Cambridge men on both sides of it. All that unpleasantness was still far away when the young John Fisher first rode down to Cambridge.

The internal reform of Cambridge can best be understood as the action of a group of influential men with similar goals. Fisher was the most outstanding, but the movement included many others of lesser fame, like William Melton and John Alcock, who were also from the North.[8] Melton was from Beverley and was already in the theology faculty when Fisher arrived; their families must have known each other. We gain a glimpse of Melton's collegiate supervisions when, forty years later, Fisher was writing in defence of the Real Presence. When encouraging strict attention to the biblical text, he compared the process with how Melton, *praeceptor meus*, used to admonish him that if he ignored even the smallest detail in a geometric diagram, he 'had not yet comprehended the true and complete mind of Euclid'.[9]

More importantly, Melton and Fisher shared the same ecclesiastical reforming goals. Melton left Cambridge in 1496 to become chancellor of York, a post he held until his death in 1528. His will includes a bequest to Michaelhouse, and also

---

[7] McConica, *English Humanists*, esp. chapters 5 and 6.
[8] Of the six Oxford and Cambridge colleges founded between 1496 and 1525, only Wolsey's Cardinal College, Oxford was not the work of a northcountryman: Jesus (1496), Christ's (1506), and St John's (1511) at Cambridge, and Brasenose (1512), Corpus Christi (1517), and Cardinal College (1525). Gray and Brittain, *Jesus College*, p. 21.
[9] J. Fisher, *De veritate corporis et sanguinis Christi* (Cologne, 1527), f. 235r. (proemium, book v).

itemises a large theological library of medieval authorities, Greek grammars and texts, and books by More, Erasmus, and Fisher. Melton only published one work himself, an *Exhortative sermon... to those who seek to be promoted to Holy Orders*, which outlines his ideal for candidates for the priesthood. Melton had a strong sense of the elevated nature of sacerdotal life, which complemented his firm belief in the Real Presence (a popular devotion in late medieval England). Just and upright behaviour was demanded of these men, and this was not thought possible without a firm grounding in good letters. Those with a knowledge of only the basics of grammar were expected to read and study until they made good this deficiency. The dissipated rural clergy, Melton observed, were also ignorant, and reading and the contemplation of holy works was a sovereign remedy against the sloth that leads to other abuses. Such reading was now made all the easier by the 'abundance of small printed books'. This brief work closes with a strong commendation by John Colet, founder of St Paul's School and intimate of More and Erasmus, recommending its use in grammar schools and universities. [10]

John Alcock was another northcountryman who thought along similar lines. He too grew up in Beverley, attended the grammar school there, and was a DCL of Cambridge (possibly Pembroke College) by 1459. Alcock's career was a blend of ecclesiastical climbing and political service which led him to the bishoprics of Rochester, Worcester, and in 1486, Ely. Along the way he served as Royal Chancellor in 1474 in Thomas Rotherham's absence, who was then also chancellor of Cambridge. Rotherham and Alcock had been contemporaries and shared similar ideas. Rotherham was provost of Beverley Minster from 1468–72. Both served the Yorkists as diplomats, yet both ended as supporters of the Tudors. Their lives and promotions were

---

[10] *BRUC*, pp. 400–1; W. Melton, *Sermo exhortatorius cancellarii Eboracensis hiis qui ad sacros ordines petunt promoveri* (Westminster: Wynkyn de Worde, 1507–10?), iiir.–v., viir.–v., and esp. viiiv., 'Precipuum autem contra inertem torporem prestat remedium lectio assidua et revolucio librorum legis dei et scripturarum: quos ante nos sancti patres et doctores ediderunt. In quorum opusculis iam per impressionem habundantibus possunt vel mediocriter eruditi varium et iocundum colligere solatium. Ad veram sacerdotii artem tale pertinet studium'.

nearly parallel, and when Rotherham was dying in May 1500 he named Alcock his executor; Alcock himself died in October of that year.[11]

Rotherham was conspicuous in his support of both Oxford and Cambridge, and in 1481 also founded a grammar college in his home town. The purpose of this school called 'Jesus College' in Rotherham was to 'preach the word of God in the parish...and diocese of York, and teach gratuitously in the rules of grammar and song, scholars from all parts of England, and especially from the diocese of York'. There was to be a provost, six choristers, and three masters, a number corresponding to the ten commandments that Rotherham had broken. The first master taught grammar, the second song, and the third 'the art of writing and accounts', for the 'many youths endowed with the light and sharpness of ability, who do not all wish to attain...the priesthood, that these may be better fitted for the mechanical arts and other worldly matters'. So, Jesus College was for both an improved clergy and a prosperous commonwealth. Besides, Rotherham wanted no parroting priests; his bequests to the school included 105 books, many of them classical.[12]

John Alcock was a similarly energetic founder and builder. Comptroller of the royal works and buildings under Henry VII, he also was involved in buildings at Ely, Cambridge (Great St Mary's and the Schools), and Malvern Priory. He too founded a grammar school, in 1479 in Hull, the home of his parents. The school was for song and grammar, free for any who attended, and the chantry obligation was to pray for the Yorkist King Edward IV, and Alcock and his heirs.[13]

Alcock's interest in Church reform is clear in his published sermons, most of which are in English. He preached at St Paul's, London on Childermas to the 'boy bishop' and his classmates, a work which recommends prayer, learning, and loyalty to the Tudors, while warning against such vanities as French slippers, the long hair and short collars of the Germans, Spanish leather,

---

[11] *BRUC*, pp. 5–6 and 489–91; Gray and Brittain, *Jesus College*, pp. 21–2.
[12] Leach, *Schools of Medieval England*, pp. 275 6. He also gave a mitre for the use of the boy bishop.   [13] *VCH*, Yorkshire, I, pp. 449–50.

and Roman hats. In Alcock's *Exhortacyon made to Relygyouse Systers in the tyme of theyr consecracyon*, he explained what the Latin of their vows meant, and the symbolism of the light and oil. In both of these works Alcock relied on the authority of Scripture and the Fathers, and his approach was pastoral and instructive.[14] Like Fisher, Melton, and Rotherham, he was firm in his belief in the sacraments and religious vocations. It was the practice, not the theology, of the English Church that they felt needed improving.

JESUS COLLEGE

The first of the Cambridge colleges that came from the zeal of these men was that 'of the Blessed Virgin Mary, St John the Evangelist, and the glorious virgin St Radegund, near Cambridge'. It has always been known as Jesus College, however, by the wish of the founder and perhaps as an echo of the Jesus College at Rotherham. The name of Jesus was another popular devotion in fifteenth-century England. Alcock's college was 'near Cambridge' in that it occupied the Benedictine nunnery of St Radegund which sat alone in its ample precincts beside the town meadows outside the King's Ditch, between the town and Barnwell Priory. Even today an aerial view shows Jesus surrounded by green, contiguous with no other buildings.

Alcock was translated from Worcester to Ely in 1486, and the following year he found the convent of St Radegund in bad order. The prioress had just died and, considering the nuns unfit to elect her successor, he appointed one. In 1495–6 Alcock again visited the sisters, and found only two still present (one reputed to be *infamis*).[15] Whether he had done anything between 1486 and 1496 to reverse this decline is unknown. That he had allowed it to continue as a justification for his next move has been suspected, although his published sermon shows his belief in the value of nunneries. At any rate, Alcock suppressed St Radegund's and founded a college in its place.

---

[14] J. Alcock, *An exhortacyon made to Relygyouse systers* (Westminster: Wynkyn de Worde, n.d.), *STC* 287; *In die innocencium sermo pro episcopo puerorum* (Westminster: Wynkyn de Worde, n.d.), *STC* 282–3.   [15] Gray and Brittain, *Jesus College*, pp. 15–16.

15 The cloister of St Radegund's Convent, adapted by Bishop Alcock for Jesus College.

Alcock neatly adapted the convent for collegiate use, shortening the chapel and converting much of the nave into three stories of chambers, and decorating the remainder in the perpendicular style. The architectural work was financed in large part by two laymen, Sir John Rysley and Sir Reginald Bray. Rysley

271

at his death in 1512 also left £160 for the completion of the chapel work.[16]

Bishop Alcock died in 1500 before he promulgated statutes for Jesus College, and the earliest enacted were those of Bishop James Stanley in 1514–15. The college did have some *normam vivendi* from the Alcock years, however. It included many of the elements associated with the succeeding Tudor colleges: preaching, lay patronage, grammar instruction, and a fellowship with connections with the new learning and the circle of Lady Margaret,[17] and the hand of John Fisher. Fisher was senior proctor in 1494–5, and was an obvious choice when his townsman Alcock began work on Jesus. The extent of this help is uncertain, but it has been shown that Fisher wrote the foundation charter of 1496, and then used it as an exemplar when suppressing the Hospital of St John in 1509 to found in its place St John's College.[18]

Alcock envisaged a master, six fellows, and six boys for Jesus College. The first master, William Chubbes, held the post until his death in 1505. He too was a Yorkshireman, MA 1469, DTh. *c.* 1487, and a past master of Pembroke College. It has been asserted that it was at his suggestion that Alcock founded the college. Chubbes was in the patronage of Lady Margaret, and she also paid a Cambridge master £2 to write out Chubbes' works.[19] The original fellows included William Atkynson of Pembroke, MA 1478, DTh. 1498, who later became a canon of St George's Chapel, Windsor, and at Lady Margaret's request in 1502 translated the *Imitatio Christi* from French.[20] Lady Margaret's aid came in more direct ways as well; £26 was given in 1503 towards the rebuilding of the chapel.[21]

The inclusion by Alcock of six boys to study grammar reflected the interest that he showed in founding his chantry school at Hull, and also echoed Archbishop Rotherham's earlier Jesus College. This inclusion of preparatory studies was not

[16] Gray and Brittain, *Jesus College*, pp. 26–8.   [17] *Docs.* III, 92.
[18] A. Gray, *The Earliest Statutes of Jesus College, Cambridge* (Cambridge, 1935), pp. 57–61.
[19] *BRUC*, p. 136; M. Underwood, 'The Lady Margaret and Her Cambridge Connections', *Sixteenth Century Journal*, 13 (1982), 68. These included a commentary on Scotus' *Sentences* I, now CUL MS Kk. 1.18.   [20] *BRUC*, p. 22.
[21] Underwood, 'Lady Margaret', p. 69.

unique, as Merton College, Oxford and several earlier Cambridge colleges had young bible clerks. Alcock presumably expected the fellows to do the teaching.

John Alcock died in 1500 before he could finalise many of his arrangements, and Bishop West's statutes of *c.* 1517 claim the college was 'begun to be founded' by Alcock.[22] Early on Jesus College acquired the endowments and lectureships that characterise the new learning. Sir John Rysley, patron of the building fund, also helped to endow a theology lectureship in 1506 jointly with John Batmanson, DCL 1493, who had served as a diplomat, gave legal advice on the will of Lady Margaret, and was present at the promulgation by Bishop Fox of the statutes of Corpus Christi College, Oxford.[23] This theology lectureship was to be held by a fellow of the college, its subject matter was restricted to the Old and New Testaments, and it could be given in either Latin or English. All fellows were required to attend.[24] The post was held by Thomas Cranmer *c.* 1516.

Sir Reginald Bray, the other patron of the building, had a career similar to Batmanson's. Of gentle birth, he was steward of Lady Margaret's household, and with Rotherham and others intrigued against Richard III. He was well rewarded after Bosworth Field: he was high steward of Oxford in 1494, possibly the same at Cambridge; speaker of the House of Commons in 1497; and at his death in 1503 was buried in his chantry chapel at St George's, Windsor. Sir Reginald's architectural interests were shown in the conversion of St Radegund's; he also completed St George's Chapel, supported Henry VII's great chapel at Westminster, and aided Bishop Alcock's rebuilding of Great Malvern Priory.[25]

Bray was a benefactor of both Pembroke and Jesus, and his

[22] Gray and Brittain, *Jesus College*, p. 25.   [23] *BRUC*, pp. 44–5.
[24] *Docs.* III, 120, 'In ista theologiae lectione nihil aliud enarrari aut profiteri volumus, quam quod in aliqua Novi aut Veteris Testamenti parte contineatur. Eam tamen vel materno vel Latino sermone interpretandam judicio magistri et lectoris permittimus.'
[25] C. H. and T. Cooper, *Athenae Cantabrigienses* (Cambridge, 1858), I, pp. 6–7; *The History of the King's Works*, ed. H. M. Colvin, III (London, 1975), pp. 6, 211, 291, 312, 314; W. G. Richardson, *Tudor Chamber Administration* (Baton Rouge, Louisiana, 1982), App. I, pp. 451–8.

widow, Lady Katherine, made the master and fellows of Pembroke party to her endowment in 1506 of a grammar master for Jesus. He was assisted by an usher who taught four boys under fourteen years of age, who served as choristers. After four years of grammar study (or fewer, if they were adept), they could enter the faculty of arts as college *juvenes*. These latter were also four in number, were under the supervision of the grammar master, and acted as organist, sacrist, bible clerk, and gatekeeper; all served at table as well. The grammar scholars were to be given preference in election to fellowships.[26] Lady Katherine reserved the right to appoint the grammar master, and also required the college to celebrate Masses for her family.

The original fellowship was six, but this was increased in 1500 by two more, endowed by the laymen Thomas Roberts and Roger Thorney. A third fellowship was given by Lady Jane Hastings in 1501, and a fourth in 1506 by Bishop Stanley of Ely. In 1518 Sir Robert Rede endowed a chantry priest at Jesus, and made the college responsible for maintaining the university professorships first established by the statutes of 1488.[27]

Bishop Stanley's statutes of 1514–15 consolidated the fellowship to eight, no doubt for financial reasons. The five foundation fellows were all to be priests, four studying theology and one law, with the other three fellowships left open. The college officers included a president, bursar, and dean: the dean supervised the Friday disputations in which all were to participate. The fellows each had a private chamber, but the three principal chambers were reserved for distinguished pensioners; from the beginning Jesus College planned on housing those outside of the fellowship.

Stanley's statutes were replaced in 1516–17 by those of his successor at Ely, Nicholas West. Among the significant innovations were the descriptions of the daily lectures in the three philosophies or logic, and one weekly lecture in mathematics

---

[26] Gray and Brittain, *Jesus College*, pp. 30–1.
[27] Gray and Brittain, *Jesus College*, pp. 31–3.

for the fellows and bachelor commoners, which complemented the work of the university mathematics professor. Whether these lectures were founded by Bishop West or only codified by him is impossible to say; there was already a theology lecture, and it is likely that the arts lectures date from the foundation as well. [28] The mutilated tax assessment for Cambridge in 1522 shows Jesus College with a membership of about forty-five to fifty. [29] The new college was prospering.

At Jesus we see all the hallmarks of the English Renaissance college coming together: ecclesiastical reform, pensioners, an emphasis on grammar, undergraduate scholars included on the foundation, college lectors, the hand of John Fisher, and heavy lay endowment by those who rose to prominence with the Tudors. With those early supporters, and with the first master and several of the fellows we encounter the household of Lady Margaret Beaufort. No one has ever done more to help the University of Cambridge into new paths than the Lady Margaret, and it was John Fisher who showed her the way.

LADY MARGARET

Lady Margaret is first known to have met Fisher when he was senior proctor in 1494–5. His duties took him to Greenwich where he recorded expenses for lunching 'at the Queen Mother's' and supping with the 'Lord Chancellor', which may refer to the royal chancellor who was then Cardinal Morton, the patron of the young Thomas More. [30] We see the patterns of patronage coming together.

Lady Margaret was fifty-one in 1494 and twice widowed. At age twelve she was married to Edmund Tudor, Earl of Richmond, who died the next year leaving her pregnant with a son who was to be King Henry VII. She married twice more, but both unions were childless. She devoted herself to her son's fortune, and throughout the Wars of the Roses promoted his

---

[28] *Docs.* III, 109–10.   [29] *LP*, Addendum, vol. I, part 1, pp. 108–10.
[30] *GBk* B, I, p. 68 (1494–5).

interests. When her plots against Richard III bore fruit in 1485 she became one of the most influential people in the kingdom.[31]

Lady Margaret had patronised popular piety before meeting Fisher; in 1494 Wynkyn de Worde had at her command printed Walter Hylton's *Ladder of Perfeccion*, and during the same period she was active in promoting Hugh Oldham and Richard Smyth, later involved in founding Corpus Christi and Brasenose Colleges, Oxford.[32]

She was evidently impressed on meeting John Fisher, and he was soon a chaplain in her household and later her confessor in succession to Richard Fitzjames, the warden of Merton College.[33] Exactly what Lady Margaret's educational convictions were is hard to say. Her piety was clearly genuine, and had already taken conventional forms; she had founded several almshouses, and in 1496 chantries in Westminster Abbey and one at Wimborne that included a grammar school. With Fisher these benefactions accelerated, and were directed towards Cambridge. We have already seen her association with Jesus College in 1497 and her patronage of Doctor Chubbes and William Atkynson. In the same year she endowed professorships in divinity at both Oxford and Cambridge. Support for this new form of academic institution must have been at Fisher's suggestion. He had already seen the success of the three Cambridge arts professors of 1488, and establishing such a chair in divinity helped to fulfil his vision of solid teaching on both the university and collegiate levels. It was also a further sign of the waning position of the friars in the theology faculty.

In December 1496 and March 1497 Lady Margaret obtained licences from her son to found two professorships in theology, one for each university, and permission to grant them lands not exceeding £20 per annum in value.[34] Several years then passed in negotiations before the ultimate form of these posts was determined although some lectures were given in the interim.[35]

---

[31] C. H. Cooper, *Memoir of Margaret, Countess of Richmond and Derby* (Cambridge, 1874), pp. 1–40.   [32] Underwood, 'Lady Margaret', p. 68.

[33] *BRUO*, II, pp. 691–2 (Richard Fitzjames).

[34] J. W. Clark, *Endowments of the University of Cambridge* (Cambridge, 1904), pp. 57–65.

[35] *GBk* B, I, p. 120 (1498–9).

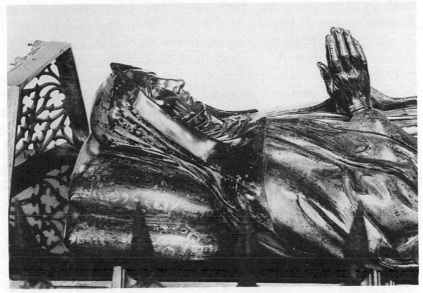

16 Lady Margaret's effigy by Pietro Torrigiano on her tomb in Westminster Abbey

In 1502, the abbey of Westminster became custodian for the benefaction, and responsible for paying £13 6s 8d per annum to the Oxford and Cambridge professors.[36] By the foundation deed each professor was required to read 'freely, solemnly, and openly' without any fee other than his salary, on every legible day in term between seven and eight in the morning, and in the long vacation until 8 September, but not during Lent, so that the auditors might occupy themselves with preaching.[37] He was to be elected biennially by a vote of the vice-chancellor and the faculty of theology, who were to swear to elect impartially the best candidate. His duties also included reciting prayers for the soul of the foundress and her ancestors. Thus Lady Margaret personally enjoyed the benefits of a chantry, while the university received financial support, and the kingdom benefited from the improved clergy. The first Lady Margaret Professor (by the 1502 charter) was Fisher himself, and it was

[36] Clark, *Endowments*, pp. 70–3.
[37] The mathematics lecture was similarly suspended in Lent. *Docs.* I, no. 136, pp. 382–3.

held by Erasmus from 1511–14.[38] The later history of the foundation parallels that of Oxford. With the dissolution of Westminster Abbey in 1540 the payment of the stipend fell to the crown, dealt with through the Court of Augmentations.[39]

Lady Margaret also endowed a preachership which, like the professorships, was not without precedent at Cambridge. In 1446 Thomas Collage, otherwise unknown, left £40 to Oxford and Cambridge to support preachers, who were to receive 6s 8d (as long as the money lasted) on each occasion they preached, 'that encouragement might be bestowed on divinity, which now was at a low ebb'.[40] We hear nothing more of how or whether this was ever implemented. In 1459 William Lasby, a clerk of Cambridge, gave Queens' College land in St Botolph's parish to provide for the delivery of sermons by college fellows who were in the theology faculty.[41] As part of the 1472 grant which supported Dame Alice Wyche's lector in the same college, it was stipulated that he should also pray for her and her husband, and preach an Easter sermon at St Dionysius' in London.[42] John Argentein, the physician and provost of King's, also endowed a preacher to complete his chantry at his college.[43]

In a sense, the preaching at St Paul's Cross in London had always been an effort by the university to bring its learning to the people. Oxford expanded this effort in 1489–90 when they wrote to the papal collector Giovanni Gigli asking for permission for the chancellor and doctors of theology to grant preaching licences. Nothing happened, however.[44]

Cambridge was more successful in getting permission to grant preaching licences. Through the efforts of Thomas Cabold of Gonville Hall, DCL and minor papal penitentiary for Britain

---

[38] cf. Underwood, 'Lady Margaret', p. 69, where a Dr Smyth is called the first professor. Smyth was paid as a lecturer. *GBk* B, 1, p. 118.

[39] Clark, *Endowments*, pp. 73–5.

[40] A. Wood, *History and Antiquities of the University of Oxford* (Oxford, 1792), 1, p. 596. It is uncertain whether the words are Wood's, or from the original documents.

[41] *BRUC*, pp. 353; Searle, *Queens' College*, 1, pp. 65–6, 'in locis quibus magis necesse est in salvationem et revelamen quamplurium animarum'.

[42] Searle, *Queens' College*, 1, pp. 80–1.

[43] King's College Archives, *Mundum Books*, 10 and *passim*.

[44] *Epistolae academicae Oxon.*, ed. Anstey, 11, pp. 564 and 567–8; *BRUO*, 11, pp. 764–5.

in 1499–1500, Cambridge was granted a bull by Alexander VI on 2 May 1503. It empowered the chancellor annually to appoint twelve doctors, masters, or graduates in priestly orders to preach throughout England, Scotland, and Ireland to the people and clergy, except in places where the bishops themselves preached, or in any church without the consent of the rector.[45] The first licences were given the next year to three men, all sympathetic to the new learning.[46]

These papal licences were remarkable in that they were initially for life. In 1511 Cambridge passed a statute to curtail any possible abuses by restricting them to two years if the candidate had not publicly preached in the university before; however, if he did so (in either English or Latin) during the two years, the licence would be extended for life. If not, the licence would expire.[47]

Between 1504 and 1522 about 175 of these licences were granted, even to Richard Reynolds, who was already professed at Syon monastery when he received his. The list reads like a *Who's Who* of Cambridge religious life.[48] After 1522, except for four granted in 1526–7, there is a gap of ten years. Evidently the right was revoked during the 1520s, for the next we hear of them is in February 1532 when the university wrote to Bishops Stephen Gardiner of Winchester and John Fisher seeking their help in restoring the papal privilege. The letters speak of the 'utter uprooting of that storm of opinions' that caused the suspension – doubtless a reference to Lutheranism at Cambridge.[49] Some temporary respite was given, for in June of that year six university preachers were appointed.[50] But then

---

45 *GBk* B, I, p. 130 (1499–1500); *BRUC*, pp. 116 and 673. For an example of such a licence with the bull rehearsed, see Lewis, *Life of Fisher*, II, pp. 261–3.

46 John Fawne, *BRUC*, pp. 221 and 675; Thomas Patenson, *BRUC*, p. 444; Geoffrey Knight, *BRUC*, p. 340.   47 *Docs.* I, 421–2; *GBk* B, I, p. 250 (1510–11).

48 See *GBk* B, I, p. 216 (1505–6) and *passim*; *GBk* B, II, p. 7 (1512), and *passim*; CUA Lic. A (1) pp. 1–16; CUA Plan Press I, Charters etc., Drawer X, and CUA Subscrip. Add. 4.

49 CUA, Epistolae academicae, pp. 122–3, 'Quare nunc post sedatam, aut potius (et spes est) funditus extractam illam opinionum tempestatem, ob quam privilegio illo nostro uti a patribus pro tempore vetiti sumus, nunc certe et nobis utile et populo necessarium esse existimamus...'

50 *GBk* Γ, p. 274 (1532–3) and CUA Subscrip. Add. 4, f. 5r.

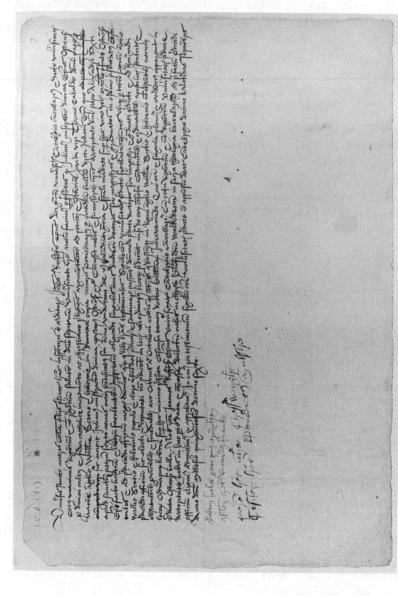

17 The preaching licence granted to Humphrey Walkden by the university in 1516, with the names of four other preachers appointed that year appended below.

there was another lapse which lasted until the Marian Restoration.[51]

Thus, when Lady Margaret endowed a preachership in 1504, it was not an entirely new idea. Like the preacherships at Queens' College it carried a chantry obligation and specified where the sermons were to be given: six each year, at St Paul's Cross or St Margaret's, Westminster, and in parishes in London, Ely, and Lincoln dioceses where Lady Margaret held land. What was unique was the generous salary attached: £10 annually, and the provision that the preacher was to be a college fellow as well. The evangelical emphasis is also clear, as by the foundation charter the first was to be John Fawne of Queens', university professor and preacher, and friend of Erasmus. Erasmus in the preface of his *De ratione concionandi* acknowledged the reforming zeal of this patronage when he spoke of Lady Margaret and John Fisher as supporters of preachers who 'brought to the people the gospel philosophy'.[52] In the next year the preachership was modified to give preference to the fellows of Christ's College, the next target for the Lady Margaret's generosity.

CHRIST'S COLLEGE

In the same year that the foundation charters of the professorship and preachership were sealed, Bishop Fisher began another project to strengthen Cambridge. Godshouse, as we have seen, was founded in the 1430s in part to produce schoolmasters. The young college had continued for the next seventy years while suffering from the usual financial problems. The statutes were not sealed until 1494; perhaps it is not a coincidence that it was the year of Fisher's senior proctorship. With its internal lector who was charged with teaching (among other things) 'the

[51] The privilege was renewed by Queen Elizabeth by letters patent in 1561 (Dyer, *Privileges*, 1, 126) and continued until 1858, when there was another lapse until the privilege was exercised in 1957. CUA Subscript. Add. 4.
[52] *Epistolae Erasmi*, XI, pp. 191–2; Underwood, 'Lady Margaret', pp. 70–1; Clark, *Endowments*, pp. 65–7. In 1679 the Lady Margaret's Preacher was excused from sermons outside the university, and so it has remained. Clark, *Endowments*, p. 58.

works of poets and orators', and its Lancastrian endowments, it was a likely candidate for Lady Margaret's liberality.

The conversion of Godshouse into Christ's College was the result of Fisher encouraging Lady Margaret to redirect benefactions originally destined for Westminster Abbey. The royal permission allowing this was given in a letter from Henry VII to his mother, 'to altre and chaunge part of a lycence which I had gyven unto you before to be put into mortmain at Westmynster; and now to be converted into the university of Cambridge for your soule helthe'. The intermediary was given as 'Master Fysher'.[53] Further endowments came from estates obtained specifically to be given to the college. In 1504 Sir Reginald Bray was surveying lands that soon were Christ's. The next year Hugh Ashton was buying livings for the same reason, and other members of her household involved in these tasks reflected the background and values of the new learning: John Fothede, master of Michaelhouse and university preacher in 1509; Robert Bekynsaw, fellow of Michaelhouse and Fisher's successor as president of Queens' College; and Henry Hornby of Yorkshire, Lady Margaret's chancellor and dean of chapel, master of Peterhouse, and instrumental in the founding of St John's College.[54]

Since Christ's College was a refoundation and there was continuity with the fellowship of Godshouse, the new college effectively dates from 1506 when new statutes were promulgated. Lady Margaret declared herself 'heir to all Henry VI's godly intentions', thus emphasising the continuity of the two colleges and the two dynasties. Even the new college motto, *Souvent me souvient* was a refashioning of Henry VI's *N'oubliez pas*.[55] But Christ's was significantly different in size and in the composition of the fellowship. The statutes compare the college to the body. The head was the master, an office filled by the last proctor of Godshouse, John Syclyng.[56] He was assisted by

[53] Cooper, *Lady Margaret*, pp. 91–2; Underwood, 'Lady Margaret', pp. 67–8.
[54] *BRUC*, pp. 238, 51–2, and 313–14; Underwood, 'Lady Margaret', pp. 69 and 73–6.
[55] See H. Rackham, ed. *Christ's College in Former Days* (Cambridge, 1939), pp. 61–4.
[56] *BRUC*, p. 572 (John Syclyng).

two deans, who were fellows. The fellowship was two-tiered and reflects the growing status of undergraduates within the colleges. There were to be twelve fellow-scholars and forty-seven pupil scholars. The fellow scholars were elected from the pupil scholars, and were required to have a BA, study theology, philosophy, or the arts, and take Holy Orders within a year of election. The purpose of the college is clear: to produce an improved clergy; and this was emphasised by the preference they were given in the election of the Lady Margaret Preacher.[57] Preference in the election of the fellows was given to natives of the northern counties, and follows an example we have already noted; Rotherham, Alcock, Fisher, Melton, Fothede, and Bekynsaw were all from the North; St John's College was to follow a similar pattern.[58] Other colleges were similarly affected. Robert Shorton, DTh. 1512, was a fellow of Jesus 1503–5, university preacher 1507–8, and master of Pembroke 1516–34. During his tenure at Pembroke eight of the twenty-one fellows elected came from Northumberland, Durham, and Westmorland.[59] This wave of northerners was due to both the intersecting patterns of patronage and the growth of religious renewal that later found expression in the Pilgrimage of Grace.

The forty-seven pupil scholars of Christ's were chosen from poor boys who knew Latin and were preparing for Holy Orders. They were to study in the arts faculty, except for six who were judged suitable to pursue the master of grammar degree, a memory of the Godshouse intention. In practice it did not work out that way; few Christ's men took the MGram., which was soon to disappear from Cambridge as the more humanist BA course became accepted as the best preparation for a schoolmaster. The six grammar students also served in hall and read the lesson on a weekly rota.[60]

The Christ's College lector, called metaphorically the 'reproductive organ' in the statutes, was the successor of his Godshouse

---

[57] Underwood, 'Lady Margaret', p. 70.
[58] Underwood, 'Lady Margaret', p. 78; T. Baker, *History of the College of St John the Evangelist*, ed. J. E. B. Mayor (Cambridge, 1869), I, 98.
[59] *BRUC*, pp. 525–6; Attwater, *Pembroke College*, p. 32.
[60] Rackham, *Early Statutes of Christ's*, pp. 103–9.

forerunner, and his duties are often described in identical words. He was to give four two-hour lectures in hall each day, again on 'sophistry, logic, philosophy, and works of poets and orators', and conduct twice-weekly disputations. Discipline was maintained by flogging and fines. These lectures were meant to complement the university instruction, and the statutes required that all college members follow the lectures and acts demanded of them by the university, as well as attend the internal exercises. The hours of the latter were specified so as not to conflict with the former.[61] The Christ's College accounts are extant from 1531 and show the payments regularly made to the lector, who was by that time aided by three salaried 'sub-lectors', an innovation that Bishop Fisher had included in his 1524 statutes for St John's.[62]

The founding of Christ's College also involved additional building. The hall and master's lodge were added, and the first floor of the lodge was reserved for the use of Lady Margaret herself and the permanent visitor, John Fisher. A window was cut between the lodge and chapel so that she could hear Mass. The accommodation for the collegians was above par, with only two to a room, although this was later changed to four. Lady Margaret's interest in the welfare of this, her first college, is seen in her personal use of the lodge, and a reputation that lingered long afterward. Thomas Fuller recounted the story that when she saw the dean correcting a scholar (no doubt with the rod), 'she said, "Lente, lente!, Gently, gently", as accounting it better to mitigate his punishment than to procure his pardon: mercy and justice making the best medley to offenders'.[63]

ST JOHN'S COLLEGE

The second college of John Fisher and Lady Margaret included many of the features of Christ's, but in a larger and more developed form. It was also more completely Fisher's creation,

---

[61] *Docs.* III, 202.
[62] Christ's College Archives, 'Accounts 1530–1545', f. 4v. and *passim*; Mayor, *Statutes of St John's*, p. 328.
[63] Fuller, *Cambridge*, p. 135, where he says he heard this anecdote used in a university sermon.

for although the idea of suppressing the Hospital of St John and founding a college on its site had been discussed by Lady Margaret's council as early as 1505, she died in 1509 and the completion of the task fell to Fisher.[64]

The first action was the suppression, which was agreed to in principle by the Countess, her stepson James Stanley, Bishop of Ely, and King Henry VII. But after the deaths of the king and his mother things became more difficult, since her will had not been changed to take this new project into account, nor had the necessary charters been obtained to suppress the hospital and found the college. These were the first obstacles. The hospital, it was claimed, was impoverished and the brethren, only three, were dissolute. The suppression was not effected until March 1511 when the last of the Austin Canons left by boat for Ely, and in April the foundation charter was given by Lady Margaret's executors. The details of the endowment were disputed, however, and in the end were not all that Fisher had wanted, according to his own account. He made good much of the shortfall out of other monies he had received from the Countess, and also secured the properties of three small religious houses. Building began in 1511 with 800,000 bricks ordered from Greenwich, and the old hospital was converted into what is now the First Court of St John's.[65] Care was taken by Fisher; the contract with a carpenter in 1516 required all parts to be as good as, if not better than, specified comparable parts of Jesus, Pembroke, and King's Colleges.[66] Although the work was not completed before 1520, the college was formally opened in July 1516.

The statutes of 1516 specified a master who was a theologian, seven senior fellows, two deans, twenty-eight foundation fellows who had at least the BA, were in Holy Orders and were studying philosophy or theology, and thirty scholars who were undergraduates in the arts faculty. In electing fellows preference was given first to college scholars and secondly to those of

---

[64] For St John's foundation, see Baker, *St John's*, I, 52–84; *VCH*, III, pp. 437–8.
[65] Willis and Clark, II, p. 240.
[66] Willis and Clark, II, p. 243; document printed in *Cambridge Commemorated*, ed. L. and H. Fowler (Cambridge, 1984), p. 23.

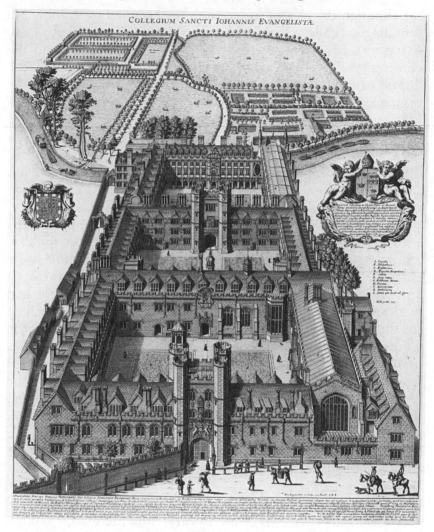

18 St John's College first court *c.* 1690. It was little changed from Fisher's time. The south side of the court was rebuilt in the eighteenth century. The chapel and the building to its north (called the 'Labyrinth') were originally part of the medieval St John's Hospital that preceded the College. The chapel and Labyrinth were destroyed in 1868–9 to make room for the present chapel.

Christ's College. In all of these positions special considerations were given to northerners.[67] Fisher also promulgated new sets of statutes in 1524 and 1530. By the 1530 formulation the foundation was set at a master, seven senior fellows, twenty-eight foundress's fellows, and twenty-two foundress's scholars, with more added by private foundations.[68]

The college was for priests or those planning to become priests. Preaching was central, 'so that theologians might come from the college and give to the people the fruit of their studies'.[69] One quarter of all the fellows were engaged in preaching to the people in English; at least eight sermons a year wherever they wanted, were demanded, and once in the college chapel: these were to be in addition to any required by the theology faculty. If any of the senior fellows were not competent preachers, they were to spend their time writing on the Sacred Scriptures or biblical languages, and in both public and college disputations. The college accounts show that these obligations were fulfilled, and that fellows were paid for preaching in country churches.[70]

The college teaching was extensive, and elaborated in each successive recodification of the statutes. Those of 1516 are similar to Christ's College. There was a lector, paid 13s 4d per quarter, who each weekday in term gave four lectures, in sophistry, logic, and two in philosophy. He was to spend at least two hours a day in *repetitiones*, explaining the lectures to the scholars. The fellows were also to appoint one of their number to lecture in the long vacation on the quadrivial sciences.

The students were to attend all required disputations in the Schools as well as those in college. They were to be examined daily by their tutors and the senior fellows on the lectures they had heard, both collegiate and university. No one in college was to take the MA unless he had publicly lectured in college or in the Schools on an assigned text of Aristotle's natural philosophy, or metaphysics. The two deans presided over the

---

[67] Mayor, *Statutes*, pp. 351–96.
[68] *VCH*, III, p. 438; M. Underwood in *Humanism, Reform, and Reformation: the Career of Bishop John Fisher*, ed. E. Duffy and B. Bradshaw (Cambridge, 1988).
[69] Mayor, *Statutes*, p. 377 (1516).
[70] Underwood, 'Lady Margaret', pp. 70–1.

19 John Fisher, proctor in 1494–5, entered his expenses for lunching with Lady Margaret Beaufort in the university account book in his own hand.

weekly disputations of the fellows in chapel; the senior dean over the theology act, and the junior over that in philosophy.[71]

These statutes were replaced in 1524 by a code based in part on that of Richard Fox for Corpus Christi College, Oxford.[72] The arts exercises were little changed from 1516, except that three sublectors were added, for sophistry, logic, and philosophy. The mathematics lecture in the long vacation was to be given by four men instead of one and, with monies bequeathed to him by Lady Margaret, Fisher established four 'examiners': for dialectic, mathematics, philosophy, and 'for studies which are called humanities'. Each of these men were to exercise the students on what they had heard in the Schools. These correspond exactly to the four Rede professors, endowed in the same year, and are a perfect example of the complementary nature of university and college lecturing.[73] On days when there were no public lectures, the philosophy and logic examiners were to review their pupils on the college lectures, the humanity examiner was to set a short oration, and the mathematics examiner was to 'explain his art'. They were all similarly to do this on days when the public lectures were 'beyond the understanding of the listeners'. Also with monies from Lady Margaret 'praelectors' in Greek and Hebrew were instituted. However, if it seemed to the master and senior fellows that the Hebrew lecture was not useful to the students, it could be changed into one in Latin on Duns Scotus.[74] Extensive pre-1530 archival material survives which shows that these statutory provisions were carried out.[75]

In the statutes for 1530 the provisions for lectures were little changed. These were in turn superseded in 1545 by a set possibly written by Sir John Cheke.[76] The lectures were the same, and the primary innovations were the inclusion of mathematics for first year scholars, and that the Greek lecture was to be given

[71] Mayor, *Statutes*, pp. 375–89.   [72] Mayor, *Statutes*, p. xiv.

[73] All colleges were required to provide such examiners by the 1570 university statutes. *Docs.* I, p. 491.

[74] Mayor, *Statutes*, pp. 326–30, 343–5, and 250–2, '...si quis forte Latiniori sermone illum donabit'.

[75] Esp. St John's College Archives, Drawer 107.1, p. 156 and Drawer 107.7, p. 18.

[76] Mayor, *Statutes*, pp. xxi and 104–6.

in the Public Schools.[77] These statutes were suspended under Queen Mary and replaced by a version based on those of 1530. On the accession of Elizabeth the statutes of 1545 were restored. They were then replaced in 1580 by yet another version which was corrected in 1586.[78] But, through all these changes the basic programme of lectures called for in the 1530 statutes remained intact: a college lector, three sublectors, four mathematical lectors, four examiners, and lectors in Greek and Hebrew.

The influence of Christ's and St John's Colleges on Cambridge was striking. Not only were their fellowships large, but they took in great numbers of pensioners. The tax census of 1522 lists between 500 and 550 members of the university; of these about 100 were at Christ's and 95 at St John's, most of them undergraduates. The next largest colleges were Trinity Hall, The King's Hall, and Jesus, with half those numbers. And in the next twenty years St John's continued to grow in wealth and endowments.[79]

One other college should be mentioned in the context of academic renewal at this time. In 1509 Pembroke obtained a theology lectureship that once again illustrates patronage between the university and influential laymen. Sir William Hussey, Lord Chief Justice, died in 1494, leaving to Pembroke enough money to purchase a farm.[80] His son, John, knighted in 1503, was a soldier, diplomat, and comptroller of the royal household. His endowments for learning took several forms; he aided Bishop William Smith of Lincoln and Sir Richard Sutton in founding Brasenose College, Oxford in 1509, was related by marriage to the humanist circle of Lord Mountjoy, Erasmus' patron, and was himself the patron of *The Mirror of Christes Passion* by John Fewterer, DTh. of Pembroke, university preacher, and later monk of Syon. Hussey was executed in 1537 for supposed complicity in the Pilgrimage of Grace.[81]

In 1507–8 the Cambridge congregation paid John Philippe, the Terence professor, two shillings for writing a letter to

[77] Mayor, *Statutes*, pp. 105–11.   [78] St John's College Archives, C1.5.
[79] *LP*, Addenda, vol. I, part 1, pp. 104–10.
[80] Attwater, *Pembroke College*, p. 24; *DNB*, X, p. 332.
[81] *DNB*, X, p. 329; McConica, *English Humanists*, p. 81.

Bishop Fox, then master of Pembroke, 'for the establishment of the theology lecture founded by Lord Hussey'.[82] It was open to the university at large, and the first lector in 1507 was Robert Shorton, formerly of Jesus College, who took his BTh. in the same year. He left Pembroke when chosen by Fisher as the first master of St John's, a post which he left in 1516 to return to Pembroke as master. Shorton was later dean of Cardinal Wolsey's chapel, and was charged with selecting Cambridge men as fellows for Cardinal College, Oxford. Shorton served Catherine of Aragon as her almoner, and died in 1535, an ally of Fisher in resisting the royal divorce.[83] Shorton's successor as Hussey lector was William Hudson, also a university preacher.[84]

ERASMUS IN CAMBRIDGE

The reshaping of the university is explained only in part by the structures of instruction and the founding of colleges. For a true change to occur in the kinds of preachers and theologians that the university produced required a different curriculum, one that specifically included Greek. By encouraging Erasmus of Rotterdam to teach in Cambridge, John Fisher obtained not only a Greek teacher, but the man who was the animating spirit, and greatest propagandist, of the northern renaissance and all that it represented. Erasmus has left no trace in the university or college archives, but his influence was real and abiding: on his pupils, by his example, and as a symbol of the chancellor's strong commitment to the reform of the curricula in both arts and theology.[85]

Erasmus' first contact with Cambridge was through three of his pupils at the Collège de Montaigu in Paris *c.* 1498. Richard Whitford was elected a fellow of Queens' in March 1497 and simultaneously given leave to study in Paris for five years. He

---

[82] *GBk* B, 1, p. 232 (1507–8).

[83] *BRUC*, 525–6; the correct date of the first lecture is found in Pembroke College Archives, Register Cδ, pp. 65–6.

[84] *BRUC*, p. 319; Pembroke College Archives, Register Cδ, pp. 70–1. This lecture disappeared after 1528.

[85] See D. F. S. Thomson and H. C. Porter, *Erasmus and Cambridge*, and the revised translations of the letters in CWE.

was later chaplain to Bishop Fox, professed as a Bridgettine in 1507, after which as the 'Wretch of Syon' he wrote a series of vernacular spiritual works.[86] Accompanying Whitford to Paris was William Blount, Lord Mountjoy, later to be a regular patron of Erasmus. The third Englishman in this group was Robert Fisher, a kinsman of the then fellow of Michaelhouse, for whom Erasmus wrote the *De conscribendis epistolis*. These three encouraged Erasmus to visit England in 1499, a trip which included his meeting John Colet during a stay in Oxford. Erasmus did not see Cambridge until 1506, however, when he was probably present at Henry VII's and Lady Margaret's visit in April, during a progress to Walsingham.[87] The royal party stayed at Queens' where Fisher was then president. Erasmus and Fisher knew each other by this time through their pupils in Paris and mutual friends in London, and it was doubtless Fisher who nominated Erasmus for the DTh. degree during this brief stay. The grace called for the usual exercises and preaching, as well as a series of lectures on *Romans*; his expertise in a new form of hermeneutics was already recognised. But Erasmus never took this degree, choosing instead the doctorate offered to him by Turin in September 1506.[88]

Erasmus returned to Cambridge from 1511 to 1514 at the invitation of Fisher as chancellor, a period that is well documented by his letters and the later reminiscences of his friends. Henry Bullock, BA 1504 was a fellow of Queens' from 1506, when he might have met Erasmus. He certainly did meet him in 1509 when Erasmus was in London, since Bullock was a familiar of the More, Colet, and Grocyn circle. Bullock was professor of mathematics in 1510–11, and his humanist hand in the Queens' account books signals his learning. It was Bullock who lent Erasmus a horse to ride up to Cambridge in August 1511.[89]

Erasmus stayed at Queens' College where tradition (now generally disbelieved) has held that he stayed in the tower room

[86] *BRUC*, pp. 635–6.
[87] 'Erasmus at Cambridge in 1506', appendix VI in *Epistolae Erasmi*, I, 590–2.
[88] *GBk* B, I, p. 222 (1506).   [89] *BRUC*, p. 105; CWE, II, no. 225, p. 168.

in Essex Court.[90] Whether he always lived in Queens' is uncertain; he speaks of the bookseller Garret Godfrey as his 'host' in later years, and possibly he lodged with him near Great St Mary's as well as dined with him there.[91] He also stayed with William Gonnell, a schoolmaster at Landbeach, during the Plague in 1513. Gonnell was later a tutor in Thomas More's household. Erasmus was not continuously in Cambridge, making several trips to London and being absent out of term and during Lent.[92]

During this fairly brief sojourn Erasmus did significant personal writing, taught Greek and theology, and formed a number of close friendships with Cambridge men who continued his work after his departure. He edited Jerome's letters; he completed his Latin translation of the Gospels and Epistles, the *Novum Instrumentum*; translated St Basil on *Isaiah*, two of Plutarch's short works, and continued with Lucian's dialogues; and worked on his own *De ratione studii*, *De copia verborum*, *De conscribendis epistolis*, and the *Disticha catonis*.[93] With his quick use of the printing press, his influence throughout Europe was immense.

In addition to this literary activity Erasmus taught Greek, the *sine qua non* for unlocking the Scriptures and the Greek Fathers. His significance here is as pioneer and propagandist. Although the first officially to teach Greek with some kind of a stipend from the chancellor, he was not the first master at Cambridge or Oxford to know the language. The idea that a knowledge of Greek made for better theologians and missionaries is at least as old as St Basil, and was encouraged by the Council of Vienne in 1312.[94] In fifteenth-century Oxford and Cambridge, however, there were not many people who could teach it. Those students interested in learning Greek usually left for Italy.

We do not know who first taught Greek privately at either

[90] Thomson and Porter, pp. 35–7.
[91] Thomson and Porter, no. 52, p. 197.
[92] For Gonnell, see Thomson and Porter, pp. 221–2.
[93] Thomson and Porter, pp. 38–61. He borrowed a Greek New Testament for Greyfriars in 1511. Moorman, *Grey Friars*, p. 58.
[94] *Chartularium universitatis Parisiensis*, ed. H. S. Denifle, II (Paris 1895), pp. 154–5.

Oxford or Cambridge. There were men at both universities who could have done so by the 1460s. The colleges provided opportunities for instruction for which no records were kept. John Farley of New College (1449–64), MA, scholar in theology, and Oxford University scribe 1458–64, was able to write some Greek.[95] He was a contemporary at Oxford of Stephano Surigone, who also knew some Greek.[96] So did George Neville of Balliol, MA 1452 and Oxford chancellor, who was a patron of the Greek scribe Emmanuel of Constantinople and John Shirwood. Shirwood knew at least some Greek, as did William Sellyng, OSB, BTh. 1458, who taught the language in Canterbury to William of Worcester.[97] William Grocyn, MA 1474 and Oxford University scribe *c.* 1470–6 could at least write his name in Greek *c.* 1470.[98] None of this proves that Greek was taught in fifteenth-century Oxford, but there were men who could have taught it.

Similar indications exist for Cambridge. John Gunthorpe, MA, BTh. 1468 and warden of The King's Hall studied between his degrees in Italy, and learned Greek at the school of Guarino da Verona.[99] Stephano Surigone left Oxford for Cambridge in the 1470s. Other evidence is equally circumstantial, like the Greek New Testament in Greyfriars library that Erasmus borrowed. An enigmatic grecian was Richard Brynkley, OFM of Cambridge Greyfriars, BTh. 1489, DTh. 1493, and years later incorporated DTh. of Oxford as well. He was a student of Greek and Hebrew and borrowed a Hebrew psalter from Bury St Edmunds in 1502; surely his study of Greek preceded Hebrew? His annotations appear in Greek psalters, Gospels (one from Oxford Greyfriars), and, among other items, a copy of the *Epistolae* of Aeneas Silvius.[100]

But we seek in vain for record of a Greek class at either university before Erasmus. He began that first autumn in 1511

95 *Epistolae academicae Oxon.*, ed. Anstey, II, pp. 367–74 (1460–3); Reg. Aa, p. 292 (1457); Weiss, *English Humanism*, pp. 137–8.
96 Trinity College, Cambridge MS 330, ff. 1r–14r.
97 BL Cotton Julius F. vii, ff. 118r., 123r., and 205r.
98 *Epistolae academicae Oxon.*, ed. Anstey, II, p. 416.   99 Weiss, *English Humanism*, p. 123.
100 *BRUC*, p. 103; Moorman, *Grey Friars*, pp. 155–6; Gonville and Caius MSS 348/59 and 403/412; Leicester, Old Town Library MS; Ipswich Central Library, Aeneas Sylvius, *Epistolae* (Nuremberg, 1481).

and wrote to his friend Andrea Ammonio in London, 'up to this moment I have been lecturing on Chrysoloras' *Grammar*, but the audience is small; perhaps more people will attend when I start Theodore's *Grammar*'.[101] Among those in attendance was Henry Bullock, whose copy of Theodore Gaza's Γραμματικὴ εἰσαγωγή is the Aldine edition of 1495. The first book and the beginning of the second have many glosses in Bullock's hand, both marginally and interlinearly. It is the work of a beginner translating words and copying the paradigms onto the margins. After folio 17, however, the book is in virgin condition. Either Erasmus' course was very basic, or Bullock attended less zealously as the weeks went on.[102] Bullock kept at it the following year, and it is from his pen in 1514–15 that the first Greek appears in the university correspondence.[103]

The Greek classes were given without charge to the scholars, as were Erasmus' theology lectures.[104] It is almost certain that he held the Lady Margaret chair, and his seeming absences from Cambridge during Lent would have been allowed by the terms of that professorship.[105] His first theology lectures were on St Jerome, which complemented his editorial work. John Caius, who came up eighteen years later, has specified that these lectures, given 'publice' were on Jerome's *Epistles* and the *Apology* against Tyrannius Rufinus.[106]

While in Cambridge Erasmus made a number of friends, some among the senior members of the university, and others from his pupils. Henry Bullock was the best of these friends and a regular correspondent in later years. He carried on Erasmus' work in the theology faculty in the spring of 1516 by lecturing on St Matthew's Gospel with the help of his master's notes.[107] John Fawne was also a member of Queens'; he was vice-chancellor in 1512–13 and succeeded Erasmus as Lady Margaret Professor.[108] Other Queensmen in the circle included Humphrey Walkeden, professor of mathematics, and John

---

[101] CWE, II, no. 233, p. 177. [102] CUL, Inc. 2.B.3.134.
[103] CUA, *Epistolae academicae* I, pp. 35, 36, 39, and 44.
[104] CWE, II, no. 296, p. 299 and no. 282, p. 267.
[105] Thomson and Porter, pp. 39–40; CWE, II, no. 233, p. 174 and no. 296, p. 299.
[106] Caius, *Annals*, p. 125. [107] CWE, IV, no. 579, p. 346.
[108] BRUC, p. 221.

Vawen, university preacher and professor. [109] John Watson was a fellow of Peterhouse during those years under the mastership of Henry Hornby, Lady Margaret's secretary. He addressed Erasmus in 1516 as 'kindest of teachers', which is probably meant literally; he knew Greek and was probably in the theology faculty when Erasmus was lecturing. [110] In 1517 Watson became master of Christ's College, again indicating the links with Fisher and Lady Margaret's benefactions. Thomas Green, late of Jesus College and later master of St Catharine's, was also among these friends. [111] Three undergraduates formed particularly close working links with Erasmus. Thomas Lupset was of the household of Dean Colet in London before coming up in 1511, and had already made the acquaintance of More, Linacre, and Erasmus. He was probably at Pembroke until 1513, and that summer was daily helping Erasmus with the revisions of the *Novum instrumentum* and the St Jerome edition, taking private tuition in Greek as his pay. [112] Lupset left Cambridge that year, and his later career saw him involved in humanist projects on the Continent, and lecturing in Greek at Corpus Christi College, Oxford, in 1519.

Robert Aldrich of King's College, BA 1512, accompanied Erasmus to Walsingham in May of that year, a visit celebrated in the *Dialogues*. [113] He also studied Seneca and St Jerome with Erasmus in Queens' College. Aldrich went on to a fellowship at King's and headmastership of Eton, before returning to Cambridge as vice-chancellor. In 1526 at Erasmus' bidding he performed a collation of Seneca manuscripts in Peterhouse and King's College libraries. [114]

A last undergraduate whom Erasmus strongly influenced was John Bryan of Eton and King's, BA 1515. By 1512 he had written a history of France now lost, and served as Erasmus' scribe. He was also a close friend of Bullock's. In a letter of

[109] *BRUC*, pp. 611 and 608.
[110] CWE, IV, no. 576, p. 343.   [111] *BRUC*, p. 270.
[112] CWE, II, nos. 270 and 271, p. 249; Thomson and Porter, pp. 222–3.
[113] 'Peregrinatio Religionis Ergo', in Erasmus, *Opera Omnia*, III (Amsterdam, 1972), pp. 470–94.
[114] Thomson and Porter, nos. 62–4, pp. 206–11.

1517 Bullock described how he learned of Erasmus' return to England while chatting with Bryan after a sermon at Blackfriars. Bryan incepted in arts the next year, and for his regency lectures he dealt with Aristotle's philosophy in the humanist, rather than the scholastic manner, presumably from the Greek text. This sort of thing was encouraged at Cambridge, and Bryan was salaried 13s 4d for his lectures in 1519–20.[115]

Erasmus left Cambridge during the Plague of Michaelmas term 1513, twenty-six months after his arrival.[116] His stay was effectively much shorter than that, since he was frequently in London. But his influence was powerful – as a teacher, scholar, and example. His pupils and friends carried on his work after he left. He embodied much of the ideal that John Fisher was supporting; a new theology for a new Church. After the statutory innovations and collegiate foundations that antedated his stay, the influence of Erasmus himself, and the curricular innovation that accelerated in the following years, Cambridge was in Erasmus' words a 'changed place'.

NEW STUDIES

In August 1516 Bullock wrote to Erasmus, 'Here [Cambridge] they are keenly studying Greek', although who the teachers were is not known.[117] Soon, however, another Greek professor was appointed, Richard Croke, a former fellow of King's College, BA 1509. Croke spent that winter in London with William Grocyn, where he began to learn the language. It was there that he first met Erasmus, who in 1511 solicited Colet for patronage on his behalf.[118] Croke continued his studies in Paris, Louvain, and Cologne, and in 1515 was appointed the first Greek professor at the University of Leipzig. He was then twenty-six years old. In the next two years he published an edition of Book IV of Gaza's *Grammar*, and a brief introduction

[115] CWE, II, no. 282, p. 266 and no. 262, p. 230; CWE, IV, no. 579, p. 346; *GBk* B, II, p. 76.
[116] For a charmingly melodramatic interpretation of his departure, see Mullinger, *Cambridge*, I, p. 506.
[117] CWE, IV, no. 449, p. 34.
[118] CWE, II, no. 277, p. 171. Colet refused, CWE, II, no. 230. pp. 173–5 and no. 237, p. 185.

to Greek.[119] He returned to Cambridge where he took his MA in 1517.[120] Croke was appointed Greek professor in the following academic year. That December Erasmus wrote 'Cambridge is a changed place. The university there has no use for this hair-splitting, which is more conducive to wrangling than religion'.[121] The following April, 1518, he wrote to Croke to congratulate him on the appointment.[122]

Croke was brought to Cambridge in the pay of Fisher. But this was not a permanent solution; the university solicited contributions from the colleges, and also wrote to Lord Mountjoy (seemingly in vain) for his help.[123] Croke's salary was assured in 1519 with the establishment by statute of the office of public orator, who was to be paid £2 per annum from the university chest. The orator was to be expert in Greek and Latin, was to compose letters for the university, and give orations to visiting worthies. Richard Croke, 'who first brought Greek literature to us' was named in the statute as the first orator, with the provision that he could hold the post for as long as he liked.[124] The first payment to him was made by the university in 1519–20.[125] The salary was raised to £4 in 1528, bringing it into line with the other professorships in arts.[126]

Not everyone was pleased with the excitement over Greek, since its impact on theology was threatening. It implied a totally new approach to Scripture and the loss of the authority of the Vulgate. Throughout sixteenth-century Cambridge Greek was applied largely to New Testament studies. The classical texts in the college libraries were given little attention when compared to this theological application. To study Greek was to break

---

[119] R. Croke, *Tabulae graecas literas discere cupientibus utiles* (Leipzig, 1516). This is a 34-page introduction for beginners. For Croke's life, see J. T. Sheppard, *Richard Croke* (Cambridge, 1919), and Thomson and Porter, pp. 86–7.

[120] *GBk* Γ, p. 144 (1516–17).

[121] CWE, V, no. 730, p. 225.

[122] CWE, V, no. 827, pp. 398–9.

[123] See King's College Archives, *Mundum Books*, 10 (1518–19), unfoliated, 'M. Croke clerico de Cancellar'; for college contributions, see Leader, 'Teaching in Tudor Cambridge', p. 109; for Lord Mountjoy, see *GBk* B, II, p. 69 (1518–19). The letter is printed in *Epistolae Erasmi*, I, appendix X, pp. 613–14 and in partial translation in Thomson and Porter, p. 69, where it is mistakenly dated 1511 or 1513 and is thought to refer to Erasmus' teaching.

[124] *Docs.* I, 431–4.   [125] *GBk* B, II, p. 84 (1519–20).

[126] *GBk* Γ, p. 237 (1528–9).

with the spirit of scholastic theology, although not necessarily its content. This was clear when Erasmus brought out his *Novum instrumentum* in 1516, and one of the more reactionary of the Cambridge colleges (unnamed) resolved that no one could bring the book onto the college grounds 'by horse, boat, wagon, or porter'. [127]

Richard Croke dealt with such attitudes in his *principium* as professor of Greek in July 1519, which strikes a balance between the irenic and the ironic. [128] In a paean to the glory that was Greece and still was Greek, he pointed out the utility of Greek for understanding the trivium and quadrivium, since the Latin authorities in those fields based their works on Greek originals. He then passed on to theology and the philosophies, praising Francis de Meyronibus, Joannes Canonicus, Thomas Aquinas, and Duns Scotus ('I openly embrace the subtlety of Scotus'), and commending the utility of disputations. He pointed out, however, that an overemphasis on these scholastic works could lead to a neglect of the more useful study of Scripture. Croke was calling for a more balanced education.

Included in this oration was an incitement to the scholars of Cambridge to compete with Oxford, which seemed to be taking the lead in this field. [129]

> Oxonians, who up to this time you surpassed in all studies, are keeping vigil, fasting, sweating, and freezing in their dedication to learning Greek; they do everything to make this their own. If they succeed, your reputation is finished.

Actually, things were much rougher for grecians at Oxford, where they lacked a chancellor who so actively promoted the new learning. In March 1518 Thomas More, with the royal court at Abingdon, addressed a letter to Oxford expressing his indignation over the attacks of the *soi-disant* 'Trojan' faction in the university, who ridiculed those who studied Greek. [130] Specifically, a doctor of theology had used a Lenten sermon at

---

[127] CWE, IV, no. 456, p. 44.
[128] R. Croke, *Orationes Richardi Croke duae, altera*...(Paris, 1520) and in partial translation in Mullinger, *Cambridge*, I, p. 534.
[129] Mullinger, *Cambridge*, I, 534, n. 1.
[130] *St Thomas More: Selected Letters*, ed. E. F. Rogers, no. 19/60, pp. 94–103 (1518).

St Mary the Virgin's to attack not only Greek, but the pro-paedeutic value of the liberal arts in general, and Erasmus' teaching in particular. By contrast, More believed that at Cambridge[131]

> those who are studying Greek are so moved by common interest in their university that they are actually making large individual contributions to the salary of the Greek professor.

The difference between the two universities was encapsulated by Erasmus in 1519:[132]

> England has two universities, hardly anywhere uncelebrated, Cambridge and Oxford. Greek literature is studied in both, but tranquilly in Cambridge, because the chancellor there is John Fisher, Bishop of Rochester, who is as theological in his studies as in his life.

Cambridge received a further boost the following spring, 1520, when the King offered Richard Pace £10 annually to lecture on Greek at Cambridge. Pace never took up the post, however.[133] Greek studies continued to grow in that decade, and attracted patronage from outside. In 1529 Bishop Cuthbert Tunstall of London presented Cambridge with a collection of classical and neo-classical Greek texts, and the university replied that it was 'as though he had transported Athens itself to Cambridge'.[134]

It was within the colleges especially that Greek flourished. The 1520s saw a new generation of young scholars whose classical fame was lasting. Sir John Cheke, BA 1529, was taught by George Day, public orator in succession to Croke and Greek praelector at St John's.[135] Cheke in turn supervised the future Lord Burghley, Roger Ascham, and William Bill. Nicholas Ridley, BA 1522 of Pembroke taught Greek within the college, where in the late 1530s he tutored Nicholas Carr, regius

---

[131] More, *Selected Letters*, no. 19/60, p. 101.
[132] *Epistolae Erasmi*, III, no. 948, pp. 546–7.   [133] *LP*, III, part 2, p. 1540.
[134] CUA, *Epistolae academicae*, I, pp. 96–8, 'ut velut Athenas ipsas in Cantabrigiam transtulisse'.
[135] *DNB*, IV, 178–83.

New studies

professor ten years later.[136] The most popular textbooks with these men were Gaza, Jacobus Ceporinus' *Compendium* and Nicholas Clenardus' *Institutiones*.[137]

The rest of the arts curriculum was evolving in the early sixteenth century as well, as it was modified to serve the newer theology, and to conform to renaissance ideals of a useful education. Grammar showed a marked change with a new emphasis on the teaching of style, signalled by the 1488 statute that established the professor of humane letters. Concomitantly, modal grammar, one of the *bêtes noires* of the humanists, was given less attention. More concerned with classical elegance and Ciceronian word selection, the friends of the new learning condemned as barbaric a grammar that championed linguistic analysis. It was neither classical nor beautiful, and it was a foundation stone of the scholastic theology that obscured the word of God. Thomas More, who must have studied (Pseudo) 'Albertus' (*De modo significandi*) in Oxford in the 1490s, later wrote of him[138]

> Albert, professing to expound grammar, gave us some sort of logic, or metaphysics, or, really, neither of the two, but substituted for grammar sheer nightmares and wild imaginations. Yet this nonsensical nonsense was welcomed into the universities...

Erasmus, who was familiar with modal grammar from Paris and the Low Countries was equally vociferous in his condemnation of the grammar of his childhood.[139] Style had taken second place to logic and metaphysics, and he singled out Alexander's *Doctrinale*, Albertus' *De modo significandi*, and John of Garland's *Compendium* as being particularly barbarous.

[136] A description of Ridley's lectures is found in N. Carr, *Demosthenes* (1570), appendix by B. Dodington to W. Mildmay, f. 58r.–v. For the controversy over the pronunciation of Greek in the early 1540s, see Mullinger, *Cambridge*, II, pp. 54–5; *Annals*, I, pp. 402–3 (1540); *GBk* B, II, p. 239 (1541–2).
[137] *STC* 4913 and 5401–4. This conclusion was reached after examining the library catalogues, works of masters, and the inventories *post mortem* of the Vice-Chancellor's Court in CUA. I am indebted to Dr Elisabeth Leedham-Green for allowing me to work with her transcripts and notes of these library inventories.
[138] More, *Selected Letters*, no. 4/15, p. 20.
[139] Erasmus, 'De pueris instituendis', *Opera omnia*, I.2 (Amsterdam, 1971), pp. 76–7.

Alexander Hegius, an elder Dutch contemporary of Erasmus even wrote a polemic against these grammarians. [140]

The humanist emphasis on classical grammar, and the stagnation of linguistic speculation, seems to have taken its toll on speculative grammar in the faculty of arts at both Oxford and Cambridge. From its important position in the curriculum of the middle of the fifteenth century, it went into decline in the early sixteenth. The *De modo significandi* was last published in England in 1515, and its falling popularity is clear in the sales record of the Oxford bookseller John Dorne in 1520. He sold six copies of it (and three commentaries on it) out of a total sale of 1,900 books. In contrast, Valla's *Elegantiae* sold fifteen copies, and Perotus' *Rudimenta grammaticae* five copies. The grammars in greatest demand were by the Magdalen School grammarians. John Stanbridge alone accounted for ninety-four sales of various grammatical works. [141]

The new grammars provided little or nothing in the way of logical analysis. Most of them were influenced by Valla's *Elegantiae*, one of the earliest humanist grammars. Although not published in England, it circulated widely there. Rather than subjecting his grammar to logic, Valla reversed those roles in his *Dialecticae disputationes*, reducing Aristotle's five categories to three (substance, quality, and action), and correlating these to nouns, adjectives, and verbs. He also 'purified' from his logic all technical terms (and ideas) which he felt were 'barbaric'.

Valla's grammar began a trend that was followed by others. Particularly popular in Cambridge in the first half of the sixteenth century was the work of Perotus (published twice in England before 1515), William Lilly of St Paul's School, and Thomas Linacre. [142] Priscian became a rare item indeed.

This new movement was successful in dislodging modal grammar and linguistic disputations from the English universities. In 1522 John Skelton, 'poet laureate' of both Oxford and Cambridge lamented the neglect of the traditional grammarians in favour of new authorities:

---

[140] Hegius, A. *Invectiva in modos significandi*, ed. J. IJsewijn, *Forum for Modern Language Studies*, 7 (1971), 299–318.   [141] 'Day Book of John Dorne', pp. 75–177.
[142] *STC* 19767.3 and 19767.7; with reference to CUA inventories *post mortem*.

Albertus de modo significandi,
And Donatus be dryven out of scole;
Priscians hed broken now handy dandy...
Alexander, a gander of Menanders pole...[143]

The collapse of grammatical disputations took place at Cambridge in 1527 when the university passed a grace[144]

It is pleasing to us that the disputations which used to be performed every Friday in grammar, henceforth be in philosophy.

The inclusion of humanist literary studies in the arts curriculum caused the BA to replace the MGram. as the mark of an accomplished schoolmaster. Until 1500 the basic parsing of Priscian remained vital to those training to teach schoolboys.[145] From about 1508, however, the MGram. came to be awarded less for study in university, and more frequently as an acknowledgement of experience already gained in teaching elsewhere.[146] By 1520 all six of the grammarians who supplicated for degrees (an unusually high number that year) had some teaching experience, and mention of grammar acts nearly disappears from the records.[147] In that year Thomas Hartwell, a priest, incepted in grammar with no university study at all, but instead with five years 'in which he publicly taught grammar in Northampton, and four years teaching in adjacent villages.'[148]

Some of the grammarians studied in the faculty of arts instead, as in the case of John Elwys, who in 1491 had his BA accepted as his complete form for his MGram.[149] John Whyteakers used six years study in 'liberal and humane arts' to the same end in 1500,[150] and Alexander Whetherwike supplicated for his MGram. in 1508 with five years study, three of which were in arts and two 'in the oratorical art' (he also

---

[143] *The Poetical Works of Skelton and Donne*, ed. A. Dyce (Boston, 1855), p. 245.
[144] *GBk* B, II, p. 139 (1527).
[145] e.g. *GBk* Γ, p. 3 (1501–2); *GBk* B, I, pp. 161–2.
[146] e.g. *GBk* Γ, p. 50 (1506–7), 60 (1507–8), and 91 (1511–12).
[147] exc. *GBk* B, II, p. 159 (1529–30).
[148] *GBk* Γ, p. 176 (1519–20).
[149] *GBk* B, I, p. 30 (1491).   [150] *GBk* B, I, p. 132 (1499–1500).

taught school in the country for three years).[151] There are similar examples of this in the same years, some with arts combined with *poetria, humanitas,* or *ars oratorica,* all alternate names for grammar. Although the faculty of grammar was very medieval in its statutes, and would soon expire quietly, it would be a mistake to see its members, few as they were, as opponents of Italianate learning. The grammarians adapted to the humanist style as quickly as did their colleagues in the faculty of arts. A similar pattern can be seen at Oxford.[152]

The humanist form that the MGram. degrees were taking was not enough to reinvigorate the faculty of grammar as an institution. By 1500 it had ceased to be primarily a teaching corporation. With the introduction of more poetry, grammar, and literature into the curriculum of the faculty of arts, the BA came to signify the professional competence in letters that the MGram. formerly had. Thus, in the 1520s the three aspects of late medieval university grammar quietly disappeared. The education of boys in Latin grammar was left to secondary schools and the few colleges, like Jesus, which offered grammar classes. The modal grammar of the arts faculty with its 'barbarous' disputations was abandoned in the 1520s. And, the adoption of humanist grammar by the members of the faculty of grammar did not prevent their disappearance. The last MGram. was awarded by Cambridge in 1548.[153]

This new understanding of what grammar was went hand in hand with classical rhetoric and all that it implied. The 1488 statute directed undergraduates in their first two years to hear the Terence or humanities professor, and the graces in the subsequent years reflect this new emphasis. John Sampson of King's College in 1503 spoke of four years of ordinary lectures 'in humanity and logic' as preparation for his BA.[154] Gilbert Geoffrey in 1506–7 phrased it as 'ordinary lectures fully heard in Terence and dialectic for four years'.[155]

---

[151] *GBk* Γ, pp. 60 (1507–8) and 70 (1508–9).
[152] D. Leader, 'Grammar in Late-Medieval Oxford and Cambridge', *History of Education,* 12 (1983), 13.
[153] *GBk* Δ, ed. J. Venn (Cambridge, 1910), p. 48 (1547–8).
[154] *GBk* Γ, p. 12 (1503). See also p. 352 (1540–1).   [155] *GBk* Γ, p. 49 (1506–7).

It is difficult to say exactly what the humanities professor lectured on, other than that Terence was a frequent text. The playwright Terence was known in medieval Cambridge, but not given special attention. This changed by the later fifteenth century. Peterhouse owned the text by 1477, and the master, John Warkworth, gave the college a further copy.[156] It was a twelfth-century transcription and is heavily annotated on four of the six plays, partly in the hand of Thomas Burgoyne, BA 1497, who would have needed it as an undergraduate.[157] A copy now in the University Library shows equally heavy late-fifteenth- and early-sixteenth-century interlinear and marginal notes on the first play, the *Andria*.[158]

Even more interesting is another copy in the University Library, written in part in the twelfth and fifteenth centuries, with annotations from our period and later. Included with the text is a 'brief description of Terence's life', and a 'scholastic lecture' by an unknown Laurentius that explains 'What is poetry? What is comedy? What is the style of comedy? Why write it? What is an argument? What is an act? A scene?', etc. The roles of the poet and orator are enumerated according to Quintilian ('A virtuous man...learned in speech') and the moral science of the playwright is explained, but there is no Christian allegorising. Scene by scene synopses follow. This could well have been the text of a Terence professor.[159]

Terence was highly thought of by the men who restructured English education; he was a fount of good style and *exempla*. The Magdalen grammarian John Anwykyll, MGram. of Cambridge 1475, published in Oxford in 1483 what proved to be a very popular *Vulgaria*, a collection of commonplaces 'taken from Terence and translated into English'.[160] William Melton had a copy of Terence's plays.[161] They were performed in The King's Hall in the early sixteenth century. John Colet recommended the 'veray Romagne tong which in the tyme of Tully

---

[156] Peterhouse MS 253.
[157] f. 84r.; Thomas Burgogne was later a fellow of Clare, but his two older brothers were fellows of Peterhouse while he was an undergraduate. *BRUC*, pp. 108–9.
[158] CUL MS Ff.IV.39. [159] CUL MS Ff.VI.4, ff. 93r.–144r., esp. 93r.–v.
[160] *STC* 696. [161] *BRUC*, pp. 400–1.

and Sallust and Virgil and Terence was vsid' for the pupils of St Paul's School, and they also performed the plays in 1528.[162] The *Comediae* were printed several times in England in the late fifteenth century, and in translation in 1520.[163] Their popularity continued undiminished throughout the sixteenth century; over one hundred copies are recorded in the Cambridge Probate Court Wills.

The revised curriculum brought the classics in general to the forefront. By 1520 every undergraduate was reading Cicero, Virgil, Quintilian, and a host of others who, although known in the medieval university, had not been considered so useful. With them were read the many works of Erasmus. They are ubiquitous in the surviving library catalogues and personal library lists of sixteenth-century Cambridge men.

With these changes came an increased use of vernacular texts outside the Schools, and more use of English in the lectures themselves. English (and French) had been used in introductory Latin grammars in the middle ages, but the only use allowed by statute was in public sermons. Medieval scholars owned vernacular treatises, and even wrote them sometimes. The Austin Friar Osbern Bokenham, DTh. and a visitor to Italy and Spain, produced many works, including English versions of the *Legenda aurea* and Claudian's *De consolatione Stilichonis* (written at Clare in 1445), as well as vernacular hagiography and a Latin treatise on astrology.[164] Henry Watson, BA, MA 1493 and fellow of Michaelhouse, translated Sebastian Brandt's *Shyppe of Fooles* for Lady Margaret.[165] Another Cambridge man, John Palsgrave of Corpus, Paris, and Louvain, wrote in 1530 *Les clarcissement de la langue francoyse*, 'a pioneering achievement in the study of vernacular languages'.[166]

By the middle of the sixteenth century the young scholars seem to have come up with less preparation in Latin than their medieval predecessors. English was being increasingly used in lectures, as at Jesus College. William Cecil's injunctions of 1562 addressed this problem directly; the humanities professor was

[162] Lupton, *Life of Colet*, p. 279.   [163] *STC* 23885–23885.5; 23894.
[164] *BRUC*, pp. 69–70.   [165] *STC* 3547–47a.
[166] *STC* 19166, McConica, *English Humanists*, p. 120.

to 'explain and interpret the required texts in English so that he can be understood'.[167]

It was the third branch of the trivium, logic, that was given less emphasis by the statutes of 1488. There was a logic professor, but he was given only the third year of the undergraduates' four, whereas under the medieval statutes logic occupied the first two and philosophy the last two, with the *Posterior Analytics* a central part of the graduate curriculum. It was a significant change. In the 1490s the logical studies were themselves unchanged: the *Organon*, Porphyry, Gilbert de la Porrée, the *Prior* and *Posterior Analytics*, and the non-Aristotelian *parva logicalia*, including treatment of terms, all of which dovetailed neatly with speculative grammar. The first English printers catered to this established taste, publishing Andreas on the *Ars vetus*, Swineshead's *Insolubilia*, Burley's *Posterior Analytics*, and the *Libelli sophistarum* for both Oxford and Cambridge, those archetypical medieval handbooks.[168]

But their days were coming to an end. A purer version of Aristotle's logic was more compatible with the humanist perspective. The change was not sudden, but it was real. By 1530 the *Libelli sophistarum* were out of print, and the rules of syllogism were learned from renaissance handbooks, rather than from commentaries on the *Posterior Analytics*.[169] The transitional years were 1520–30, when the medieval writers were still being read along with the newer authors. But in the 1530s their place was taken by the texts of Valla, Trapezuntius, Rudolph Agricola, Melanchthon, and Joannes Caesarius. These works gave little attention to the syllogism and analysis of terms. Valla, like Cicero, gave more attention to *inventio*, the procedures for selecting and classifying material for use in discourse. In this way, for Agricola and other humanists, dialectic, the *ars disserendi* is virtually inseparable from its application to rhetoric, and there is accordingly an insistence on the use of elegant Latin.[170]

---

[167] *Statuta academiae Cantabrigiensis* (Cambridge, 1785), p. 217.   [168] *STC* 15576.6–15578.7.

[169] Although there are examples of medieval logical texts being used later in the century, they are very rare.

[170] For an introduction to this problem, see L. Jardine, 'The Place of Dialectic Teaching in Sixteenth Century Cambridge', *Studies in the Renaissance*, 21 (1974), 31–62, and 'Humanism and the Sixteenth Century Cambridge Arts Course', *History of Education*, 4 (1975), 16–31.

From this time onward the medieval commentaries on Aristotle and the tracts of *logica moderna* appear only rarely in Cambridge. It was a moribund tradition, as logic became subject to excessive simplification and misinterpretation by rhetorically-oriented writers in the later sixteenth century.[171]

A student can only be taught so much in a few years at university. In the fifteenth century the subtleties and intricacies of logic were thought worthy of several years of the scholar's time. The arts course was a unified programme, and grammar, logic, philosophy, theology, and law were all interrelated; to change one would be to weaken another, or render it superfluous. The decline of speculative grammar lessened the preparation and aptitude that young students brought to bear on logic.[172] Equally important to the equation was the changing nature of theology, and the imminent elimination of canon law from the university. With the increasing emphasis on Scriptural exegesis, and the parallel decline in scholastic theology, students had less reason to master the syllogism. A knowledge of Greek was a more useful tool for the new theology. Scholastic theology did not disappear entirely, nor did the logic or natural philosophy that served it. The central roles of these interdependent studies did change, however.

Cambridge philosophy between 1480 and 1620 remained primarily Aristotelian. The introduction of new translations, humanist approaches, Ramist attacks, newer commentaries, and Platonic lectures, made the product more eclectic, but it almost always remained in the peripatetic tradition. The questions disputed at Commencement in 1600 would have been familiar to the fifteenth-century graduate. What did change significantly were the texts which were given the most attention, and the commentators read with them. Natural philosophy lost its primacy to ethics and politics, and philosophy in general occupied a less important position within the curriculum of the arts faculty.

Philosophy was given its own professor in 1488, who lectured

---

[171] I. Thomas, 'Medieval Aftermath: Oxford Logic and Logicians of the Seventeenth Century', In *Oxford Studies Presented to Daniel Callus*, O.P. OHS, n.s. 16 (1964), pp. 297–311.
[172] Heath, 'Logical Grammar'.

to fourth-year students in natural philosophy or metaphysics.[173] The bachelor preparing for the MA was still obliged to hear 'Aristotle's philosophy in the Schools',[174] but this time was shared with the mathematics lecture. The relatively fewer hours given to philosophy at the undergraduate level were reflected in the graces which speak only of logical and humanistic studies. Incepting masters still claimed studies 'both metaphysical and philosophical', or more often 'with ordinary lectures in philosophy and metaphysics'.[175]

The dominance of Aristotle is clear in both university and college statutes, but the commentators changed from those popular in the fifteenth century. In the medieval university the texts were read alongside commentaries which were often in the *questio* form which was tailored for use in disputations. The most popular of these were the *Questiones* on the *Physics* by Joannes Canonicus and on the *Metaphysics* by Antonius Andreas. Both of these men were Catalonian Scotists who followed the Subtle Doctor on most of his points of doctrine. Other commentaries in more traditional formats by Aquinas, Averroes, Walter Burley, and Giles of Rome circulated widely. In moral philosophy the field was led by Giles' *De regimine principum*.[176]

From the late fifteenth century, continental textual developments were felt in Cambridge. Newer translations of Aristotle were introduced, although often with older commentaries, and after 1500 the commentaries and paraphrases of Lefèvre d'Etaples became increasingly popular.[177] From 1500 to 1520 these co-existed with the older commentaries and *questiones*.[178] Bryan Rowe, vice-provost of King's, had together in his library in 1521 both Lefèvre d'Etaples and Buridan on the *Ethics*.[179] John Cheswryght, MA 1513, had at his death in 1537 a mixed collection of medieval and humanist authorities, with Lefèvre d'Etaples' paraphrases of Aristotle's philosophy next to Scotus

---

[173] *Docs.* I, no. 87, p. 361 and no. 140, pp. 384–5.
[174] *Docs.* I, no. 86, pp. 360–1.
[175] *GBk* Γ, pp. 12, 49, 72, and 104 (1502–13).
[176] See Chapter 6.
[177] C. B. Schmitt, *Aristotle in the Renaissance* (London, 1983), p. 20; e.g. Royal MS 9.E.i, Bruni's translation of the *Ethics* with Aquinas' commentary.
[178] For the similar situation at Oxford, see 'Day Book of John Dorne', pp. 71–177.
[179] F. J. Norton, 'The Library of Bryan Rowe, Vice-Provost of King's College (d. 1521)', *Transactions of the Cambridge Bibliographical Society*, 2 (1958), 339–51.

on the *Metaphysics* with Andreas' *Questiones*. [180] Even at St John's College where the new learning was most welcome, an undated college order (*c.* 1525) assigned philosophic *problemata* from Andreas, Scotus, Buridan, or Joannes de Magistris. [181]

The medieval texts went into eclipse between 1520 and 1540. The surviving manuscripts which show so many annotations from the fifteenth century, were left undisturbed on the library shelves. The probate court inventories which begin in the 1530s highlight this change. Of the 11,000 books recorded, Giles of Rome and Joannes Canonicus never appear. There are only two mentions of Andreas, and one of Burley on the *Ethics*. When the Royal Injunctions of 1535 forbade the use of these medieval philosophic commentaries, they were only codifying a change that was already well under way in the faculty of arts. [182]

The Cambridge masters have left few examples of their philosophic enquiries from 1488 to 1536. Robert Hacumblen, MA 1480 and DTh. 1507, copied Aristotle's *Ethics* with an anonymous commentary, but it is in the medieval tradition. [183] Plato was not widely studied, and such works as Doket's commentary on the *Phaedo* from the 1460s had no children. The first example of the new learning impinging on philosophy (other than by new translations) was when John Bryan lectured from the Greek text of Aristotle *c.* 1517. It was not until the Edwardian Injunctions of 1551 that all lectures in Aristotle, both university and collegiate, were to be in Greek; but that was modified in 1560 by the proviso 'as far as possible'. [184]

The early years of the sixteenth century saw the beginnings of a shift in importance from natural to moral philosophy, due primarily to theological developments. Ethics and politics took first place. The older studies were still read, but were not as central to the studies of the future theologian as they had been to his predecessors who focused on the commentaries of Scotus.

[180] M. H. Smith, 'Some Humanist Libraries in Early Tudor Cambridge', *Sixteenth Century Journal*, 5 (1974), 26–9, an article which makes a false dichotomy between 'humanist' and 'conservative' libraries.   [181] St John's College Archives, C7.11, f. 8v.
[182] A similar change occurred throughout Europe. See Schmitt, *Aristotle*, pp. 46–7 and 50.
[183] *BRUC*, p. 278; King's College MS 11.
[184] *Statuta academiae Cantabrigiensis* (1785), pp. 172 and 209.

This change was codified in the Edwardian statutes which called for the philosophy professor to lecture on Aristotle's *Problemata, moralia, et politica,* Pliny, and Plato.[185] This is repeated verbatim in the Elizabethan statutes, and metaphysics are never mentioned in them.[186]

The change can be traced in the inventories which show the mixture of medieval and renaissance texts owned by masters in the first half of the century. Richard Bullar of Christ's (MA 1540; d. 1540) owned Aristotle's *Physics* and *libri naturales,* along with the *Compendium physicae* of Franz Titelmann, Johannes Velcurio on the *De anima,* and the epitome of Bricot.[187] In moral philosophy Lefèvre d'Etaples stood alone. Henry Dilcock, MA of Christ's (d. 1551) was unusual in the number of medieval authorities he still had: Scotus on the *Metaphysics,* Bricot on the *Physics,* combined with Lefèvre and Donato Acciaivoli on the *Ethics,* Buridan on the *Politics,* and Joachim Perion's new translation of it, and Melanchthon's *Epitome moralis philosophiae.* Christopher Mulcaster of Christ's (MA 1556; d. 1556) inherited this library. William Johnson of St John's (BA 1559; d. 1559) is more typical of his decade in the absence of the medieval Aristotle from his library, with its place taken by Jacques Louis D'Estrebray's translation of the *Ethics* and Perion's attack on it, Jacob Schegk's compendium, and also the first copy of Ramus' *Dialectica* to appear in Cambridge records.[188]

It was the quadrivial studies that enjoyed a flowering in the new curriculum, something that did not happen at Oxford. We have seen Melton teaching Euclid to the young Fisher in Michaelhouse, and the Euclidean writing of the first mathematics professor, Roger Collyngwode. This post was held successively by men of the new learning, like Henry Bullock; Erasmus noted his knowledge of the stars.[189] Bishop Fisher gave mathe-

---

[185] J. Lamb, *A Collection of Letters, Statutes and other Documents from the Manuscript Library of Corpus Christi College, Illustrative of the History of the University of Cambridge During the Period of the Reformation from* AD MD *to* AD MDLXXII (London, 1838), pp. 124 and 281.

[186] *Docs.* I. 457. For a medieval metaphysical manuscript annotated by William Golding of Gonville Hall in 1559, see Gonville and Caius MS 335/724.

[187] CUA, Inventories post mortem, bundle 1.

[188] For the Perion controversy, see Schmitt, *Aristotle,* pp. 76–7.

[189] CWE, II, no. 255, p. 168.

matics an important place in St John's, requiring proficiency before taking the MA or becoming a fellow.[190] Its study is particularly associated with the Johnians Thomas Smith, Roger Ascham, John Cheke, and Cheke's protégé William Buckley.[191]

A new element was added to the mathematics lecture from 1532 to 1535 when it was to be given on 'Pomponius Mela or some other geographical author', perhaps in response to an interest in the New World discoveries.[192] During these years Richard Eden began his studies at Christ's and Queens'. He was later to achieve a reputation as an alchemist and cosmographer, serving the court of Edward VI as an expert in exploration.[193]

The assigned texts for the mathematics professor were next specified in the 1549 statutes, and did not change in the subsequent recodifications. When he taught cosmography he was to use Mela, Pliny, Strabo, or Plato (not the most useful texts available); for arithmetic Cuthbert Tunstall or Cardanus; for geometry Euclid; and for astronomy, Ptolemy. However, he should especially teach arithmetic, and the others 'as much as possible'.[194] The inventories indicate that many other quadrivial texts were popular as well. Gemma Frisius' *Arithmeticae practicae methodus facilis* appears twenty times, especially during the reign of Elizabeth, supplanting Tunstall's *De arte supputandi* which was more common earlier (seventeen copies). Other frequently mentioned works included Robert Record's vernacular *Arithmetike* (thirteen copies), and Lefèvre d'Etaples' *Epitome arithmeticae Boethii* (six copies). To these must be added William Buckley's brief poem *Arithmetica memorativa* that was published with Seton's best selling *Dialectica* after 1563.

Related to the mathematical sciences were the studies of the medical faculty, which although remaining very small, was revivified by the use of Greek texts and the increasing contact with the more humanistic schools of Italy.[195] The leading English physician of the time was Thomas Linacre, a man of

[190] Mayor, *Statutes*, p. 389 (1516).

[191] Leader, 'Teaching', pp. 107–8.

[192] *GBk* Γ, pp. 272–302 (1532–5).

[193] D. Gwynn, 'Richard Eden, Cosmographer and Alchemist', *Sixteenth Century Journal*, 15 (1984), 13–34.

[194] Lamb, *Documents*, pp. 124–5 (where *Ptolomeum* is transcribed as *Platonem*).

[195] Although Erasmus found Cambridge's physicians wanting: CWE, II, no. 285, p. 276.

many talents: priest, royal physician, grammarian, translator of Galen, and founding president of the College of Physicians. Although an Oxford man, he provided in his will for two professors of medicine at Oxford and one at Cambridge, since 'as yet ther has been none certayn substanciall nor perpetuall lectures of physick'.[196] The Cambridge arrangement involved monies and lands given to St John's College for the support of a professor to lecture in the Schools, but chosen by the master of St John's, and paid £12 annually. The choice of Fisher's college was an obvious one for Linacre, as he and Fisher shared the acquaintance of More, Tunstall, and John Stokesley, all of whom were executors of Linacre's will. The first Linacre professor of medicine was George Day in 1525, who the next year succeeded Richard Croke as public orator.[197]

In the theology faculty the increased concern with preaching, exemplified by the Lady Margaret Preachership, the annual university preachers, and the preaching demands on the St John's fellowship, was complemented by the increased emphasis on classical oratory for undergraduates. We have seen this synthesis as early as the late 1470s when Lorenzo Traversagni di Savona wrote a rhetorical text that doubled as a preaching handbook.[198] The study of Greek made possible the positive Scriptural theology, as well as opening up a whole range of hitherto little-known Greek Fathers. These humanist interests took place in the first decades of the sixteenth century against a background of continuing scholasticism.

Erasmus was quite polemical in his battles with the Thomists and Scotists,[199] but most theologians accepted the old along with the new. And among the humanists there was no strong agreement between men like Erasmus and Colet about the interpretation of Scripture. Erasmus was no literalist, and like the medievals placed great emphasis on the spiritual sense. It was the old glosses and the way the spiritual sense was interpreted that he rejected. Soon Protestant theologians like

---

[196] J. M. Fletcher, 'Linacre's Lands and Lectureship', in F. Maddison *et al.* (eds). *Essays on the Life and Work of Thomas Linacre c. 1460–1524* (Oxford, 1977), esp. pp. 107–97; St John's College Archives, Bursar's Accounts SB3.1 (1526–7).

[197] St John's College Archives M3. 4, Master's Accounts 1525–6.   [198] See pp. 120, 242.

[199] e.g. CWE, II, no. 227, p. 170.

William Tyndale were to take exception to these uses of allegory. [200]

Fisher's statutes included Duns Scotus as an option for the Hebrew lecture at St John's, and Scotus was similarly assigned for the theology professor of Wolsey's Cardinal College, Oxford. [201] The old and new continued together, as the theology statutes requiring Lombard's *Sentences* remained in force until 1536. Humphrey Walkeden of Queens', the intimate of Erasmus, is a good example. His grace for incepting DTh. in 1519-20 shows him giving his college's lectures on Scotus' *Sentences* and being responsible for four sermons in Queens' and three in another college. [202] He was accordingly dispensed with his university sermons provided he preach at St Paul's Cross and give another lecture on Scotus' *Sentences* (beyond the collegiate one) during the long vacation. [203] Scotus' name and the *Sentences* commentary tradition were not yet poison: not with Fisher, not with Erasmus' Cambridge friends, and not even in the colleges in the forefront of humanism.

The libraries of more anonymous men tell a similar story. In the first two decades of the sixteenth century the doctors of theology show no particular humanist slant. Thomas Colyer was a fellow of Fisher's Michaelhouse, MA 1499, DTh. 1504-5. When he died a year later he gave books to Michaelhouse (the list is now lost), Christ's College, and Greyfriars, Richmond, Yorkshire. The benefactions included Aristotle's *Metaphysics*, *Ethics*, (in Bruni's translation), unnamed natural philosophy texts, a *De modo significandi*, Lombard, Gregory, Boethius, Anselm, Scotus' *Sentences*, Chrysostom's *Sermones*, Richard Rolle, and an anthology of Augustine. But a sense of humanism is seen in Aeneas Silvius' *Epistolae*, a *Centilarium poetarum*, Lactantius, the *De bello troiano*, and the *Epistolae virorum illustrium*. [204]

John Sampson of King's incepted DTh. in 1517 and died the same year. His bequests to King's are even more conservative,

---

[200] Thomson and Porter, *Erasmus*, pp. 18 and 95–6.
[201] Gregor Duncan, typescript of Oxford Statutes, p. 6.
[202] The Queens' College records say it was on Aquinas (Queens' College Archives, *Journale*, 2, f. 18r.). Bullock gave the Scripture lecture in the same year. These two men filled the offices from 1516 to 1521. [203] *GBk* Γ, p. 185 (1519–20).
[204] *BRUC*, p. 151

and he corrected and revised the *Sarum Antiphoner*, for which the vice-provost Bryan Rowe wrote a preface.[205] With Rowe we find a theologian in his late 30s when he died in 1521. He had proceeded MA 1507, BTh. in 1514–15, and so could well have attended Erasmus' lectures. His personal library of 101 books included medieval philosophers, theologians, and preachers, but these were overshadowed by the far more numerous humanist items: many works by Erasmus, More's *Utopia*, Valla, Pico della Mirandola, Politian, Ficino, Boccaccio, Clichtoveus, Polydore Virgil, the classics and Fathers, several Greek grammars (Gaza, Croke, Calepinus, and Amerotius), Lucian, Chrysostom in Greek, and even two Hebrew grammars.[206] Rowe had early been singled-out for his eloquence – he disputed before Henry VII in 1506 and composed a poem for the occasion, and gave an oration on Wolsey's visit in 1520 – and he is exceptional in that sense. But possession of these works of the new learning did not exclude him from owning *Sentences* commentaries, Holcot, Peter Comestor, or Hugh of St Victor. They were still the bread and butter of the disputations required to take degrees in theology.

The college libraries were even more conservative. St John's in 1544 was still heavily medieval.[207] It was not until after 1535 that the medieval foundations of the theology faculty were removed, and even then individual doctors continued to own, read, and quote Aquinas and Scotus.

The early sixteenth century also saw a number of Cambridge theologians embrace religious reform in a more complete way. The dual convent of Bridgettines at Syon on the Thames was a house of very strict observance, in close contact with the Carthusians across the river at Sheen and those in the London Charterhouse. The Carthusians and Bridgettines were the exceptions in the humanists' condemnation of monasteries. Founded

[205] *BRUC*, p. 505.   [206] Norton, 'Library of Bryan Rowe'.

[207] D. McKitterick, 'Two Sixteenth Century Catalogues of St John's College Library', *Transactions of the Cambridge Bibliographical Society*, 7 (1978), 135–55. See also J. M. Fletcher and J. K. McConica, 'A Sixteenth-Century Inventory of the Library of Corpus Christi College, Cambridge', *Transactions of the Cambridge Bibliographical Society*, 3 (1961), 187–99; E. Leedham-Green, 'A Catalogue of Caius College Library, 1569', *Transactions of the Cambridge Bibliographical Society*, 8 (1981–5), 29–41.

in the early fifteenth century, Syon had from the beginning a 'constant tradition of learning'.[208] Thomas Westhaugh of Pembroke, DTh. in 1459, joined the Sheen Charterhouse before moving over to Syon, giving them sixty-two books. His contemporary at Pembroke, Hugh Damlett, remained a secular cleric but was a Syon benefactor as well. John Steke, BA 1468–9, joined and gave over seventy books.[209] During the century of its existence at least six fellows of Pembroke joined Syon (it never had more than seventeen brethren in Holy Orders at any one time), and its Cambridge connections increased after 1500; they were also closely connected with the circle of Lady Margaret and John Fisher. William Bond of Northumberland and Queens', MA 1504, gave the college philosophy lecture in the same year,[210] and in 1509–10 took his DTh. and was elected a university preacher. Bond joined Syon later, giving the convent his library of medieval theology, mostly Aquinas and sermon collections.

Three other men had even more striking connections with the new learning in Cambridge. We have already met Richard Whitford of Queens', who had studied in Paris with Lord Mountjoy under Erasmus. Whitford joined Syon *c.* 1507, and under the pseudonym 'The Wretch of Syon' wrote a series of vernacular treatises which exemplify Erasmian piety. But his personal books show the eclecticism of this circle, with Lyra and Gorran sharing the shelf with Cicero, Perotus, and Chrysostom.[211] John Fewterer of Pembroke, university preacher 1510–11, BTh. 1514–15, and confessor general of Syon had a similarly mixed library.[212] Richard Reynolds, BA of Christ's and DTh. while a fellow of Corpus, outdid these others in his intellectual achievements. Learned in Greek and Hebrew, he left the abbey ninety-four books which show the breadth of his learning in both the new and more traditional theology.[213]

With the brethren of Syon we see the ideal of Fisher at its most successful: the new learning put into the service of spiritual

---

[208] D. Knowles, *The Religious Orders in England*, III (Cambridge, 1959), p. 213.
[209] *BRUC*, pp. 176, 630–1, and 686; M. Bateson, *Catalogue of the Library of Syon Monastery, Isleworth* (Cambridge, 1898), p. xxvii.
[210] *BRUC*, p. 72.   [211] *BRUC*, pp. 635–6.
[212] *BRUC*, pp. 226–7.   [213] Knowles, *Religious Orders*, III, pp. 214–15.

reform, propagating the Word through preaching, writing, and example. There is a peaceful synthesis of old and new. The past is renewed, rather than rejected.

There were, of course, men who objected to the changes within Cambridge. John Skelton, 'poet laureate', condemned in 1522 the displacement of speculative grammar by Plautus, Quintilian, and Greek.[214] Erasmus spoke of his battles with Thomists and Scotists and the college that banned his *Novum instrumentum*. But the shifting academic climate occurred more smoothly than at Oxford, and the changes took place within the lifetime of the scholars of the 1480s. Erasmus wrote that in those years,[215]

> nothing was taught in the university at Cambridge except Alexander of Villa Dei, what they called the *Parva logicalia* and the traditional doctrines of Aristotle with Scotist *questiones*. As time went on the humanities were added [Terence lecture]; then mathematics [the mathematics lecture]; then a new, or at least new-fangled Aristotle; then the knowledge of Greek; then all those authors whose names were unknown in the old days even to the brahmins of philosophy Iarcas-like enthroned. And what, pray, was the effect of all this on your university? Why, it flourished to such a tune that it can challenge the first universities of the age...

Elsewhere, Erasmus specified that the centres of the new studies were Fisher's colleges – Christ's, St John's, and Queens' – and that it was the chancellor's protection and encouragement that allowed this reform to take place.[216]

The impact of this new curriculum was intensified by the printing press, which extended Erasmus' influence beyond the Cambridge lecture halls. Erasmus' works, both secular and theological, were ubiquitous in the personal libraries of Cambridge men in the 1520s and 1530s. In the early sixteenth century the Cambridge book trade was dominated by others from the Low Countries. Nicholas Spierink and Sygar Nicholson had shops in town, as did Garret Godfrey, friend and possibly

[214] See pp. 302–3.
[215] CWE, IV, no. 456, p. 52.
[216] CWE, VI, no. 948, pp. 316–17.

landlord of Erasmus.[217] They offered for sale the fruits of the continental presses which in those years produced a wider range of texts than did the English presses.

It was due to another foreigner, John Siberch *alias* Lair, from the region of Cologne that printing itself came to Cambridge. Siberch was drawn through the encouragement of Richard Croke and the circle of humanists. He was loaned £20 by the university in 1520–1 to set up his press, and the guarantors of the loan included Robert Ridley, Henry Bullock, and Robert Wakefield (who studied abroad, and later lectured in Hebrew at Oxford, and lived at Syon for a time).[218] Siberch was bankrupt by 1526 and the university lost its loan, but not before he had printed works by Bullock, Fisher, Lucian, Linacre's translations from the Greek, a pirate edition of Erasmus' *De conscribendis epistolis*, Sir Thomas Eliot, Archbishop Baldwin's *De altaris Sacramento*, and Alexander Barclay's *First Egloge* in the vernacular.[219]

By 1520 then, Cambridge was quite a different place from the university the young John Fisher had first seen on riding down from Yorkshire. It was prosperous, and had grown to rival Oxford in size. Its arts faculty was attracting increasingly more men of gentle background. The friars, although still vital, no longer dominated the theology faculty. The colleges had increased in size and number, and now offered courses of instruction for their many undergraduates. Erasmus had spread Cambridge's European reputation, and Fisher had funnelled the wealth of the Tudors towards it. From the early humanist view of the Britons as barbarous, they were now known for their polish in polite letters, the land of More, Fisher, Colet, Linacre, Grocyn, and the friend of polite learning, Henry VIII.[220] This awareness was increased by English scholars abroad, Cambridge

[217] Thomson and Porter, *Erasmus*, pp. 75–6; M. H. Black, *Cambridge University Press* (Cambridge, 1984), pp. 10–21.   [218] Cooper, *Athenae*, I, 63–4.

[219] O. Treptow, *John Siberch*, ed. and trans. J. Morris and T. Jones. Cambridge Bibliographical Society, Monograph 6 (Cambridge, 1970), esp. pp. 21–37 and 52–9; scribes, illuminators, and stationers had been under the jurisdiction of the Archdeacon of Ely since *c.* 1276 (*Vetus Liber Archidiaconi Eliensis*, ed. Feltoe and Minns, p. 21); *GBk* Γ, p. xxii; Erasmus claimed in 1511 he could not find a good scribe in Cambridge. CWE, II, no. 246, p. 206.

[220] C. B. Schmitt, 'Thomas Linacre in Italy', in *Essays on Linacre*, ed. F. Maddison, M. Pelling, and C. Webster, pp. 74–5.

men like Croke, Whitford, Collyngwode, and a host of lesser men who from 1500 to 1530 studied in such varied places as Angers, Turin, Ferrara, Padua, Valencia, Freiburg, and Louvain.[221] Cambridge was in the mainstream of humanist reform, and was an instrument of internal reform for the English Church.

The Catholicism of the age was exemplified in King's College Chapel, brought to a glorious conclusion in these years. The craftsmen were an international group, but the programme for the windows was devised by Richard Fox, patron extraordinary. Renaissance images illustrate salvation history as understood by Catholic theology: the typology of Old and New Testaments, and the integral role of Mary, immaculately conceived and later assumed and crowned Queen of Heaven.[222] But even as the windows were installed, there were theologians within Cambridge who were denying that whole tradition.

[221] All mentioned in the *Grace Books*.
[222] H. Wayment, *The Windows of King's College Chapel, Cambridge*. Corpus Vitrearum Medii Aevi, Great Britain, Supplementary Volume 1 (London, 1972), pp. 2, 5–9.

Chapter 13

THE HENRICIAN REFORMATION

UNORTHODOX REFORMERS

Geoffrey Knight of Norfolk, MA 1482, DTh. 1500–1, was one of the successful, though now forgotten theologians of this period. He was a good scholar, served Cambridge as vice-chancellor (1503), was one of the first university preachers (1504), and held several benefices. When he died in 1520 he left funds to Gonville Hall to maintain two priests studying theology or arts, and also monies with which his executrix, Dame Katherine Heydon, founded a college lectureship in 1528.[1] Knight bequeathed a ring to Our Lady of Walsingham, and to the prior of that shrine 'all my newe warke called Lutherus and dilecti Erasmi cum annoctationibus et replicacionibus Lie contra Erasmum'. It was a balanced group, Erasmus and his former English friend Edward Lee, and this 'newe warke' of Luther given to a man whose livelihood was based on the old piety.[2]

This mixture of orthodoxy and the new which characterised Fisher's Cambridge would soon become untenable. In December 1520, a month after Dr Knight died, Luther was excommunicated. Fisher shared this abhorrence of Luther and his heresy, and the university acted against him too. In the Easter term of 1521 at Cardinal Wolsey's command Cambridge sent four representatives to London for the formal examination of the German's works. They were not reactionaries, but Erasmus' closest Cambridge friends: Henry Bullock, Humphrey Walkeden, John Watson, and Robert Ridley, men at the

---

[1] *BRUC*, p. 340; Caius, *Annals*, pp. 21 and 25; Gonville and Caius College Archives, XVIII Pattesley 1 and 5, and Reg. Mag. p. 273, no. 1, p. 18, no.5.
[2] *DNB*, XI, pp. 788–90.

forefront of the new learning in England. The condemnation was pronounced by Wolsey on 12 May at St Paul's Cross, and Fisher preached after the burning of Luther's books. The university followed suit, and 2s were spent for refreshments at the bonfire of his works held shortly afterwards in front of Great St Mary's.[3]

But the contagion was not so easily checked. The university and kingdom were strictly orthodox in the 1520s, when Henry earned the sobriquet *fidei defensor* for his polemic against Luther. Fisher waged the battle on the academic front as well, publishing his *Assertionis Lutheranae confutatio* in 1523. But men believe what they will, and Luther had his supporters from the beginning. Peter Valence, possibly a young Norman pensioner of Gonville Hall, defaced a papal condemnation posted on the Schools doors, scribbling on it 'Happy the man who places his trust in the name of the Lord, and decries these false and mindless vanities'. He was caught, and recanted.[4]

Others were more Fabian and thus more successful in their opposition. The works of Luther continued to circulate after the prohibition and were privately read in study groups. The booksellers of Cambridge included Dutchmen and Germans who felt even less loyalty to royal prohibitions. Sygar Nicholson, a tenant of Gonville Hall (1520–4) was charged with circulating Luther's works and imprisoned, but not until 1531.[5] After the climate changed in 1534 he served as university stationer.[6]

Those reading Luther's works in the 1520s gathered informally at the White Horse Inn (called popularly 'Little Germany'), which was on King's Parade between King's College and St Catharine's; a site uncommemorated and now a

---

[3] *GBk* B, II, pp. 91–3 (1520–1).

[4] This is dated 1517 by Fuller, *Cambridge*, pp. 145–6, but a more probable date is 1521. See C. N. L. Brooke in *Humanism, Reform, and Reformation*, ed. B. Bradshaw and E. Duffy (Cambridge, 1988). See also van Ortroy, *Analecta Bollandiana* 10 (1891), 229–35. In 1533 Valence was French Tutor to Cromwell's son.

[5] Nicholson claimed he was tortured by Thomas More (*Latimer's Sermons*, ed. G. E. Corrie, II, 321). More denied the charge (T. More, *The Apology*, ed. J. Trapp in *The Complete Works of Thomas More*, IX (New Haven and London, 1979), p. 119). See *GBk* B, II, p. 163 (1530–1) for the expenses for his imprisonment and fagots to burn books.

[6] G. Gray, *The Earlier Cambridge Stationers*, Oxford Bibliographical Society (Oxford, 1904), p. 35; M. H. Black, *Cambridge University Press*, pp. 12–14.

passageway. There could not have been anything very secret about meetings in an inn, but there were no stormtroopers of orthodoxy in Cambridge, and when authority did intervene, it was for what these men later said very publicly from the pulpit. There were no membership cards at the White Horse, and the circle no doubt varied.[7] It even included men like Stephen Gardiner, whose sympathy for Luther proved very transient. There is rarely intellectual discipline among early revolutionaries.

But there was a cadre in Cambridge in those years who, if not Lutherans, proved zealous in the pursuit of reform outside of Church authority. Thomas Bilney of Trinity Hall, BCn.L 1520–1, was a seminal figure, and he converted Hugh Latimer to the reformed cause.[8] Together they applied their evangelical beliefs by visiting the sick and prisoners in the Tollbooth and Castle, and taking long walks together on 'Heretics' Hill.'[9] Robert Barnes, the Augustinian prior, was perhaps the most Lutheran of the Cambridge reformers, and used his pulpit at Austin Friars to that end. He had earlier studied in Louvain, was a familiar of Erasmian learning, and had taught Terence, Plautus, and Cicero in his convent. He made the step to Lutheranism easily.[10] Among his pupils were Miles Coverdale, who left the order in 1528 to preach against Catholicism.[11] George Stafford, a northcountryman of Pembroke, BTh. 1524, knew Greek and Hebrew, and lectured for the next four years on the Scriptures rather than the *Sentences* (both were required to earn a theology doctorate).[12] Thomas Becon of St John's, BA 1530–1, looking back many years later, recalled this time in a rosy glow, citing a 'common saying' that 'when Master Stafford read, and Master Latimer preached, then was Cambridge blessed'.[13] Others of similar feeling in Cambridge in the 1520s included Thomas Cranmer and Matthew Parker, future Archbishops of Canterbury; Nicholas Shaxton, future Bishop

[7] cf. Mullinger, *Cambridge*, I, p. 573, '...nominally under the presidency of Barnes'.
[8] Latimer, *Sermons*, I, pp. 334–5. [9] The location is now unknown.
[10] *DNB*, I, pp. 1173–6. [11] *DNB*, IV, pp. 1289–97.
[12] Cooper, *Athenae*, I, p. 39.
[13] T. Becon, 'Jewel of Joye', in *Catechism*, ed. J. Ayre, Parker Society, 3 (Cambridge, 1844), pp. 425–6.

of Salisbury; John Bale, future Bishop of Ossory; William Tyndale, the Bible translator; and many other actors in the English Reformation.[14]

Cambridge University would officially have none of this, and Rome had its defenders. Fisher was unwavering, if distant. On the scene others stood firm. Perhaps Erasmus laid the egg that Luther hatched, but many of Erasmus' circle of the 1510s were not helpful. We have already seen Bullock, Walkeden, Watson, and Robert Ridley at Luther's first condemnation in London. Bullock and Walkeden died in the middle of the decade, but John Watson was master of Christ's College 1517–32 and served as vice-chancellor several times. He prosecuted Lutherans in Cambridge, and in 1531 attempted to require all graduates in theology to repudiate by oath the errors of Hus, Wyclif, and Luther, and to affirm Catholic doctrines.[15] Watson wrote to Erasmus in 1516 on the publication of his New Testament that it shed 'a wonderful flood of light on Christ, and earned the gratitude of all who are devoted to it'.[16] There was no contradiction there. Too much has been made of the use of Scripture by reformers like Stafford. That was neither unknown nor forbidden in Cambridge in the 1520s. It was the conclusions that the reformers drew that were unacceptable, not their sources.

The persecution of the reformers began in earnest in 1525 when Friar Barnes was accused of heresy by the vice-chancellor, Dr Edmund Natares, the master of Clare. Barnes was sent to London for examination, recanted at St Paul's, and was imprisoned at the Augustinian friars' houses in London and Northampton. He later escaped to Germany.[17] In the same year Latimer was confronted by Bishop West of Ely for his preaching in Great St Mary's. He was taken to London for examination by Wolsey, but was released after giving assurances. George Joye of Peterhouse was similarly summoned in 1527 and promised to conform.[18]

[14] Porter, *Reformation*, pp. 41–9.   [15] Porter, *Reformation*, p. 61.
[16] CWE, IV, no. 450, p. 36.
[17] Cooper, *Athenae*, I, pp. 74–5; Mullinger, *Cambridge*, p. 583.
[18] Cooper, *Annals*, I, p. 325.

In 1529 Latimer preached his celebrated 'Card Sermon' in Advent in St Edward's Church, and the controversy became wide open. Using the analogy of card games such as were popular in the colleges at Christmastime, Latimer attacked Catholic belief and practice. Dr Robert Buckenham, the prior of Blackfriars, replied from the same pulpit in January 1530 with his 'Dice Sermon', which used a related analogy to refute the attack. Latimer responded the next Sunday. Convocation was called to judge this dispute, and a kind of peace was made within the theology faculty.[19] It was the last time these views were to be so easily reconciled. The next year Bilney was burned in the Lollard's Pit in Norwich as a relapsed heretic. But by then the sides were much further apart. The Catholics contended with defenders of royal supremacy, while both pursued the protestants. The catalyst for this new development was the Divorce.

THE DIVORCE

There had always been royal aid and interference in the English universities, but they increased in pace under the Tudors and took on a more direct form under Henry VIII. It was by royal fiat and funds that Richard Pace was appointed Greek professor in 1520 (although he did not take up the post). The following year Queen Catherine forced Queens' College to accept John Lambert, BA, as a fellow against their wishes.[20] That was not without medieval precedent, but such interference soon became endemic. What was new was the use of the universities to serve much larger political ends. Both Oxford and Cambridge acquiesced in this, since with royal favour could come great short-term rewards.

Cardinal Wolsey as Lord Chancellor was integral to this process. He was an Oxford man who had taught in the Magdalen College Grammar School and, for all his faults, was a promoter of the new learning. His contact with Cambridge began in 1514 when Bishop Fisher tried to resign as chancellor,

[19] Lamb, *Documents*, pp. 14–18.
[20] Searle, *Queens' College*, I, pp. 164–6; Cooper, *Athenae*, I, p. 67; Cooper, *Annals*, I, p. 417 (1544). He was burned as a heretic in 1538.

and suggested that Wolsey be asked to replace him. Wolsey declined, claiming too many other offices pressed him (not usually a problem with him). Fisher was then re-elected for life.[21] In 1520 Wolsey was the honoured guest of Cambridge, and the oration Henry Bullock gave for the occasion was the first work printed by Siberch's press.[22] In 1524, when Wolsey was at the apogee of his power, the university followed Oxford's lead by voting the Cardinal the power to revise their statutes at his pleasure – though both had other men as chancellors.[23] It was a remarkable sign of pandering for corporations that had traditionally guarded their rights so jealously.

Wolsey never acted on the statutes since he was busy founding his great Cardinal College in Oxford. It was endowed through the suppression of selected small monasteries, was to have a humanist curriculum, and was staffed by such luminaries as the Bavarian mathematician Nicholas Kratzer and the Spaniard Juan Luis Vives. Wolsey also brought over from Cambridge promising young scholars as fellows, which was not unusual since the intercourse between the two universities had been increasing since 1500.[24] Some of these Cambridge men brought with them their Lutheranism, and the conflict intensified in Oxford.[25] The fifteenth-century roles had been reversed, and it was now Cambridge that seemed to be the fount of heresies.

It was a change which benefited Cambridge under Henry VIII. Oxford was beloved by Wolsey, Thomas More, and Archbishop Warham. Their authority passed to men of a different stamp, Thomas Cromwell and Thomas Cranmer. Cranmer we have already seen as a theology lector at Jesus and Buckingham Colleges; with the change in religious climate his fortunes soared. Cromwell was not a university man. He was Wolsey's secretary, and very capable; he survived his patron's fall to become the most powerful man in the kingdom under the king. Cambridge was more sympathetic to these mens' aims

---

[21] *Annals*, I, p. 296 (1514).   [22] Treptow, *Siberch*, p. 52.

[23] Cooper, *Annals*, I, pp. 307–9 (1524); E. Mullally, 'Wolsey's Proposed Reform of the Oxford University Statutes: A Recently Discovered Text', *Bodleian Library Record*, 10 (1978), 22–7.

[24] McConica, *English Humanists*, p. 85. For a raucous debate between Oxford and Cambridge men in 1532, see Fuller, *Cambridge*, pp. 154–5; Caius, *Annals*, p. 28; Cooper, *Athenae*, I, p. 135.   [25] Mullinger, *Cambridge*, I, pp. 549 and 604.

than was Oxford. While Cardinal College was left to wither
after 1530, Cambridge University and Cambridge men profited
from being on the proper bandwagon.

It was Cranmer, in 1529 a widowed don of about forty, who
first suggested that the universities be canvassed for support in
the King's Great Matter.[26] The papacy was adamant on the
question, and eventually the royal divorce required the concomitant renunciation of papal authority. 'Catholic Reform' came
to an end in Cambridge. The middle ground of satire and
internal reorganisation of Erasmus and his disciples, of More
and Fisher, disappeared. In a sense the changes in Cambridge
were independent of the European Reformation, for they did
not include (despite Cranmer's wishes) the thorough institution
of advanced protestantism in England or the universities. Often
the same sorts of men who went to the stake under More's
chancellorship were burned under Cromwell. Academic freedom
continued to conform to royal wishes, only now quite
independently of Rome.

Whether the renaissance of Fisher's Cambridge was destroyed
by Henry VIII depends on a historian's perspective.[27] For many,
royal supremacy was the culmination of the teaching and
curricular reforms of the previous four decades. But while the
reforms of Fisher's tenure aimed at renewing the national clergy
and international Christianity, the Henrician years saw a
narrower goal, in which national politics and religion were
much more closely allied. The Crown could never completely
dictate academic life, and under Elizabeth the non-conformists
in Cambridge would prove far more intractable than ever the
Catholics were. But there was a qualitative change in the
universities' roles in England between the time when Erasmus
lectured and 1535, when the curriculum and even the internal
financing were dictated by royal injunction.

John Fisher's vision of a renewed Cambridge was materially
supported by royal favour and, from Fisher's perspective, it was
destroyed spiritually by royal favour as well. The Crown,

[26] Hughes, *Reformation*, I, p. 241.
[27] See M. Couve de Murville and P. Jenkins, *Catholic Cambridge* (London, 1983), for a recent
Catholic view.

having given so much to Cambridge, began giving directions as well. Some Cambridge men welcomed this, and accepted the suppression of Catholic theology and law with the same zeal as they accepted the royal bounty of St John's and Christ's Colleges. Few besides Fisher opposed the royal will for long.

The debate over Latimer's 'Card Sermon' and Dr Buckenham's reply was brought to a head by a letter from Edward Fox, DTh. and provost of King's, royal almoner, and relative of Richard Fox.[28] Fox commanded both sides to silence, while observing that opposition to Latimer was in part due to his support of the King's Cause.[29] Already the Divorce question was a protective issue for reformers, and the university could not escape committing itself. The universities of Europe had already been canvassed and bribed with little success; two of the King's agents in Italy had been Edward Fox and Richard Croke. The issue culminated in February 1530 when William Buckmaster, the vice-chancellor, received a second letter from Fox, with veiled threats, asking the university to determine 'whether it is prohibited by divine and natural law to marry the childless widow of one's brother'.[30]

We have accounts by both Fox and Stephen Gardiner, then master of Trinity Hall, as to how the verdict was determined. It was not easy, since there was organised opposition. Congregation was summoned and after a long discussion no decision was reached. The next day a grace favourable to the King was proposed by Buckmaster, but was defeated on a first vote. The second vote was a deadlock. It was finally passed when the opponents abstained. Then a panel was chosen, composed heavily of the King's supporters, to make the final decision. On 9 March 1530 Cambridge decided that indeed Henry's marriage to Catherine was invalid if her marriage to Prince Arthur had been consummated. Many Cambridge men were unhappy with this decision, and Buckmaster complained that 'All the world almost cryeth out of Cambridge for this act and specially on me'.[31]

[28] Cooper, *Athenae*, I, p. 66.   [29] Lamb, *Documents*, pp. 14–15.
[30] Lamb, *Documents*, p. 19.
[31] Lamb, *Documents*, pp. 23–5, and also printed in Mullinger, *Cambridge*, I, pp. 618–20.

Oxford was similarly summoned somewhat in retard of Cambridge to decide this question of canon law, but was not initially cowed. The faculty of arts refused to be left out of the decision, which caused the King to threaten these 'mere subjects' who declined to follow the lead of their elders. Henry concluded 'it is not good to stir-up hornets'.[32] The artists' objections were restrained, and ultimately Oxford took the same position as Cambridge.

Of course, these determinations were morally worthless to Henry, since the Queen was insistent that her first marriage was unconsummated. But conditional clauses are forgotten in political controversy, and the King got what he wanted. The universities would not stand up to him – wealthy now, they could not disperse as they had done when threatened by King John – and the most learned theologians and canon lawyers in England had effectively sanctioned schism with Rome. In the atmosphere of heresy they had to know the consequences. When Dr Buckmaster visited the King in Greenwich to tell him of Cambridge's decision he was showered with compliments and royal favour, which must have alleviated some of the criticism he had received closer to home.[33]

After this, the road was much clearer for the less extreme of the Cambridge reformers. They had favoured the Divorce and now reaped the benefits. In theory, Cambridge was still orthodox; the following year Dr Watson imposed the oath renouncing Hus, Wyclif, and Luther on Nicholas Shaxton and others before allowing them to take their theology degrees.[34] The next year this was dropped. In practice, reform had its day. Latimer, once prosecuted within the university, was now Anne Boleyn's chaplain. The bookseller Sygar Nicholson was appointed one of the university stationers in 1533. The wind now blew from a different direction.

On 15 May 1532 the English bishops agreed to the Submission of the Clergy act, which acknowledged Henry as 'Supreme Head of the English Church and clergy', but with the proviso 'as far as the law of Christ allows'. That condition was the last

---

[32] C. E. Mallet, *A History of the University of Oxford* (London, 1924), I, pp. 443–5.
[33] Lamb, *Documents*, pp. 23–5. [34] *Annals*, I, p. 345 (1531–2).

bit of loyalty shown to Rome; the Submission was the 'suicide of [independent] ecclesiastical authority'. Henceforth matters of doctrine and discipline were in the King's lay hands. The next day More resigned as Lord Chancellor.[35]

The culmination for Cambridge came in the spring of 1534 when they were asked to determine on the royal supremacy. The question was phrased, 'Whether the bishop of Rome has, by God in Sacred Scripture, been given greater authority and power in the Kingdom of England than any other foreign bishop'. Again there was some resistance. Cranmer wrote to Cromwell singling out Friar Oliver, the Dominican prior for his preaching against the royal supremacy. Cranmer claimed he was 'of very small learning, sinister behaviour, ill qualities, and of suspected conversation and living'.[36] After long study and public disputation Cambridge decided in favour of the King. The document was sealed 2 May 1534.[37] Oxford followed suit on 27 July. The Convocations of Canterbury and York had already agreed, and Parliament that spring had passed the laws of succession and royal supremacy that made it treason to believe otherwise. An oath to that effect was required of the whole population. The clergy and laity overwhelmingly complied, and England was no longer part of the Roman Catholic Church.

The Cambridge chancellor was not among this multitude. He was summoned to appear at Lambeth on 13 April to take the oath, along with the London clergy. Fisher knew what would happen, and before leaving Rochester settled his estate, leaving money to his servants and the town poor, £100 to Michaelhouse, and his library to St John's College; but it was all seized by the crown.[38] Thomas More described the Lambeth gathering as a happy occasion for most, with Latimer and Cranmer laughing and hugging in the garden while others called for beer at the buttery hatch.[39] Fisher refused to sign and was sent to the Tower, where in May 1535 he learned he had been made a cardinal. The honour in no way helped his

[35] Hughes, *Reformation*, I, p. 237.
[36] Quoted in *VCH*, II, pp. 274–5.
[37] *Annals*, I, p. 367 (1534).
[38] Van Ortroy, 'Fisher', pp. 276–9.
[39] More, *Selected Letters*, no. 54/200, pp. 218–19.

20 John Fisher in his sixties, drawn by Holbein.

situation, and the King reportedly said that when the hat arrived Fisher would have no head on which to wear it.[40] The trial was in June 1535, and he was condemned to be hanged, drawn, and quartered as a traitor. Henry remitted the sentence to beheading instead, probably from fear that the old man would have died while being dragged on the hurdle the four miles to Tyburn. He was sixty-nine, and the year in the Tower and his ascetic regime had weakened him. Instead, on 22 June Fisher was taken to Tower Hill where, 'a very image of death' he was executed, the naked body left in the sun, and the head parboiled and set up on London Bridge.

[40] Van Ortroy, 'Fisher', p. 311. For Fisher's execution, see E. E. Reynolds, *St John Fisher* (London, 1955), pp. 281–6.

The death shocked contemporary Europe, and even later protestant historians have made little effort to portray John Fisher as anything less than a victim of a cruel time.[41] The Roman reaction is more surprising; his martyrdom for that Church did not lead to canonisation until 400 years later.

Cambridge University retained him as their chancellor until his death, long after he had become an embarrassment. St John's remained loyal as well, sending a delegation to him while in the Tower (although in part to get his signature on the statutes).[42] But after the death Thomas Cromwell was picked as his successor, Fisher's virtual executioner, and since January 1535 the King's vice-regent in matters spiritual. 'As lay a person and devoid of spiritual aura as could be found in England,'[43] he was not a Cambridge man, but a very wise choice for a more political era. He also had some interest in academic matters. The striking contrast of Cromwell and Fisher puts into relief the changes that had occurred within the university and in its relations with royal authority. Among Cromwell's first acts was to have all evidence of his predecessor removed from Cambridge; the fish and ear of wheat rebuses in the St John's chapel were defaced, and the inscription above his would-be chantry chapel, 'I shall make you fishers of men'.[44] Cromwell's triumph was brief, for with Fisher he is numbered among the five Tudor chancellors to die on the scaffold.[45]

But Cromwell's tenure was a pivotal five years which saw direct royal authority used to consolidate the new learning, the new theology, and the new teaching structures that had developed in the Fisher years. With this came a tradition of external control from the court that was far more effective than

[41] e.g. T. Macaulay, *History of England*, in (ed.) C. H. Firth (London, 1914), II, p. 620, 'a man worthy to have lived in a better age, and to have died in a better cause'. Fisher has not been subjected to revisionist views in recent years, as has More.

[42] Van Ortroy, 'Fisher', pp. 133–4. The delegation was distinguished: John Redman, later first master of Trinity; Richard Brandesby, Linacre Professor of Medicine; and John Seton, college lector and later author of the most widely used logical work in Elizabethan England.

[43] G. R. Elton, *Reform and Reformation: England, 1509–1558* (Cambridge, Mass., 1977), p. 191.

[44] Reynolds, *Fisher*, p. 287; Baker, *St John's*, II, 567.

[45] Porter, *Reformation*, p. 3. The others were Somerset (1552), Northumberland (1553), and Essex (1601). See H. Trevor-Roper, 'Foreword' to *The Lisle Letters: An Abridgement*, ed. M. St Clair Byrne (Chicago, 1983), p. ix, 'The Tudor Revolution in government had the true character of a revolution: it devoured its children'.

anything Rome or the Bishop of Ely had been able to muster in the preceding centuries.

ROYAL INJUNCTIONS

In the autumn of 1535 the full weight of Cromwell's plans for the universities became known. By early October (the document is undated) the King issued injunctions and appointed Cromwell visitor of the university.[46] After a preamble deploring the barbarism and ignorance of Cambridge, and expressing a desire to promote piety and extirpate heresy and superstition, the injunctions demanded

1 that allegiance under the common seal of the university to the statutes regarding royal succession and supremacy be sworn by all
2 that in all of the colleges there should be founded at their own expense two daily public lectures, one in Greek and the other in Latin
3 that no lectures be given in the Schools, colleges, or hostels, on the *Sentences* or any doctor who commented on them but rather all theology lectures should be on the Bible 'according to the true sense thereof and not after the manner of Scotus, etc.'
4 that all students be allowed to read the Bible privately and attend lectures on it
5 that the study of canon law and degrees in it be abolished
6 that all ceremonies, constitutions and observances that hinder polite learning should be abolished
7 that instruction in the subjects of the faculty of arts should be in Aristotle, Rudolphus Agricola, Philip Melanchthon, Trapezuntius, etc., and not the 'frivolous questions and obscure glosses of Scotus, Burley, Anthonius Trombetta, Bricot, Bruliferius, etc.'
8 that all college and university statutes not in accord with these injunctions be void

[46] The Injunctions are in Peterhouse Archives, Register, f. 169r., and printed in *Statuta academiae Cantabrigiensis*, pp. 134–41, and Fuller, *Cambridge*, pp. 160–2, and in translation in Cooper, *Annals*, I, pp. 374–5 and Mullinger, *Cambridge*, I, p. 630 and II, pp. 7–13.

9 that officers of colleges and hostels be sworn to observe these injunctions

Cromwell did not exercise his powers of visitation personally, but instead appointed Thomas Leigh, DCL of King's College, who had already served Cromwell as a diplomat and an overbearing suppressor of monasteries.[47] Leigh promulgated further injunctions from Cambridge on 22 October. In addition to insisting on similar points of discipline as the earlier ones, they also required

1 that all scholars observe the statutes and customs of the university and colleges that were not repugnant to the injunctions
2 that college fellowships were not to be sold
3 that geographical and collegiate factionalism cease, and elections to fellowships and offices be freely made on merit
4 that the university, college, and hostel officers deliver up their papistical muniments, and an inventory of their rentals and moveable property to Cromwell 'to await his good pleasure'
5 that the university maintain at its own expense a public lecture in either Greek or Hebrew
6 that all attend a commemorative Mass in Great St Mary's for the college and university founders and benefactors, and also for the King and 'Lady Anne, his lawful wife, and Queen of the realm'
7 that the injunctions be publicly read monthly and allowed to be transcribed

J. B. Mullinger has described these injunctions as 'the line that in university history divides the mediaeval from the modern age'.[48] Politically this is true in representing the subjugation of the university and colleges in administration, curriculum, and internal custom to the King. No longer did the corporation of scholars have the exclusive right to make their own statutes. In teaching, however, they codified trends that were already well under way: the use of renaissance commentators in the arts

---

[47] *DNB*, XI, pp. 861–2; Knowles, *Religious Orders*, III, pp. 272–90.
[48] Mullinger, *Cambridge*, I, p. 631.

faculty; the non-medieval study of Scripture in theology; and the founding of college lectureships and university professorships.

For the university the first business was to get their 'bullas papisticas' reconfirmed in the King's name, and to send an exact rental of their lands and inventory of their goods. The vice-chancellor was in London for thirty-eight days at considerable expense to achieve this.[49] The colleges likewise made their submissions.[50] Their lists of values are now lost, but the threat of dissolution must have been quite real, and was to hang heavily for the next ten years. The oath demanding allegiance to the Church of England and Royal Supremacy was implemented, and in modified forms was required by the university until 1871, and by some colleges until the mid-twentieth century.[51] As for the prohibition on regional considerations in the election of college fellows, this injunction was quietly ignored.

The most fundamental innovation was the abolition of canon law. What had in the medieval university rivalled arts in numbers of scholars had been made meaningless by Royal Supremacy. Its days had been numbered since the Submission of the Clergy in 1532. By that act the bishops and clergy had promised not to make any new canons unless licensed by the King, and had offered up the existing body of canon law to a commission appointed by the King. That commission first met in 1551, but no revision was ever carried out. The last canon law degrees were granted in the summer of 1535.[52] Canon law was still practised within the established Church, but by civil lawyers.

The theology faculty was required to lecture on Scripture in the undefined 'true sense thereof'. More significantly, not only were *Sentences* commentaries forbidden, but the use of any theologian who had commented on them. This eliminated the

---

[49] *GBk* Γ, pp. 310 and 320–1 (1535–6); *GBk* B, II, pp. 197–200 (1535–6) and pp. 207–8 (1536–7).   [50] e.g. Gonville Hall, printed in Fuller, *Cambridge*, pp. 164–6.

[51] Shadwell, *Enactments*, pp. 118–19; *Annals*, I, p. 382 (1536) and p. 408 (1544).

[52] Hughes, *Reformation*, I, p. 239.

study of nearly every theologian of the previous four hundred years. Perhaps this was not the intent, but only a prohibition on their particular commentaries on the *Sentences*. In any case, the works of Scotus, Aquinas, and others were still owned, read, and annotated by masters throughout the sixteenth century, albeit in greatly reduced numbers. Some even quoted medieval theologians in their works. [53]

The injunctions relating to arts studies codified an existing change; what is curious is the list of proscribed texts. Walter Burley and Scotus were of course popular, but what of Bricot, Trombetta, and Bruliferius? They were continental logical writers of the previous fifty years who were practically unread in Cambridge. Their inclusion implies that whoever aided Cromwell in writing the injunctions had no familiarity with Cambridge, and was perhaps a graduate of Paris. But the 'etc.' that followed those names was taken to include all the medieval logicians.

The recommended texts – Agricola, Melanchthon, and Trapezuntius – were known and used, although they posed problems for the beginner. A solution appeared with the *Dialectica* of John Seton of St John's. An MA of 1532, he was sublector within his college in 1533–4, principal lector the following year, and probably in later years as well. [54] It was this experience that prompted him to write an introductory logic of his own, which circulated in manuscript before being published in 1545. In his dedication to Chancellor Stephen Gardiner (Seton was one of his chaplains), he describes how he wrote the book while a lector at St John's, 'for after the royal injunctions there were a great number of outdated dialectical texts and I had at hand no suitable author whom I might teach to the young students'. Aristotle and Melanchthon were too difficult, and Agricola had already provided a handbook on *inventio*. So, he wrote an accessible Aristotelian text out of necessity. Seton recounts how it gained popularity as outsiders came across it, and eventually John Cheke and Thomas Watson

---

[53] e.g. Pembroke MS 207, an anonymous work *c.* 1600, esp. pp. 1 and 269. For evidence of continuing ownership, see CUA, Vice-Chancellor's Court Inventories Post Mortem.
[54] St John's College Archives, SB3. 9–10.

(*amici mei*), fellow lectors of St John's, encouraged him to prepare an edition.[55]

Seton's *Dialectica* restated, in simple terms and with schemata, terms, types of propositions, and ways of disputing. In essence, he 'reduces the *Organon* to the *Topics* alone'.[56] This book was the most frequently used introductory logic in Tudor Cambridge. It gave its name to lectureships at Trinity, Queens', and Corpus Christi; at Trinity it preceded the lecture on Agricola, so that both *iudicium* and *inventio* were taught to beginners. Its popularity was proverbial, and it was published eight times between 1563 and 1639.[57]

The establishment of university professorships in Greek or Hebrew, and college lectors in Greek and Latin, was really nothing new. The financing of the university professorships was left undefined, but the question was settled by Parliament in reference to a tax exemption. The universities were traditionally exempted from the exaction of subsidies, although this was not done without some effort by Cambridge in 1521–2 and 1531–2.[58] In 1534 they were made liable for payment of first-fruits and tenths and were not exempted, but Parliament then dovetailed the usual exemption with the demands of the Royal Injunctions.[59] On 4 February 1536 they granted a permanent exemption 'in consideration of which' the colleges and hostels of both universities were perpetually to support a 'King Henry the eight his lecture' in whatever discipline the king should assign.[60]

The university fulfilled the injunction beyond the letter of the law, establishing both Greek and Hebrew professors in the

---

[55] *STC* 22250. [56] Jardine, 'Dialectic', p. 55.
[57] e.g. Gabriel Harvey in his poem 'The Schollers Love' spoke of 'all the predicaments that are in John Seton'. BL Sloane MS 93, f. 65v.
[58] *Annals*, I, pp. 246 (1496–7), 254 (1500), 272 (1503–4), 295 (1513), 296 (1514), 370 (1534). For 1521–2, see *GBk* B, II, pp. 101–2, when representatives were sent to Oxford to determine how they were dealing with the problem. Cambridge did make up a list of the value of all their members' benefices, *LP* Addendum vol. I, part I, pp. 105–10. For 1531–3, see *GBk* Γ, p. 263 (1531–2), *GBk* B, II, p. 174 (1532–3), and CUA Epistolae academicae, I, ff. 63r.–v.
[59] Stat. 26 Henry VIII, c. 3; Shadwell, *Enactments*, pp. 106–8.
[60] Stat. 27 Henry VIII, c. 42; Shadwell, *Enactments*, pp. 108–9; *Annals*, I, pp. 379–81 (1535). The same Parliament passed a statute against non-residence of beneficed persons, exempting legitimate scholars, professors, and lectors. Stat. 28 Henry VIII, c. 13; *Annals*, I, pp. 382–4 (1536).

Schools for a time. The Hebrew lecture was financed by suspending the mathematics professor from 1535 until 1539, and diverting the funds to the new position.[61] This temporary measure was ended in 1539 with the appointment of Roger Ascham as professor of mathematics.[62] The inclusion of Hebrew on the university level fulfilled the Erasmian ideal of twenty years earlier, but which had hitherto been taught only within the colleges.

The chair in Greek was paid for by the colleges, as the injunctions required.[63] The first professor of Greek under this new scheme was Nicholas Ridley from 1535 to 1537–8, when he was replaced by John Ponet, who held the post until 1541, except for the year 1538–9 when it was Roger Ascham's. Each of the colleges paid a quarterly assessment through the senior bedell.[64] This varied between the colleges and from year to year. In addition, The King's Hall seems to have supported both Greek and Hebrew lectures in the Schools from 1535–40, as well as paying towards the lecturer supported by the other colleges.[65]

This arrangement was changed in 1540, again through external intervention. In that year the bishopric of Westminster was established, and was charged with maintaining at each university regius professorships in divinity, Greek, Hebrew, medicine, and law, each with a stipend of £40 per annum.[66] This programme, which probably came from the pen of Bishop Gardiner, chancellor of Cambridge in succession to Cromwell, also named men to these chairs. They were all filled by 1542.[67]

The institution of a civil law professorship was an effort to promote a study diminished within the university by the

---

[61] *GBk* Γ, pp. 310, 315, and 327 (1535–9). [62] *GBk* B, II, p. 226 (1539–40).

[63] Oxford did likewise. F. Logan, 'The Origins of the So-Called Regius Professorships', in D. Baker, ed. *Renaissance and Renewal in Christian History, Studies in Church History*, 14 (1977), p. 274.

[64] e.g. Peterhouse Archives, Computus Rolls (1537–41), 'Et ix s. vi d pro lectoribus hebraicis et grecis'. For like entries with varying payments, see Queens' College Archives, *Journale*, II, p. 20 (1535–6), f. 21r. (1537–8), etc.; King's College Archives, *Mundum Books*, 11 (1535–6) unfoliated; Christ's College Archives, Accounts 1530–45, f. 111r. (1536–7), etc.

[65] Cobban, *King's Hall*, p. 85. [66] Logan, 'Regius Professorships', p. 275.

[67] See Clark, *Endowments*, p. 156 and R. Ascham, *The Whole Works*, ed. J. Giles (London, 1864), I, i, pp. 25–6, no. 12.

abolition of canon law. Roman law was used in the university courts and was valued in the diplomatic service and Church courts. An Act of Parliament in 1545 gave doctors of civil law who had been properly deputed the right to exercise ecclesiastical jurisdiction, as they had been doing since the abolition of canon law.[68] The second regius professor of law, Thomas Smith, further enhanced the study through his own illustrious career. But civil law still languished, and an effort by the Edwardian commissioners in 1549 to found a college for its study by dissolving Clare and Trinity Hall was blocked by Bishop Gardiner, master of the latter.[69] Trinity Hall continued as a centre of civil law study, however, and many of its graduates were members of Doctors' Commons, the professional society of ecclesiastical lawyers in London, and there was liaison between the two institutions for several centuries more.

The colleges, like the university, fulfilled what was demanded of them concerning lectures. At Gonville Hall the lectureship in 'humanity, logic, or philosophy' either 'in the latyn tong or the Greek tong' founded in 1528 through Sir Geoffrey Knight's bequest was considered by the college as compliance enough.[70] At King's College in 1535–7 Martin Tyndal was paid for the Latin lecture, and Henry Pamplyn for one in Greek.[71] After a gap in the records until 1541, the accounts show eight men paid for offices which included teaching duties: three as deans, three for giving undergraduate lectures, and one each in Greek and Hebrew. This pattern was little changed throughout the century.[72] At Queens' in 1535–6 the college was supporting the Wyche lecture in theology, as well as paying for two arts lectures, one of which was on Plautus. That year Thomas Smith was paid £2 for the new college Greek lectureship, a post which he held until 1538.[73] Further lectures were added later in the century. For other colleges the records are either incomplete,

[68] 37 Henry VIII, c. 17; Shadwell, *Enactments*, pp. 147–9.
[69] *Annals*, II, pp. 25, 32–6 (1540–9); *DNB*, XVIII, pp. 532–5; G. D. Squibb, *Doctors' Commons*, Oxford, 1977.
[70] Caius, *Annals*, p. 25; Gonville and Caius College Archives XXVIII, Pattesley no. 5; *Docs.* II, pp. 253–6.
[71] King's College Archives, *Mundum Books*, 11 (1535–7), unfoliated.
[72] King's College Archives, *Mundum Books, passim*.
[73] Queens' College Archives, *Journale*, 3, p. 1 and ff. 21r., 32r., and 44r.

or the lectors received no separate payments. But the pattern is one of compliance.[74] In December 1536 King's College paid to have the injunctions displayed on a board.[75] Christ's College tried to ingratiate itself to Cromwell and his agents with £9 1s 6d in gifts.[76] The university had corporatively shown similar favour in 1533–4 when, as 'our singular patron', it voted him an annuity of £2.[77]

The texture of Cambridge life changed after Dr Leigh's visit in 1535. Corpus Christi College ceased its annual procession and sold its liturgical implements. The townsmen were furious, not out of abused piety, but for being denied the feast which the college provided after the procession. A suit ensued with the town claiming that the college had forfeited their premises (originally gifts from townsmen) by default. Royal commissioners held in favour of the college.[78]

More importantly, the religious orders were on their way out. Religious houses had already been suppressed in Cambridge to found Jesus and St John's Colleges. All monastic foundations worth less than £200 a year were suppressed in 1536, but the friars were excluded. Thus there was no immediate effect on Cambridge. The King's injunctions for monasteries in 1535 had even favoured the universities since they had required the heads to keep or find one or two monks in the universities to study and eventually return home to instruct their brethren.

Buckingham College was included by name in the university injunctions requiring colleges to maintain daily Greek and Latin lectures.[79] But the reprieve was short-lived. It was not a separate corporation but a cell of Crowland Abbey. Thus when the parent was dissolved in 1538–9 the college fell into the hands of the crown, and the former monks left. The site was soon acquired by Sir Thomas Audley, yet another Lord Chancellor, who in April of 1542 founded Magdalene College in the old monastic buildings. Audley died in 1544, and the college

---

[74] Leader, 'Teaching', pp. 117–18.
[75] King's College Archives, *Mundum Books*, 11 (1535–6), unfoliated.
[76] Christ's College Archives, Accounts 1530–45, ff. 53v.–54r.
[77] It was voted during yet another quarrel with the townsmen. GBk B, ii, p. 184 (1533–4) and GBk Γ, p. 286.
[78] Fuller, *Cambridge*, pp. 70–1.   [79] *Annals*, i, p. 374 (1535).

remained poor and disorganised for many years. Its early history more properly belongs to Elizabethan Cambridge.

The axe did not fall on the mendicant friars until 1538, but Cromwell's intentions were clear from 1534. In that year the royal supporter John Hilsey, prior of London Blackfriars, along with George Brown, an Austin Friar, were commissioned to visit all of the orders with equal jurisdiction.[80] In the same year Dr Robert Buckenham, sometime prior of Blackfriars, Cambridge, and opponent of the new religion, fled the kingdom, and Thomas Diss, warden of Greyfriars, Cambridge, suffered a nervous breakdown while in the pulpit, protesting that he was 'yntangled with worldly busynes concernynge yᵉ howse'.[81] The end was in sight for the Cambridge friaries, and those who did not flee seem to have busied themselves dismantling their convents. The junior proctor's accounts for 1536–7 show that the Austin and Blackfriars were selling and 'lending' their lead roofs for repairing the libraries in the Schools.[82] The commissioners who visited Greyfriars in 1538 reported that they had 'no substance of leade, save only som...smale gutters'.[83]

Queens' College, under president William May, made several arrangements with the neighbouring Carmelites. The friars were probably trying to make the best of a bad situation, while Queens' saw their chance to get room to grow. In February 1537 some of the friars dined at Queens' and arranged to sell the college the wall that served as their common boundary. Shortly afterwards the college took twelve cartloads of rubble and 1,000 tiles from the nearly deserted convent. In August the college tried to absorb all of it; the prior and the last three remaining friars surrendered the house, not to the Crown, but to Queens'.[84] But the crown would not confirm this, and it was not until 1541 that the buildings were sold to Queens' by the Court of Augmentations, and a few years later Queens' obtained the title to the land as well.

The surrender of the priories took place in the late summer

---

[80] *LP*, VII, pp. 530, 665.
[81] *GBk* A, p. 229 (The Esquire Bedell John Mere's Diary).
[82] *GBk* B, II, pp. 208–10 (1536–7).
[83] Moorman, *Grey Friars*, pp. 130–1.
[84] Searle, *Queens' College*, I, pp. 194–6, 222–3; *LP* ix, 246.

or early autumn of 1538 (the deeds are undated and unsealed). The houses were nearly deserted and the numbers signing are far below what they should have been: twenty-four Franciscans, sixteen Dominicans, four Carmelites, and four Augustinians.[85] Clearly any who had prospects elsewhere had left in the previous years. All the empty convents were quickly scavenged for building materials. There was no resistance to the surrenders. Those unwilling to conform had already fled, like the Blackfriar Buckenham. For martyrs one must look to Cambridge men who had joined other communities, like Richard Reynolds of Syon.

TRINITY COLLEGE

The university had conformed to the King and his new religious discipline, and Cambridge was a changed place. Internally, the developments of the Fisher years had been solidified with the founding of the stable professorships especially in Greek and Hebrew, the languages of Scriptural study. A new use of Scripture was codified, and the *Sentences* gave way to the Fathers and the new reformers. For the beginner the Latin of Cicero was normative, and he read his Aristotle with newer, if not necessarily better, commentaries.

There was a new enthusiastic generation of Cambridge men, both teaching within the university and aiding it from without. They were children of the new learning who had been tutored by the former pupils of Erasmus. They included Thomas Smith of Queens', Matthew Parker of Corpus, and a host from St John's.[86] One of the most important for Cambridge's future prosperity was John Redman. A relative of Bishop Tunstall, Redman had studied at Corpus Christi College, Oxford, and Paris, but took his BA in 1526 from St John's. He was a fellow by 1530, doctor of theology and public orator in 1537, and held the Lady Margaret Professorship from 1538–44 and in

---

[85] Moorman, *Grey Friars*, pp. 127–41; Gumbley, *Dominicans*, pp. 38–9; *VCH*, II pp. 274–5, 281, 285–6, 289–90.

[86] Porter, *Reformation*, p. 3. 'The Cambridge of Fisher was the seed-time of a strange harvest: the corn would have been alien to him...' Referring to Fisher's Christ's and St John's, 'He looked that it should bring forth grapes, and it brought forth wild grapes'.

1549. He was also an accomplished Greek scholar. Redman was warden of The King's Hall from 1542–6, and was undoubtedly instrumental in protecting Cambridge's colleges from suppression and guiding the foundation of Trinity College, of which he was the first master.[87]

John Cheke was also of St John's. A local boy, he was elected to a fellowship in 1529, served as regius professor, tutor to Prince Edward, and from 1548 as provost of King's College.[88] Among his pupils at St John's were William Cecil, William Bill, and Roger Ascham. Ascham, BA 1534, was later a regius professor of Greek (as well as mathematics), public orator, and tutor to Princess Elizabeth.[89] In his *Toxophilus* (1544) he recalled Cheke's exercises in his chambers on Homer, Aristotle, Plato, and the Greek tragedians and historians.[90] In a letter of 1542 to his fellow Johnian Richard Brandesby he speaks of the great improvements at Cambridge, listing the regius professors, and adding, 'Aristotle and Plato, who have been lectured on for fifteen years, are now heard by the boys in the original. Herodotus, Thucydides, Xenophon are read more than Cicero and Terence'. All of this Ascham attributed to Cheke's regius professorship. He concludes the letter with salutations to Cheke, John Madew, John Seton, Roger Tonge, Alban Langdale, and William Bill, all former classmates.[91] They were accomplished scholars, held college lectureships, and were enthusiasts of the new learning. Tonge, Madew, and Bill would prove themselves loyal to the new religion as well; Seton and Langdale returned to the Old Faith, dying abroad in the reign of Elizabeth.

On the episcopal bench Cambridge men were making a strong showing; Cranmer at Canterbury, Edward Lee in York, Gardiner in Winchester, Nicholas Shaxton in Salisbury, Edward Fox in Hereford, Latimer in Worcester, and others.[92] It was a trend that continued under Elizabeth, with Matthew Parker, Edmund Grindal, and John Whitgift holding the see of Canterbury in succession.

[87] *DNB*, XVI, 825.
[88] *DNB*, III, pp. 178–83.
[89] *DNB*, I, pp. 622–31.
[90] Cooper, *Athenae*, I, p. 167.
[91] Ascham, *Whole Works*, I, i, pp. 24–7.
[92] Mullinger, *Cambridge*, II, p. 18, n. 1.

But the Cambridge of the 1540s shared the uncertainty of the last years of Henry VIII. Although claims of decay are a commonplace among university men, Cambridge had declined in size since the 1520s.[93] The situation was apparent to reformers like Latimer who, preaching to King Edward in 1549 stated 'indeed the universities do wonderously decay already', due to the wealthy students taking the fellowships of the poor and godly.[94] Thomas Lever, BA 1541–2 of St John's, preaching at St Paul's Cross at the end of that decade also linked this decline to the movement of pensioners out of the hostels and into the college fellowships, thus thwarting the charitable intentions of King Henry.[95]

A far greater threat appeared in 1544 when an Act of Parliament gave the King the power to dissolve any college chantry at either university.[96] What had recently been given or enhanced by the crown could equally well be taken away, for greed was the dark side of the English reform. Actually, Henry's intention was probably to raise money by taking chantry lands away from the colleges, not dissolving the colleges themselves. But others were less concerned with education, and some courtiers asked the king to have the possessions of Oxford and Cambridge surveyed, no doubt to know what to request later.[97]

Oxford and Cambridge men were aware of the importance of these events, and they made a concerted effort to influence the king in their favour. Two obvious friends of Cambridge were John Redman's former pupils John Cheke, then tutor to Prince Edward, and Thomas Smith, a clerk of the Queen's council. The Senate wrote to Smith in particular to solicit his aid. By the account of Matthew Parker, then vice-chancellor, the friends of the university decided to request an enquiry into the affairs of the colleges, which would be conducted by Cambridge men. The King agreed, and in January 1546 Parker, John Redman (warden of The King's Hall and royal chaplain), and William May (president of Queens') were commissioned to

---

93 *GBk* B, II, p. viii.
94 Latimer, *Sermons*, II, p. 102.
95 Lever, *Sermons*, pp. 120–2.
96 Stat. 27 Henry VIII, c. 4, s. 6.
97 W. W. Rouse Ball, *Cambridge Papers* (London, 1918), p. 4.

report on the revenues of the colleges and the number of students maintained by them.[98] They were aided by eleven clerks from the Court of Augmentations in the actual survey.

While this enquiry was under way, Cambridge made further efforts to help itself by putting its belongings at the service of the King, while pointing out its value to the state and begging for his protection. They also wrote asking Queen Catherine Parr, through Thomas Smith, for her support. Her reply to Smith was encouraging. Although she complained that he could have just as well written to her in English as Latin, she said that she had advocated their case to the King, that he was favourable to them, and had plans (vaguely expressed) to 'advance learning and erect new occasion thereof'.[99]

The Queen's reply is dated 26 February 1546, by which time the commissioners had completed their survey. It was a very long and creative piece of accounting; nearly all the colleges showed themselves to be operating on deficits. When they presented an abstract of this document to the King at Hampton Court he perused it and remarked (Parker says in admiration) that 'he had not in his realm so many persons so honestly maintained in living by so little land and rent'. But the King did question how this was possible if the colleges lost money every year. They replied that it was partly from fines from farmers renewing their leases, and partly by selling wood. Henry must have realised the weakness of this answer, but he clearly had no interest in dissolving the colleges, much to the disappointment of the courtiers in the room.[100] Cambridge was safe and, equally encouraging, the benefaction suggested in the Queen's letter was under way the next month.

It is said that Henry's idea of founding Trinity College originated with John Redman.[101] But Henry's reign had seen

---

[98] Lamb, *Documents*. pp. 58–9; M. Parker, *Correspondence*, ed. J. Bruce and T. Perowne, Parker Society (Cambridge, 1853), pp. 34–6; *LP*, XXI, pt (i) p. 68; Mullinger, *Cambridge*, II, pp. 76–80.

[99] *LP*, XXI, pt (i), nos. 203 and 204; Parker, *Correspondence*, p. 36; Rouse Ball, *Cambridge Papers*, pp. 6–7.

[100] Lamb, *Documents*, p. 59; *Docs.* I, pp. 105–294; Parker, *Correspondence*, pp. 35–6.

[101] Rouse Ball, *Cambridge Papers*, pp. 8–9.

Wolsey's great plans for Cardinal College, which the King turned into the stillborn King Henry's College before refounding it this same year as Christ Church. It is more likely that Trinity College was Henry's own solution for giving Cambridge a comparable college, and Redman was surely an advocate of the plan. Once Henry had decided to act he proceeded with haste. The plans were under way by March under the supervision of Redman, and a scheme was prepared by the Court of Augmentations. For a site the King chose the existing royal foundation, The King's Hall, and the neighbouring Michaelhouse and Physwick Hostel, a dependency of Gonville Hall. They were taken over by May, although the surrender and dissolution of these medieval houses was not formalised until December.[102] There was no question of their condition being fallen; rather it was thought that their lands, buildings, and resources could be put to better use. Trinity College became a going concern that Michaelmas term.

The charter of foundation, dated 19 December 1546, expresses a purpose not dissimilar from the medieval colleges; for the glory and honour of Almighty God and the Holy and Undivided Trinity, the increase of Christian religion in the realm, leading youths to piety, and the extirpation of pestiferous heresy. To these were added the furthering of good letters and tongues, and the fight against the enormities of the Roman Pope.[103] Statutes were not promulgated until 1552, so the college was governed by the schema drawn up by the Court of Augmentations in collaboration with Dr Redman. There was a master who, like the warden of The King's Hall, was appointed by the crown.[104] Redman was, not surprisingly, the first to hold this office. He ruled a house of fifty graduate fellows and ten undergraduate scholars, and forty grammarians under the discipline of a schoolmaster and usher. This grammar school was short-lived, for in 1549 the Edwardian commissioners had these scholars absorbed into the college fellowship; but even from

---

[102] *Annals*, I, pp. 442, 446–52.   [103] *Docs.* III, 365–70.
[104] Since its foundation in 1960, the mastership of Churchill College shares this peculiarity.

1546 ten of the forty foundation 'grammarians' were already matriculated in the university. [105]

By 1548 the college had 143 men on the foundation: the master, one other doctor of theology, nine bachelors of theology, twenty-seven MAs, thirteen BAs, ten *dialectici* (corresponding to the medieval *sophister generalis*), forty-two *grammatici* (scholars in their first two years), six men kept on from The King's Hall and Michaelhouse, eight Bible clerks, and twenty-five *pauperes*. [106] To these were added by the 1552 statutes fifty-four pensioners, who had to pass an entrance examination. The college also had two chaplains and a large corps of servants.

It is in the teaching provisions of Trinity College that we see the complete development of humanist ideals furthered by an extensive programme of internal lectures and tutorials, closely coordinated with the university professorships. Again, they were meant to complement each other, not compete. There were nine salaried internal lectors who appear in the college accounts from 1547, and whose duties are explained in the statutes of the next decade. The senior lector taught bachelors Aristotle's natural philosophy at 6 a.m. He had four assistant lectors for the undergraduates; these men were known by the texts they taught: the *Topics*, the *Sophistic Refutations* (or the *Posterior Analytics* or Agricola's *De inventione dialectica)*, Porphyry (or other books from the *Organon*), and for the beginners, John Seton's *Dialectica*. In addition to their lectures, they were all to meet their classes after morning prayers, asking individual scholars to interpret the authors covered and, after a text had been finished, to make the whole class go through it rapidly, reducing the headings and divisions to a table, and making the book into a compendium.

The five lectors were supported by four others. The lector of Greek language was heard by all scholars, except those whom the senior lector judged advanced enough to hear the regius professor in the Schools instead. A second Greek lector used

---

[105] Trinity College Muniments, Box 29, c.II.A; the 1546 plan is described in detail in Rouse Ball, *Cambridge Papers*, pp. 13–19.
[106] Trinity College Muniments, Senior Bursar's Ledger, I, f. 47v.–50r.

Clenardus, Ceporinus, or Gaza's introductory texts to teach the memorisation of inflections to beginners. Both lectors also held repetitions for their pupils every Saturday. The Latin lector taught Cicero to undergraduates and at the end of each term, verse composition. The fourth lector was for mathematics, and taught the quadrivium to bachelors.[107]

The Trinity statutes also formalised the position of tutors, requiring all scholars to have one. This had appeared in some colleges much earlier, as we have seen at The King's Hall. The role of tutors was codified on the university level by the Edwardian injunctions of 1549 which ordered that 'tutors should diligently teach their pupils, correct them, and not allow them to wander loosely in the city'.[108] At Trinity we find the most complete record of the tutor–pupil relationship in the accounts that the future Archbishop Whitgift kept of his pupils' expenses while at Trinity in the 1570s.[109] Whitgift bought books for his pupils, paid for their room and board, paid their fees to the college lectors, and also made separate payments to other tutors from whom they received instruction.

The Trinity College teaching was designed to complement the professors in the Schools, and the nexus was administratively even closer. When Trinity and Christ Church, Oxford were founded in 1546, Westminster Cathedral, which had formerly paid the regius professors, granted the crown lands worth £400 per annum, and was thus relieved of supporting the Oxford and Cambridge posts.[110] Instead, Trinity College was given the responsibility of providing £40 per annum to the Cambridge professors of divinity, Greek, and Hebrew, while the two other chairs, in civil law and medicine, were financed through the Court of Augmentations.[111] The Trinity statutes specified that

107 Trinity College Muniments, Senior Bursar's Ledger, I, f. 24r.; Admissions and Admonitions 1560–1759, p. 61 and *passim*; Trinity College Add. MS a. 178. I am indebted to the former librarian, Dr P. Gaskell, for volunteering his personal notes on these college lectureships. See also Mullinger, *Cambridge*, II, pp. 579–627 for selections from the 1552 statutes.

108 *Statuta academiae Cantabrigiensis*, p. 67, and repeated by the Elizabethan statutes and injunctions. Lamb, *Documents*, p. 303 (1559). *Docs.* I, 492 (1570).

109 S. R. Maitland, 'Archbishop Whitgift's College Pupils', *British Magazine*, 32 (1847), 361–79, 508–28, 650–6; 33 (1848) 17–31, 185–96, 444–65.

110 Logan, 'Regius Professorships', p. 276. 111 Logan, 'Regius Professorships', p. 276.

these three men were to lecture at least four times a week even during the long vacation.[112] They were elected by the vice-chancellor, the master of Trinity and its two most senior fellows, and the heads of King's, St John's, and Christ's. A procedure for the public examination of candidates was provided, and Trinity fellows were to be preferred *ceteris paribus*. Although the elections were subject to royal confirmation, no notice was to be taken of royal attempts at interference.[113]

Trinity College included all the features of St John's College, while being blessed with even greater resources. It soon rivalled it in size, and took its first four masters from among the Johnians. But it was its wealth that set Trinity in a class of its own. It was enriched with all the holdings of both Michaelhouse and The King's Hall, worth about £360 per year. To this was added the plunder of the monasteries: forty advowsons and nearly a dozen manors. The total endowment of Trinity when it opened was assessed at £1,678 3s 9¼d.[114] To house the college the remnants of The King's Hall, Michaelhouse, and Physwick Hostel were modified, and new buildings constructed with stone quarried from the abandoned husk of Greyfriars, which was included in the endowment. Along with the land came possession of the thirteenth-century conduit the friars had built from Madingley to bring them pure water. The fountain in Great Court is still served by the same Franciscan flow, 'whose splash at midnight has been grateful to the ears of so many generations of dwellers in the Great Court'.[115]

[112] The statute of 1552 in question is printed in Clark, *Endowments*, pp. 156–61. This was dispensed with in 1568. BL Lansdowne MS 10, art. 53, ff. 163r.–164r.

[113] By contrast, the professorships of law and medicine were crown appointments.

[114] *Annals*, I, 445–51 (1546).

[115] G. M. Trevelyan, *Trinity College*, 2nd edn (Cambridge, 1972), p. 14. A standpipe outside Great Gate until recently preserved 'the memory of the former public use outside the house of the Friars Minor' (Lloyd, *Early Christ's*, p. 70, n. 1). Serious damage to the conduit was discovered in 1971 but, to the credit of Trinity, the expense was paid to refurbish it. *ex info.* Trinity Clerk of the Works Office. To build Trinity 3,000 loads of materials were taken from Greyfriars to Trinity in 1556 alone (Willis and Clark, II, p. 562).

CONCLUSION

With the founding of Trinity College our story ends. The evolution that had begun one hundred years earlier had come to term. The university was larger, richer, and from being decidedly secondary, now rivalled Oxford in prestige and influence. The hostels were gone, and nearly all the university members were now college members as well. With this came the disappearance of necessary regency lectures, replaced by salaried professorships and college lectors and tutors. The curriculum was now solidly humanistic, with humane letters and moral philosophy taking precedence over medieval logic and natural philosophy. Aristotle was still The Philosopher, but it was a less scholastic Aristotle. With the dominance of the language arts, 'the strong philosophical and scientific heart was cut away'.[116]

Both university and colleges were now regularly subject to control by the crown, and the pattern of royal commissions, injunctions, and statutes accelerated: by Edward in 1549, by Mary in 1554, by Elizabeth in 1559, and again in 1570. In the battle of religious and political beliefs begun by the Reformation and furthered by the printing press, the universities were too useful as friends and too dangerous as enemies to be left alone. The crown could never really 'control' the universities, but it could exercise considerable influence through coercion. Besides, Cambridge was for the most part sympathetic to the Tudors, and provided many of the great Elizabethan politicians and ecclesiastics who, like Burghley, Parker, Whitgift, and Mildmay, were benefactors of Cambridge as well.

Calvinism was the orthodoxy of the divinity faculty by the 1570s. Resistance to the religious settlement came for the most part from the extreme left, with precise protestants objecting to the wearing of the surplice in chapel, 'that rag of popery'. It was only a symbol, but it became a shibboleth to the vociferous party that felt that the Reformation had not been carried to a

[116] C. B. Schmitt, *John Case and Aristotelianism in Renaissance England* (Kingston and Montreal, 1983), p. 20, n. 24 and pp. 13–76.

proper conclusion. There was to be much life but little peace in the divinity faculty for the next hundred years.[117]

The greatest outward changes resulted from the break with Rome. The once thriving canon law faculty had disappeared, and with it the friars and monks. Their convents were desolate for a time and then converted to new uses: Buckingham College to Magdalene College, and the Carmelites' house into the Walnut Court of Queens' College.[118] What was left of Greyfriars by the Trinity builders was adapted into Sidney Sussex College in 1596, and Blackfriars was turned into Sir Walter Mildmay's puritan Emmanuel College in 1584; the Dominican chapel is now a hall, and their fishpond still graces the college's gardens.[119] Only the Austin Friars' convent was divided piecemeal, and the site is now covered by the Science Area. The great libraries of these convents were dispersed and for the most part lost (along with most of the college libraries) although some of the Dominican and Franciscan codices, after passing through several hands, ended up in the Vatican Library.[120]

With the accession of Elizabeth in 1559 the liturgical accoutrements that had survived Kings Henry and Edward, or which had been restored by Queen Mary, were removed for the last time.[121] With the fluctuations of those years came a fluctuation of consciences, or at least conformity. After 1560 the old Catholics caused little trouble. If they were uncomfortable they left, like John Seton and his fellow logician John Sanderson. A Lancastrian, Sanderson came up to Trinity in 1554, held the college lectorships in Seton and Porphyry, and was elected Rede professor of logic in 1562–3.[122] He did not finish the year, being expelled for giving commonplaces in

---

[117] Porter, *Reformation*.
[118] Stained glass from the Carmelites is now in the windows of the college's Old Library, overlooking its former home.
[119] The Blackfriars' statue of Our Lady of Grace attracted so many pilgrims during the Stourbridge Fair in 1538 that Cromwell had it removed. *LP*, XIII (2) 224. It is possibly the figure now in the Catholic Church in Hills Road.
[120] N. R. Ker, 'Cardinal Cervini's Manuscripts from the Cambridge Friars', in *Xenia medii aevi historiam illustrantia*, pp. 51–71.
[121] See Porter, *Reformation*, pp. 68–9, 109–10, and 114–18.
[122] Trinity College Muniments, Admissions and Admonitions 1560–1759, pp. 61–2; Jesus College Archives, A/C.1.2.; *DNB*, XVII, 753–4.

chapel that contained Catholic doctrine on fasting and feast days, and for using allegorising and citing Plato while interpreting Scripture. Sanderson finished his life in Douai and Reims. But he is exceptional, and the more normal victims of persecution for alleged Catholic beliefs were older men like Dr Caius and Provost Baker of King's, who stored away copes and crucifixes 'against the day' when they might be used again. [123]

That day was far away. Between the 1440s and 1540s the medieval university had been transformed. The relative independence of the small medieval guild was gone, but so was its insignificance. It had become larger, and by the late sixteenth century an intensely protestant university, a place of the individual conscience, of scientific enquiry, a more severe school than its medieval ancestor. And, it was far more influential in the English Church and State. As an institution it would not again see such a period of change until the century from 1870 to 1970.

[123] Cooper, *Athenae*, II, pp. 322–3; Brooke, *Gonville and Caius College*, pp. 72–4.

BIBLIOGRAPHY

MANUSCRIPTS CITED

Bordeaux, Bibliothèque Municipale
    MS 44 15th cent., theology

Cambridge, University Library
  Cambridge University Archives
    UA/Collect. Admin. 1 Senior Proctor's Book
    UA/Collect. Admin. 2 Junior Proctor's Book
    UA/Collect. Admin. 3 Old Proctor's Book
    UA/Collect. Admin. 9 Black Parchment Book
    UA/Collect. Admin. 13 Utinam Book
    UA/Collect. Admin. 19 1785 Statute Book
    Ely Diocesan Archives, G/1/5 Register of Bishop William Grey
    Ely Diocesan Archives, G/1/6 Register of Bishop John Alcock
    UA/Lic. A (1) 1–16 Preaching Licences
    UA/Luard 152 Preaching Licences
    UA/Luard 159 Rede Endowment
    UA/Matric. 1 Matriculations
    UA/Misc. Coll. 5 Bedell Buck's Book
    UA/Misc. Coll. 10 Disputed Questions
    UA/Subscript. Add. 4 Preaching Licences and Subscriptions
    UA/VCP/4 Vice-chancellor's court probate inventories
    UA/Comm. Court I–III Court records
  Cambridge, University Library
    MS Dd.V.27 15th cent., sermon collection
    MS Ee.III.61 15th cent., scientific tracts
    MS Ff.IV.39 15th cent., Terence
    MS Ff.VI.4 15th cent., Terence
    MS Gg.I.34(2) 15th cent., moral philosophy
    MS Gg.VI.20 15th cent., sermon tracts
    MS Kk.I.18 15th cent., theology

Bibliography

Cambridge, Christ's College, Archives
    Bursar's accounts, 1530–45
Cambridge, Corpus Christi College
  Archives
  Registrum ciste magistri Billingford
  Library
    MS 68 15th cent., theological items
    MS 423 15th cent., sermon tracts
    MS 480 15th cent., Greek psalter
    MS 496 15th cent., moral philosophy
Cambridge, Gonville and Caius College
  Archives
    XVIII Pattisley Will of Dr Geoffrey Knight
  Library
    MS 35/141 15th cent., scientific tracts
    MS 54/31 13th–14th cent., legal treatises [on canon and Roman law]
    MS 114/183 15th cent., Patristic texts, etc.
    MS 141/191 14th cent., computistic and mathematical texts
    MS 167/88 15th cent., scientific [comm. Aristotle's *Physics*]
    MS 182/215 15th cent., lecture notes on logic
    MS 203/109 14th cent., grammar texts
    MS 335/724 15th cent., philosophical texts
    MS 348/541 15th cent., Greek psalter
    MS 368/590 15th cent., comms. on *Physics* and *Metaphysics*
    MS 369/591 15th cent., comms. on *Metaphysics* and *Ethics*
    MS 377/597 15th cent., grammatical texts
    MS 385/605 13th cent., misc. texts, partly grammar
    MS 403/412 12th cent., Greek Gospels
    MS 417/447 15th cent., grammar texts, etc.
    MS 466/573 13th cent., philosophical texts
    MS 469/576 13th cent., Aristotle
    MS 483/479 13th–14th cent., *Digest*
    MS 507/385 15th cent., scientific texts [Albertus Magnus, etc.]
    MS 593/453 13th, 15th cent., grammar texts
Cambridge, Jesus College, Archives
    Account rolls I and II
    Audit book A/C.I.2
    Bursar's accounts A/C.I.1–3
Cambridge, King's College
  Archives
    Allen's catalogue Miscellaneous

Bibliography

Computi bursarum   15th cent., account rolls
Ledger book I   Includes bequests and benefactions
Liber protocoli, 1500–78   Entrances of fellows and licences to study
       abroad
Mundum books I–XX   College accounts from 1456
   Library
      MS 9   15th cent., theological texts
      MS 11   15th cent., comm. on *Ethics*
Cambridge, Pembroke College
   Archives
      Register AA   College accounts and misc.
      Register CS   College accounts and misc.
   Library (deposited in Cambridge University Library)
      MS 38   14th cent., Gospel of John
      MS 122   14th cent., Aquinas' *Summa*
      MS 123   14th cent., Aquinas' *Summa*
      MS 124   14th cent., Aquinas' *Summa*
      MS 125   14th cent., Aquinas on *Sentences*
      MS 130   14th cent., *Metaphysics*
      MS 137   14th cent., Avicenna
      MS 141   13th cent., Bible
      MS 142   12th cent., Bible
      MS 157   14th cent., Burley on *Ethics* and *Politics*
      MS 158   15th cent., Burley and Giles of Rome
      MS 173   14th–15th cent., comm. on *Epistles*
      MS 175   14th–15th cent., theology
      MS 181   15th cent., biblical comm.
      MS 186   13th cent., comm. on St Paul
      MS 201   14th cent., canon law
      MS 207   16th cent., theology questions
      MS 223   15th cent., biblical comms.
      MS 230   14th, 15th cent., theological tracts
      MS 242   15th cent., theological tables
      MS 245   15th cent., theology
      MS 255   15th cent., theological tracts
      MS 263   15th cent., sermon collections
Cambridge, Peterhouse
   Archives
      Bursar's rolls, 1388–9
      Computus rolls, 1537–41
   Library (deposited in Cambridge University Library)
      MS 23   15th cent., biblical comm.

Bibliography

MS 38 14th cent., biblical gloss
MS 46 13th cent., Bible
MS 49 14th–15th cent., Aquinas on *Sentences*
MS 58 13th cent., Aquinas on *Sentences*
MS 91 15th cent., theological comms.
MS 99 15th cent., theological tracts
MS 102 14th cent., philosophical and logical tracts
MS 117 13th cent., Aquinas on *Sentences*
MS 120 14th cent., pastoralia
MS 124 14th cent., Aquinas' *Summa*
MS 135 13th, 15th cent., theological tracts
MS 143 14th, 15th cent., philosophical tracts
MS 157 14th cent., philosophical tracts
MS 160 15th cent., sermon tracts
MS 166 13th cent., sermons
MS 169 15th cent., theological items
MS 174 13th cent., sermons
MS 183 14th cent., comm. on *Physics*
MS 188 15th cent., philosophical items
MS 195 14th cent., theological and philosophical tracts
MS 200 14th cent., sermon tracts
MS 239 15th cent., philosophical tracts
MS 240 15th cent., philosophical tracts
MS 246 14th cent., theological tracts
MS 250 15th cent., astronomical tracts
MS 253 12th cent., Terence
MS 267 15th cent., astronomical tracts
MS 272 14th cent., Dumbleton's logic
Cambridge, Queens' College, Archives (deposited in Cambridge University Library)
    Auditor's books IX–XI
    Journale, I–V, 15th–16th cent.
Cambridge, St John's College, Archives
    C1.2 Statutes of 1516 and 1524
    C1.5 Statutes of 1586
    C1.12 Statutes of 1580–5 and misc.
    C1.40 Statutes of 1516 and 1524
    C17.1 College Revenues of 1546
    C17.2 College Revenues of 1556
    C17.24 Value of College lands 1517–18
    Drawer 107.1 Master's accounts 1510–14
    Drawer 107.6 Master's accounts 1535–6

Drawer 107.7 Master's accounts 1527
Drawer 107.8 Master's accounts 1518–23
M3.1-10 Master's accounts 1514–23
SB3.1 Bursar's accounts 1526–46
'Thin Red Book' misc., including statutes
Cambridge, Sidney Sussex College, Library
    MS Δ.3.11   15th cent., poetic texts
Cambridge, Trinity College
  Archives
    Admissions and admonitions 1560–1759
    Box 29.c.II. A, College expenses 1546
    Box 29.c.III.d, Regius professorships
    King's Hall accounts 22–6, for 1517–43
    Senior Bursar's accounts 1–2, for 1547–83
    Senior Bursar's ledger, for 1547 and after
  Library
    MS 330 (B.14.47)   Surigone's *De institutionibus boni viri*
    Add. MS a.177–82   Dr Gaskell's notes on college history

Dublin, Trinity College Library
    MS A.5.3   15th cent., theological and misc.

Gdansk, Bibl. Civ.
    MS 2370   15th cent., logical texts

Leicester, Old Town Library
    New Testament in Greek

London, British Library
    MS Add. 10344   15th cent., comm. on *Phaedo*
    MS Add. 15673   15th cent., theology texts
    MS Arundel 66   15th cent., astronomical items
    MS Arundel 249   15th cent., grammar tracts
    MS Cotton Julius F.vii   William of Worcester's commonplace
    MS Egerton 889   15th cent., astronomical tracts
    MS Egerton 2622   15th cent., quadrivial tracts
    MS Harleian 1587   14th, 15th cent., grammar texts
    MS Harleian 1705   15th cent., Plato
    MS Harleian 2178   15th cent., logical tracts
    MS Harleian 5356   17th cent., Robert Booth on philosophy
    MS Harleian 5398   15th cent., theological items
    MS Harleian 7037   Baker MS 10, Cambridge items

Bibliography

MS Harleian 7039   Baker MS 12, Cambridge items
MS Lansdowne 10   Burghley Papers
MS Lansdowne 20   Burghley Papers
MS Royal 3.D.I   15th cent., theological tables
MS Royal 5.C.III   15th cent., theological and philosophical texts
MS Royal 6.B.V   15th cent., misc.
MS Royal 7.D.I   13th cent., theological items
MS Royal 8.E.VII   15th cent., Cambridge histories
MS Royal 8.E.XII   15th cent., sermons
MS Royal 9.E.I   15th cent., Aristotle's *Ethics*
MS Royal 9.E.II   14th cent., canon law texts
MS Royal 12.B.XIX   15th cent., logical texts
MS Royal 12.C.XVII   14th cent., astronomical tracts
MS Royal 12.C.XXI   15th cent., Frontinus
MS Royal 12.D.VI   15th cent., astronomical tracts
MS Royal 12.E.XI   15th cent., rhetorical items
MS Royal 12.G.I   15th cent., astronomical tables
MS Royal 14.C.IV   15th cent., epistolaries
MS Sloane 93   16th cent., poetry
MS Sloane 407   15th cent., astronomical texts
London, Lambeth Palace Library
    MS 70   15th cent., logical texts
    MS 97   13th cent., philosophical texts
    MS 111   13th cent., philosophical texts
    MS 141   13th cent., Augustine
    MS 145   15th cent., theological texts
    MS 393   15th cent., logical texts
    MS 396   15th cent., philosophical texts
    MS 675   15th cent., natural philosophy
London, Public Record Office
    PRO/SP Hen. VIII, 233.
London, Society of Antiquaries
    MS 39   15th cent., scientific items

New York City, New York Academy of Medicine Library
    Former Phillips MS 9418   15th cent., medical tract

Oxford, Oxford University Archives
    Register of Congregation G   1505–17
    Register of Congregation H   1518–35
Oxford, Bodleian Library
    MS Ashmole 1437 (s.c. 7775)   15th cent., medical texts

MS Ashmole 1522 (s.c. 6750)   14th cent., quadrivial texts
MS Bodley 300 (s.c. 2474)   15th cent., misc.
MS Bodley 487 (s.c. 2067)   15th cent., commonplace
MS Bodley 507 (s.c. 2171)   15th cent., scientific texts
MS Bodley 587 (s.c. 2359)   15th cent., rhetorical tracts
MS Bodley 676 (s.c. 2593)   15th cent., scientific texts
MS Bodley 832 (s.c. 2538)   15th cent., commonplace
MS Digby 15 (s.c. 1616)   15th cent., quadrivial items
MS Digby 29 (s.c. 1630)   15th cent., medical and astronomical texts
MS Digby 48 (s.c. 1649)   15th cent., scientific texts
MS Digby 57 (s.c. 1658)   15th cent., scientific texts
MS Digby 104 (s.c. 1705)   13th–14th cent., misc.
MS Digby 147 (s.c. 1748)   14th cent., scientific tracts
MS Hatton 15 (s.c. 4121)   14th cent., philosophical texts
MS Lat. misc. d.34 (s.c. 36217)   15th cent., rhetorical tracts
MS Laud misc. 594 (s.c. 1030)   14th, 15th cent., scientific tracts
MS Laud misc. 674 (s.c. 504)   15th cent., astronomical texts
MS Laud misc. 706 (s.c. 809)   15th cent., theology and science
MS Rawlinson C. 677 (s.c. 12521)   14th cent., philosophical and logical
                                                          tracts
MS Rawlinson G. 25 (s.c. 14758)   15th cent., New Testament
MS Saville 38 (s.c. 6584)   15th cent., astronomical items
Oxford, Balliol College Library
MS 27   14th cent., theological texts
MS 28   15th cent., theological text
MS 35B   15th cent., theological texts
MS 93   15th cent., philosophical texts
MS 124   15th cent., philosophical and misc. notebook
MS 276   15th cent., rhetorical tracts
MS 310   15th cent., epistolaries
Oxford, Corpus Christi College (deposited in Bodleian Library)
MS 103   15th cent., logical tracts
MS 116   15th cent., logical and philosophical tracts
MS 126   15th cent., logical and philosophical tracts
MS 151   14th cent., astrology
MS 225   14th cent., philosophical tracts
MS 228   15th cent., logical and philosophical tracts
MS 251   14th cent., quadrivial tracts
Oxford, Lincoln College (deposited in Bodleian Library)
MS 21   15th cent., Aristotle's *Ethics*
MS 60   15th cent., rhetorical tracts

MS 90   15th cent., theology

MS 117–18   Thomas Gascoigne's *Liber Veritatum*

Oxford, Magdalen College (deposited in Bodleian Library)

MS 38   15th cent., logical and philosophical tracts

MS 47   15th cent., logical tracts

MS 49   15th cent., Aristotle's *Ethics* and *Politics*

MS 92   15th cent., logical and philosophical texts

MS 162   15th cent., logical texts

MS 166   15th cent., rhetorical texts

Oxford, Merton College

MS C.2.11   15th cent., grammar and logical tracts

MS C.2.12   14th cent., quadrivial tracts

Oxford, New College (deposited in Bodleian Library)

MS 127   15th cent., epistolaries

MS 162   15th cent., scientific tracts

MS 238   15th cent., philosophical tracts

MS 242   14th cent., philosophical texts

MS 249   15th cent., rhetorical texts

MS 289   15th cent., logical texts

Oxford, Oriel College (deposited in Bodleian Library)

MS 35   15th cent., philosophical texts

MS 48   14th cent., philosophical texts

MS 54   14th cent., rhetorical texts

Vatican City, Biblioteca Apostolica Vaticana

MS Ott. Lat. 69   14th cent., theological texts

MS Ott. Lat. 196   14th cent., theological texts

MS Ott. Lat. 202   13th cent., Aquinas' theology

MS Ott. Lat. 211   13th cent., Aquinas' theology

MS Ott. Lat. 229   13th cent., Gregory's theology

MS Ott. Lat. 2088   14th cent., Ockham on *Sentences*

MS Urb. Lat. 1180   15th cent., grammar texts

Worcester, Cathedral Library

MS F.118   14th cent., logical texts

PRINTED BOOKS

Booklists and library catalogues

Bateson, M. *Syon Monastery Library Catalogue*, Cambridge, 1898.

Boyle, L. E. and Rouse, R. H. 'A Fifteenth Century List of the Books of Edmund Norton', *Speculum*, 50 (1975), 284–8.

Bibliography

Bradshaw, H. 'Two Lists of Books in the University Library', *CAS, Proceedings*, 2 (1863), 239–78.

Cargill-Thompson, W. D. J. 'Notes on King's College Library, 1500–1750', *Transactions of the Cambridge Bibliographical Society*, 2 (1954), 38–54.

Corrie, G. E. 'A Catalogue of the Books Given to Trinity Hall, Cambridge, by the Founder', *CAS, Report*, 11 (1861), 73–8.

'A Late Fifteenth Century St Catharine's Booklist', *CAS, Quarto Publications*, 1 (1840), 1–5.

'A List of Books Presented to Pembroke College, Cambridge, by Different Donors, During the Fourteenth and Fifteenth Centuries', *CAS, Report*, 10 (1860), 11–23.

Coxe, H. O. *Catalogus codicum MSS qui in collegiis aulisque Oxoniensibus hodie adservantur*, 2 vols., Oxford, 1852.

Craster, H. H. E. 'Index to Duke Humphrey's Gifts to the Old Library', *Bodleian Quarterly Review*, 1 (1914–16), 131–5.

Curtis, M. H. 'Library Catalogues at Tudor Oxford and Cambridge', *Studies in the Renaissance*, 5 (1958), 111–20.

Fletcher, J. M. 'Addendum to "Provost Argentine of King's and His Books"', *Transactions of the Cambridge Bibliographical Society*, 3 (1961), 263.

'A Fifteenth Century Benefaction to Magdalen College Library', *Bodleian Library Record*, 9 (1973–8), 169–72.

Fletcher, J. M. and McConica, J. K. 'A Sixteenth Century Inventory of the Library of Corpus Christi College, Cambridge', *Transactions of the Cambridge Bibliographical Society*, 3 (1961), 187–99.

Gaskell, P. 'Books Bought by Whitgift's Pupils in the 1570s', *Transactions of the Cambridge Bibliographical Society*, 7 (1979), 284–93.

Halliwell, J. O. 'A Catalogue of the Books Bequeathed to Corpus Christi College, Cambridge (A. D. 1439) by Thomas Markaunt with their Prices', *CAS, Quarto Publications*, 14 (1847), 15–20.

Hunt, R. W. 'The Manuscript Collection of University College, Oxford', *Bodleian Library Record*, 3 (1950–1), 13–34.

'Medieval Inventories of Clare College Library', *Transactions of the Cambridge Bibliographical Society*, 1 (1949–53), 105–25.

Jacob, E. F. 'An Early Booklist of All Souls College', *Bulletin of the John Rylands Library*, 16 (1932), 469–81.

James, M. R. 'A Catalogue of the Library of the Augustinian Friars at York', *Fasciculus Ioanni Willis Clark Dicatus*, Cambridge, 1909, pp. 2–16.

'A Catalogue of Thomas Markaunt's Library from MS Corpus Christi College, Cambridge, 232', *CAS, Octavo Series*, 32 (1899), 76–82.

Bibliography

A Descriptive Catalogue of the Western Manuscripts in the Library of Clare College, Cambridge, Cambridge, 1905.

A Descriptive Catalogue of the Manuscripts in the Library of Corpus Christi College, Cambridge, 2 vols., Cambridge, 1912.

A Descriptive Catalogue of the Manuscripts in the Library of Gonville and Caius College, Cambridge, 2 vols., Cambridge, 1907–8 (with supplement, 1914).

A Descriptive Catalogue of the Manuscripts other than Oriental in the Library of King's College, Cambridge, Cambridge, 1895.

A Descriptive Catalogue of the Manuscripts in the Library of Pembroke College, Cambridge, Cambridge, 1905.

A Descriptive Catalogue of the Manuscripts in the Library of Peterhouse, Cambridge, 1899.

A Descriptive Catalogue of the Manuscripts in St Catharine's College, Cambridge, Cambridge, 1925.

'Greek Manuscripts in England before the Renaissance', *The Library*, 7 (1927), 337–53.

Jayne, S. *Library Catalogues of the English Renaissance*, Berkeley, 1956.

Ker, N. R. 'Cardinal Cervini's Manuscripts from the Cambridge Friars' in *Xenia medii aevi historiam illustrantia oblata Thomae Kaeppeli, OP*, 2 vols., ed. R. Creytens, OP and P. Kunzle, OP (Storia e Letteratura: Raccolta di Studi e Testi, 141, 142, Rome, 1978), 1, pp. 51–71.

Medieval Libraries of Great Britain, Royal Historical Society Guides and Handbooks, 3, 2nd ed. London, 1964.

'Oxford College Libraries Before 1500', in *Les Universités à la fin du Moyen Age*, ed. J. Paquet and J. IJsewijn, Louvain, Institut d'études médiévales, 1978, pp. 293–311.

Records of All Souls College Library, 1437-1600, Oxford, Oxford Bibliographical Society, 1971.

Leach, A. F. 'Wyckham's Books at New College' in M. Burrows (ed.), *Collectanea*, 3, Oxford Historical Society, 32, 1896, pp. 213–44.

Leedham-Green, E. 'A Catalogue of Caius College Library, 1569', *Transactions of the Cambridge Bibliographical Society*, 8 (1981–5), 29–41.

Liddell, J. R. 'The Library of Corpus Christi College, Oxford', *The Library*, 18 (1938), 385–416.

McKitterick, D. 'Two Sixteenth Century Catalogues of St John's College Library', *Transactions of the Cambridge Bibliographical Society*, 7 (1977–80), 135–55.

Munby, A. N. L. 'Notes on King's College Library in the Fifteenth Century', *Transactions of the Cambridge Bibliographical Society*, 1 (1949–53), 280–6.

Mynors, R. A. B. *Catalogue of the Manuscripts of Balliol College, Oxford*, Oxford, 1963.

Bibliography

Norton, F. J. 'The Library of Bryan Rowe, Vice-Provost of King's College (d. 1521)', *Transactions of the Cambridge Bibliographical Society*, 2 (1958), 339–51.

Oates, J. C. T. 'The University Library Catalogue of 1556: An Addendum', *Transactions of the Cambridge Bibliographical Society*, 4 (1964), 79–82.

Oates, J. C. T. and Pink, H. L. 'Three Sixteenth Century Catalogues of the University Library', *Transactions of the Cambridge Bibliographical Society*, 1 (1949–53), 310–40.

Pantin, W. A. *Canterbury College, Oxford*, Oxford Historical Society, 3 vols., n.s. 6–8, 1947–50.

Powicke, F. M. *The Medieval Books of Merton College*, Oxford, 1931.

Rhodes, D. E. 'Provost Argentine of King's and His Books', *Transactions of the Cambridge Bibliographical Society*, 2 (1956), 205–12.

Royal Commission on Historical Manuscripts, First Report, London, HMSO, 1874.

Sayle, C. E. 'King's Hall Library', *CAS, Report*, 72 (1923), 54–76.

Searle, W. G. 'Catalogue of the Library of Queens' College, 1472', *CAS, Quarto Series*, 1 (1840), 165–93.

Smith, M. H. 'Some Humanist Libraries in Early Tudor Cambridge', *Sixteenth Century Journal*, 5 (1974), 15–34.

Ullman, B. L. 'Manuscripts of Duke Humphrey of Gloucester', in *Studies in the Italian Renaissance*, Rome, Edizioni di Storia e Letteratura, 1955, pp. 345–55.

Weiss, R. 'The Earliest Catalogue of the Library of Lincoln College', *Bodleian Quarterly Review*, 8 (1935–8), 343–59.

'Henry VI and the Library of All Souls College', *English Historical Review*, 57 (1942), 102–5.

Other books and articles

Alcock, J. *In die innocencium sermo pro episcopo puerorum*, Westminster, Wynkyn de Worde, n.d.

An Exortacyon Made to Relygyouse Systers, Westminster, Wynkyn de Worde, 1496.

Allen, P. S. 'Erasmus at Cambridge in 1506', in P. S. Allen (ed.) *Epistolae Erasmi*, 1, Oxford, 1906, pp. 590–3.

Allen, P. S. and H. M. (eds.) *The Letters of Richard Foxe*, Oxford, 1929.

Amundsen, D. W. 'Medieval Canon Law in Medical and Surgical Practice by the Clergy', *Bulletin of the History of Medicine*, 52 (1978), 22–44.

Anianus, *Le Comput Manuel de Magister Anianus*, ed. D. E. Smith, Paris, 1928.

Anstey, H. (ed.) *Epistolae Academicae Oxon.*, 2 vols., Oxford Historical Society 35 and 36, Oxford, 1898.

Bibliography

Ascham, R. *Epistolae*, ed. W. Elstob, Oxford, 1703.

The Whole Works, 3 vols., ed. J. Giles, London, 1865.

Ashworth, E. J. *Language and Logic in the Post Medieval Period*, Dordrecht, 1974.

'The *Libelli Sophistarum* and the Use of Medieval Logic Texts at Oxford and Cambridge in the Early Sixteenth Century', *Vivarium*, 17 (1979), 134–58.

'The Eclipse of Medieval Logic', in *The Cambridge History of Later Medieval Philosophy*, ed. N. Kretzmann, A. Kenny, and J. Pinborg, Cambridge, 1982, pp. 787–96.

Aston, T. H. 'The Date of John Rous's List of the Colleges and Academical Halls of Oxford', *Oxoniensia*, 42 (1977), 226–36.

'Oxford's Medieval Alumni', *Past and Present*, 74 (1977), 3–40.

Aston, T. H. (ed.) *History of the University of Oxford*, I: *The Early Oxford Schools*, ed. J. Catto; III: *The Collegiate University*, ed. J. K. McConica, Oxford, 1984, 1986.

Aston, T. H., Duncan, G. D., and Evans, T. A. R. 'The Medieval Alumni of the University of Cambridge', *Past and Present*, 86 (1980), 9–86.

Attwater, A. *Pembroke College, Cambridge*, ed. S. C. Roberts, Cambridge, 1936.

Baker, T. *History of the College of St John the Evangelist*, 2 vols., ed. J. E. B. Mayor, Cambridge, 1869.

Bartlett, K. 'The Decline and Abolition of the Master of Grammar at Cambridge', *History of Education*, 6 (1977), 1–8.

Barton, J. L. *Roman Law in Britain*, Ius Romanum Medii Aevi Pars V, 13, Milan, 1971.

'The Study of Civil Law before 1380', in *The History of the University of Oxford*, I, ed. J. Catto, Oxford, 1984, pp. 519–30.

Bateson, M. (ed.) *Grace Book B*, 2 vols., Cambridge, 1903–5.

Becon, T. 'Jewel of Joye', in *Catechism*, ed. J. Ayre, Parker Society 3, Cambridge, 1844.

Bell, H. E. 'The Price of Books in Medieval England', *The Library*, 17 (1937), 312–32.

Bennett, H. S. *The Pastons and their England*, Cambridge, 1951.

Bennett, J. A. W. *Chaucer at Oxford and Cambridge*, Toronto, 1974.

Black, M. H. *Cambridge University Press, 1584–1984*, Cambridge, 1984.

Bodenstedt, M. I. *The Vita Christi of Ludolphus the Carthusian*, Washington, 1944.

Bowker, M. *The Henrician Reformation in the Diocese of Lincoln*, Cambridge, 1981.

Secular Clergy in the Diocese of Lincoln, 1495–1520, Cambridge, 1968.

363

Bibliography

Boyle, L. E. 'Aspects of Clerical Education in Fourteenth Century England', *The Fourteenth Century, Acta*, 4 (1977), 19–32.

'Canon Law Before 1380', in *The History of the University of Oxford*, I, ed. J. Catto, Oxford, 1984, pp. 531–64.

'The Constitution *Cum ex eo* of Boniface VIII', *Mediaeval Studies*, 24 (1962), 263-302.

'The Curriculum of the Faculty of Canon Law at Oxford in the First Half of the Fourteenth Century', in *Oxford Studies Presented to Daniel Callus, OP*, Oxford Historical Society, New Series 16, Oxford, 1964, pp. 135–62.

'The *Oculus Sacerdotis* and Some Other Works of William of Pagula', *Royal Historical Society Transactions*, 5th Series, V (1955), pp. 81-110.

Bradshaw, H. 'An Early University Statute Concerning Hostels', *CAS Publications*, 2 (1864), 279–81.

Bradwardine, T. *Thomas Bradwardine: His Tractatus de Proportionibus*, ed. H. L. Crosby, Madison, Wisconsin, 1955.

Brewer, J. S. and Gairdner J. (eds.) *Letters, Papers, Foreign and Domestic, of the Reign of Henry VIII, 1509–47*, 21 vols., London, 1862–1910.

Brocklebank, T. 'Sir Thomas Rede', *CAS, Communications*, I (1851–9), 365–74.

Brooke, C. N. L. 'The Churches of Medieval Cambridge', in *History, Society, and the Churches*, ed. D. Beales and G. Best, Cambridge, 1985, pp. 49–76.

A History of Gonville and Caius College, Woodbridge, Suffolk, 1985.

'John Fisher as University Chancellor', in *Humanism, Reform and the Reformation: the Career of Bishop John Fisher*, ed. B. Bradshaw and E. Duffy, Cambridge, forthcoming.

Brooke, C. N. L. and Highfield, J. R. L. with photographs by W. Swaan, *Oxford and Cambridge*, Cambridge, 1988.

Bullough, V. L. 'The Medieval Medical School at Cambridge', *Mediaeval Studies*, 24 (1962), 160–8.

Burley, W. 'The *De potentiis animae* of Walter Burley', ed. M. J. Kitchel, *Mediaeval Studies*, 33 (1971), 85–113.

Bushell, W. D. *Church of St Mary the Great*, Cambridge, 1948.

Caius, J. *The Annals of Gonville and Caius College*, ed. J. Venn, CAS, Octavo Series 40, Cambridge, 1904.

'Historiae Cantabrigiensis Academiae, Liber Primus', in *The Works of John Caius*, ed. E. S. Roberts, Cambridge, 1912.

De Antiquitate Cantabrigiensis Academiae, London, 1568; also in Caius, *Works*, ed. E. S. Roberts, Cambridge, 1912.

Bibliography

Calendar of Patent Rolls, Henry VI, 1422–29, Public Record Office Texts and Calendars, London, 1901.

Cantelow, N. 'De Antiquitate et Origine Universitatis Cantabrigiensis', in T. Sprott, *Chronica*, ed. T. Hearne, Oxford, 1719, pp. 221–80.

Carmody, F. J. *Arabic Astronomical and Astrological Science in Latin Translation*, Berkeley, 1956.

Caroë, W. D. *King's Hall, Trinity College, Cambridge*, CAS, Quarto Publications, New Series 2, Cambridge, 1909.

Carpenter, N. C. *Music in the Medieval and Renaissance Universities*, Norman, Oklahoma, 1958.

Carr, N. *Demosthenes...Olynthiacae Orationes*, London, 1571.

Caxton, T. *Caxton's Eneydos*, ed. W. T. Culley and F. J. Furnivall, Early English Text Society, Extra Series 57, London, 1890.

Chandler, R. *The Life of William Waynflete*, London, 1811.

Cheney, C. R. *Medieval Texts and Studies*, Oxford, 1973.

Chibnall, A. C. *Richard de Badew and the University of Cambridge 1315–1340*, Cambridge, 1963.

Clark, J. H. P. 'Thomas Maldon, O. Carm., A Cambridge Theologian of the Fourteenth Century', *Carmelus*, 29 (1982), 193-235.

Clark, J. W. *Endowments of the University of Cambridge*, Cambridge, 1904.

'On the Charitable Foundations in the University Called Chests', *CAS, Proceedings*, New Series 5 (1903–4), 78–101.

'On the History of the Library', in *A Descriptive Catalogue of the Manuscripts of Peterhouse*, ed. M. R. James, Cambridge, 1899, pp. xvii–xxxii.

Clark, J. W. and Gray, A. *Old Plans of Cambridge*, Cambridge, 1921.

Cobban, A. B. 'Decentralised Teaching in the Medieval English Universities', *History of Education*, 5 (1976), 193–204.

'Edward II, Pope John XXII, and the University of Cambridge', *Bulletin of the John Rylands Library*, 47 (1964–5), 49–78.

The King's Hall within the University of Cambridge in the Later Middle Ages, Cambridge, 1969.

'The Medieval Cambridge College: A Quantitative Study of Higher Degrees to *c.* 1500', *History of Education*, 9 (1980), 1–12.

The Medieval Universities: Their Development and Organisation, London, 1975.

'Origins: Robert Wodelarke and St Catharine's', in *St Catharine's College, 1473–1973*, ed. E. E. Rich, Leeds, 1973, chap. 1.

'Theology and Law in the Medieval Colleges of Oxford and Cambridge', *Bulletin of the John Rylands Library*, 65 (1982), 57–77.

Colvin, H. M. (ed.) *The History of the King's Works*, 6 vols., London, 1963–73.

Bibliography

Constable, G. *Letters and Letter Collections*, Typologie des sources du moyen âge occidental, fasc. 17, Turnhout, 1976.

Cooper, C. H. *Annals of Cambridge*, 5 vols. (v ed. J. W. Cooper), Cambridge, 1842–1908.

Memoir of Margaret, Countess of Richmond and Derby, Cambridge, 1874.

Cooper, C. H. and T. *Athenae Cantabrigienses*, 2 vols., Cambridge, 1858–61.

Corpus Juris Canonici, 2 vols., ed. E. Friedberg, Leipzig, 1879–81.

Corrie, G. E. *Brief Historical Notes on the Interference of the Crown with the Affairs of the English Universities*, Cambridge, 1839.

Costello, W. T. *The Scholastic Curriculum at Early Seventeenth Century Cambridge*, Cambridge, Mass., 1958.

Courtenay, W. J. 'The Effect of the Black Death on English Higher Education', *Speculum*, 55 (1980), 696–714.

Couve de Murville, M. and Jenkins, P. *Catholic Cambridge*, London, 1983.

Cranage, D. H. S. and Stokes, H. P. 'The Augustinian Friary in Cambridge and the History of the Site', *CAS, Proceedings*, 22 (1917–20), 53–75.

Cranmer, T. *Miscellaneous Writings*, Parker Society 15, Cambridge, 1846.

Crawley, C. *Trinity Hall*, Cambridge, 1976.

Croke, R. *Orationes Richardi Croci Duae, Altera...*, Paris, 1520.

Croke, R. *Tabulae Graecas literas discere cupientibus utiles*, Leipzig, 1516.

Curia Regis Rolls, 9–10 Henry III, Public Record Office Texts and Calendars, London, 1957.

Curtis, M. *Oxford and Cambridge in Transition 1558–1642*, Oxford, 1959.

Dale, A. W. W. (ed.) *Warren's Book*, Cambridge, 1911.

Davis, N. (ed.) *The Paston Letters*, II, Oxford 1976, p. 203.

Denifle, H. S. (ed.) *Chartularium Universitatis Parisiensis*, 4 vols., Paris, 1894–7.

DNB: Dictionary of National Biography.

Documents relating to the University and Colleges of Cambridge, 3 vols., London, 1852.

Dorne, J. 'The Daily Ledger of John Dorne, 1520', ed. F. Madan in *Collectanea*, I, ed. C. R. L. Fletcher, Oxford Historical Society 5, Oxford, 1885, pp. 73–177.

Dyer, G. (ed.) *The Privileges of the University of Cambridge*, 2 vols., London, 1824.

Elmham, T. of *Vita et Gesta Henrici Quinti Anglorum Regis*, ed. T. Hearne, Oxford, 1727.

Elton, G. R. *Reform and Reformation: England, 1509–1558*, Cambridge, Mass., 1977.

Bibliography

Emden, A. B. *A Biographical Register of the University of Cambridge to 1500*, Cambridge, 1963.

A Biographical Register of the University of Oxford to AD 1500, 3 vols., Oxford, 1957–9.

A Biographical Register of the University of Oxford AD 1501 to 1540, Oxford, 1974.

'Northerners and Southerners in the Organisation of the University to 1509', in *Oxford Studies Presented to Daniel Callus, OP*, Oxford Historical Society, New Series 16, Oxford, 1964, pp. 1–30.

An Oxford Hall in Medieval Times, Oxford, 1927.

'Oxford Academical Halls in the Later Middle Ages', in *Medieval Learning and Literature: Essays Presented to Richard William Hunt*, ed. J. J. G. Alexander and M. T. Gibson, Oxford, 1976, pp. 353–65.

Erasmus, D. *The Correspondence of Erasmus*, ed. J. K. McConica *et al.*, Collected Works of Erasmus 1–5, Toronto, 1974–9.

Opera Omnia, 9 vols., ed. J. H. Waszink *et al.*, Amsterdam, 1969–85.

Opus Epistolarum, 12 vols., ed. P. S. Allen, Oxford, 1906–58.

Erfurt, T. of *Grammativa Speculativa*, ed. G. L. Bursill-Hall, Classics of Linguistics 1, London, 1972.

Excerpta e Statutis Academiae Cantabrigiensis, Cambridge, 1785.

Fairbank, A. and Dickins, B. *The Italic Hand in Tudor Cambridge*, Cambridge Bibliographical Society Monograph 5, London, 1962.

Fasciculus Zizaniorum, ed. W. Shirley, Rolls Series 5, London, 1858.

Feingold, M. *The Mathematician's Apprenticeship*, Cambridge, 1984.

Feltoe, C. L. and Minns, E. H. (ed.) *Vetus Liber Archidiaconi Eliensis*, CAS, Octavo Series 48, Cambridge, 1917.

Fisher, J. *De Veritate Corporis et Sanguinis Christi*, Cologne, 1527.

Fletcher, J. M. 'Change and Resistance to Change: A Consideration of the Development of English and German Universities during the Sixteenth Century', *History of Universities*, 1 (1981), 1–36.

'Linacre's Lands and Lectureships', in *Linacre Studies: Essays on the Life and Works of Thomas Linacre c. 1460–1524*, ed. F. Maddison, M. Pelling, and C. Webster, Oxford, 1977, pp. 107–97.

'The Teaching of Arts at Oxford, 1400–1520', *Paedagogica Historica*, 7 (1967), 417–54.

Fletcher, J. M. (ed.) *Registrum Annalium Collegii Mertonensis 1521–1567*, Oxford Historical Society, New Series, 23, Oxford, 1974.

Forte, S. L. 'A Cambridge Dominican Collector of *Exempla* in the Thirteenth Century', *Archivum Fratrum Praedicatorum*, 38 (1958), 115–48.

Foster, J. E. *Churchwarden's Accounts of St Mary the Great*, CAS, Octavo Series 35, Cambridge, 1905.

Bibliography

Fowler, L. and H. *Cambridge Commemorated*, Cambridge, 1984.

Foxe, J. *Acts and Monuments*, 8 vols., ed. G. Townsend, London, 1843–9.

Fuller, T. *The History of the University of Cambridge*, ed. J. Nichols, London, 1840.

Gabriel, A. L. *Summary Bibliography of the History of the Universities of Great Britain and Ireland up to 1800*, Notre Dame, 1974.

Gairdner, J. 'A Letter Concerning Bishop Fisher and Sir Thomas More', *English Historical Review*, 7 (1892), 713–15.

Gairdner, J. (ed.) *Three Fifteenth Century Chronicles*, Camden Society, New Series 28, Westminster, 1880.

Gascoigne, T. *Loci e Libro Veritatum*, ed. J. E. Thorold Rogers, Oxford, 1881.

Gaskell, P. *Trinity College Library: The First 150 Years*, Cambridge, 1980.

Gibbon, E. *Memoirs of My Life*, ed. B. Radice, Harmondsworth, 1984.

Gibson, S. 'The Order of Disputations', *Bodleian Quarterly Review*, 6 (1930), 107–12.

Statuta Antiqua Universitatis Oxoniensis, Oxford, 1931.

Godfrey, W. R. 'John Colet of Cambridge', *Archiv für Reformationsgeschichte*, 65 (1974), 6–18.

Gottfried, R. S. *Epidemic Disease in Fifteenth Century England*, New Brunswick, NJ, 1978.

Grant, E. *Much Ado About Nothing*, Cambridge, 1981.

A Source Book in Medieval Science, Cambridge, Mass., 1974.

Gray, A. *The Dual Origins of the Town of Cambridge*, CAS, Quarto Publications, New Series 1, Cambridge, 1908.

The Priory of St Radegund, Cambridge, CAS, Quarto Publications 31, Cambridge, 1898.

Gray, A. (ed.) *The Earliest Statutes of Jesus College, Cambridge*, Cambridge, 1935.

Gray, A. and Brittain, F. *A History of Jesus College, Cambridge*, London, 1979.

Gray, G. J. *The Earlier Cambridge Stationers*, Oxford Bibliographical Society, Oxford, 1904.

Gray, J. M. *The School of Pythagoras*, CAS, Quarto Publications, New Series 4, Cambridge 1932.

Gumbley, W. *The Cambridge Dominicans*, Cambridge, 1938.

Gwyn, D. 'Richard Eden, Cosmographer and Alchemist', *Sixteenth Century Journal*, 15 (1984), 13–34.

Hackett, M. B. *The Original Statutes of Cambridge University: The Text and its History*, Cambridge, 1970.

Bibliography

Halliwell, J. O. *College Life in the Time of James the First as Illustrated by an Unpublished Diary of Sir Symonds D'Ewes*, London, 1851.
Rara mathematica, London, 1841.

Harpsfield, N. *The Life and Death of Sir Thomas More*, ed. E. V. Hitchcock and R. W. Chambers, Early English Text Society 186, London, 1932.

Harrison, W. *Description of England*, ed. G. Edelen, Ithaca, 1968.

Haskins, C. H. 'The Life of Medieval Students as Seen in their Letters', *American Historical Review*, 3 (1897), 203–29.

Haslam, J. 'The Development and Topography of Saxon Cambridge', *CAS, Proceedings*, 72 (1982–3), 13–29.

Hays, R. W. 'Welsh Students at Oxford and Cambridge Universities in the Middle Ages', *Welsh Historical Review*, 4 (1968 9), 325 61.

Heath, T. 'Logical Grammar, Grammatical Logic, and Humanism in Three German Universities', *Studies in the Renaissance*, 18 (1971), 9–64.

Hegius, A. 'Invectiva in modo significandi', ed. J. IJsewijn, *Forum for Modern Language Studies*, 7 (1971), 299–318.

Herryson, J. *Abbreviata Chronica ab anno 1377 usque ad annum 1469*, ed. J. J. Clark, Cambridge, 1840.

Heytesbury, W. *On 'Insoluble' Sentences*, ed. P. V. Spade, Toronto, 1979.

Heywood, J. *The Ancient Laws of the Fifteenth Century for King's College*, London, 1850.

Heywood, J. and Wright, T. *Cambridge University Transactions during the Puritan Controversies of the Sixteenth and Seventeenth Centuries*, 2 vols., London, 1854.

Hoccleve, T. *De regimine principum*, ed. T. Wright, Roxburghe Club 79, London, 1860.

Howard, H. F. *An Account of the Finances of the College of St John the Evangelist*, Cambridge, 1935.

Howell, W. S. *Logic and Rhetoric in England, 1500–1700*, Princeton, 1956.

Hughes, P. *The Reformation in England*, rev. edn, 3 vols. in 1, London, 1963.

Hunt, R. W. 'Oxford Grammar Masters in the Middle Ages', in *Oxford Studies Presented to Daniel Callus, OP*, Oxford Historical Society, New Series 16, Oxford, 1964, pp. 163–93.

In Hoc Opusculo..., Paris, Guy Marchant, 1496.

Jacob, E. F. 'English University Clerks in the Later Middle Ages: The Problem of Maintenance', *Bulletin of the John Rylands Library*, 29 (1946), 304–25.

Jardine, L. 'Humanism and the Sixteenth Century Cambridge Arts Course', *History of Education*, 4 (1975), 16–31.

'The Place of Dialectic Teaching in Sixteenth Century Cambridge', *Studies in the Renaissance*, 21 (1974), 31–62.

Bibliography

Jerman, C. 'Hugh of St Cher', *Dominicana*, 44 (1959), 338–47.

Joseph, R. *The Letter Book of Robert Joseph*, ed. H. Aveling and W. A. Pantin, Oxford Historical Society, New Series 19, Oxford, 1967.

Karpinski, L. C. 'The Algorism of John Killingworth', *English Historical Review*, 29 (1914), 707–17.

Kibre, P. 'Lewis of Caerleon: Doctor of Medicine, Astronomer, and Mathematician', *Isis*, 43 (1952), 100–8.

Kingsford, C. L. *English Historical Literature in the Fifteenth Century*, Oxford, 1913.

'A London Chronicle, 1446–50', *English Historical Review*, 29 (1914), 505–15.

Knowles, D. *The Religious Orders in England*, 3 vols., Cambridge, 1948–59.

Lamb, J. *A Collection of Letters, Statutes, and Other Documents from the Manuscript Library of Corpus Christi College, Illustrative of the History of the University of Cambridge, During the Period of the Reformation, from AD MD to AD MDLXXII*, London, 1838.

Langlois, C. V. 'Nicholas de Lyre, frère mineur', *Histoire Littéraire de la France*, 36 (1927), 355–400.

Latimer, H. *Sermons*, ed. G. E. Corrie, 2 vols., Parker Society, Cambridge, 1844–5.

Lawrence, C. H. 'The Origins of the Chancellorship at Oxford', *Oxoniensia*, 41 (1976), 316–23.

Lawrence, C. H. 'The University in State and Church', in J. Cato, ed. *HUO*, I, Oxford, 1984, pp. 97–150.

Leach, A. F. *Educational Charters and Documents 598 to 1909*, Cambridge, 1911.

The Schools of Medieval England, London, 1915, repr. London, 1969.

Leader, D. R. 'Grammar in Late Medieval Oxford and Cambridge', *History of Education*, 12 (1983), 9–14.

'John Argentein and Learning in Medieval Cambridge', *Humanistica Lovaniensia*, 33 (1984), 71–85.

'Philosophy at Oxford and Cambridge in the Fifteenth Century', *History of Universities*, 4 (1984), 25–40.

'Professorships and Academic Reform at Cambridge: 1488–1520', *Sixteenth Century Journal*, 14 (1983), 215–27.

'Teaching in Tudor Cambridge', *History of Education*, 13 (1984), 105–19.

Leathes, S. M. *Grace Book A*, Cambridge, 1897.

Leland, J. *The Itinerary of John Leland, 1535–43*, 10 vols., ed. L. T. Smith, London, 1906–9.

Lerner, R. G. 'Poverty, Preaching, and Eschatology in Revelation Commentaries of "Hugh of St Cher"', in *The Bible in the Medieval World*,

Bibliography

Essays in Memory of Beryl Smalley, ed. K. Walsh and D. Wood (Studies in Church History Subsidia 4, London, 1985), 157–89.

Lever, T. *Sermons*, ed. E. Arber, London, 1870.

Lewis, J. *Life of Dr John Fisher*, 2 vols., London, 1855.

Libellus Sophistarum ad usum Cantab. London, 1497.

Libellus Sophistarum ad usum Oxon. London, c. 1500.

Little, A. G. 'The Friars and the Foundation of the Faculty of Theology in the University of Cambridge', in *Mélanges Mandonnet*, Bibliothèque Thomiste 14, Paris, 1930, II, 389–401.

'The Friars vs. the University of Cambridge', *English Historical Review*, 50 (1935), 686–96.

Grey Friars in Oxford, Oxford Historical Society 20, Oxford, 1892.

Little, A. G. and Pelster, F. *Oxford Theology and Theologians, c.* AD *1282–1302*, Oxford Historical Society 96, Oxford, 1934.

Lives of the Brethren of the Order of Preachers, trans. P. Conway, ed. B. Jarrett, London, 1924.

Lloyd, A. H. 'The College Game of Swans', in *Christ's College in Former Days*, ed. H. Rackham, Cambridge, 1939, pp. 64–75.

The Early History of Christ's College, Cambridge, Cambridge, 1934.

Lobel, M. D. and Johns, W. H. (eds.) *Atlas of Historic Towns*, 2 vols. [3rd in press], Oxford, London, 1975.

Logan, F. D. 'The Origins of the So-Called Regius Professorships: An Aspect of the Renaissance in Oxford and Cambridge', in *Renaissance and Renewal in Christian History, Studies in Church History*, 14, Oxford, 1977, pp. 271–8.

Lohr, C. H. 'Medieval Latin Aristotle Commentaries, A–F', *Traditio*, 23 (1967), 313–413; 'G–I', *Traditio*, 24 (1968), 149–245; 'J', *Traditio*, 26 (1970), 135–216; 'J–My', *Traditio*, 27 (1971), 251–351; 'Na–Ri', *Traditio*, 28 (1972), 281–396; 'Ro–Wi', *Traditio*, 29 (1973), 93 197; 'Supplementary Authors', *Traditio*, 30 (1974), 119–44.

Lucas, P. J. 'John Capgrave, OSA (1393–1464), Scribe and Publisher', *Transactions of the Cambridge Bibliographical Society*, 5 (1969), 1–35.

Lupton, J. H. *A Life of John Colet, D.D.*, London, 1909.

Lytle, G. F. 'Social Origins of Oxford Students in the Late Middle Ages 1380–1510', in *Les Universités à la Fin du Moyen Age*, ed. J. Paquet and J. IJsewijn, Institut d'études médiévales, Louvain, 1978, pp. 426–54.

Macaulay, T. *History of England*, 6 vols., ed. C. H. Firth, London, 1913–15.

McConica, J. K. *English Humanists and Reformation Politics*, Oxford, 1965.

'Humanism and Aristotle in Tudor Oxford', *English Historical Review*, 94 (1979), 291–317.

Bibliography

McDowall, R. W. 'Buckingham College', *CAS, Proceedings*, 44 (1951), 1–12.

McFarlane, K. B. 'William Worcester: A Preliminary Survey', in *Studies Presented to Sir Hilary Jenkinson*, ed. J. C. Davies, London, 1957, pp. 196–221.

Maitland, F. W. *Township and Borough*, Cambridge, 1898.

Maitland, S. R. 'Original Papers relating to Archbishop Whitgift', *The British Magazine*, 32–3 (1847-8).

Major, J. *Historia maioris Britanniae tam Angliae quam Scotiae*, Paris, 1521.

Mallet, C. E. *A History of the University of Oxford*, 3 vols., London, 1924–7.

Martin, C. 'Walter Burley', in *Oxford Studies Presented to Daniel Callus, OP*, Oxford Historical Society, New Series 16, Oxford, 1964, pp. 194–230.

Masters, R. *A History of the College of Corpus Christi and the Blessed Virgin Mary*, Cambridge, 1753.

Maxwell-Lyte, H. C. *A History of the University of Oxford*, London, 1886.

Mayor, J. E. B. *Early Statutes of the College of St John the Evangelist in the University of Cambridge*, Cambridge, 1859.

Melton, W. *Sermo Exhortatorius Cancellarii Eboracensis hiis qui ad Sacros Ordines Petunt Promoveri*, Westminster, 1507/10.

Metham, J. *The Works of John Metham*, ed. H. Craig, Early English Text Society, Old Series 132, London, 1916.

Mitchell, R. J. *John Free*, London, 1955.

Mitchell, W. T. *Epistolae Academicae 1508–1596*, Oxford Historical Society, New Series 26, Oxford, 1980.

Moore Smith, G. C. 'University Praelectors in Mathematics, Philosophy, Logic, and Rhetoric', *Cambridge Review*, 53 (1914), 276–8.

Moorman, J. R. H. *The Grey Friars in Cambridge, 1225–1538*, Cambridge, 1952.

More, T. *The Apology*, ed. J. Trapp, Complete Works of Thomas More 9, New Haven and London, 1979.

Selected Letters, ed. E. F. Rogers, New Haven, 1961.

Morison, S. E. *The Founding of Harvard College*, Cambridge, Mass., 1935.

Mullally, E. 'Wolsey's Proposed Reform of the Oxford University Statutes: A Recently Discovered Text', *Bodleian Library Record*, 10 (1978), 22–7.

Mullinger, J. B. *St John's College*, London, 1901.

The University of Cambridge from the Earliest Times to the Royal Injunctions of 1535, Cambridge, 1873.

The University of Cambridge from the Royal Injunctions of 1535 to the Accession of Charles the First, Cambridge, 1884.

Munby, A. N. L. *The History and Bibliography of Science in England: The First Phase, 1833–45*, Berkeley, 1968.

Bibliography

Neale, C. M. *The Early Honours Lists of the University of Cambridge (1498–9 to 1746–7)*, Bury St Edmund's, 1909.

New Catholic Encyclopedia, 17 vols., New York, 1967–79.

Oates, J. C. T. *Cambridge University Library: A History*, 1 Cambridge, 1986.

Orme, N. *Education in the West of England 1066–1548*, Exeter, 1976.

Ortroy, F. van 'Vie du Bienheureux Martyr Jean Fisher, Cardinal Evêque de Rochester (d. 1535)', *Analecta Bollandiana*, 10 (1891), 121–365, and 12 (1893), 97–287.

Owst, G. R. *Preaching in Medieval England*, Cambridge, 1926.

Pantin, W. A. *The English Church in the Fourteenth Century*, Cambridge, 1955.

'The Halls and Schools of Medieval Oxford: An Attempt at Reconstruction', in *Oxford Studies Presented to Daniel Callus, OP*, Oxford Historical Society, New Series 16, Oxford, 1964, pp. 31–100.

'A Medieval Treatise on Letter Writing, with Examples from the Rylands Latin MS 394', *Bulletin of the John Rylands Library*, 13 (1929), 326–82.

Oxford Life in Oxford Archives, Oxford, 1972.

Pantin, W. A. and Mitchell, W. T. *The Register of Congregation 1448–1463*, Oxford Historical Society, New Series 22, Oxford, 1972.

Paris, Matthew, *Chronica Majora*, 7 vols., ed. H. R. Luard, Rolls Series 57, London, 1872–83.

Historia Anglorum, 3 vols., ed. F. Madden, Rolls Series 44, London, 1866–9.

Parker, M. *De Antiquitate Britannicae Ecclesiae*, London, 1572.

Correspondence, ed. J. Bruce and T. T. Perowne, Parker Society, Cambridge, 1853.

Parker, R. *Town and Gown*, Cambridge, 1983.

Paston Letters and Papers of the Fifteenth Century, 2 vols., ed. N. Davis, Oxford, 1971–6.

Peacock, G. *Observations on the Statutes of the University of Cambridge*, London, 1841.

Pearce, E. C. 'College Accounts of John Botwright, Master of Corpus Christi 1443–74', *CAS, Proceedings*, 22 (1917–20), 76–90.

Peck, F. *Desiderata curiosa*, London, 1779.

Peek, H. E. and Hall, C. P. *The Archives of the University of Cambridge*, Cambridge, 1962.

Perreiah, A. 'Logic Examinations in Padua *c.* 1400', *History of Education*, 13 (1984), 85–103.

Philpott, H. (ed.) *Documents Relating to St Catharine's College, Cambridge*, Cambridge, 1861.

Pollard, A. W. and Redgrave, G. R. *Short-Title Catalogue of Books Printed in England, Scotland, and Ireland, and of English Books Published Abroad,*

1475–1640, vol. I, A–Z, London, The Bibliographical Society, 1963: 2nd edn, by W. A. Jackson and F. S. Ferguson, completed by K. F. Pantzer, vol. II, I–Z, London, The Bibliographical Society, 1976.

Pollard, G. 'The Legatine Award to Oxford in 1214 and Robert Grosteste', *Oxoniensia*, 39 (1974), 62–73.

'Mediaeval Loan Chests at Cambridge', *Bulletin of the Institute of Historical Research*, 17 (1939–40), 113–29.

'The University and the Book Trade in Medieval Oxford', *Beiträge zum Berufsbewusstsein* (*Miscellanea Mediaevalia*, Band 3, 1964), 336-45.

Porphyry the Phoenician, *Isagoge*, trans. E. W. Warren, Toronto, 1975.

Porter, H. C. *Reformation and Reaction in Tudor Cambridge*, Cambridge, 1958.

Pseudo-Albertus Magnus, *Questiones Alberti de Modis Significandi*, ed. and trans. L. G. Kelly, Studies in the History of Linguistics 15, Amsterdam, 1977.

Rackham, H. *Christ's College in Former Days*, Cambridge, 1939.

Rackham, H. (ed.) *The Early Statutes of Christ's College, Cambridge, with the Statutes of the Prior Foundation of Godshouse*, Cambridge, 1927.

Rashdall, H. *The Universities of Europe in the Middle Ages*, 3 vols., new edition by F. M. Powicke and A. B. Emden, Oxford, 1936.

Register of the University of Oxford, ed. A. Clark, II, 2 parts, Oxford Historical Society 10–11, Oxford, 1887.

Régistres de Gregoire IX, Les, ed. L. Auvray. Librairie des écoles Françaises d'Athènes et de Rome, II, Paris, 1908.

Reynolds, E. E. *St John Fisher*, London, 1955.

Rhodes, D. E. *John Argentein, Provost of King's: His Life and Library*, Amsterdam, 1967.

'The Princes in the Tower and Their Doctor', *English Historical Review*, 77 (1962), 304–6.

Rice, E. F. 'Humanist Aristotelianism in France', in *Humanism in France*, ed. A. H. T. Levi, Manchester, 1970, pp. 132–49.

Richards, G. C. and Salter, H. E., ed. *The Dean's Register of Oriel 1446–1661*, Oxford Historical Society 84, Oxford, 1926.

Richardson, H. G. 'The Schools of Northampton in the Twelfth Century', *English Historical Review*, 56 (1941), 595–605.

Richardson, W. G. *Tudor Chamber Administration*, Baton Rouge, Louisiana, 1982.

Ridley, N. *The Works of Nicholas Ridley*, ed. A. Christmas, Parker Society, Cambridge, 1841.

Rijk, L. M. de '*Logica Cantabrigiensis*: A Fifteenth Century Cambridge Manual of Logic', *Revue Internationale de Philosophie*, 29 (1975), 297–315.

Bibliography

'*Logica Oxoniensis*: An Attempt to Reconstruct a Fifteenth Century Oxford Manual of Logic', *Medioevo*, 3 (1977), 121–64.

'The Place of Billingham's *Speculum Puerorum* in Fourteenth and Fifteenth Century Logical Tradition with the Edition of Some Alternative Tracts', *Studia Mediewistyczne*, 16 (1975), 99–153.

Risse, W. *Bibliographia Logica, Band I, 1472–1800*, Hildesheim, 1965.

Roach, J. P. C. (ed.) *A History of the County of Cambridge and the Isle of Ely*, III, Victoria County History, London, 1959.

Roberts, H. (ed.) *Calendar of Wills Proved in Vice-Chancellor's Court at Cambridge, 1501–1765*, Cambridge, 1907.

Roberts, S. C. *A History of the Cambridge University Press 1521–1921*, Cambridge, 1921.

Rose, P. L. 'Erasmians and Mathematicians at Cambridge in the Early Sixteenth Century', *Sixteenth Century Journal*, 8 (1977), 47–59.

Roth, F. *The English Austin Friars, 1249–1538*, 2 vols., New York, 1966.

Rouse Ball, W. W. *Cambridge Papers*, London, 1918.

Royal Commission on Historical Monuments, *An Inventory of the Historical Monuments in the City of Cambridge*, 2 vols., London, 1959.

Rubin, M. *Charity and Community in Medieval Cambridge*, Cambridge, 1986.

Ruysschaert, J. 'Lorenzo Guglielmo Traversagni di Savone', *Archivum Franciscanum Historicum*, 46 (1953), 195–210.

Salter, H. E. *Mediaeval Archives of the University of Oxford*, II, Oxford Historical Society 73, Oxford, 1921.

'An Oxford Hall in 1424', in *Essays in History Presented to R. L. Poole*, ed. H. W. C. Davis, Oxford, 1927, pp. 421–35.

Snappe's Formulary, Oxford Historical Society 80, Oxford, 1923.

Salter, H. E. (ed.) *Registrum Annalium Collegii Mertonensis 1483–1521*, Oxford Historical Society 76, Oxford, 1923.

Registrum Cancellarii Oxoniensis 1434–1469, 2 vols., Oxford Historical Society 93–4, Oxford, 1932.

Sammut, A. *Unfredo Duca di Gloucester e gli Umanisti Italiani*, Padua, 1982.

Schmitt, C. B. *Aristotle in the Renaissance*, London and Cambridge, Mass., 1983.

John Case and Aristotelianism in Renaissance England, Kingston and Montreal, 1983.

'Philosophy and Science in Sixteenth Century Universities: Some Preliminary Comments', in *The Cultural Context of Medieval Learning*, ed. J. E. Murdoch and E. D. Sylla, Dordrecht, 1975, pp. 485–537.

'Thomas Linacre in Italy', in *Linacre Studies*, ed. F. Maddison, M. Pelling, and C. Webster, Oxford, 1977, pp. 36–75.

Bibliography

Scofield, C. L. *The Life and Reign of Edward the Fourth*, 2 vols., London, 1923.

Searle, W. G. *Grace Book Γ*, Cambridge, 1908.

The History of the Queens' College of St Margaret and St Bernard, I, CAS, Octavo Series 9, Cambridge, 1867.

Seebohm, F. *The Oxford Reformers*, 3rd edn, London, 1914.

Seton, J. *Dialectica*, London, 1568.

Shadwell, L. L. ed., *Enactments in Parliament*, I, Oxford Historical Society 58, Oxford, 1912.

Sheppard, J. T. *Richard Croke: A Sixteenth Century Don*, Cambridge, 1919.

Shrewsbury, J. F. D. *A History of Bubonic Plague in the British Isles*, Cambridge, 1970.

Siraisi, N. G. *Arts and Sciences at Padua: The Studium of Padua before 1350*, Toronto, 1973.

Skånland, V. 'The Earliest Statutes of the University of Cambridge', *Symbolae Osloenses*, 40 (1965), 83–98.

Skelton, J. *The Poetical Works of Skelton and Donne*, ed. A. Dyce, Boston, 1855.

Smalley, B. *The Study of the Bible in the Middle Ages*, 2nd edn, Oxford, 1952.

Southern, R. W. 'From Schools to University', in *The History of the University of Oxford*, I, ed. J. Catto, Oxford, 1984, pp. 1–36.

Squibb, G. D. *Doctor's Commons*, Oxford, 1977.

Stamp, A. E. *Michaelhouse*, Cambridge, 1929.

Statuta Academiae Cantabrigiensis, Cambridge, 1785.

Statutes of the Colleges of Oxford, with Royal Patents of Foundation, 3 vols., London, 1853.

Stokes, H. P. *The Chaplains and the Chapel of the University of Cambridge 1256–1568*, CAS, Octavo Series 41, Cambridge, 1906.

The Esquire Bedells of the University of Cambridge, CAS, Octavo Series 45, Cambridge, 1911.

The Mediaeval Hostels of the University of Cambridge, CAS, Octavo Series 49, Cambridge, 1924.

Stone, L. (ed.) *The University in Society*, 2 vols., Princeton and London, 1975.

Storey, R. L. 'The Foundation and the Medieval College, 1379–1530', in *New College, Oxford, 1379–1979*, ed. J. Buxton and P. Williams, Oxford, 1979.

Talbot, C. H. *Medicine in Medieval England*, London, 1967.

Talbot, C. H. and Hammond, E. A. *The Medical Practitioners of Medieval England – A Biographical Register*, London, 1965.

Bibliography

Thomas, I. 'Medieval Aftermath: Oxford Logic and Logicians of the Seventeenth Century', in *Oxford Studies Presented to Daniel Callus, OP*, Oxford Historical Society, New Series 16, 1964, pp. 297–311.

Thomas, K. *Man and the Natural World*, New York, 1983.

Thomson, D. F. S. and Porter, H. C. (eds.) *Erasmus and Cambridge*, Toronto, 1963.

Thorold Rogers, J. E. *History of Agriculture and Prices in England*, 7 vols., Oxford, 1866–1902.

Toner, N. 'Augustinian Spiritual Writers of the English Province in the Fifteenth and Sixteenth Centuries', *Sanctus Augustinus (Analecta Augustiniana)*, II, Rome, 1959, pp. 493–523.

Traversagni di Savona, L. G. *Nova Rhetorica seu Margarita Eloquentiae Sacrae Castigatae ad Eloquendum Divina*, St Albans, 1480.

Treptow, O. *John Siberch*, ed. and trans. J. Morris and T. Jones, Cambridge Bibliographical Society 6, Cambridge, 1970.

Trevelyan, G. M. *Trinity College*, 2nd edn, Cambridge, 1972.

Trevor-Roper, H. 'Forward', in *The Lisle Letters: An Abridgement*, ed. M. St Clair Byrne, Chicago, 1983.

The Rise of Christian Europe, London, 1965.

Ullmann, W. 'The Decline of the Chancellor's Authority in Medieval Cambridge: A Rediscovered Statute', *The Historical Journal*, 1 (1958), 176–82.

'The University of Cambridge and the Great Schism', *Journal of Theological Studies*, 9 (1958), 53–77.

Underwood, M. G. 'The Lady Margaret and Her Cambridge Connections', *Sixteenth Century Journal*, 13 (1982), 67–81.

Venn, J. *Early Collegiate Life*, Cambridge, 1913.

Venn, J. (ed.) *Grace Book Δ*, Cambridge, 1910.

Venn, J. et al. *Biographical History of Gonville and Caius College*, 7 vols., Cambridge, 1897–1978.

Venn, J. and J. A. (eds.) *Alumni Cantabrigienses to 1751*, 4 vols., Cambridge, 1922–7.

Vinsauf, Geoffrey, *Poetria Nova*, ed. M. F. Nims, Toronto, 1967.

Walsingham, Thomas, *Historia Anglicana*, ed. H. T. Riley, 2 vols., Rolls Series 28, London, 1864.

Ward, J. O. 'From Antiquity to the Renaissance: Glosses and Commentaries on Cicero's *Rhetorica*', in *Medieval Eloquence*, ed. J. J. Murphy, Berkeley, 1978, pp. 25–67.

Wayment, H. *The Windows of King's College Chapel, Cambridge*, Corpus Vitrearum Medii Aevi, Great Britain Supplementary 1, London, British Academy, 1972.

Bibliography

Weisheipl, J. A. 'Classification of the Sciences in Medieval Thought', *Mediaeval Studies*, 27 (1965), 54–90.

'Curriculum of the Faculty of Arts at Oxford in the Early Fourteenth Century', *Mediaeval Studies*, 26 (1964), 143–85.

'Developments in the Arts Curriculum at Oxford in the Early Fourteenth Century', *Mediaeval Studies*, 28 (1966), 151–75.

'John Canonicus', in *New Catholic Encyclopedia*, VII, New York, 1967, p. 1038.

'The Nature, Scope, and Classification of the Sciences', *Studia Mediewistyczne*, 18 (1977), 85–101.

'Ockham and Some Mertonians', *Mediaeval Studies*, 30 (1968), 163–213.

'The Place of John Dumbleton in the Merton School', *Isis*, 50 (1959), 439–54.

'The Place of the Liberal Arts in the University Curriculum during the Fourteenth and Fifteenth Centuries', in *Actes du Quatrième Congrès International de Philosophie Médiévale*, Montreal, 1969, 209–13.

'Repertorium Mertonense', *Mediaeval Studies*, 31 (1969), 174–224.

'The Structure of the Arts Faculty in the Medieval University', *British Journal of Educational Studies*, 19 (1971), 163–71.

Weiss, R. *Humanism in England during the Fifteenth Century*, 3rd edn, Oxford, 1967.

Wendover, Roger of, *Flores Historiarum*, ed. H. Hewlett, 3 vols., Rolls Series 84, London, 1886–9.

Wilkins, D. (ed.) *Concilia Magnae Britanniae*, 4 vols., London, 1737.

Williams, G. 'Notices of William Millington', *CAS, Proceedings*, 1 (1859), 287–328.

Williamson, R. R. 'The Plague in Medieval Cambridge', *Medical History*, 1

Willis, R. and Clark, J. W. *The Architectural History of the University of Cambridge and of the Colleges of Cambridge and Eton*, 4 vols., Cambridge, 1886.

Wood, A. *History and Antiquities of the University of Oxford*, Oxford, 1792.

Worcestre, W. *Itineraries*, ed. J. H. Harvey, Oxford Medieval Texts, Oxford, 1969.

Wordsworth, C. (ed.) *The Ancient Kalendar of the University of Oxford*, Oxford Historical Society 65, Oxford, 1904.

Wyclif, J. *Sermons*, ed. J. Loserth, 4 vols., London, Wyclif Society, 1887–90.

Wylie, J. A. H. and Collier, L. H. 'The English Sweating Sickness (*Sudor Anglicus*): A Reappraisal', *Journal of the History of Medicine and Allied Sciences*, 35 (1981), 425–45.

Bibliography

UNPUBLISHED DISSERTATIONS

Egan, K. J. 'The Establishment and Early Development of the Carmelite Order in England', unpublished Ph.D dissertation, Cambridge, 1965.

Fletcher, J. M. 'The Teaching and Study of Arts at Oxford, *c.* 1400–*c.* 1520', unpublished DPhil. dissertation, Oxford, 1962.

Keir, G. 'The Ecclesiastical Career of George Neville, 1432–1476', unpublished BLitt. thesis, Oxford, 1970.

Leader, D. R. 'The Study of Arts at Oxford and Cambridge at the End of the Middle Ages', unpublished Ph.D dissertation, Toronto, 1982.

INDEX

University institutions are indexed under Cambridge; colleges, halls, and hostels separately. Numbers in italics refer to pages with illustrations.

Index

Index

Index

Index

Index

Index

Index

Index

Index

Index

Index

397

Index

Index

399